Heritages of Portug[illegible] Influence: Histories, Spaces, Texts, and Objects

Fall 2021/Spring 2022

Tagus Press
Center for Portuguese Studies and Culture
University of Massachusetts Dartmouth
Portuguese Literary & Cultural Studies (PLCS) 36/37

PREVIOUS ISSUES

Fronteiras/Borders (PLCS 1)
Edited by Victor J. Mendes, Paulo de Medeiros, and José N. Ornelas

Lídia Jorge in other words / por outras palavras (PLCS 2)
Edited by Cláudia Pazos Alonso

Pessoa's Alberto Caeiro (PLCS 3)
Edited by Victor J. Mendes

2001 Brazil: A Revisionary History of Brazilian Literature and Culture (PLCS 4/5)
Edited by João Cezar de Castro Rocha

On Saramago (PLCS 6)
Edited by Anna Klobucka

A Repertoire of Contemporary Portuguese Poetry (PLCS 7)
Edited by Victor K. Mendes

Cape Verde: Language, Literature & Music (PLCS 8)
Edited by Ana Mafalda Leite

Post-Imperial Camões (PLCS 9)
Edited by João R. Figueiredo

Reevaluating Mozambique (PLCS 10)
Edited by Phillip Rothwell

Vitorino Nemésio and the Azores (PLCS 11)
Edited by Francisco Cota Fagundes

The Other Nineteenth Century (PLCS 12)
Edited by Kathryn M. Sanchez

The Author as Plagiarist—The Case of Machado de Assis (PLCS 13/14)
Edited by João Cezar de Castro Rocha

Remembering Angola (PLCS 15/16)
Edited by Phillip Rothwell

Parts of Asia (PLCS 17/18)
Edited by Cristiana Bastos

Facts and Fictions of António Lobo Antunes (PLCS 19/20)
Edited by Victor K. Mendes

Garrett's Travels Revisited (PLCS 21/22)
Edited by Victor K. Mendes and Valéria M. Souza

Economies of Relation: Money and Personalism in the Lusophone World (PLCS 23/24)
Edited by Roger Sansi

Lusofonia and Its Futures (PLCS 25)
Edited by João Cezar de Castro Rocha

Literary Histories in Portuguese (PLCS 26)
Edited by João Cezar de Castro Rocha

The South Atlantic, Past and Present (PLCS 27)
Edited by Luiz Felipe de Alencastro

Fernando Pessoa as English Reader and Writer (PLCS 28)
Edited by Patricio Ferrari & Jerónimo Pizarro

The Eighteenth Century (PLCS 29)
Edited by Bruno Carvalho

Transnational Africas: Visual, Material and Sonic Cultures of Lusophone Africa (PLCS 30/31)
Edited by Christopher Larkosh, Mario Pereira & Memory Holloway

Luso-American Literatures and Cultures Today (PLCS 32)
Edited by Christopher Larkosh with Maggie Felisberto, Jo-Anne Ferreira and Emanuel da Silva

Ocean Crossings (PLCS 33)
Edited by André Nóvoa

The Open Veins of the Postcolonial: Afrodescendants and Racisms (PLCS 34/35)
Edited by Inocência Mata and Iolanda Évora

Heritages of Portuguese Influence: Histories, Spaces, Texts, and Objects (PLCS 36/37)
Edited by Miguel Bandeira Jerónimo, Anna M. Klobucka, and Walter Rossa

Portuguese Literary & Cultural Studies (PLCS) is an interdisciplinary, peer-reviewed hybrid online and print journal that publishes original research related to the literatures and cultures of the diverse communities of the Portuguese-speaking world from a broad range of academic, critical and theoretical approaches. PLCS is published semi-annually by Tagus Press in the Center for Portuguese Studies and Culture at the University of Massachusetts Dartmouth.

Manuscript Policy

Portuguese Literary & Cultural Studies welcomes submission of original and unpublished manuscripts in English or Portuguese appropriate to the goals of the journal. Manuscripts should be between 6,000–8,500 words in length and must be accompanied by an abstract. Manuscripts should be in accordance with the *MLA Style Manual and Guide to Scholarly Publishing* (latest version) or *The Chicago Manual of Style* (latest version) with parenthetical documentation and a list of works cited. The author is responsible for the accuracy of all quotations, titles, names, and dates. Manuscripts should be double-spaced throughout. All of the information must be in the same language (e.g., abstract, body of the article, bio-blurb). Updated guidelines are available at https://ojs.lib.umassd.edu/index.php/plcs/index. PLCS encourages submission of manuscripts in the form of a single attached MS Word document.

Portuguese Literary & Cultural Studies 36/37

Heritages of Portuguese Influence: Histories, Spaces, Texts, and Objects

Edited by Miguel Bandeira Jerónimo,
Anna M. Klobucka, and Walter Rossa

Tagus Press
UMass Dartmouth
Dartmouth, Massachusetts

Portuguese Literary and Cultural Studies 36/37
Center for Portuguese Studies and Culture/Tagus Press
University of Massachusetts Dartmouth

Manufactured in the United States of America
Copyedited by Grace Holleran
Designed by Richard Hendel
Cover design & typesetting by Inês Sena

For all inquiries, please contact:
Center for Portuguese Studies and Culture/ Tagus Press
University of Massachusetts Dartmouth
285 Old Westport Road
North Dartmouth MA 02747–2300
Tel. 508–999–8255 / Fax 508–999–9272
https://www.umassd.edu/portuguese-studies-center/

Cover Image: Walter Rossa, *Fiends Market showcase*, Providence, 2019.

ISSN: 1521-804X (print)
ISSN: 2573-1432 (online)
ISBN: 978-1-951470-13-5 (pbk.: alk. paper)
ISBN: 978-1-951470-19-7 (Ebook)

Library of Congress Control Number: 2022940594

5 4 3 2 1

Contents

Reviews

Heritages of Portuguese Influence: Histories, Spaces, Texts, and Objects

MIGUEL BANDEIRA JERÓNIMO, ANNA M. KLOBUCKA, AND WALTER ROSSA

Editors' Introduction

In the editorial article published in the *International Journal of Heritage Studies* in late 2012, addressing the creation of the Association of Critical Heritage Studies in that same year, Laurajane Smith stresses that for scholars invested in the new, "critical" paradigm of studying heritage the resolute focus on cultural dimensions is crucial. Heritage is "*primarily* a cultural phenomenon, and not something simply subject to technical and policy debate" (535; emphasis added). It is a "political act" embedded in specific political contexts and dynamics and subject to particular power relations, as the manifesto of the newly formed association emphasized. Many methodological and analytical consequences resulted from this repositioning of heritage. Its foundational corollary was the need to critically question the formation of what Smith called the "Authorized Heritage Discourse" (AHD), the dominant, patently Eurocentric discourse that shapes the "matter" of heritage studies and the "international value and legitimacy of heritage itself," frequently obscuring its political (and social and cultural) causes, uses, and consequences—as well as its various connections to configurations of identity and personal and interpersonal relations among its actors—and valuing instead "technical" appreciations and economic rationales and interests. In many ways, heritage is a political resource, contentious and consequential, begging for a constant reflection on its definition—from an exclusively material delineation to one more attentive to "the complexities of the cultural activities" it mediates—as well as on its uses and implications (537, 540).

Echoing and extending these ideas in a widely cited 2013 article, "Clarifying the Critical in Critical Heritage Studies," Tim Winter describes the dominant contemporary directions in the field as "bringing a critical perspective to bear upon the socio-political complexities that enmesh heritage" and "tackling the thorny issues those in the conservation profession are often reluctant to acknowledge," while offering his aspirational definition of the "critical" perspective on heritage as aimed at "better understanding [of] the various ways in which heritage now has a stake in, and can act as a positive enabler for, the complex, multi-vector challenges that face us today, such as cultural and environmental sustainability, economic inequalities, conflict resolution, social cohesion and the future of cities, to name a few" (533). The dynamically evolving objectives and the expansive scope of scholarly work that falls under the umbrella of critical heritage studies are well represented in this issue of *Portuguese Literary and Cultural Studies*, which addresses itself not only to the geocultural territories that coincide with the historical reach of the Portuguese Empire but also to the diasporic heritage practices of Portuguese-speaking immigrant communities in other parts of the world, in this case represented by the United States.

The idea of organizing an issue of PLCS around the topic of Lusophone heritage(s) arose in the context of Miguel Bandeira Jerónimo's appointment as Hélio and Amélia Pedroso/Luso-American Foundation Endowed Chair in Portuguese Studies at the University of Massachusetts Dartmouth in Spring 2019, when he co-organized (with Anna M. Klobucka and Walter Rossa) a state-of-the-art conference on "*Heritages(s) of Portuguese Influence: Histories, Spaces, Texts, and Objects*" on April 5, 2019. As editors of the volume that grew out of the conference, we are grateful to all of the participants for their brilliant presentations, several of which form the core of this issue, as well as to all of the sponsors whose support made the conference and its satellite events possible: the Hélio and Amélia Pedroso/Luso-American Foundation Endowment and the Center for the Portuguese Studies and Culture and the Department of Portuguese at UMass Dartmouth; the PhD program in Heritages of Portuguese Influence and the UNESCO Chair in Intercultural Dialogue in Heritages of Portuguese Influence at the University of Coimbra; Camões, I.P.; the Calouste Gulbenkian Foundation; and the Fundação para a Ciência e Tecnologia, through the funded research project "The worlds of (under)development: processes and legacies of the Portuguese colonial empire in a comparative perspective (1945-1975)" (PTDC/HAR-HIS/31906/2017 | POCI-01-0145-FEDER-031906).

Although most articles in this volume reference extended timelines, often spanning several centuries, they are arranged here in a roughly chronological order, following Jerónimo and Rossa's introductory article, which surveys the history of heritagization in "spaces of Portuguese influence" during the late colonial period and the first decades after decolonization. Arguing that "the study of the historical intersections between trajectories of decolonization, heritage discourses and repertoires, and international and local dynamics is crucial to a much-needed critical history of heritagization," Jerónimo and Rossa lay out this process's main temporal and epistemic markers and identify its leading dynamics and challenges, producing a concise prospective framing for the more focused and detailed analyses that follow.

A period of more than a century within the temporal span of Portugal's so-called Third Empire (from the independence of Brazil in 1822 to decolonization) is surveyed in Joana Brites's article on the establishment and evolution of colonial public works services, which details their evolving organization and the politics inflecting their development, beginning with the original legal decree that addressed this matter in 1869 and ending with the demise of the Estado Novo regime in 1974. While Pedro Schacht Pereira's contribution also considers the *longue durée* of the Portuguese empire, his medium is that of intellectual history, more specifically an archeological excavation of the historical roots and building blocks of the still-influential doctrine of Lusotropicalism, which buttressed Portugal's colonial claims in the twentieth century and continues to haunt the Lusophone postcolony as arguably the most pervasive ideological legacy of the imperial era.

The focus on material heritage, albeit from a perspective that is keenly attentive to the political and symbolic dimensions of heritage building, returns in Walter Rossa's likewise *longue durée* examination of the city of Goa, from its designation as the center of the Portuguese Estado da Índia in the 1530s and its consequent urban development; its decline and decay over several centuries; and the inclusion of its "churches and convents" in UNESCO's World Heritage List in 1986, two and a half decades after Goa's decolonization and incorporation into the Republic of India. The heritage-building process is also the subject of Márcia Chuva's article on the evolution and the present state of cultural heritage policies and the uses of the past in Brazil. Following a detailed description of the presence of Brazilian objects in UNESCO's lists of World Heritage and Heritage of Humanity, both material and intangible, and an assessment of the heritage policies implemented by Brazil's National Historical and Artistic Heritage Institute, Chuva takes up as her case study the heritagization of the Ruins of São Miguel das Missões, an arena on which distinct paradigms of heritage definition and preservation can be observed to coexist and compete.

The expansive and problematizing view of what counts as "heritage" that this issue seeks to foster is borne out by Abel Djassi Amado's examination of the Cabo Verde branch of União Nacional, the political party supporting the Estado Novo dictatorial regime. The complex and intricate process of establishing the branch in the second half of the 1930s offers the opportunity to examine the articulation of regional political ideas and ideologies in the context of the competing interests of nativism and what Amado dubs as "metropolitanism," as well as the clash between different sectors of local elites (representing, respectively, Praia and Mindelo). Moving closer to our twenty-first-century present, the following two articles concern themselves with the memorialization of imperial history in contemporary Portugal. Elsa Peralta demonstrates that major public representations of the nation's collective identity remain dependent on the memory of the Portuguese empire, with the casting of Portugal as the modern-world pioneer of cultural dialogue on a global scale having become a core feature of the country's contemporary brand image. For her part, Inês Beleza Barreiros examines the political forces at work in evolving conceptualizations of the "heritage of Portuguese influence," arguing that earlier Portuguese concepts of heritagization (such as "World's Luso Heritage," "Portuguese Origin," "Portuguese World Art," and "Portuguese Heritage around the World") have often erased the colonial violence inherent in the scattering of this heritage around the world and has promoted instead the construction of an aestheticized and sanitized vision of Portugal's imperial past.

Outside of the state-sponsored and academic spheres where formal processes of heritagization are developed and conceptualized lie the many creative uses to which twentieth- and twenty-first-century Lusophone artists have put the remnants of the Portuguese empire. In her contribution to this issue, Ana Balona de Oliveira surveys a wide spectrum of works by African and Portuguese artists, whose birth dates range from 1958 to 1983, examining them as ethico-political interventions that appropriate and disrupt sculptural, architectural, and linguistic structures left behind by the empire and its history in order to confront systemic coloniality in the postcolonial present and to imagine decolonized futures. Similarly, albeit with reference to a different art form, Mirian Tavares considers the ways in which several cinematographers from former Portuguese colonies in Africa (Mozambique, Cabo Verde, and Guinea-Bissau) "inhabit the ruins" of colonialism, facing the past "não numa atitude de lamentação, mas sim numa postura de reconstrução, ou melhor, de adaptação e mudança, de transformação."

The final two articles in the volume situate their inquiries in immaterial heritage building by Portuguese-speaking communities on the East Coast of the United States, more specifically in New York and New Jersey. Kimberly DaCosta Holton explores the evolution of fado performance in New Jersey following the closing of Newark's last casa de fado, which led to the hybridization of performance spaces and audiences as well as to the emergence of a more heterogenous collective of fado performers and aficionados, setting her discussion against the background of a history of ethnic tensions in Newark's Ironbound neighborhood. In the second article, which centers on a comparative analysis of the annual celebrations of the Portugal Day in Newark in June and Brazilian Day in New York City in September, Krista Brune reflects on how the two main Lusophone diasporic communities in the New York metropolitan area articulate their respective forms of community, collective memory, and embodied culture through these festivals.

The two reviews that complement the article section reinforce the diversified and expanded understanding of "heritages of Portuguese influence" pursued throughout this issue. Daniel da Silva's review of Rui Vieira Nery's history of fado stresses the always already multicultural and multiracial roots and developmental pathways of this quintessentially Portuguese musical art form. Carmen Ramos Villar reviews Alberto Peña Rodríguez's history of the Portuguese American press as a revealing study of political and cultural community building in the diaspora. All in all, we hope that this volume of *PLCS* contributes to the ongoing developments and debates in the field of Lusophone critical heritage studies in ways that are at the same time constructive and deconstructive but that, in any case, expand the field's boundaries and productively complicate the paradigms governing its concerns, definitions, and policies.

MIGUEL BANDEIRA JERÓNIMO is Associate Professor of History at the University of Coimbra (Portugal).

ANNA M. KLOBUCKA is Commonwealth Professor of Portuguese and Women's and Gender Studies at the University of Massachusetts Dartmouth.

WALTER ROSSA is Professor in the Department of Architecture at the University of Coimbra.

MIGUEL BANDEIRA JERÓNIMO AND WALTER ROSSA

Heritage(s) of Portuguese Influence: History, Processes, and Aftereffects

ABSTRACT: Portugal was a late decolonizer (1975). The "winds of change" had a delayed impact on Portuguese colonial territories. The authoritarian nature of empire and resilient forms of imperial nationalism fostered imperial permanence, and the transformative energies of global decolonization were mostly refused. Since the 1950s, a modernizing momentum occurred, transforming urban and rural colonial landscapes and multiplying infrastructures, from railways to ports, dams, and numerous public facilities. This momentum coexisted with the beginning of the colonial wars, from 1961 onward. The colonial attempts of heritagization were severely constrained by these factors. The same happened in the post-independence period, characterized by civil wars and political and economic disarray in most territories of former Portuguese Africa. Heritage discourses and policies hardly had space to emerge. Only in the 1990s were they embraced by governments, in a reticent manner and more in theory than in practice. This text addresses these issues, touching upon some examples and arguing that the study of the historical intersections between trajectories of decolonization, heritage discourses and repertoires, and international and local dynamics is crucial to a much-needed critical history of heritagization.

KEYWORDS: Portuguese decolonization, development, heritage, Africa

RESUMO: Portugal foi um descolonizador tardio (1975). Os "ventos da mudança" tiveram um impacto moroso nos territórios coloniais portugueses. A natureza autoritária do império e as formas resilientes de nacionalismo imperial promoveram a permanência imperial. As energias transformadoras da descolonização global foram maioritariamente recusadas. A partir da década de 1950 ocorre um impulso modernizador, transformando as paisagens coloniais, urbanas e rurais, e multiplicando as infraestruturas, desde ferrovias a portos, barragens e inúmeros equipamentos públicos. Esse ímpeto coexistiu com o início das guerras coloniais, desde 1961. As tentativas coloniais de patrimonialização foram severamente restringidas por esses fatores. O mesmo aconteceu no momento pós-independência, caracterizado, na maior parte dos territórios da ex-África portuguesa, por guerras civis e desordem política e económica. Discursos e políticas de património dificilmente tiveram espaço para emergir, e só na década de 1990 foram adotadas pelos governos, de forma reticente, mais na teoria do que na prática. Este texto trata dessas questões, abordando alguns exemplos e argumentando que o estudo das intersecções históricas entre trajetórias de descolonização, discursos e repertórios patrimoniais, e dinâmicas locais e internacionais, é crucial para uma muito necessária história crítica da patrimonialização.

PALAVRAS-CHAVE: descolonização portuguesa, desenvolvimento, património, África

---

Winds of (Imperial) Permanence

Portugal was a late decolonizer. The anticolonial "winds of change" had a delayed impact on Portuguese colonial territories, which were not ceded until 1975. Characterized by a racialized, exclusionary politics of difference, despite the widespread rhetoric that promoted assimilation and integration, the authoritarian nature of empire favored imperial resilience in many ways. Publicizing the existence of a "multiracial, pluricontinental nation," the authorities repeatedly pushed back against the transformative energies of global decolonization and strove to monitor and control the growing international intervention in their political and cultural internal affairs. Since the 1950s, combined policies of ethnic (white) colonization and socioeconomic developmentalism had reigned, with the addition of enhanced social and military control connected to the liberation wars in 1961. Changes aimed at preserving Portugal's status as a colonial power were actively promoted in many areas, with different consequences but with a similar rationale.

The late colonial period (1945–1975) was characterized by a tentative enhancement of colonial rule, consisting of political, economic, and, to a lesser extent, sociocultural integration and managed transformation. The Constitutional Revision of 1951 brought the end of "empire" and the birth of "overseas provinces," enabling a "semantic decolonization." In 1961, the creation of the "Portuguese economic space" (espaço económico português) occurred, with a single market and a common currency, the Escudo Area, aiming at economic integration of the metropole and its overseas provinces. The longstanding "colonial pact" of no direct metropolitan investment in the colonies was abandoned. Portuguese

Henrique Galvão, *Portugal não é um país pequeno* (Portugal is not a small country). (Penafiel: Municipality of Penafiel, 1934).

capital transfers and investments rose, trade liberalization ensued, and foreign investment (e.g., the Point Four Program, associated with the Marshall Plan and fostered by the United States) was partially allowed.

At the same time, discourses and institutions of imperial and colonial change emerged. The idea of colonial planning became common currency, a process that was in some ways similar to the direction followed by other European colonial empires. The need to cope with the wanted and unwanted dynamics of urbanization and "detribalization," to foster rural development, to promote social welfare, and, of course, to perfect colonial extractivism and productivism led to the expansion of the "imperialism of knowledge" (Cooper 1997, 64). Diverse epistemic communities of experts and areas of expertise, including the fields of rural and urban development, multiplied. These dynamics also led to the enlargement of the colonial state, at least on paper. In a sense, an administrative revolution took place: the plethora of bureaucracy was evident. This expansion included several agencies with a mandate of socioeconomic development.

Beira Airport tower (Mozambique). Built in 1958.

Port of Luanda (Angola). Building process since the 1940s.

The spatialization of state power grew significantly. In some areas, this occurred for the first time. In a related development, new forms of population politics became crucial: ethnic (white) colonization was sponsored; urban and rural reorganization was tentatively enacted; surveys designed to promote and demonstrate an alleged shared "lusotropical" identity were disseminated (Anderson, Roque, and Santos 2019); and initiatives of population transfer and villagization emerged, both dictated by political-securitarian and economic goals. Repressive developmentalism was characteristic of this period, merging developmental and security-oriented rationales and dynamics (Jerónimo 2018). These are some of the most important processes that defined the transformative politics of imperial permanence, the set of policies and related institutional frameworks set forth by the Portuguese empire-state with a view to consolidating the existing colonial empire and reacting to the evolving internal and external pressures toward decolonization.[2]

A Modernizing Empire?

Since the 1950s, combined dynamics of population politics, socioeconomic developmentalism, and administrative governance prevailed in Portuguese colonial policy; in addition, 1961 brought the advent of enhanced social control and military intervention. A modernizing momentum, also related to the strategies of imperial relegitimization, was evident at home and abroad. From 1953 onward, various "development plans" (planos de fomento) were implemented, with significant impact on many aspects of the colonial societies, such as territorial scientific knowledge (e.g., cartography and various sciences); the use of resources (water supply and agriculture, forestry and livestock development, fishery, energy, and extractive and transformative industries); transportation and communication (roads, railways, ports, airports, and telecommunications); education, health, and social assistance (e.g., building and refurbishment of schools and hospitals); and various other areas such as housing, urbanization, and sanitation. These plans were connected to grand infrastructure projects (e.g., ports and railways), settlement plans, and dams and irrigation projects (Jerónimo and Pinto 2015; Castelo 2014). The sociopolitical and spatial consequences of these dynamics were clear, transforming both urban and rural colonial landscapes.

Plans or projects of white settlements, such as Cela in Angola and Limpopo in Mozambique, coexisted with (forced) native settlements. The former were "utopias of Portugueseness" (Castelo 2016), as evidenced by their transposition of

Dam of Cahora Bassa on the Zambeze River (Mozambique). Built 1969-1974.

Prenda Neighborhood within Luanda's *mussekes* (*shanty-towns* in Kimbundo language). Built over the 1960s.

architectural models from Portugal, while the latter were spaces of proto-urban population concentration and control (Jerónimo 2017; Curto, Cruz, and Furtado 2016).

The Estado Novo's African developmentalism entailed the expansion of infrastructures, however limited, from railways to ports, dams, and numerous public facilities. Incipient industrialization produced new urban and rural problems, and new policies arose in response to these challenges. Alongside the promotion of urban concentration and outsized dominance of the capital cities, the related administration of ethnic and racial difference became urgent; the case of the contrast between the shanty-town peripheral belt of Lourenço Marques (now Maputo) in Mozambique and the so-called "cement city" (the urban core) was exemplary of these new problems. The preservation of a segregated white city and widespread adoption of modernist architecture and urbanism went hand in hand, both as an aesthetic declaration and a political statement.[3] Its postcolonial aftereffects are manifest, although they are clearly understudied.

A Central Aspect: International Dynamics

All the factors outlined above relate more or less to inter and transnational political and economic dynamics. The "modernizing empire" engaged variously with international organizations, participating in different ways in the global spread of "international development."[4] While the relation with the International Labor Organization proved instrumental (Monteiro 2018), the relationship with the United Nations (since Portugal joined it in 1955) and with UNESCO was far more problematic, before and after the country's formal admission to the latter in 1965. In 1966, UNESCO's Resolution 11 gave permission to the Director-General to impede any kind of technical assistance to the Portuguese due to the colonial situation. In 1972, the year in which the Convention Concerning the Protection of the World Cultural and Natural Heritage was approved, Portugal left the organization. While UNESCO countries were ratifying the Convention, the Portuguese were dealing with strenuous wars in Africa and the third colonial Development Plan (1967–73) was on its way.[5]

The third plan significantly reinforced existing socioeconomic projects. While the criticism of the Modern Movement in architecture and the institutionalization of cultural-heritage agendas gained momentum in developed countries, Portugal and its then-colonies in Africa and Asia dealt with violent decolonization and, in Africa, with long-lasting civil wars. Heritage discourses and policies hardly had space to take root or gain any kind of centrality in policy making.

Portugal returned to UNESCO after the Carnation Revolution of 1974, which led to the definitive decolonization in 1975, and it ratified the convention in June 1979. The first set of Portuguese assets was inscribed in the World Heritage List (WHL) in 1983. Only in the 1990s were the principles of the convention embraced by the governments of the new Lusophone nation-states, and in a reticent manner at that, more in theory than in practice and under difficult conditions.

The history of the heritages of Portuguese influence is a revealing example of the rewards resulting from pursuing analytical intersections between trajectories of decolonization, heritage discourses and repertoires, and international and local dynamics, which can be particularly fruitful in the rethinking of the global histories of heritagization. In fact, without the proper study of these intersections, many of them still to be fully apprehended, the history of the heritages of Portuguese influence and its aftereffects can hardly be understood.

The Heritage during Colonial Rule

Twentieth-century colonial modernizing momentum transformed the urban and rural landscapes of Portuguese colonies significantly. Naturally, so did the wars that had shaped the last years of the colonial empire since 1961. The building of roads and other infrastructures associated with the war effort was one example. These dynamics fostered initiatives of cultural-heritage preservation. It is impossible to describe their comprehensive track record here, but two significant moments can be highlighted.

In 1940, the Estado Novo promoted its first great centenary commemoration cycle, dedicated to the "foundation" of Portugal in 1140 and the Restoration of Independence in 1640. The main event was the Exhibition of the Portuguese World, in Lisbon, which addressed a wide assortment of cultural expressions (*Os anos 40* 1982). In the metropole, a substantial program of building restoration was implemented, all of it chronologically and programmatically related to the foundation of "Portugueseness" (portugalidade). From the 1940s until the commemoration, in 1960, of the fifth centenary of Henry the Navigator's death—a second and last great cycle of commemorations, which were promoted as being more scientific and cultural (that is, doctrinal) than their precedents—similar actions addressed the colonial territories, partially connected to the developmentalist drive described above. For instance, the systematic survey and listing of colonial cultural heritage assets began to be composed. Survey missions and conservation projects were devised in order to monumentalize the colonies.

A program aiming at the erection of new monuments, such as statues, obelisks, and totems, ensued. The repercussions of these initiatives were severely constrained by the start of the colonial war in Angola and also by the emancipatory events in Goa, Daman, and Diu in India, both of which occurred in 1961. The winds of permanence started to be slightly restrained, both from within in the colonies and from the outside, internationally.

Notwithstanding this increasingly unfavorable context, the developmental momentum continued to foster initiatives of cultural-heritage protection. Despite the Estado Novo's ambivalent relationship with UNESCO, the Portuguese authorities did not ignore the organization's norms and practices on cultural heritage. By 1968, a commission to promote the "valorization, defense, and preservation of the monumental, artistic, and cultural heritage of the overseas provinces" (Mariz 2016, 187), including sites of archeological and historical relevance, was created, exactly a decade after a decree that aimed to concentrate the inventory, classification, and restoration of the monuments of national interest at the Overseas Ministry. A 1958 decree aimed to unify norms and practices across the overseas provinces. A decade later, one of the commission's first proposals was to send works published by UNESCO to the colonies (including their translations into Portuguese) in order to establish a modicum of regulation internationally recognized as good practice in heritage preservation. Documents about similar contexts, such as Rhodesia, were also sent to the colonies. However, circumstances shaped by the escalating colonial wars and the marginal international support for the Portuguese colonial persistence meant the marked politicization of heritage, in which political assessments tended to prevail over technical rationales. While development was generally fertilized by security-driven rationales and goals, heritagization tended to be shaped by discourses of identity, political visions, and propagandistic aims. The demonstration of Portugueseness of all colonial territories was seen as fundamental, one of the ways in which the political concept of a so-called pluricontinental nation could persevere.

In December 1973, the Provincial Secretary of Public Works of Angola, António Guedes de Campos, synthesized the political perspective on the policies of heritage: "Today, when battles are fought with ideas as they are with guns, and when victories are ephemeral if not based on principles sustained by historical continuity, it is indispensable to make an effort to preserve and improve our monuments in Angola, symbols of a secular presence and of the values of the race, with a view to revitalizing them for the present" (Mariz 2016, 409).[6] However, the norms and guidelines emanating from the metropole were mostly ignored locally, given the lack of human and material resources. The available resources were frequently directed toward more pressing needs. The traditional divergences between central and local authorities, between the metropole and the overseas provinces, surely shaped these dynamics. Centralized governance was rarely a reality, for many reasons. As a consequence, for instance, interventions targeting specific monuments were often performed without the authorization of those in charge, in the metropole but also locally. Moreover, specialized personnel was scarce, failing to match the ambitious nationalist rhetoric. In 1972, for Mozambique and Angola, the law only determined the existence, in the service of the colonial state, of one architect who was an expert in restoration. The situation in other overseas provinces was even more dramatic. Despite references to the guidelines defined by the Venice Charter for the Conservation and Restoration of Monuments and Sites (1964) or to the debates that occurred at the 15th meeting of UNESCO (Paris, 1968), the overall picture was grim (Mariz 2016, 191–92, 196).

Aftereffects

The end of the small Portuguese colonies in South Asia in December 1961, and the protracted recognition of their integration into the Republic of India by the Portuguese (which did not happen until 1974), led to the suspension of official cultural relations between the two countries. Contrary to what happened in former Portuguese Africa, where the Portuguese language was the shared communicational currency, in the former Portuguese settlements in India, English and native languages (Konkani, Marathi, Indi) thrived. In the new African countries, post-independence dynamics were not homogeneous. Pacific transition processes (Cabo Verde) coexisted with long and devastating civil wars (Angola and Mozambique) and with some coups d'état and civil turbulence (in São Tomé and Príncipe and, to a greater extent, in Guinea-Bissau). The engagement of the new states with the Portuguese colonial cultural legacy has also been diverse (Chabal 1996, 2002). It is not possible to summarize this diversity here, but four illustrations can be provided to highlight some important aspects. These cases share a common feature: they are all inscribed in the WHL. They also demonstrate the efforts of post-independence authorities to preserve and promote colonial cultural heritage as tokens of their own identity and unity.

The first example is Goa, a small and recently formed Islamic town when it was conquered by the Portuguese in 1510. It became the center of Portuguese action in the East in the 1530s, and Catholic churches and convents were erected around the city. However, Goa barely supported its role as capital city, especially due to sanitary issues. The population slowly started to abandon the place. A plan to move the capital to another location appeared in the last decade of the seventeenth century, but the resistance of the Church and the shift of the Portuguese colonial focus to Brazil made it impossible. This changed with the liberal revolution of 1820 in Portugal and the associated expulsion of religious orders in 1834; a new capital, Panjim, was designated in 1843. From then on, Goa—now called Old Goa—was neglected. The reuse of building materials became organized and systematic. The main religious complexes prevailed and shared the landscape with coconut trees. However, the shrine to Saint Francis Xavier at Bom Jesus church remains the focus of Catholic devotion in Asia. With antecedents that go back to the beginning of the Portuguese Republic (1910), colonial authorities strove to monumentalize Old Goa in the late 1950s. A new plan that obliterated the previous urban structure was devised. The integration of the territory in the Republic of India, in 1961, only delayed the obliteration, as Indian authorities went on to execute the plan. What we see in Old Goa today is the result of that project. Indian authorities proposed listing the "Churches and Convents of Goa" in the country's first application to the WHL, which was recognized by UNESCO in 1986. Their description on the WHL website states that they "illustrate the evangelization of Asia."

The second example is the Island of Mozambique, which, since the beginning of the Portuguese presence in the East, was a mandatory pit stop for all the vessels of Carreira da Índia.[7] It also became crucial to the provision of slaves to Brazil. As a consequence, it turned into a multiethnic trade outpost at the Swahili coast under Portuguese dominance. After the independence of Brazil in 1822 and the ensuing Portuguese project of creating "new Brazils in Africa," the island became the capital of Mozambique. Local dynamics, including competition with other colonial powers, led to the selection of Lourenço Marques (now Maputo) as the new capital, 1,500 kilometers to the south, and the island lost its territorial and strategic relevance. But it remained as the main territorial reference of unity for all Mozambicans, even during the Civil War (1977–1992). The authorities applied for its inclusion in the WHL, which was granted in 1991. It is still the only Mozambican WHL site.

The third example is Ribeira Grande, now Cidade Velha (Old City), on Santiago Island, Cabo Verde, which was the first human settlement in the archipelago in 1462 (Pires 2007). It was the colony's capital until 1757, the year it was replaced by Praia, founded in the sixteenth century on the same island but in a more ideal location. Ribeira Grande has never been a large town, as its topography prevents the formation of a regular urban pattern. Nonetheless, it has the oldest and some of the most valuable examples of built heritage in Cabo Verde, despite decades of extreme poverty, reinforced by its neglect by the Estado Novo regime. The developmental drive never truly reached the archipelago, while emigration continued to be a crucial, structural reality in the country. In the past, however, Cabo Verde had played an important role in Atlantic transcontinental connections as a stopover and also a warehouse for the slave trade. Following the heritage preservation actions of the 1960s, the inventory of heritage was concluded in 1971. In 1980, five years after Cabo Verde's independence, UNESCO sent an expert to evaluate the archipelagos's heritage. In the 1990s, the government started the process that led to the inclusion of Ribeira Grande in the WHL in 2009. Cabo Verde's circulatory centrality in the Atlantic, as a platform in the transcontinental slave trade, was key to the success of the application, more so than the site's material and architectural dimensions. Ribeira Grande remains Cabo Verde's only WHL site.

The fourth example is Mbanza Kongo, the political and religious capital of the Kingdom of Kongo, and the oldest inhabited African city south of the equator.[8] During the colonial period, it was renamed by the Portuguese as São Salvador, one of the measures that aimed at the Christianization of the area and its elites. After Angola's independence, the city returned to its secular name. Angolan authorities applied for its inclusion in the WHL, which was granted in 2017 under the name of "Mbanza Kongo, Vestiges of the Capital of the former Kingdom of Kongo." The WHL website states that Mbanza Kongo "illustrates, more than anywhere in sub-Saharan Africa, the profound changes caused by the introduction of Christianity and the arrival of the Portuguese into Central Africa." It is the only Angolan WHL site.

With the relative exception of Mbanza Kongo, all these sites are former colonial capitals. And this shared feature is significant because it shows clearly how the new independent states have valued and promoted such sites as their most expressive material cultural heritage.

Clube Ferroviário da Beira (Railroad Club of Beira, Mozambique) Swimming Pool. Built in 1970.

Building for Companhia Universal de Seguros (Universal Insurances Company, Lobito, Angola). Built in 1967.

Conclusions

As noted above, the Portuguese empire's late colonial moment was marked by a "second colonial occupation" (Low and Lonsdale 1976, 12), which had noticeable consequences for the urban and rural landscapes of colonial societies, generating new dynamics with long-lasting effects on, for example, the quantity and quality of infrastructures and edified heritage, from public buildings to private, multinational undertakings. Unfortunately, the historical context of the emergence of these objects and structures; the social, political, and economic dimensions of their uses; and, as importantly, the historical dynamics of their preservation, readaptation, or destruction after independence, continue to be understudied phenomena. Without this analytical move, our understanding of the crucial historical intersections between late colonialism, trajectories of decolonization, heritage discourses and repertoires, and respective international and local dynamics is significantly compromised. Moreover, in the spaces of "Portuguese influence," the violent imperial disengagement and the post-independence civil wars impeded an immediate and more or less systematic engagement with the issues of cultural heritage, from infrastructural and edified to natural and cultural.

The questioning or redefinition of colonial practices of heritage or the reenactment of networks of expertise or of institutions devoted to the topic proved impossible for decades and has begun to take place only recently. At the same time, despite the growing post-independence engagement with international organizations, the difficult economic circumstances and the political disarray that marked respective societies entailed other priorities. This meant that the heritagization of spaces of Portuguese influence was a protracted and turbulent process. Signs of change are emerging, but there is still much to consider and do in response to the issue. Even the touristification of the past, colonial or not—a process so crucial to the rebuilding of epistemic communities and institutions devoted to the study and development of heritage discourses and practices—is a recent phenomenon. These are perhaps the most important aspects that help us to understand the feeble and erratic nature of the engagement with heritage preservation in the Portuguese-speaking world, in addition to the ambivalent uses of the colonial past in the process.

NOTES

1. For all these points and more, see Jerónimo and Pinto (2015). For a comparative assessment of decolonization, see Thomas, Moore, and Butler (2008). On colonial architecture, see Milheiro (2012) and Tostões (2014).

2. For a recent summary of the Portuguese process of decolonization, see (MacQueen 2018).

3. For a more comprehensive account of this issue, see Rossa (2016).

4. For an excellent overview of the intersection between developmentalism and international organizations, see Unger (2018). See also Frey, Kunkel, and Unger (2014).

5. For more on the 1972 UNESCO Convention, see Cleere (2011). For the geographical expansion of the convention, see Cleere (2003).

6. This and all other translations from Portuguese are by the authors.

7. On the Island of Mozambique, see Ilha de Moçambique (1985) and Lobato (1945). For related heritage issues, see Rossa, Lopes, and Gonçalves (2018).

8. On Mbanza Kongo, see Thornton (2000). For the Kingdom of Kongo, see Bostoen and Brinkman (2018).

WORKS CITED

Anderson, Warwick, Ricardo Roque, and Ricardo Ventura Santos, eds. 2019. *Luso-Tropicalism and Its Discontents: The Making and Unmaking of Racial Exceptionalism*. New York: Berghahn Books.

Bostoen, Koen, and Inge Brinkman, eds. 2018. *The Kongo Kingdom: The Origins, Dynamics and Cosmopolitan Culture of an African Polity*. Cambridge: Cambridge University Press.

Castelo, Cláudia. 2014. "Developing 'Portuguese Africa' in Late Colonialism: Confronting Discourses." In *Developing Africa*, edited by Joseph M. Hodge, Gerald Hodl, and Martina Kopf, 63–86. Manchester: Manchester University Press.

———. 2016. "Reproducing Portuguese Villages in Africa: Agricultural Science, Ideology and Empire." *Journal of Southern African Studies* 42 (2): 267–81.

Chabal, Patrick, ed. 2002. *A History of Postcolonial Lusophone Africa*. Bloomington: Indiana University Press.

———. ed. 1996. *The Postcolonial Literature of Lusophone* Africa. London: Hurst.

Cleere, Henry. 2011. "The 1972 UNESCO World Heritage Convention." *Heritage & Society* 4 (2): 173–86.

———. 2003. "The World Heritage Convention in the Third World." In *Cultural Resource Management in Contemporary Society*, edited by Francis P. McManamon and Alf Hatton, 99–106. London: Routledge.

Cooper, Frederick. 1997. "Modernizing Bureaucrats, Backward Africans, and the Development Concept." In *International Development and the Social Sciences: Essays in the History and Politics of Knowledge*, edited by Frederick Cooper and Randall Packard, 64–92. Berkeley: University of California Press.

Curto, Diogo Ramada, Bernardo Cruz, and Teresa Furtado. 2016. *Políticas coloniais em tempo de revoltas — Angola circa 1961*. Porto: Afrontamento.

Frey, Marc, Sonke Kunkel, and Corinna Unger, eds. 2014. *International Organizations and Development (1945–1990)*. Basingstoke: Palgrave Macmillan.

Ilha de Moçambique: Relatório. 1985. Maputo: Secretaria de Estado da Cultura de Moçambique/Arkitektskolen i Aarhus.

Jerónimo, Miguel Bandeira. 2017. "'A Battle in the Field of Human Relations': The Official Minds of Repressive Development in Portuguese Angola." In *Decolonization and Conflict*, edited by Martin Thomas and Gareth Curless, 115–36. London: Bloomsbury.

———. 2018. "Repressive Developmentalisms: Idioms, Repertoires, Trajectories in Late Colonialism." In *The Oxford Handbook of the Ends of Empire*, edited by Andrew Thompson and Martin Thomas, 537–54. Oxford: Oxford University Press.

Jerónimo, Miguel Bandeira, and António Costa Pinto. 2015. "A Modernizing Empire? Politics, Culture and Economy in Portuguese Late Colonialism." In *The Ends of European Colonial Empires*, edited by Miguel Bandeira Jerónimo and António Costa Pinto, 51–80. Basingstoke: Palgrave Macmillan.

Lobato, Alexandre. 1945. *A Ilha de Moçambique: Monografia*. Lourenço Marques: Imprensa Nacional de Moçambique.

Low, D. A., and John Lonsdale. 1976. "Towards the New Order, 1945–1963." In *History of East Africa*, edited by D. A. Low and Alison Smith, 3: 1–63. Oxford: Clarendon Press.

MacQueen, Norrie. 2018. "Portugal: Decolonization without Agency." In *The Oxford Handbook of the Ends of Empire*, edited by Andrew Thompson and Martin Thomas, 162–78. Oxford: Oxford University Press.

Mariz, Vera. 2016. "A 'memória do Império' ou o 'Império da memória': A salvaguarda do património arquitectónico português ultramarino (1930–1974)." PhD diss., University of Lisbon.

Milheiro, Ana Vaz. 2012. *Nos trópicos sem Le Corbusier: Arquitetura luso-africana no Estado Novo*. Lisboa: Relógio d'Água.

Monteiro, José Pedro. 2018. *Portugal e a questão do trabalho forçado: Um império sob escrutínio (1944–1962)*. Lisboa: Edições 70.

Os anos 40 na arte portuguesa. 1982. 5 vols. Lisboa: Fundação Calouste Gulbenkian.

Pires, Fernando. 2007. *Da cidade da Ribeira Grande à Cidade Velha em Cabo Verde: Análise histórico-formal do espaço urbano, séc. XV–séc. XVIII*. Praia: Universidade de Cabo Verde.

Rossa, Walter. Forthcoming. "Goa's Heritage of Portuguese Influence in a Global Context." In *African-Asian Portuguese Interactions*, edited by Robert Newman and Delfim Correia da Silva. Goa and Coimbra: Goa University Press and Imprensa da Universidade de Coimbra.

———. 2016. "Luanda and Maputo: Accounts of the Two Capitals in Urban Heritage Discourse." *Journal of Lusophone Studies* 1 (1): 107–16.

Rossa, Walter, Nuno Lopes, and Nuno Simão Gonçalves, eds. 2018. *Oficinas de Muhipiti: Planeamento estratégico, património, desenvolvimento*. Coimbra: Imprensa da Universidade de Coimbra.

Thomas, Martin, Bob Moore, and Larry Butler. 2008. *Crises of Empire*. London: Hodder.

Thornton, John K. 2000. "Mbanza Kongo/São Salvador: Kongo's Holy City." In *Africa's Urban Past*, edited by David Anderson and Richard Rathbone, 67–84. London: James Currey.

Tostões, Ana, ed. 2014. *Arquitetura moderna em África: Angola e Moçambique*. Lisboa: Fundação para a Ciência e Tecnologia.

Unger, Corinna. 2018. *International Development: A Postwar History*. London: Bloomsbury.

MIGUEL BANDEIRA JERÓNIMO (PhD King's College London, 2008) is an Associate Professor of History at the University of Coimbra (College of Arts and Humanities). He was a Visiting Assistant Professor at Brown University (2011 and 2012) and Hélio and Amélia Pedroso/Luso-American Foundation Endowed Chair in Portuguese Studies (Spring 2019) at the University of Massachusetts Dartmouth. His research interests focus on the comparative and connected histories of imperialism, colonialism and internationalism in the nineteenth and twentieth centuries. Among other publications, he authored *The 'Civilizing Mission' of Portuguese Colonialism (c.1870–1930)* (2015) and coedited *Internationalism, Imperialism and the Formation of the Contemporary World* (2017) and *Education and Development in Colonial and Postcolonial Africa* (2020). He coordinates the international research project "The Worlds of (Under)Development: Processes and Legacies of the Portuguese Colonial Empire in a Comparative Perspective (1945–1975)," funded by the Portuguese Foundation for Science and Technology (2018–22). He also coedits the book series "História & Sociedade" at Edições 70 (Portugal) and "The Portuguese Speaking World: Its History, Politics, and Culture" at Sussex Academic (United Kingdom).

WALTER ROSSA holds a PhD in Architecture and an MA in Art History. He is Professor in the Department of Architecture, a researcher at the Center for the History of Society and Culture, and UNESCO Chair in Intercultural Dialogue in Heritages of Portuguese Influence at the University of Coimbra. He also co-shares the Cunha Rivara Chair at Goa University. Rossa researches the theory and history of architecture and urbanism, especially on town planning, the landscape, and the cultural heritage of the former Portuguese colonial universe. He has dedicated his recent academic efforts to cooperation and the operative relation between heritage, history, planning, and development to establish interactions between his academic activity and development actions.

JOANA BRITES

Colonial Public Works Services in Portugal's Third Empire (1869–1975)[1]

ABSTRACT: This paper analyzes the establishment and evolution of colonial public works services in Portugal's Third Empire, from the original, prototypical establishment of their organization, in 1869, until the end of Portuguese colonial rule, in 1975. The creation and successive restructuring of these services are analyzed in relation to the colonial policies undertaken throughout this period, shedding light on the gap between normative texts and their effective implementation on the ground. At the same time, the paper highlights how lawmaking can provide insight into the way the authority over a colonial empire was conceptualized and how the appearance of control was a key factor both internally and externally. Finally, by embracing a *longue durée* perspective, this analysis identifies common denominators and global trends, and questions the impact of political turning points on the process at hand.

KEYWORDS: public works, Portuguese colonialism, Africa, legislation

RESUMO: Este artigo analisa o estabelecimento e a evolução dos serviços de obras públicas no terceiro império português, desde o decreto que, em 1869, primeiro estipulou o protótipo da sua organização, até ao fim do domínio colonial português, em 1975. A criação e sucessiva reestruturação destes serviços é posta em relação com as políticas coloniais seguidas no período examinado. Clarifica-se o fosso entre os textos normativos e a sua efetiva implementação no terreno. Ao mesmo tempo, o artigo sublinha o modo como a produção de legislação pode contribuir para esclarecer a forma como se concebeu a autoridade sobre um império colonial e como a aparência de controlo foi crucial interna e externamente. Finalmente, adotando-se uma perspetiva de longa duração, identificam-se pontos comuns e tendências, e questiona-se o impacto das viragens políticas no processo em análise.

PALAVRAS-CHAVE: obras públicas, colonialismo português, África, legislação

1. Introduction

The present article is the first (and partial) output of a broader research project dedicated to the role of architecture in the legitimation of late Portuguese colonialism in Africa. The presumed absence or significantly lesser extent of the state's control over architectural designs in these territories, when compared to the dictatorially ruled metropole, has been a widely shared premise of mainstream historiography on the architecture built in formerly Portuguese Africa during the second half of the twentieth century.[2] However, an in-depth, *longue durée*, and cross-scale analysis of the spheres, mechanisms, and circuits of public architecture monitoring, appraisal, and execution in former Portuguese African colonies remains unfulfilled, despite important contributions.[3] This avenue of inquiry is critical to the discussion of the agency of colonial modernism and can further dispute the still-lingering, albeit highly questionable and already contested, deterministic linkage between modern architecture and political and social progressiveness.[4] Moreover, architecture viewed as a terrain of negotiation and contingent accommodation, with an impact on perceptions and behaviors, can offer a fruitful contribution to the understanding of colonial rule, in terms of both discourse and practice. It can shed light on its implementation and operativity, its challenges and shortcomings, its compromises and strategies of survival. It can elucidate how order and predictability coexisted with situational contingency and inventiveness.

The problem under analysis is a composite one. In a first phase, it implies on the one hand the study of the organization of colonial public works services on the ground; on the other, of the metropole bodies with responsibilities regarding the very same works. It is crucial to examine how these entities, on the scale of both the colonies and the metropole, evolved and interacted, thus revealing the circuits of design making, approval and implementation, related motivations, opportunities and constraints, and actual accomplishments. One must consider and illustrate the gap between normative texts and reality; in other words, one cannot confuse the regulation of public works services with their practice. Nevertheless, with the necessary methodological precautions, lawmaking can offer a fruitful insight into the way the authority over a colonial empire was conceptualized and how the appearance of control was a key factor, internally and externally. Moreover, there is much to be learned from the legislation's shortcomings, delays, and resistance towards its application, as this article seeks to demonstrate. Therefore, it is essential to cross-examine and confront the normative formulations with archival materials from the former colonial territories and the metropole.

In a second stage, where my investigation currently stands, other layers of analysis, located upstream and downstream of the architectonic object, need to be included and cross-examined. Land property, labor conditions in the construction sector, the organization and functioning of building sites, and the process of forming and circulating transnational expertise directly or indirectly related to architecture are, in my view, among the most pressing research topics. The constellation of actors, social relations, dynamics, realities, and institutional frameworks connected to and residing within the architectonic object is a rich and meaningful ground for detailed analysis.

The following text focuses solely on the organization of public works services in the colonies. Although the subject of this paper is only a part of a multifaced process, and thus insufficient to grasp the entire set of conditions shaping the production of colonial architecture, this choice of focus allows me the necessary space to explain the emergence and reshaping of these services from the nineteenth century until the end of the Portuguese rule in Africa in 1975. The historical reconstruction of the organics of public works services implies a permanent dialogue with the colonial policies implemented throughout this period. The goal is not to use this context simply as a scenario but to assess how colonial public works were a critical part of these policies and, in turn, clarify broader frameworks and the mindsets that governed them. Furthermore, the extensive timeframe covered here, together with the detachment of the analysis from political turning points, allows the mapping of continuities and the consequent questioning of singularities and fine-tuning of specificities.

2. The Emergence of a Global Legal Frame for Public Works Services in the Portuguese Colonies

The refocusing of Portugal's imperial core and rationale toward its African possessions was a multifaced process launched in the nineteenth century, following Brazil's independence in 1822 and the subsequent search for alternative stages and strategies for economic growth, geopolitical repositioning, and a national sense of historical purpose (a teleological mythology with an imperial vocation at its center). Additionally, the increasing contemporaneous disputes over African territories between rival colonial powers and the resulting struggle to assure their "effective" occupation weighed heavily on this transition and the management of the third and last phase of the Portuguese colonial empire. These internal and external agendas and pressures, together with the construction of the liberal state in Portugal from 1834 onward, translated, among many other dimensions, into a reboot of the colonial administration.[5] Consecutive waves of legal transformations aimed to restructure, rebuild, and modernize the empire, whose African territories were still largely unknown to the colonizers and precariously held, despite Portuguese presence on the continent dating back to the fifteenth century.

For their pivotal structural and discursive role in the colonial development, public works soon became the target of this torrent of juridical innovation and transformation. Therefore, they are a rich analytical avenue to observe the push toward and resistances against the construction of a modern state and the modernization of the colonial system, along with the survival of the *ancien régime*'s practices and mindsets within a renewed legal framework. Public works constitute a particularly illustrative sector of the overall substantial chasm between the law and practical achievements.

The general legal frame for the organization of public works services in Portuguese colonies, whose effects would prove to be meager, was decreed on December 3, 1869,[6] two days after the comprehensive reform of the administrative institutions in the overseas territories,[7] which was infused with a wishful decentralizing spirit. As far as I have been able to determine, this decree, issued by the Ministry of Navy and Overseas Affairs, was the first ever to conceive a single organization model for the public works services of all the Portuguese colonies. Its introduction should be understood in the light of a liberal-driven global effort, not devoid of obstacles and setbacks, to establish an administrative and legal uniformization of colonial possessions. The empire was starting to be considered and addressed as a whole. The exercise was remote, largely abstract, and highly disconnected from the empirical knowledge on the ground.

The decree in question aimed to serve as a blueprint. As it stipulated, five years from its promulgation, the colonies were to have their own public works services regulated in accordance with the 1869 diploma.[8] One exception was granted, for the time being: the so-called Portuguese "Estado da Índia," comprising the territories of Goa, Daman, and Diu, would maintain the existing organization of public works in place, until further assessment. The presence of military engineering personnel in this possession postponed an immediate application of the decree. The singularity of human resources available in

Estado da Índia demanded a closer examination of needs prior to the adoption of the broader organization model prescribed for the territories of Angola, Mozambique, Cabo Verde, Portuguese Guinea (today Guinea-Bissau), São Tomé and Príncipe, Macau, and Timor. But just over two months later, on February 26, 1870, Luís Augusto Rebello da Silva, at the time Minister and Secretary of State for Navy and Overseas Affairs, deemed it beneficial to extend the range of the 1869 model to the Portuguese Estado da Índia, believing that its "higher degree of civilization" would actually facilitate the implementation of the new system.[9]

The major, yet frail, accomplishment of the 1869 decree was the establishment and organization of a human resources template for the task at hand. In the words of Rebello da Silva, this task was, right after education, "the second powerful instrument of progress."[10] The tale of progress, flourishing rampantly both nationally and internationally, had a systematic presence in nineteenth-century colonial discourse and jurisprudence. With the turn of the century, the word "development" would replace "progress" in this normative sphere, prolonging its linear view of history and the modernist belief in the ability to reshape both human beings and nature. For their impact on the territory and its population, infrastructures were an evident priority, tool, and laboratory of this narrative.

The operations of the standard colonial public works service comprehended public road works, civil and military constructions, wetland depletion, river channeling, soil exploitation and statistics, as well as a mining branch where justifiable. This heterogeneous scope of intervention was supervised in each colony (at the time formally denominated "province") by a director of public works (either a civil or military engineer), to whom the remaining employees (engineers; technicians, generally from the army and responsible for conducting and managing the works; technical designers; and craftsmen) would answer. In turn, the public works' director followed the orders of the governor-general of the colony, who chaired the colonial Technical Council. This body, established by the decree of December 3, 1869, in order to (ideally) cease decision-making devoid of technical expertise, oversaw all matters related to public works. Taking into consideration the input of this council, the governor-general would decide which works would be carried out (after their design evaluation), what elements should accompany the projects, what system ought to be followed for their execution (either by direct or outsourced management, fully or in part), what conditions must be regarded to guarantee budget compliance and technical proficiency, and what rules the accounting management would follow.

Regarding the recruitment of personnel for the colonial public works services, it targeted first and foremost the military, a pool considered to have the "most valuable" men for the job.[11] The attempt to maintain a permanent workforce for the public works of each overseas territory was deemed imprudent in the preamble of the 1869 decree. Instead, these workers were labeled as providers of a commission service and placed into a flexible category called *situação de serviço* (service situation), created at the time of the decree. This resolution allowed the central government to designate a fluctuating body of technicians, according to short-term needs and available budget, which was required to accept the call to serve in any of the colonies. For service in the western African territories of Cabo Verde, São Tomé and Príncipe, and Angola, technicians were chosen among those trained and graduated in the metropole. For other colonies—Mozambique, the Estado da Índia, Macau, and Timor—the workforce would be supplied by the Estado da Índia, which had its own technical training capacity. The criterion of geographical specialization applied at this time in the organization of colonial public works services and their personnel would soon prove to be inefficient, however, and was abandoned later in the nineteenth century.

All those appointed to the *situação de serviço* received a pay supplement and benefited from career progression measures. However, this arrangement would soon prove to be unfit for attaining an indispensable level of competence within the technical corps. The incentives fell short, particularly in the African colonies, given the challenges of the tropical climate, perceived as pathological both physically and morally, and the negligible healthcare assistance.[12]

The gradual replacement in the twentieth century of the public works' expert corps composed of military personnel with a workforce comprising civil engineers, urban planners, and (albeit relatively fewer) architects, similarly to other European colonial powers (Silva 2015a, 9), did not, however, solve Portugal's chronic shortage of human resources in its colonies. The lack of sufficiently skilled staff would indeed come to be one of the most persistent arguments for significant legal upgrades to public works services in the African colonies until the end of the Portuguese rule in 1975. Far from being restricted to public works, the debate over personnel persistently encompassed every area of colonial activity, starting with the political administration itself.

In terms of monitoring mechanisms, the 1869 decree established regular annual inspections of the public works services and extraordinary inspections when required by the metropole or the governor-general of the colony.

Furthermore, an annual report on works, together with suggestions of improvements deemed necessary for the service, was to be compiled by the director of public works in each colony and submitted to the government. This measure reinforced an ordinance dating back to 1857, in turn clarified and expanded in 1868, which established a chain of quarterly reports on ongoing works that was to be compiled by the director of public works, presented to the governor-general of the colony, and then sent to the respective ministry in Lisbon.[13] The frequent need to insist on previously ruled topics elucidates the time window required to internalize legal standards and procedures.

The immense lack of human and material resources, the lingering attachment of the colonial administrative apparatus to its former *raison d'être* (largely shaped by the slave trade, whose formal abolition, in 1836, had meager effects), the precapitalist mindset of potential domestic investors, as well as the dispersion of competing, narrow, and short-term goals of metropolitan and colonial elites severely limited the reach of the 1869 diploma. At the time, the investment of the Portuguese government in the infrastructural development of its overseas territories was still virtually inexistent, despite its relative increase.

In the overall budget for the fiscal year 1852/53, an amount just under 39 million réis (or 39 contos) was allocated to the public works in the entire Portuguese colonial space.[14] In order to grasp how negligible this sum was, the budget of the central metropolitan administration for the same year was equivalent to 12,889 contos (Valério 2001, 47–48). The first amount was therefore only about 0.3 percent of the latter. Secondly, the disparity of the areas' size must be highlighted, notwithstanding the dramatic and expectable differences in population density. Continental Portugal (with around 91,624 km^2 [Law 2011, 297]) occupied approximately 0.0046 percent of the combined territory of its two largest colonies in Africa: Angola, with over 1.2 million km^2, and Mozambique, with 783,000 km^2 (Alexandre 2004, 111).[15]

In 1870, 81 million réis (81 contos) were allocated to public works in the overseas budget.[16] The sluggishly rising funding rested mostly on a specific tax on imports and exports in various colonies, created and adjusted repeatedly from the late 1850s to the early 1870s (Silva 1904, 305–6) and drawn on to partially or fully finance the public works in those territories. Custom houses (*alfândegas*) were the primary source of public revenue throughout the second half of the nineteenth century, since the capacity to collect direct taxes, like the fiscal system in general, was in an embryonic stage.[17] In the preparatory report of the 1874/75 budget, a total of 176 million réis (176 contos) from the aforementioned tax revenues were distributed among Cabo Verde, São Tomé and Príncipe, Angola, Mozambique, and India.[18] The funding was nevertheless still meager.

The shortcomings of a self-financed colonial development scheme had become apparent at a time when African possessions were increasingly regarded as a priority among national political elites. Although temporary and far from forming national consensus, this shift strengthened the position of those who argued for some degree of metropolitan sacrifice, which would correspond to the increase of indebtedness abroad rather than to the reduction of domestic investment. The law of April 12, 1876, authorized the government to take out a loan up to the amount of 1 billion réis (1000 contos) to be applied to the construction, maintenance, or upgrade of public works exclusively in the African colonies.[19] Other, smaller loans would follow from the late 1870s to the early 1890s (Silva 1904, 307–8). The priority was clearly given to transport infrastructures, followed by personnel. Taking Mozambique as an example, from the total sum assigned to this territory in 1876 (400 million réis), the most substantial cuts were allocated to subsidizing the construction of the Lourenço Marques (today Maputo) railway (22.5 percent); to ports, roads, and bridges (16.75 percent); and to technical and secretarial staff (15 percent).[20]

The awareness of King Leopold II's colonial projects and the rising tensions prior to the Berlin Conference (1884–85) made both the timing and the targeted investment unsurprising, as urban planning and infrastructure were perceived as tools of colonial legitimization and territory control. They were key arguments to back up the historical rights claimed by the Portuguese in the "scramble for Africa." The security nexus, already palpable here, will indeed be the long-lasting characteristic of colonial developmentalism until the end of Portuguese rule.[21] And the same link, as Sara Lorenzini (2019) points out, can be argued for the entire history of development from the nineteenth century to the present.

The outcome of this gradual, albeit slow and insufficient, increase of financing pace is identified, in an early 1890s retrospective analysis, with the launch of a public works expedition to Africa in 1877 (in articulation with a larger, multifaceted campaign of scientific exploration) and the development of some public works perceived as significant, mainly in Angola and Mozambique.[22] The efforts and appeals toward the exploration and field research and documentation of African territories, regarded as key to Portugal's claims of "effective domain" over them, cannot be separated from the creation of the Sociedade de Geografia de Lisboa (Geographical Society of Lisbon) in 1875.[23] The prioritization of cartography would soon be adopted by the government, with the establishment of a Central Cartography Commission within the Ministry of Navy and Overseas Affairs. It also received the endorsement and close attention of the Associação Comercial de Lisboa (Commercial Association of Lisbon). This alignment of private and public interests was critical to the undertaking of expeditions and the multiplication of voices in the ongoing colonial debate. Like other European geography societies, the Geographical Society of Lisbon became a central locus for the discussion of colonial strategies.

However, the tangible impact of the aforementioned expeditions, which emulated those previously promoted by other European colonial powers, remains ill-defined and questionable. As for the public works, only with the financial relief from the loan authorized in 1876 could their implementation be ruled at a more concrete and operative level. In other words, public works services, structured some years before according to the 1869 decree, existed in a largely virtual state until the establishment of a more practical set of guidelines regarding the launching, approval, and management of public works, as well as the execution of expenses. A "regulation for the administration and supervision of public works" was issued for Mozambique on December 23, 1876; for Angola on February 19, 1877; for Cabo Verde on September 4, 1877; and for São Tomé and Príncipe on October 19, 1877 (Silva 1904, 306).[24]

However, by the late 1870s, the framework for public services issued in 1869 was already perceived as needing some refinement, particularly in view of the additional funding authorized in May 1878, June 1879, and June 1880. As a result, on December 23, 1880, an additional diploma was decreed, exclusively targeting public works services in Portugal's African colonies.[25] It did not revoke the 1869 organization of these services but further specified their scope and monitoring. The introduction in this document of geodesy, surveying, and hydrography, with consequent efforts to enhance respective cartography, is highly elucidative of the endeavors to get to know and assess African territories, as well as to produce a simulacrum of Portuguese domain over them. The fine-tuning of terminology—such as replacing "soil exploration," present in the 1869 formula, with "geology, mapping, and mining"—reiterates the impact of colonial scientific exploration and research. In turn, the 1880 diploma also covered bridges, railways, telegraphs, seaports, and lighthouses, thus reflecting the growing attention paid to transport and communication infrastructures. In terms of monitoring, two key aspects were inserted. For the first time, the Technical Council implemented in each colony had its tasks specified. Secondly, there was a precise determination of who possessed the authority to approve a public work project according to its foreseen cost, following the abovementioned "regulations for the administration and supervision of public works" issued for the various African colonies between 1876 and 1877.

This surge of energy in thc 1870s did not turn the page of public works development, however, nor could it have done so. The basic need for a network of transport infrastructure, railways in particular, was far from being met, and Portugal was not able to finance such a network. Indeed, it only took off from the late 1880s onward under the leadership of concession companies and private investors, who had parallel agendas in parallel geographies and often gained an ample authority over these territories.

The perceived flaws of the 1869 decree would be tackled in a conjuncture of an economic and financial crisis and a more radicalized and encompassing imperial nationalism. The latter was spurred by the so-called British Ultimatum (1890), which crushed the ambitious Portuguese aspirations of securing a coast-to-coast land corridor connecting Angola to Mozambique (rendered in the so-called "rose-colored map"). A wider readjustment of the colonial system was on the way, with implications ranging from protectionist trade tariffs to labor regime (Pedreira 1998, 278–85). The striving to capitalize on human and natural African resources went hand in hand with violent military campaigns that aimed to shatter local sovereigns, on the one hand, and with the growing "privatization of control, administration, and taxation" (Jerónimo 2018a, 13) entrusted to chartered companies, on the other.[26] The engineering of power balances and strategies of compromise that aimed to counteract the limited capacity of Portuguese rule would come to be another enduring feature of Portugal's colonial empire, one that would cross different internal political regimes and transmute according to distinct world orders. Public works reflected this modus operandi at many levels, one of the clearest being the evolution of construction priorities.

Ruled on August 20, 1892, the "Organization Plan for Public Works and Industry Services in the Directorate General of Overseas and Overseas Provinces" conveyed the conviction that public works overseas needed to be tackled on two articulated fronts: locally, by restructuring the public works services in the colonies, and in the metropole, by reorganizing the division that, within the framework of the Directorate General of Overseas (in turn part of the Ministry of Navy and Overseas Affairs), was responsible for the central administration of public works in overseas territories, among its other responsibilities, since the mid-nineteenth century.[27]

The restructuring of the services addressed the need to tighten the supervision of works, which grew to absorb larger hydraulics works, agronomy, forestry, and postal services, as well as the manufacturing industry. Moreover, it aimed to further control and reduce the expenditure of funds only "to the absolutely necessary" and attract and secure qualified and experienced personnel in the overseas territories.[28] It was also time to expand the efforts toward unification and uniformization. The laws and regulations governing the public works in the metropole would, as a rule, apply to colonial public works. The overseas technical staff could no longer embody a separate and rather volatile workforce category. Integration mechanisms, on the one hand, and equivalence measures between civilian and military employees, on the other, were therefore prioritized.

3. The Portuguese First Republic and the Longevity of Its Legislative Work

The Portuguese First Republic (1910–26) reinforced imperialist nationalism and made efforts toward an "effective" occupation. Following the creation, in August 1911, of the Ministry of Colonies (the first autonomous government department solely dedicated to the overseas territories), the global legal framework of colonial public works services was again reshaped.[29] The decree of November 11, 1911, established the new "General Regulation of the Directories and Inspections of Public Works in the Colonies," replacing the 1892 rule and the complementary and episodic legislation that followed.[30]

Matching the decentralizing spirit of the republican regime's proposals, the organization defined for colonial public works services was intended to act as a set of general principles. It did not fix the structure of these services but instead determined a list of responsibilities and the flow of authority, giving each colony permission to create permanent sections to divide and conduct the listed tasks. As an example, Angola's regulation, issued in 1912, established four technical sections (Ramos 1970, 687). To operationalize the general regulation of public works services and their inspection, each colony proposed the organization of their technical personnel and other minor adjustments that it considered convenient, which were subject to the government's final approval. But, once again, the transformative power of legislation is highly questionable, both in general and particularly with regard to the ability to transfer and/or share control with local authorities. And the law itself ended up demonstrating its limits, as well as the gap between its spirit and its letter. The diploma of November 11, 1911, provides clear evidence of this for one immediate reason: it remained in place until 1964. This means that the republican-inspired organization of the public works service in the Portuguese colonial empire would also come to accommodate and enable the intents and courses of action of the military dictatorship (1926–32) and of more than two thirds of the long-lasting right-wing dictatorship that followed, the Estado Novo, or New State (1933–74), both characterized by muscular administrative centralization. Legal continuities, rather than apparently drastic legislative changes, shed a helpful light onto the past, questioning the validity of turning points as much as the historians' drive to establish them.

The 1911 decree was flexible enough to act as a vessel for different political typologies and imperial projects, in turn interacting with disparate internal and external contexts. This situation is, nevertheless, far from exceptional and only at first sight surprising. Legislation constrains but does not determine behavior, and the exercise of rule comprises a dynamic interaction with those over whom it is imposed. Exclusively top-down and essentialized interpretations of both decentralization and centralization procedures often dismiss the complex and multi-layered nature of agency, the enduring dynamics of the interaction with local powers, and the possibilities and limitations inherent to those procedures. Narrow understandings neglect the unavoidable appropriation and reinterpretation of rules and regulations, the conflict and fusion between the elusive nature of law and its materiality, dispersed, shared, and delivered by individuals with their own accumulated experience and ingrained operating schemes. Moreover, the legal endurance in the public works sector offers some insight into a larger phenomenon: as pointed out by Andrew Roberts, the Estado Novo soon realized that it could capitalize on the republican inheritance and "adopt with few alterations" the policies of the First Republic (1986, 500).

The 1911 regulation introduced an unprecedented level of comprehensiveness and detail, embodying a tendency that would further intensify throughout the century: the significant increase and specialization of bureaucracy in an attempt to eliminate the arbitrary and the subjective from decision-making procedures. As a result, hierarchies and circuits of power were clearly codified, and mechanisms to document, inspect, reward, and punish performance in the sphere of public administration were implemented or fine-tuned. Although archival documentation illuminates the systematic shortcomings and slowness of the efforts to gradually automate decisions, the legal endeavor at stake here is revealing.

It would frame the administrative mindset over the following decades. Equally significant is the fact that the 1911 decree covered two phenomena often regulated autonomously: the organization of colonial public works services and the concrete rules governing the approval of works' execution.

The scope of action of the colonial public works directorates was enlarged and endowed with higher specificity, thus revealing a growing awareness of tangible challenges on the ground, and the need to extend the state's supervision to private enterprises. For the first time, the verb "to study" preceded the list of activities in most of the areas of intervention ascribed to public works directorates, thus echoing the growing global perception of the importance of knowledge-based practices. The interconnected drive to plan and program ahead propelled the creation of a mandatory general plan, of works in each colony, ideally immune to interference from casual demands. Moreover, each section of the public works services was to have prototype projects of the most common constructions, approved at a higher level and ready to be applied. The same purpose of standardizing and/or detailing assignments and procedures was evident in the reorganization of colonial Technical Councils, the regulation of public works services' inspections, and the scheduling and normalization of reports submitted to the metropole.

Naturally, this detailed regulatory drive also encompassed personnel: workers' admission and promotion (for which experience was valued and, for higher positions, required), salaries, tasks, absences, and leaves, as well as disciplinary penalties. Furthermore, while admitting the possibility of recruiting workers for a limited time and on an ad hoc basis (through service contracts), the new diploma revealed a more stable future horizon in comparison with that of 1869. The 1911 colonial prospects called for the stabilization of a body of experts on the ground. As such, the law established a permanent technical staff composed of engineers, architects, and site managers, along with auxiliary construction employees dedicated to the maintenance of infrastructures.

For the first time, the position of architect appeared recognized in the legislation related to the colonies. However, in daily practice, the architects' duties often extended to activities beyond their specific training.[31] Furthermore, the formalization of the architect's role in the twentieth-century Portuguese colonial space should not be understood as foreshadowing a looming hegemony of this professional in the construction sphere. Such dominance never existed. As far as my research, which focuses on the former Portuguese colonies in Africa, and in particular on Mozambique, has been able to determine, the number of architects in colonial public works services was systematically small until the end of Portuguese rule. Until 1950, the Mozambican services had only one architect.[32] In 1964, when the services and corresponding personnel were restructured, architect vacancies in the permanent staff of Mozambique's public works reached seven, an unprecedented peak, while the same reform foresaw thirty-seven positions for engineers (in the areas of civil and mechanical engineering, geography, and agronomy).[33] According to the research I conducted at the Historical Archive of Mozambique, the frequent demands addressed to colonial and metropolitan authorities protesting the persistent understaffing of these services barely included mention of architects. Colonial public works were indeed a preserve of engineers, even when building designs carried out on the ground came from the hands of metropolitan architects. It was the engineers who, increasingly detached from the military sphere and trained in different specialties, conceptualized, conducted, and monitored public works programs in the colonies. The same phenomenon can be verified not only in the vast campaign of public works launched in the metropole during the Estado Novo but also in other colonial empires (see, among others, Ravesteijn and Nispen 2007).

The growing complexity and bureaucratization of public works services also translated into the reinforcement of two categories of staff. The first was the secretariat personnel, who played a crucial role in assembling the paper trail of the services' activities. These would, in theory, be observable and verifiable through multiple compulsory logbooks, carefully examined during inspections. Secondly, the 1911 diploma gave prominence to the intermediate management layer, formed by section heads of the public works services. The delegation and specialization of oversight responsibilities enabled a more thorough and extensive examination of the work conducted on the ground. These mid-level managers also acted as intermediaries, providing the director of public works services in each colony, whose supervisory role was broadened, with monthly, quarterly, biannual, and annual reports. Consequently, the director was granted superior knowledge of the actions and performance of all personnel and sectors, which was crucial to the setting of intervention priorities.

4. A Normative Zenith in the Twilight of the Portuguese Colonial Empire

The last major reform of colonial public works services in Portugal's Third Empire took place in 1964. Since the First Republic, additional legislation with an impact on public works had been issued, but the 1911 decree was broadly kept in place for more than five decades.[34] Along with continuities—such as racial discrimination, coercive labor, and economic exploitation—significant changes had nonetheless occurred between 1911 and 1964. For example, the transition from a military to a civil administration in the colonies had been completed; the colonies' degree of autonomy was significantly reduced following the 1926 coup d'état; the nationalist-driven 1930 Colonial Act, together with the 1933 Organic Charter of Portugal's Colonial Empire and the Overseas Administrative Reform, set up the centralizing policy of the Estado Novo; the settler population grew steadily;[35] the place and role of the Catholic missionary movement in the colonial project strengthened, and its "civilizing" potential was framed by the state via the Missionary Agreement (1940) and the Missionary Statute (1941).[36] Furthermore, the need to reshape and secure Portuguese imperial and colonial legitimacies in the post–World War II context propelled numerous readjustments. The constitutional revision of 1951 stipulated the formal end of the colonial empire, a makeover that turned "colonies" into "overseas provinces." The launch of development plans from 1953 onward bred a particular strand of "welfare colonialism" that did not pave the way to a significant inequality reduction. Albeit coping with this aspiration, the plans did, in fact, assert the internal and external legitimacy of the authoritarian rule as an alternative modernizing path (Jerónimo 2018b, 537–54; Castelo 2014, 63–86). By the same token, they enlarged the scope of counter-subversion, security, and coercive societal control measures, particularly crucial in the face of the rise of the independence wars, with armed struggles erupting in Angola (1961), Guinea-Bissau (1963), and Mozambique (1964). The ambivalent integration of key international organizations, with emphasis on the United Nations and several of its agencies, placed the Portuguese colonial empire under increasing scrutiny. The handling of forced labor (its justification, resilience, and circumvention in the face of complaints and international inspections), formally abolished in 1962, is a pivotal example of the dynamics in place in late Portuguese colonialism (Monteiro 2020; Monteiro 2018; Jerónimo and Monteiro 2000).

The "Organic Diploma of Public Works and Transport Services in the Overseas Provinces," ruled in 1964 (Decree 45575, of February 26),[37] was part of the wider overhaul of the regulation of the different branches of public service overseas, determined by the Organic Law of the Portuguese Overseas Provinces, issued on June 24, 1963.[38]

In the 1964 diploma, the use of the word "plan" grew exponentially, in accordance with the approach of the development programs implemented from the

1950s. In addition to the general plans for improvements and public works projected since 1911, the new reorganization of services determined the elaboration of district plans, along with plans for key sectoral interventions, such as roads, urban planning, electrification, or the hydrometric management of water resources.

The developmental discourse of late Portuguese colonialism was in evidence in the 1964 decree. When characterizing the remit of public works and transport services, the emphasis was placed on the interconnected notions of "efficient occupation," "orderly progress," and "rational use." In turn, the number of articles dedicated to urban issues confirms the ongoing transformation in the past decades: the gradual replacement of directionless and/or isolated actions by an articulated view and conception, a network-based approach. In fact, the word "network" appears as normalized in the legal formula. The execution of land use schemes, as well as regional and local urbanization plans for each population center or group of centers, was inscribed for the time in the scope of tasks handed to the abovementioned services. The public buildings started to be thought of holistically, as an integral part of a broader intervention.

In Angola and Mozambique, public works and transport services constituted Provincial Directorates of Public Works and Transport Services. In the remaining "overseas provinces," these services had a less organic complexity and used the designation of Provincial Departments of Public Works and Transport Services. Several brigades and missions, created in particular from the end of the 1940s to study and act in specific areas of public works, had been progressively integrated into these services since May 1962.[39] The 1964 diploma represented the culmination of the concentration efforts to bring together, under a single organic framework, all sectors and agencies in the field of public works and transport. In the short term, the remaining autonomous councils, commissions, offices, and brigades were also absorbed. This movement also included the specialized colonial commissions that oversaw heritage preservation.[40] These commissions came to incorporate the organizational structure of the public works and transport services. Heritage became an area of intervention coupled with the construction of new public buildings, hence confirming its growing importance and instrumentalization for the legitimation of Portuguese colonialism.

The Provincial Directorates for Public Works and Transport Services, exclusive to Angola and Mozambique, were composed of central and regional services. The former, in addition to the Directorate's Office, comprised the following: an Administrative Services Department, composed of several specific divisions; a

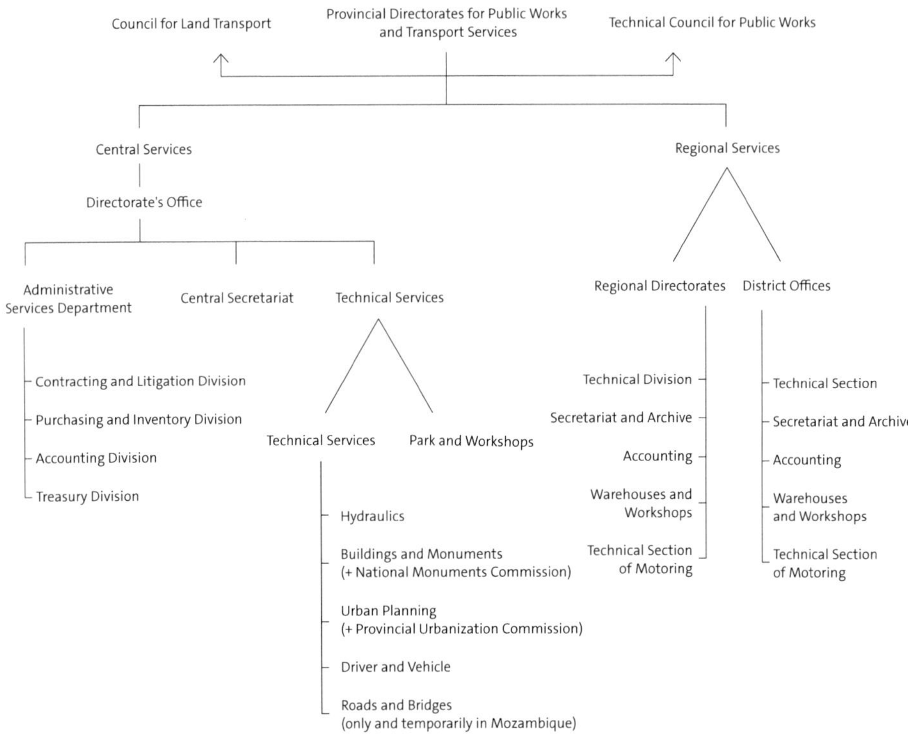

Fig. 1: Organizational chart of the Provincial Directorates for Public Works and Transport Services (Angola and Mozambique), elaborated according to the one included in the Organic Diploma ruled in 1964 (Decree 45575, February 26).

Central Secretariat, with a section of daily office procedures and an archive, a personnel section, and a library; and the various Technical Services Departments. These included, along with a sector of Parks and Workshops, the following: a Hydraulics Department; a Buildings and Monuments Department (next to which the National Monuments Commission acted as an advisory body); an Urban Planning Department (next to which the Provincial Urbanization Commission functioned as an advisory board); and a Driver and Vehicle Department. In Mozambique, a Department of Roads and Bridges was also projected "as long as circumstances dictate."[41] The regional services in the Angola and Mozambique provinces constituted executive bodies that operated at the headquarters of district governments. When a regional directorate covered more than one district, there was a district office in each. The district directorates and offices comprised the following: a technical division or section; a secretariat and archive section; an accounting section; a warehouses and workshops section, and a technical section of motoring. The resulting organizational chart (fig. 1) demonstrates the exponential growth in the segmentation and specialization of work.

In the "overseas provinces" of Guinea, São Tomé and Príncipe, Cabo Verde, Macau, and Timor, the provincial departments of public works and transport services had a technical division (which included the various specialized intervention sections) and an administrative division, with sections dedicated to secretarial work, accounting, warehouses, and purchasing.

Alongside all Provincial Directorates and Departments of Public Works and Transport Services, the Technical Council for Public Works and the Council for Land Transport functioned as advisory bodies to the provincial governments. They issued nonbinding assessment reports, leaving to the governor-general the power to approve or disregard their technical advice. No work could be carried out, whatever the source of the funds to cover its cost (general budget, district, county, or any other funds), without the respective project being approved by the governor of the province, following the assessment of the director or head of public works services.

The Decree 45575 came into force in the "provinces" of Angola, Mozambique, and Macau sixty days after its publication, on February 26, 1964, in the *Diário do Governo* (the Portuguese government bulletin). Each province was to submit the draft regulations necessary for the decree's implementation to the governor for approval. In the other "overseas provinces," the decree would only come into force after the respective governments weighed the availability of financial resources to cope with the increase in expenditure, which would not come to fruition in all cases. Although this reorganization of services was to be applied in the Portuguese Estado da Índia "as soon as the situation of occupation by enemy forces currently verified ceases," according to the end of the 1964 diploma, Portugal had already irreversibly lost control over that territory.[42] At the time, the priority was to halt the nationalist movements in Africa. The decree, in its apparent alienation from realities on the ground, conveys the government's belief in and efforts toward boosting the resilience of the Portuguese colonial empire. Far from being disconnected, military strategies and public works policies intersected in a comprehensive and decisive way, which went beyond the impact of the former on the priorities set for the latter or on the timetable for their pursuit. Although this subject has yet to be thoroughly examined in relation to Portugal's

Third Empire, it is safe to assume the critical role of infrastructures in military logistics. The supply and transportation of human and material needs, as well as the provision of communication services and medical aid, are two among various areas that evidence a clear connection between the two.

The 1964 reorganization of colonial public works services, complemented by occasional updates and supplementary provisions, was not the final one during Portugal's Third Empire.[43] Nevertheless, one can argue that it was the last to have operative bearing. In fact, the final organic revision of colonial public works and transport services—Decree 470/72—was published in the *Diário do Governo* as late as November 23, 1972. It followed the revision of the Organic Law of the Overseas Territories, enacted on June 19, 1972,[44] which, in turn, would give rise to the promulgation of new political and administrative statutes for the various "overseas provinces."[45] Decree 470/72 came into force formally in the "provinces" on January 1, 1973, leaving each territory 120 days to submit to the provincial governor the specific regulations that would implement the general normative text. A year later, the revolution that put an end to the Estado Novo took place on April 25, 1974. This time window was extremely narrow to apply and naturalize any legal restructuring, let alone among a flurry of legislative transformations and at the climax of the ongoing independence wars, which also increasingly united the internal opposition to the regime. With the Carnation Revolution of April 1974 came the gradual recognition of the independence of the various overseas territories between 1974 (Guinea-Bissau) and 1975 (Mozambique, Cabo Verde, São Tomé and Príncipe, Angola, and Timor). Macau would remain under feeble Portuguese sovereignty until 1999, when it was formally handed over to the People's Republic of China.

5. Conclusion

As noted early on, this article is a first contribution to the understanding of a larger research question. As such, it does not attempt to grasp the full complexity of colonial public works, their contexts and trajectories, or their intersections with other social, political, military, or economic dynamics. Having mainly addressed how Portugal envisioned the setting and functioning of public works services in its colonies, the study has left aside, for the time being, other vital lenses of analysis, some of them connected to the abovementioned dynamics. The understanding of the reading and undertaking of this process from a colonial point of view is of first importance. Moreover, intertwined with this article is the thorough examination of colonial public works' place and handling within the metropolitan government, before and after the creation of the Ministry of Colonies, following the increase of these works' importance and the subsequent specialization, bureaucratization, and expertise employed to address them at this level, too. The creation of the Lisbon-based Colonial Urbanization Office in 1944 is the most well-known outcome of this process. My ongoing research intends to contribute to a further understanding of this office by casting light on how the technical staff on the ground, namely the colonial public works services analyzed in this text, dealt with the establishment of this body and the plans and designs that it radiated. But additional scales—such as the transnational and transimperial; the international and the global—are also critical to puzzle out a phenomenon that by no means was thought out or handled in a vacuum, i.e., in a single and singular imperial bubble. Moreover, a more comprehensive collation of legislative sources with archive material is paramount to mapping further and scrutinizing the gap between the normative universe and its effective implementation on the ground.

Colonial public works is, by its very nature, a research topic that requires a multifaceted approach. One cannot tackle any given infrastructure nor the service responsible for its design or execution without bringing into the equation and interconnecting the internal and external politics, the economic and financial policies, and the social and cultural fabric. Before aesthetic exegesis and debates over form comes a world—perhaps less attractive, but of primary importance—of normative underpinnings, administrative procedures, the expansion of bureaucracy, contested policy formulation, decision-making circuits, personnel, and expense rationales, among others.[46] It is a world of imagined control and order, where failures and delays can bear as much analytical value as enforcements and accomplishments; a world where continuities—either on paper, in practice, or both—challenge straightforward analytical clippings, as much as the inclination to mistake law for reality.

While acknowledging that disparate ideologies and political regimes have differences in terms of colonial policies, it is particularly relevant to highlight, in conclusion, common denominators and global trends identified in the structuring of Portuguese colonial public works services throughout the significant period examined in this article. From 1869, when the first modular organization of colonial public works services was decreed for Portugal's multiterritorial empire, until the end of Portuguese colonialism in 1975, successive legislative reforms set out to establish and fine-tune a domain of critical intervention.

Colonial public works were above all driven by the need to secure dominance, especially over the African territories. Although these territories were at first ill-defined, unknown, and highly coveted, they came under increasing international scrutiny after 1945, and Portuguese rule over them became challenged by the growth of independence movements and their respective domestic and foreign support. The discourse of "progress" and "development" that transpires in the legislation analyzed here is entangled with security needs and schemes rather than being its redeeming aspect. The meaning of control evolved, as well as the ways in which control was pursued. But colonial public works were always a part of this toolbox. Therefore, they are a fruitful analytical avenue to observe how Portugal viewed and handled its colonial empire in a *longue durée* perspective. Control, one might argue, is never fully guaranteed, and its virtual dimension is an enduring feature of control exercise itself. The case of the Portuguese Third Empire is a particularly elucidative example of a colonial rule that, despite its growing tangibility, was always limited and frail, hence heavily reliant on power compromises and attentive to optics. Consequently, the formal existence of public works services—i.e., the definition of a structure dedicated to their execution regardless of the difficulties to achieve actual palpable works—has an importance that should not be underestimated.

The recognition of legal possibilities and predicaments is the reflexive recoil of all the legislative endeavors examined here: the decree of 1869 and its consecutive transformations and upgrades in 1880, 1892, 1911, 1964, and 1972. The emergence of each decree followed a report submitted by a commission appointed to study the subject. These diplomas, issued in the metropole, gradually took less time to be implemented on the ground, via corresponding regulations approved for every colony. The 1972 decree is the exception that confirms the rule since context-based factors severely restrained its operativeness.

The shortage of qualified personnel and the struggle to attract and retain a technical workforce were the most stable arguments for the legal reshaping of the colonial public works services. Engineers were the driving force of the colonial public works conception and execution during the Portuguese Third Empire. Military background, a prime condition for their selection in the nineteenth century, steadily faded with the turn of the twentieth century. But the importance of the profession, and of its blossoming specific fields, remained undisputed. The literature on public works does not, however, necessarily reflect this balance of power since it has been far more attentive to architects and their works.

Finally, two trends must be stressed. Firstly, with each legal reshaping of colonial public works services, the level of complexity rose. Diplomas became progressively longer, more detailed, and increasingly bureaucratic. Mechanisms of supervision and the dissection and specialization of work were enhanced. Circuits of decision-making became formally lengthier. Secondly, the level of planning and the weight of lawmaking based on scientific and technical expertise grew firmly, and at a faster rate in the second half of the twentieth century.

NOTES

1. This text was produced within the frame of the research project "The Worlds of (Under)Development: Processes and Legacies of the Portuguese Colonial Empire in a Comparative Perspective (1945–1975)" (PTDC/HAR-HIS/31906/2017 | POCI-01-0145-FEDER-031906).

2. See, among others, Magalhães and Gonçalves (2009, 18); Rodrigues (2010, 47); Milheiro (2012, 449, 454); Mendes (2012, 246); Alcântara (2013, 189); Miranda (2013, 35); Tostões (2014b, 66); Silva (2015a, 10); and Grande (2016, 109).

3. Among others, Henriques (2004), Fonte (2007), Milheiro (2012; 2013), Silva (2015b; 2016), and Marçal (2016).

4. Two examples of different approaches to the relationship between modern architecture and colonialism are Tostões (2014a) and Lagae and Van Craenenbroeck (2015). For a critical assessment of Portuguese architectural historiography on the topic in question, see Domingos (2015).

5. Following the stabilization of liberalism in Portugal, the designation of "colonies" was eradicated from the official language and documents. These territories were named "overseas provinces," thus marking them as part of the Kingdom of Portugal and expressing the "assimilation" policy of the time. I choose to keep the designation of "colonies" since, regardless of their formal labeling, that was the real identity and function of these territories.

6. Portugal. Ministério dos Negócios da Marinha e Ultramar, *Diário do Governo* 284 (December 14, 1869): 1572–73 [Decree of December 3, 1869].

7. Portugal, *Decreto de 1 de Dezembro de 1869. Carta orgânica das instituições administrativas nas províncias ultramarinas annotada por J. A. Ismael Gracias* (Nova Goa: Imprensa Nacional, 1894), 1–5.

8. As an example, in the case of Mozambique, the 1869 decree was published in the official bulletin of the colony five years later, on November 7, 1874, and the local regulation of Mozambican public works service took place in December of the same year. See Governo Geral da Província de Moçambique, *Boletim Official* 45 (November 7, 1874): 197–202; Governo Geral da Província de Moçambique, *Boletim Official* 50 (December 12, 1874): 231–33.

9. Portugal, *Collecção da Legislação Novíssima do Ultramar: vol. VIII, 1870-1874*, 2nd ed. (Lisboa: Imprensa Nacional, 1896), 3 [Decree of February 26, 1870].

10. Portugal. Ministério do Ultramar, *Relatórios do Ministro e Secretário de Estado dos Negócios da Marinha e do Ultramar apresentados às cortes na sessão legislativa de 1870: Edição comemorativa do I Centenário da Reforma Administrativa de 1 de Dezembro de 1869* (Lisboa: Ministério do Ultramar, 1969), 255.

11. Preamble of the Decree of December 3, 1869. Portugal. Ministério dos Negócios da Marinha e Ultramar, *Diário do Governo* 284, 1572.

12. For a discussion of the Western pathologization of African environment see, among others, MacKenzie (1990), Livingstone (2002), Driver (2004), Driver and Martins (2005), Eves (2005), Chakrabarti (2014), and Mahony and Endfield (2018).

13. Portugal, *Collecção da Legislação Novíssima do Ultramar, vol. VII, 1868–1869*, 2nd ed. (Lisboa: Imprensa Nacional, 1896), 126 [Ordinance of December 29, 1868].

14. Portugal, *Collecção Official de Legislação Portugueza: anno de 1892* (Lisboa: Imprensa Nacional, 1893), 623 [report that served as a preamble to the "Organization Plan for Public Works and Industry Services in the Directorate General of Overseas and Overseas Provinces," ruled on August 20, 1892].

15. In the 1850s, the frontiers of Portuguese colonies in Africa were still ill-defined and far from fixed, hence the areas mentioned here are merely indicative, reflecting future territories established and stabilized as part of Portuguese domain. This process took place from the end of the nineteenth century to the first decades of the twentieth century.

16. Preamble of the Decree of December 3, 1869. Portugal. Ministério dos Negócios da Marinha e Ultramar, *Diário do Governo* 284, 1572.

17. See, among others, Havik, Keese, and Santos 2015; Alexopoulou and Juif 2017; Alexopoulou 2018.

18. Portugal, *Collecção Official de Legislação Portugueza: anno de 1892*, 623 [report that serves as a preamble to the "Organization Plan for Public Works and Industry Services in the Directorate General of Overseas and Overseas Provinces," ruled on August 20, 1892].

19. Portugal, *Collecção da Legislação Novíssima do Ultramar: vol. IX, 1875-1878* (Lisboa: Imprensa Nacional, 1880), 319–20 [Law of April 12, 1876].

20. Portugal, *Collecção da Legislação Novíssima do Ultramar: vol. IX, 1875-1878*, 397 [ordinance of December 28, 1876].

21. For a pertinent multidisciplinary reading of the multifaced and cross-cutting presence of the security nexus in the late Portuguese Empire, see Cruz (2000).

22. Portugal, *Collecção Official de Legislação Portugueza: anno de 1892*, 623 [Report that serves as a preamble to the "Organization Plan for Public Works and Industry Services in the Directorate General of Overseas and Overseas Provinces," ruled on August 20, 1892].

23. See, for instance, Guimarães (1984), Santos (1986), and Centro de Estudos Africanos da Universidade do Porto and Instituto de Investigação Científica Tropical (2013).

24. These decrees were then published in the respective government bulletin of each colony. For example, the Regulation for the Administration and Supervision of Public

Works was issued for Mozambique in the metropolitan legislation on December 23, 1876, and then published by the Governo Geral da Província de Moçambique in its *Boletim Official* 12 (March 19, 1877): 65–67.

25. Portugal, *Collecção Official de Legislação Portugueza: anno de 1880* (Lisboa: Imprensa Nacional, 1881), 410–11.

26. For a more comprehensive discussion of these developments, see Jerónimo (2013).

27. To grasp the still considerable (albeit decreasing) time interval between the promulgation of the organization of colonial public works services and its application and specific regulation at the level of each colony, consider, as an example, that the 1892 diploma gave origin to the "Regulation for the Administration, Supervision, and Payments of Public Works in Mozambique" in 1894. Governo Geral da Província de Moçambique, *Boletim Official* 9 (March 3, 1894): 110–11.

28. Portugal, *Collecção Official de Legislação Portugueza: anno de 1892*, 625.

29. Portugal. Assembleia Nacional Constituinte, "Decretos de 23 de agosto de 1911," *Diário do Governo* 197, 1st series (August 24, 1911): 3573–74.

30. Portugal. Ministério das Colónias, "Regulamento geral das direcções e inspecções de obras públicas nas colónias," *Diário do Governo* 268, 1st series (November 16, 1911): 4603–10 [republished with corrections in *Diário do Governo* 274, 1st series (November 23, 1911): 4679–86].

31. Portugal, *Diário da Câmara dos Deputados*, session n.º 66 (May 10, 1917): 14. http://debates.parlamento.pt/catalogo/r1/cd/01/02/02/066/1917-05-10.

32. Historical Archive of Mozambique (AHM), General Government of Mozambique, box no. 2482, file "Colony of Mozambique. Directorate of Public Works Services. Report for the year 1949" (report no. 311).

33. Portugal. Ministério do Ultramar, "Decreto n.º 45575. Diploma orgânico dos serviços provinciais de obras públicas e transportes do ultramar," *Diário do Governo* 48, 1st series (February 26, 1964): 346.

34. See, namely, Portugal. Ministério das Colónias, "Decreto n.º 21430," *Diário do Governo* 151, 1st series (June 30, 1932): 1352–53; and Portugal. Ministério das Colónias, "Decreto-Lei n.º 29821," *Diário do Governo* 188, 1st series (August 12, 1939): 877. These laws introduced some changes in the general regulation of the directions and inspections of public works in the colonies, which had been approved by the decree with the force of law of November 11, 1911.

35. See Castelo (2007; 2009); Morier-Genoud and Cahen (2012).

36. For a discussion of this topic, see Jerónimo (2012), Dores (2015), Morier-Genoud (2019).

37. Portugal. Ministério do Ultramar, "Decreto n.º 45575. Diploma orgânico dos serviços provinciais de obras públicas e transportes do ultramar," *Diário do Governo* 48, 1st series (February 26, 1964): 331–53.

38. Portugal. Presidência da República, "Lei n.º 2119," *Diário do Governo* 147, 1st series (June 24, 1963): 769–74.

39. As determined by Decree 44364, of May 25, 1962. See Portugal. Ministério do Ultramar, "Decreto n.º 44364," *Diário do Governo* 119, 1st series (May 25, 1962): 756–58.

40. For an in-depth study of colonial heritage preservation, see Mariz (2016).

41. Portugal. Ministério do Ultramar, "Decreto n.º 45575. Diploma orgânico dos serviços provinciais de obras públicas e transportes do ultramar," 333.

42. Portugal. Ministério do Ultramar, "Decreto n.º 45575. Diploma orgânico dos serviços provinciais de obras públicas e transportes do ultramar," 346.

43. See, namely, the following: Portugal. Ministério do Ultramar, "Portaria n.º 21355," *Diário do Governo* 139, 1st series (June 25, 1965): 871; Portugal. Ministério do Ultramar, "Decreto n.º 47499," *Diário do Governo* 14, 1st series (January 17, 1967): 86–97; Portugal. Ministério do Ultramar, "Decreto n.º 47519," *Diário do Governo* 27, 1st series (February 1, 1967): 149–56; Portugal. Ministério do Ultramar, "Portaria n.º 23201," *Diário do Governo* 28, 1st series (February 2, 1968): 195; Portugal. Ministério do Ultramar, "Decreto n.º 48294," *Diário do Governo* 73, 1st series (March 26, 1968): 400; Portugal. Ministério do Ultramar, "Decreto n.º 48607," *Diário do Governo* 236, 1st series (October 7, 1968): 1553–56; Portugal. Ministério do Ultramar, "Decreto-Lei n.º 48860," *Diário do Governo* 33, 1st series (February 8, 1969): 137–40; Portugal. Ministério do Ultramar, "Decreto n.º 49446," *Diário do Governo* 294, 1st series (December 18, 1969): 1798–808; Portugal. Ministério do Ultramar, "Portaria n.º 516/70," *Diário do Governo* 240, 1st series (October 16, 1970): 1495; Portugal. Ministério do Ultramar, "Decreto n.º 469/72," *Diário do Governo* 273, 1st series (November 23, 1972): 1716–18.

44. Portugal. Presidência da República, "Lei n.º 5/72," *Diário do Governo* 145, 1st series (June 23, 1972): 807–19.

45. See, for instance, Portugal. Ministério do Ultramar, "Decreto n.º 544/72," *Diário do Governo* 296, 1st series (1st supplement), (December 12, 1972): 2030(23)–2030(31) [Political and administrative status of the Overseas Province of Angola]; Portugal. Ministério do Ultramar, "Decreto n.º 545/72," *Diário do Governo* 296, 1st series (1st supplement), (December 12, 1972): 2030(31)–2030(40) [Political and administrative status of the Overseas Province of Mozambique].

46. A remarkable example of such historiographical enterprise can be found in Peter Scriver's (2007) analysis of the Public Works Department of British India.

WORKS CITED

Alcântara, Daniela. 2013. "Arquitetura moderna: Do Brasil a Portugal e África—alguma investigação e leitura." In *Portugal, Brasil, África: Urbanismo e arquitectura; Do ecletismo ao modernismo*, edited by José Manuel Fernandes and Maria Lucia Bressan Pinheiro, 183–97. Casal de Cambra: Caleidoscópio.

Alexandre, Valentim. 2004. "The Portuguese Empire (1825–1890): Ideology and Economics." In *From Slave Trade to Empire: European Colonisation of Black Africa 1780s-1880s*, edited by Olivier Pétré-Grenouilleau, 110–32. London: Routledge.

Alexopoulou, Kleoniki. 2018. "An Anatomy of Colonial States and Fiscal Regimes in Portuguese Africa: Long-term Transformations in Angola and Mozambique, 1850s–1970s." PhD diss., Wageningen University.

Alexopoulou, Kleoniki, and Dacil Juif. 2017. "Colonial State Formation Without Integration: Tax Capacity and Labour Regimes in Portuguese Mozambique (1890s–1970s)." *International Review of Social History* 62 (2): 215–52.

Castelo, Cláudia. 2014. "Developing 'Portuguese Africa' in Late Colonialism: Confronting Discourses." In *Developing Africa: Concepts and Practices in 20th Century Colonialism*, edited by Joseph Hodge, Gerald Hödl, and Martina Kopf, 63–86. Manchester: Manchester University Press.

———. 2009. "Migração ultramarina: Contradições e constrangimentos." *Ler História*, no. 56, 69–82.

———. 2007. *Passagens para África: O povoamento de Angola e Moçambique com naturais da Metrópole (1920–1974)*. Porto: Afrontamento.

Centro de Estudos Africanos da Universidade do Porto and Instituto de Investigação Científica Tropical, eds. 2013. *O colonialismo português: Novos rumos da historiografia dos PALOP*. V.N. Famalicão: Húmus, 2013.

Chakrabarti, Pratik. 2014. *Medicine and Empire: 1600–1960*. Basingstoke: Palgrave Macmillan.

Cruz, Bernardo Pinto. 2020. *(Des)controlo em Luanda: Urbanismo, polícia e lazer nos musseques do Império*. Lisboa: Outro Modo.

Domingos, Nuno. 2015. "Colonial Architectures, Urban Planning and the Representation of Portuguese Imperial History." *Portuguese Journal of Social Science*, no. 14, 235–55.

Dores, Hugo. 2015. *A missão da República: Política, religião e o império colonial português (1910–1926)*. Lisboa: Edições 70.

Driver, Felix. 2004. "Imagining the Tropics: Views and Visions of the Tropical World." *Singapore Journal of Tropical Geography* 25 (1): 1–17.

Driver, Felix, and Luciana Martins, eds. 2005. *Tropical Visions in an Age of Empire*. Chicago: University of Chicago Press.

Eves, Richard. 2005. "Unsettling Settler Colonialism: Debates over Climate and Colonization in New Guinea, 1875–1914." *Ethnic and Racial Studies* 28 (2): 304–30.

Fonte, Maria Manuela Afonso da. 2007. "Urbanismo e arquitectura em Angola de Norton de Matos à Revolução." PhD diss., Universidade Técnica de Lisboa.

Grande, Nuno. 2016. "Cosmopolitisme dans un climat tropical." In Les universalistes: 50 *ans d'architecture portugaise*, edited by Nuno Grande, 109. Paris: Fundação Calouste Gulbenkian.

Guimarães, Ângela. 1984. *Uma corrente do colonialismo português: A Sociedade de Geografia de Lisboa*, 1875–1895. Lisboa: Livros Horizonte.

Havik, Philip J., Alexander Keese, and Maciel Santos. 2015. *Administration and Taxation in Former Portuguese Africa*, 1900–1945. Newcastle upon Tyne: Cambridge Scholars Publishing.

Henriques, Isabel Castro. 2004. *Território e identidade: A construção da Angola colonial (c. 1872–c. 1926)*. Lisboa: Centro de História da Universidade de Lisboa.

Jerónimo, Miguel Bandeira. 2012. *A diplomacia do império: Política e religião na partilha de África (1820-1890)*. Lisboa: Edições 70.

———. 2018a. "Portuguese Colonialism in Africa." In *Oxford Research Encyclopedia of African History*, edited by Thomas Spear et al., 1–31. Oxford: Oxford University Press. https://oxfordre.com/africanhistory.

———. 2018b. "Repressive Developmentalisms: Idioms, Repertoires, Trajectories in Late Colonialism." In *The Oxford Handbook of the Ends of Empire*, edited by Andrew Thompson and Martin Thomas, 537–54. Oxford: Oxford University Press.

———. "The States of Empire." 2013. In *The Making of Modern Portugal*, edited by Luís Trindade, 65–101. Cambridge: Cambridge Scholars Press.

Jerónimo, Miguel Bandeira, and José Pedro Monteiro. 2000. "Colonial Labour Internationalized: Portugal and the Decolonization Momentum (1945–1975)." *The International History Review* 42 (3): 485–504.

Lagae, Johan, and Ludwine Van Craenenbroeck. 2015. "'Congobéton Léopoldville: Congés payés du 1/1/57 au 31/12/57'; Postwar Architecture, Construction Work, and Local Labor in a Belgian Colony." ABE Journal 8. https://doi.org/10.4000/abe.2797.

Law, Gwillim. 2011. *Administrative Subdivisions of Countries: A Comprehensive World Reference, 1900 through 1998*. Jefferson, NC: McFarland.

Livingstone, David N. 2002. "Race, Space, and Moral Climatology: Notes toward a Genealogy." *Journal of Historical Geography* 28 (2): 159–80.

Lorenzini, Sara. 2019. *Global Development: A Cold War History*. Princeton, NJ: Princeton University Press.

MacKenzie, John M., ed. 1990. *Imperialism and the Natural World*. Manchester: Manchester University Press.

Magalhães, Ana, and Inês Gonçalves. 2009. *Moderno tropical: Arquitectura em Angola e Moçambique (1948–1975)*. Lisboa: Tinta da China.

Mahony, Martin, and Georgina Endfield. 2018. "Climate and Colonialism." *WIREs Climate Change* 9 (2). https://doi.org/10.1002/wcc.510.

Marçal, Bruno José Navarro. 2016. "Um império projectado pelo 'silvo da locomotiva': O papel da engenharia portuguesa na apropriação do espaço colonial africano; Angola e Moçambique (1869–1930)." PhD diss., Universidade Nova de Lisboa.

Mariz, Vera. 2016. "A 'memória do império' ou o 'império da memória': A salvaguarda do património arquitectónico português ultramarino (1930–1974)." PhD diss., Universidade de Lisboa.

Mendes, Rui Paes. 2012. "O modernismo e suas abordagens em Moçambique e Angola." *Urbe: Revista Brasileira de Gestão Urbana* 4 (2): 245–57.

Milheiro, Ana Vaz, ed. 2013. *Construir em África a arquitectura do Gabinete de Urbanização Colonial em Cabo Verde, Guiné-Bissau, São Tomé e Príncipe, Angola e Moçambique: 1944–1974*. Lisboa: ISCTE.

———. 2012. *Nos trópicos sem Le Corbusier: Arquitectura luso-africana no Estado Novo*. Lisboa: Relógio D'Água.

Miranda, Elisário. 2013. "Liberdade & ortodoxia: Infraestruturas de arquitectura moderna em Moçambique (1951–1964)." PhD diss., Universidade do Minho.

Monteiro, José Pedro. 2020. "From 'Natives' to 'Aborigines': Late Colonialism, Indigenous Rights and the Global Politics of Sovereignty (1953–1962)." *The Journal of Imperial and Commonwealth History* 48 (5): 934–57.

———. 2018. *Portugal e a questão do trabalho forçado: Um império sob escrutínio (1944–1962)*. Lisboa: Edições 70.

Morier-Genoud, Eric. 2019. *Catholicism and the Making of Politics in Central Mozambique, 1940–1986*. Rochester, NY: Rochester University Press.

Morier-Genoud, Eric, and Michel Cahen, eds. 2012. *Imperial Migrations: Colonial Communities and Diaspora in the Portuguese World*. Basingstoke: Palgrave Macmillan.

Pedreira, Jorge M. 1998. "Imperialismo e economia." In *História da expansao portuguesa*. Vol. 4, *Do Brasil para a África (1808–1930)*, edited by Francisco Bethencourt and Kirti Chaudhuri, 268–301. Lisboa: Círculo de Leitores.

Ramos, Francisco Pinto. 1970. *Resumo sinóptico de legislação da província de Angola publicada no Boletim Oficial nos últimos setenta anos: 1900-1969*. Viseu: Tipografia Guerra.

Ravesteijn, Wim, and Marie-Louise Ten Horn-Van Nispen. 2007. "Engineering an Empire: The Creation of Infrastructural Systems in the Netherlands East Indies, 1800–1950." *Indonesia and the Malay World* 35 (103): 273–92.

Roberts, Andrew. 1986. "Portuguese Africa." In *The Cambridge History of Africa*. Vol. 7, *1905 to 1940*, edited by A. D. Roberts, 494–536. Cambridge: Cambridge University Press.

Rodrigues, Inês Lima. 2010. "Quando as nossas casas modernas viajaram pelo mundo: Desde Portugal a outros países de expressão portuguesa (1940–1974)." *Cadernos PROARQ*, no. 14, 34–52.

Santos, Maria Emília Madeira. 1986. "Das travessias científicas à exploração regional em África: Uma opção da Sociedade de Geografia de Lisboa." *Boletim da Sociedade de Geografia de Lisboa*, no. 7–12: 113–22.

Scriver, Peter. 2007. "Empire-Building and Thinking in the Public Works Department of British India." In *Colonial Modernities: Building, Dwelling and Architecture in British India and Ceylon*, edited by Peter Scriver and Vikramaditya Prakash, 69–92. London: Routledge.

Silva, Carlos Nunes. 2015a. "Colonial Urban Planning in Lusophone African Countries: A Comparison with Other Colonial Planning Cultures." In *Urban Planning in Lusophone African Countries*, edited by Carlos Nunes Silva, 7–28. Farnham: Ashgate.

———, ed. 2016. *Governing Urban Africa*. London: Palgrave MacMillan, 2016.

———, ed. 2015b. *Urban Planning in Lusophone African Countries*. Farnham: Ashgate.

Silva, J. J. da. 1904. *Repertorio alphabetico e chronologico ou índice remissivo da legislação ultramarina: Desde a epocha das descobertas até 1902 inclusivé*. Lisboa: Typographia de J. F. Pinheiro.

Tostões, Ana, ed. 2014a. *Arquitetura moderna em África*. Lisboa: Caleidoscópio.

———. 2014b. "Visões cruzadas: Um laboratório de arquitetura entre global e local." In *Arquitetura moderna em África: Angola e Moçambique*, edited by Ana Tostões, 62–121. Lisboa: Caleidoscópio.

Valério, Nuno, coord. 2001. *Os orçamentos do Estado Português: Propostas governamentais, orçamentos aprovados e rectificados e contas de execução (1837–2001)*. Lisboa: Instituto Nacional de Estatística.

JOANA BRITES holds a PhD in History with a specialization in Art History from the University of Coimbra, where she is a tenured Assistant Professor of Art History in the College of Arts and Humanities and a Researcher in the Center for Interdisciplinary Studies (CEIS20). Among other research projects, she is a member of "WUD—The Worlds of (Under)Development: Processes and Legacies of the Portuguese Colonial Empire in a Comparative Perspective (1945–1975)." Her research focuses on modernism and fascism; modern architecture, colonialism, and development; sculpture of the late modern period; and dissonant heritage.

PEDRO SCHACHT PEREIRA

The (In)Tangible Legacy of "Generic Lusotropicalism": Unexamined Links in the Textual History of "Portuguese Humane Colonialism"

If this passage has attracted appropriate attention here and there, never—and one should ask why—have the commentators bothered to know what could have been its documented source.
—Pierre Franklin-Tavares, *Hegel et l'Abbé Grégoire*[1]

Sources are always about something else.
—Michel-Rolph Trouillot, *Silencing the Past: Power and the Production of History*

ABSTRACT: For quite some time, Portuguese scholars have proposed that the success of the cooptation of Gilberto Freyre's Lusotropicalism by the colonial discourse of Portugal's Estado Novo can be explained in part due to the preexistence of a colonial discourse that contained similar ideas, at least as far back as the late eighteenth century. In this article, I trace the textual history of what has been called "generic Lusotropicalism" in order to establish some of the known and lesser-known sources of this ideological construct. Whereas the authority of sources has continually been claimed both by proponents of generic Lusotropicalism—as historical corroboration—and by scholars who have studied it, I claim here that this textual history is more heterogeneous than may have been previously thought and has not always been wielded with the same rhetorical or political purposes.

KEYWORDS: Lusotropicalism, humane colonialism, Hegel, Henry Koster, Jaime Cortesão

RESUMO: A existência de um ideário de feição lusotropicalista em Portugal prévio à apropriação do lusotropicalismo de Gilberto Freyre pelo discurso colonial do Estado Novo, e que se manifestaria desde pelo menos os finais do séc. XVIII, tem sido explicada pelos estudiosos como uma razão do sucesso dessa apropriação. Este artigo segue no encalço da história textual daquilo a que se chamou "lusotropicalismo genérico," de forma a estabelecer algumas das fontes conhecidas e menos conhecidas desse construto ideológico. Enquanto que a autoridade das fontes tem sido uma constante entre os defensores do lusotropicalismo genérico—que veem nela uma corroboração histórica—e os seus estudiosos, neste artigo proponho que a história textual em questão é mais heterogénea do que antes se pensava e nem sempre foi usada com os mesmos propósitos retóricos e políticos.

PALAVRAS-CHAVE: Lusotropicalismo, colonialismo humano, Hegel, Henry Koster, Jaime Cortesão

---

In recent years, pointed controversies have emerged in the Portuguese public sphere regarding the memory of Portuguese colonialism and the country's role in the history of transatlantic slavery. Whether they were ignited by a Lisbon municipal project for a so-called "Museum of the Discoveries," a historically inaccurate speech delivered by the president while on state visit in Senegal that attempted to paint the country's legal abolition precedent as the de facto historical abolition of slavery,[2] or the widespread hostility towards the increasingly visible affirmation of Black political identities and their vocal rejection and denunciation of police brutality, these debates once again exposed the degree to which ideas and beliefs loosely or closely associated with the discursive field known as Lusotropicalism—that is, simply put, Portuguese racial exceptionalism—remain pervasive in the national psyche almost fifty years after the end of Portuguese colonial rule in Africa. Beyond the chatter on social media, where the belief in Portuguese "benign colonialism" is very conspicuous, many conservative pundits and public figures have authored newspaper op-eds where the ideology we have come to associate with the Brazilian sociologist, anthropologist, and cultural historian Gilberto Freyre (1900–1987) constitutes a tacit grammar. Perhaps more surprisingly, in at least one instance Lusotropicalism was openly defended as a political project for the present era.[3] Perhaps more uncanny than the remarkable resilience that colonialist ideology has managed to enjoy in a postcolonial age is the candor with which arguments that were already shown to be faulty when Lusotropicalism was timidly challenged for the first time in a scholarly publication are again recuperated, as if the independence of the five Portuguese-speaking African countries had never taken place. Indeed, readers familiar with the controversy surrounding the publication of Charles Boxer's *Race Relations in the Portuguese Colonial Empire* in 1963, and particularly with the brief exchange that took place between the British historian and the Portuguese agronomist, historian, and cartographer Armando Cortesão (1891–1977), may be puzzled when recognizing in newspaper articles of the late 2010s the same arguments and tone that characterized the militant, pro-colonialist stance of Oliveira Salazar's defenders in the 1960s. These articles read as if the steady stream of scholarship, as well as the manifestoes and speeches of Lusophone Africa's intellectuals and independence leaders, published and discussed in the last sixty years, had never existed.[4]

In this article, I study one piece of the puzzle of this apparent cognitive dissonance by analyzing a textual chain that has not attracted much scholarly attention. There are many factors that explain the longevity and resilience of ideas loosely or directly associated with Lusotropicalism in the Portuguese national psyche, and certainly the fact that the Estado Novo used Freyre and some of his writings to shore up Portugal's colonialist discourse after the 1950s has played a significant role (Castelo 1999, 2019). That role has also been scrutinized sharply and abundantly, starting as early as 1955 with the publication of "Qu'est-ce que le 'luso-tropicalismo'?" by Buanga Fele (the pseudonym of a leader of Angola's independence movement, Mário Pinto de Andrade) in *Présence africaine*, picking up again in the 1960s and 1970s with Eduardo Lourenço (1984 [1961]) and Valentim Alexandre (1973, 1979), and continuing throughout the 1990s with many scholars from different disciplines, including Cláudia Castelo, Miguel Vale de Almeida (2004), Cristiana Bastos (1998, 2019), Boaventura de Sousa Santos (2002), and many others. More recently, several edited volumes and special issues of academic journals, in English and French, where Lusotropicalism is directly or indirectly scrutinized have been published, and at least one was entirely devoted to discussing the topic.[5] What has not received necessary attention is the study of why Freyrean Lusotropicalism found such fertile ground for taking root in late colonial and postcolonial Portugal, despite the Estado Novo's initial reluctance to embrace it. I argue that it is due to what I, following Almeida, call "generic Lusotropicalism," that is, "an inclination, a commonsense interpretation, sometimes . . . official representation" by way of which "Luso-Tropicalism has become a social fact" (Almeida 2004, 63). This is discernible in the long duration, which explains why ideas we now intuitively associate with Freyre were consensual even for opponents of the Estado Novo regime, including intellectuals associated with the Republican project of 1910–26, such as Jaime Cortesão (1884–1960).[6] Built over centuries, and emerging in periods characterized by crises of imperial expansion or contraction, generic Lusotropicalism is a discourse that fertilizes the ground, as it were, for the longstanding success of Lusotropicalism proper in the Portuguese national psyche, and so often is conflated with it. This may be because Freyre's initial claim that the Portuguese possessed a special ability to adapt to life in the tropics—based on the categories of mobility, miscibility, and acclimatability, or more generally from the presupposition that the Portuguese were prone to miscegenation beyond self-interest—encourages a leap of faith toward legitimating the idea of an exceptional, more humane Portuguese colonialism. I do not offer a contrastive analysis of these two different and often conflated claims in this article; I merely signal this possibility as a valid avenue for future research. Instead, I pursue a reading of sources that allow me to trace a provisional history of the idea of Portuguese "humane colonialism" and discuss examples of its early instrumentalization by arguably unexpected actors.

To be fair, awareness of this generic, resilient precursor and survivor of Lusotropicalism is not new. Anna Klobucka (2002) has studied Camões's *The Lusiads* (1572) and its episode of the Isle of Love as an antecedent to Freyre's formulations, and Miguel Vale de Almeida (2004) also pointed out the felicitous coincidence of Freyre's exceptionalist interpretation of Portuguese colonialism with its preexisting iterations in the discourse of the social sciences, literature, and the commonsensical self-representations of Portuguese national identity, which he located in the second half of the nineteenth century. Monica Grin (2012) compared the role of exceptionalist representations of the Portuguese empire in Portugal with that of the related myth of "racial democracy" in Brazil, and in what was arguably a pioneering formulation in post-1975 scholarship, Valentim Alexandre suggested in the preface to Cláudia Castelo's well-known study that the Lusotropicalist image

> tem raízes antigas: a ideia de uma particularidade portuguesa, no domínio colonial, pode ser rastreada pontualmente já desde o século XVIII. Mas é no último quartel de Oitocentos que ela começa a ganhar consistência, pela articulação de elementos de diversa natureza. (Castelo 1999, 5)

> has old roots: the idea of a Portuguese particularity in the colonial domain can be traced already in the eighteenth century. But it is in the last quarter of the nineteenth century that it begins to acquire consistency, through the articulation of different elements of various nature.

Taking Pierre Franklin Tavares's observation in my first epigraph to task, I have pursued a textual history that includes writings by G. W. F. Hegel (1770–1831) and the Portuguese-born British traveler, part-time slave-owner, and abolitionist Henry Koster (1793–1820), and is bookended closer to us by passages from the Portuguese historian Jaime Cortesão and, on the opposite chronological end, by excerpts from the French bishop, revolutionary leader, and abolitionist author Henri Grégoire (1750–1831). Some of these texts are known and have been discussed in different contexts, but reconstituting the links that associate them to generic Lusotropicalism allows us to understand one aspect of the grammar of Portuguese racial exceptionalism: the uncritical acceptance of textual sources at face value. These names are just pieces in the much larger puzzle that is the modern philosophical discourse on history, which encompasses many literary genres, travel writing in particular, and in Hegel knows one of its principal moments.[7] What the rehearsal of this particular textual genealogy—a genealogy without a discernable origin or Archimedean point, as it were—shows is that the increasing consolidation of the discourse of exceptional Portuguese colonialism occurred in and responded to a specific historical context, that of the debates about the abolition of the slave trade in the early nineteenth century, and served distinct, sometimes opposite political motivations. In its early manifestations, generic Lusotropicalism embodied the complex intersection between a selective interpretation of empirical evidence about miscegenation in the Portuguese Atlantic (motivated by pragmatic political goals, whether it was the abolition of the slave trade or its staunch refusal) and the rhetorical needs of a philosophical discourse of history that built its claims to universality on the fissures of the testimonial discourse found in European travel narratives, whose political motivations or textual histories more often than not have gone unchecked.

Jaime Cortesão and "Humane Colonialism"

In August 1959, just one year before his death, and two years before the start of the African wars of liberation that eventually brought about the demise of the Portuguese empire, the Portuguese historian Jaime Cortesão gave an interview to *Diário Ilustrado*, a now-defunct Lisbon evening tabloid. In this interview, he was asked for an opinion about Freyre's concept of Lusotropicalism. That a tabloid would have an interest in the views of an intellectual who earlier in the century had twice endured exile for his views on Salazar's dictatorial regime suggests the degree to which Freyre's cooptation by Portuguese imperial discourse was reaching the popular imagination by the end of the 1950s. The historian's response to the question about Lusotropicalism, as well as the ensuing exchange with the interviewer, constitutes an invaluable document:

> Acho muito interessante o tema [do Lusotropicalismo], mas as teorias de Gilberto Freyre excedem o meu campo próprio de investigação. De qualquer forma tenho-me encaminhado também para procurar a existência de um laço cultural comum numa ampla comunidade que envolva sobretudo Portugal e o Brasil, comunidade que, a meu ver, deveria ir até à estruturação política. (Cortesão 1959, 1)

> I find the topic [of Lusotropicalism] very interesting, but Gilberto Freyre's theories exceed my field of research. In any case, I have also been searching for the existence of a common cultural bond among an ample community that should involve mainly Portugal and Brazil, a community that, in my view, should go as far as [assuming the shape of] a political structure.

The first couple of sentences frame the tone and tenor of Cortesão's testimony in this interview, which we could characterize as politely dismissive of the presumed central role played by Freyre. What can be read as a candid admission of lack of scientific competence serves also to quickly and effectively point out that Cortesão's own work had already for a time pursued a path that was presumably comparable to that of Freyre's Lusotropicalism; otherwise, the mention of his own research trajectory would be uncalled for. If it is possible to read Cortesão's position as one of heuristic caution, motivated by his awareness of the different disciplinary fields in which both men operated, it is also important to point out that, for Cortesão, Lusotropicalism may have been a matter for anthropology and sociology to deal with, but exceptional Portuguese colonialism seems to belong to the field of history, as the continuation of the interview will show.

According to the Portuguese historian, his path culminates in the affirmation of a political entity that would affirm the "common cultural bond" that mainly Portugal and Brazil should share. Before proceeding to investigate what this cultural bond might consist of, it is worth noting that these statements give embryonic form to what since the early 1980s has been called "Lusofonia," the postcolonial Portuguese brethren to ideas such as "Francophonie," or "Commonwealth," or even "Hispanidad." Equally conspicuous is the conflation of (or at least the immediate progression from) Freyre's Lusotropicalism with the idea of a community of Portuguese-speaking nations, a project that actually did materialize in some fashion with the creation in 1996 of the Community of Portuguese-Speaking Countries (CPLP).[8] This conflation is striking in that it speaks to the degree to which, by the time the anticolonial movements in Africa were celebrating their first victories, a Portuguese Republican intellectual respected for his antifascist credentials was preconditioned to recognize, in Freyre's ideas of felicitous Portuguese miscegenation in the tropics, the ideals of Portuguese humane colonialism, the true seed that should blossom as the project for a new transnational Portuguese-speaking community. This precondition is powerful enough to explain the gesture of what I called the renunciation of reading, which we will witness in a moment, although we will have to understand such gesture as an instance of a certain history of reading, the pivotal moments of which I attempt to outline here.

But it could just as well be said that Cortesão's statements conspicuously outlive the collapse, in the 1820s, of the Luso-Brazilian empire they nostalgically commemorate. The African liberation movements that at the time this interview took place were about to initiate a fourteen-year-long armed struggle against Portuguese rule do not seem to occupy a place of any preeminence in Cortesão's imagined community, perhaps because the subaltern status of those territories was discouraging to a historian intent on determining Portuguese national character and tracing the history of the community it supposedly made possible. But could it also be that the "common cultural bond" sought by Cortesão would not survive critical scrutiny or the sobering reality check provided by the oppressive circumstances of daily experience for Africans living under Portuguese late colonialism? I believe the historian's writing warrants both the questions and the ambivalence, which in my view spring from his peculiar word choice. Allow me to repeat one of the key sentences from Cortesão's response: "I have also been searching for the existence of a common cultural bond among an ample community that should involve mainly Portugal and Brazil." To *search for the existence* places the emphasis on "existence," not on "common cultural bond." It might mean to locate something one is convinced is already in existence, as the idea of a common cultural bond implies: the existence of the community alluded to is justified only by the linguistic, legal, religious, and racial bonds that somehow preexist it and that therefore incite the historian to search. But it can equally convey the act of conjuring up something that does not yet exist, as the subjunctive mode ("que envolva") in the original Portuguese, as well as the historical evidence that such a community did not in fact exist at that time, amply attest. Thus, the ascription to the same utterance of what speech act theory calls a constative and a performative value is what contributes to the ambivalence I indicated above—an ambivalence that to me suggests that in this interview Cortesão alludes in fact to the idea of conjuring up a past, of inventing what one is already certain to exist or having existed; of inventing certainty, as much as certifying invention. Before I can clarify the stakes of this apparent hermeneutic circle, it is important to have a fuller sense of the line of argumentation followed by Cortesão in the continuation of the interview:

> — Parece-lhe que, na verdade, o comportamento dos portugueses perante outras etnias se reveste da invulgaridade que pode derivar-se das teorias do lusotropicalismo?
> — A minha opinião é de que o português foi, em relação às etnias diferentes, de uma forma geral, mais tolerante e compreensivo que os outros povos coloniais. Em apoio desta minha opinião cito-lhe nada menos do que este nome: Hegel na *Filosofia da História* e precisamente por comparação com os outros povos.
> — Será que nos estamos mantendo dentro do mesmo caminho?
> — Creio que o português, por herança cultural e temperamental, continua a ter, do ponto de vista individual, o mesmo comportamento. (Cortesão 1959, 1, 3)

> — Does it appear to you that Portuguese behavior towards other ethnicities is in fact imbued with the exceptionalism we may derive from Lusotropicalist theories?
> — My opinion is that, generally speaking, the Portuguese were, in relation to other ethnicities, more understanding and tolerating than the other colonial powers. In support of this opinion I cite you none other than this name: Hegel in the *Philosophy of History*, and precisely in comparison with the other powers.
> — Do you think we are still treading the same path?
> — I believe that the Portuguese, because of their cultural and temperamental heritage, maintain at the individual level, the same behavior.

As we can now tell, the "common cultural bond" that would inform a transatlantic political community of the Portuguese language is informed by the belief in an exceptionalist Portuguese colonialism, based on a unique sense of understanding and tolerance for the otherness of others. So unique, I might add, that when one looks for any evidence of it, something that could dissolve for us the oxymoron implicit in the idea of "understanding and tolerant colonialism," what we find instead is a recourse to the authority of none other than Hegel. That is, we remain entrapped in the circular logic of the invention of certainty, the conjuring up of a past that for now seems to exist only within the narrative chain of citation. On the other hand, it is important to note that in Cortesão's discourse "understanding" and "tolerance" are predicated as cultural and temperamental legacies of the Portuguese, a gesture prompted by the reporter's line of questioning. This interview should thus be considered as an iconic instance of the conflation, in a modern Portuguese context associated with popular culture, of two discourses of exceptionalism: Lusotropicalism and Portuguese "humane colonialism."

Before pursuing this chain of argument to the extent allowed by the archival research I have been able to conduct thus far, let me briefly sketch out the latest developments in the discussions of Lusotropicalism. Around the same time that Cortesão's interview took place, international scholars like Charles Boxer and Marvin Harris were already scrutinizing the exceptionalist claims put forth by official Portuguese historiography. After the 1974 revolution that put an end to Portugal's decades-long dictatorship as well as its African empire, other scholars, such as Gerald Bender, kept up with that pioneering effort. In the context of the Portuguese language, we need to recognize the anticolonial discourses of the African liberation movement leaders in Cabo Verde/Guinea Bissau and Mozambique—Amílcar Cabral and Eduardo Mondlane, respectively—as the first instances of a critique of Lusotropicalism in Portuguese. In Portugal, as early as the 1960s, the philosopher and essayist Eduardo Lourenço published articles about the subject, later compiled in volumes in 1984 and 2014, and in the 1970s and 1980s we must acknowledge the historian Valentim Alexandre (1973, 1979) and the literary scholar and pioneer of postcolonial studies Alfredo Margarido (2000). Alexandre and Margarido have even suggested that earlier, European sources should be pursued in the search for the origins of Lusotropicalism, without clarifying, however, which sources they had in mind. More recently, Almeida has claimed that the late nineteenth-century context of imperial expansion in the wake of the so-called scramble for Africa should be considered a credible precursor to Freyre's 1930s formulations. And in 2010, when my research for this project was just beginning, I proposed in an article that Freyre's Portuguese-educated mentor Manoel de Oliveira Lima was the missing link between Portugal's fin de siècle imperial malaise and Brazil's first efforts to celebrate miscegenation (Pereira 2009). What I had not been able to find until recently was any substantive documentary evidence for the various claims regarding the European genealogy of the idea of the humane and tolerant nature of Portuguese colonialism in the tropics. As I intend to demonstrate, my discovery of such evidence came hand in hand with the realization that, rather than proving the preeminence of a European over a Brazilian genealogy, in both contexts the same arguments used to justify Lusotropicalist discourse constitute the most persuasive grounds for its dismissal. And now we can go back to the interview with the Portuguese historian better equipped to consider the strange appearance of Hegel on the Lusotropical scene.

You will remember that in the interview Cortesão uses Hegel to claim that the humane and tolerant nature of Portuguese colonialism is a historically grounded idea. This is a claim that one can trace back to Cortesão's publications from the early 1930s, and again to a public lecture delivered in 1941 to the Liceu Literário Português in Rio de Janeiro, when he was already exiled in Brazil. In this lecture, Cortesão prompts his audience to "go, compare, weigh it on the scales of historical justice and then tell me which among the colonizing powers was the most humane and tolerant" and then informs them that such view is vindicated by "one of the greatest geniuses of modern philosophy and the philosophy of all times" (1941, 93). Indeed, in Appendix 1b to Hegel's (1975, 165) Introduction to the *Lessons on the Philosophy of World History* we read:

> The Portuguese were more humane than the Dutch, Spanish, and English. For this reason, it was easier on the coast of Brazil than elsewhere for slaves to gain their freedom, and large numbers of free Negroes were to be found in this region. . . . An English writer reports that, among the wide circle of his acquaintances, he had encountered instances of negroes becoming skilled workers and tradesmen, and even clergymen and doctors, etc.

The first thing that meets the eye in this passage is that Hegel engages, just as Cortesão does, in an exercise of comparative colonialisms; then, he associates Portugal's comparatively superior display of humanity to the abundance of freed slaves in Brazil's coastal cities. Upon closer examination, an attentive reader will realize the extemporaneous nature of Hegel's claim, as it does nothing to shore up the overall argument he attempts to develop in this section of the Introduction, that of the comparatively higher susceptibility that Africans rather than Amerindians supposedly showed to European culture in the eighteenth century. Finally, Hegel anticipates another one of the gestures found in Cortesão's interview, that is, he resorts to giving full credence to the authority of unexamined sources, in this case the writings of an undisclosed English writer who linked the abundance of freed slaves in Brazilian coastal cities to the evidence of a more humane disposition of the Portuguese colonizer. The similarity of this gesture does not however hide the difference of the consequences: whereas Hegel momentarily but rather unconvincingly usurps the seat of authority in Portuguese imperial history, Cortesão willingly gives up his genuine credentials as a historian of the early modern Portuguese expansion and of the formation of Brazil. Moreover, in this gesture, he also relinquishes his authority as a direct witness to Brazil's race-based socioeconomic inequality, and entirely skirts the evidence of the discontent felt by African subjects that at the time of his interview was continuously emanating from the African territories under Portuguese rule.

In any case, the argument about the comparative abundance of freed blacks in colonial Brazil was worth pursuing, as was Hegel's unnamed English source. The fact that Hegel's library may not be entirely reconstituted, and that the *Lectures on the Philosophy of World History* were posthumously published from extant notes by Hegel himself and by his students, raises important challenges to this research, as some references are virtually impossible to locate, given their possible misspellings.[9] These difficulties notwithstanding, it is fairly easy to determine which English travelers to colonial Brazil Hegel may have read. The British scholar Leslie Bethel compiled a list of British and Irish authors who visited Brazil between the sixteenth century and the present day, an obvious point of departure. I then crossed Bethel's information with the bibliographies cited by authors such as Boxer and Freyre, among many others, and I extensively perused Google Books, a valuable resource of our times. I can now safely determine that, among the relatively small universe of English-language works penned by travelers to colonial Brazil, the writings of Henry Koster (1793–1820) are the ones that most likely inspired Hegel's extemporaneous remark.

Although all the English-language visitors to Brazil I cross-checked comment on the ubiquity of Africans and their descendants in Brazilian life, it is in Koster that I found the most detailed references to the institution of slavery, as well as a systematic attempt to develop arguments about the supposedly lenient treatment dispensed to Brazilian slaves by their Portuguese masters, and, most importantly, a clear effort to prove that it was indeed easier in Brazil for enslaved Africans and their descendants to obtain their freedom.

(In)Accurate Koster

Henry Koster was born in Lisbon in 1793 to a British merchant with interests in the Portuguese-speaking territories of South America. Traveling to what is now the state of Pernambuco in northeastern Brazil in search of better health, at a time when Portugal was occupied by the Napoleonic troops and thus off limits, Koster wound up spending the greater part of his brief adult life there, with two short trips to England in 1816 and 1819. He rented a sugar cane *fazenda*, or estate, in the Jaguaribe region of Pernambuco, which came with a good number of slaves, whose lives he describes in his writings. Upon a new bout of what researchers think may have been tuberculosis, he traveled further inland in search of a better climate and left lively impressions of his travels. He died in 1820 in the city of Recife, where he was buried in an unknown location in the city's British Cemetery.

Koster's fluent Portuguese was somewhat deceitful to Brazilians, who preferred to address him as Henrique da Costa. This perception might not have been entirely inaccurate, as Koster states in his writings that "England is my country, but my native soil is Portugal" (Koster 1816, 334), thus suggesting that he was mindful of the difference between citizenship and birthright, and arguably about the varying degrees of emotional attachment that come with both. He left two writings that remained largely influential for a long time after his premature demise: a two-volume book entitled *Travels in Brazil*, which would be cited frequently by travelers and naturalists of various nationalities, and a pamphlet with the title "On the Amelioration of Slavery," which came out in the same year as *Travels* and was influential in abolitionist and anti-abolitionist circles alike, and later on among historians of Brazil and scholars of slavery. *Travels in Brazil* was first published in England in 1816. A second edition came out the following year in London and in Philadelphia, followed by German and French translations. The first Portuguese version was prepared by Antônio de Pimentel for the *Revista do Instituto Arqueológico Pernambucano* in Brazil but never saw the light of day until Câmara Cascudo published it in 1942 (Koster 1942). To this day, there is no edition of Koster's book in Portugal, which alone should not be enough to explain the lack of awareness in Portuguese historiography about the author's pivotal role in the international debates about abolition and Portuguese racial exceptionalism.

In fact, and for all its popularity, *Travels in Brazil* still awaits any substantive scholarly attention, in Portugal or elsewhere. One can trace its influence in recent studies by historian Herbert Klein (2012), and Stuart Schwartz (1982) has also studied some specific arguments Koster advances in his book about the treatment of slaves in Brazil's Benedictine estates. In *Casa-grande & senzala*, Freyre mentions Koster a total of twenty-four times. He credits the Portuguese-born English traveler along with his friend Robert Southey, who met Koster in Lisbon in 1800, during Southey's second trip to Portugal, for what he deemed as their pioneering expression of the idea of Portuguese lack of racial prejudice towards the colonized peoples of Brazil, and their awareness that economic necessity rather than humanitarian imperative played a role in bringing about that felicitous colonial practice.[10] In a letter to John May, Southey described Koster as "a man more conversant than most of the English here, and whose opinions call forth somewhat more freedom of conversation than I allow myself elsewhere" (Southey 1856, 114). In his commentary on Southey and Koster, Freyre writes:

> Observou Southey que o sistema colonial português se revelara mais feliz do que nenhum outro no tocante às relações do europeu com as raças de cor mas salientando que semelhante sistema fora antes "filho da necessidade" do que de deliberada orientação social e política. . . . "Esta vantagem," escreveu Koster, referindo-se à ausência de discriminações aviltantes da parte dos portugueses contra os indígenas, "provém mais da necessidade que de um sentimento de justiça." (2002, 120)

> Southey observed that the Portuguese colonial system had shown itself to be more felicitous than any other in what pertains to the relations of the European with the colored races, although he pointed out that such system came about out of necessity rather than through deliberate social and political orientation. . . . "This advantage," Koster wrote, referring to the absence of degrading discrimination by the Portuguese against indigenous people, "comes more from necessity than from a sense of justice."

Arguably, and in recent times, the Brazilian anthropologist Manuela Carneiro da Cunha has offered what is the closest scrutiny of Koster's two known publications, in two articles published five years apart. On the one hand, she emphasizes the instrumental role Koster's pamphlet "On the Amelioration of Slavery" (published in 1816) played in English debates about the abolition of the slave trade and of slavery; but she also highlights how both texts rely heavily on the testimonial for the validation of ideas that British abolitionists had been advancing in the public sphere for years: "what remains to be seen by historians of Brazil is whether or to what degree such description was in turn influenced by the debate which was taking place in England in 1815 and 1816" (Cunha 1990, 373). This suggests that Koster's keen interest in the matter of slavery might have preceded his arrival on Brazilian shores. What this means, even if Cunha does not make such assertion, is that Koster's favorable views of Brazilian slavery might respond not so much to the observed historical reality as to the needs of an argument that was taking place elsewhere. The plausibility of my claim can be established if we keep in mind that Koster conducted substantial research for both his book and his abolitionist pamphlet in Southey's famous library, where works by the likes of the Abbé Henri Grégoire (1754–1831) were to be found. Indeed, some of the arguments presented by Koster in *Travels in Brazil* can be traced back to Grégoire's *De la littérature des nègres* (1808), which was published in English in 1810. Pierre-Franklin Tavares (1993) actually bypasses Koster entirely when he looks for Hegel's source in the *Philosophy of World History* and locates it in Grégoire, perhaps because he is primarily interested in studying the French dimension of this textual history: "Impossible not to recognize here the mark of the most famous of Abbé Grégoire's publications: *De la littérature des nègres*. It is staring us in the face! However, one must note that until now nobody has realized it" (495).

In pursuing Hegel's likely English source, it took me almost no time to stumble on a relevant French one. The fact that Hegel does refer to "an English writer," and that therefore Tavares is jumping one link in the textual chain does not mean that his insertion of Abbé Grégoire into the fray is not pertinent, and we will pursue that link a bit closer to the end of this article. At this point, it has already become apparent that the idea of preeminently humane Portuguese colonialism has been a continually appropriated trope in different cultural, political and linguistic contexts and serving different interests: to argue for abolition of the slave trade and the institution of slavery in early-nineteenth century France and England; to provide supposed empirical evidence to shore up the foundations of a philosophy of history in mid-nineteenth century Germany; and, finally, to polish the pedigree of Portuguese republican historiography at a time when its obsolescence was masked by the increasing visibility of Freyre's Lusotropicalism.

Interestingly, no Portuguese author is constituted as a direct interlocutor in this almost two-hundred-year-long conversation, something that seems to have escaped Jaime Cortesão as much as his foreign counterparts. For his part, Koster, who, despite his defense of gradual emancipation, owned slaves during his period in Brazil, did not choose to make his fellow Brazilian slave owners his interlocutors in the debate about abolitionism. Could this be the reason why it took more than one hundred years for his book *Travels in Brazil* to be translated into Portuguese, and why to date it is still not available in Portugal?

To the naked eye, statements such as the following may be read as encouraging a Lusotropicalist worldview, and indeed one of the confessed goals of Koster's study of Brazilian slavery was to collect information that would allow him to make a compelling case against slavery in the British plantations in the Caribbean. That has to be the reason why Koster decided to reiterate in the pamphlet "On the Amelioration of Slavery" most of the arguments found in *Travels in Brazil*. The pamphlet was in fact envisioned as a targeted response to an invective that the representative of the Columbian islands to the British Parliament had published against the first timid abolitionist moves by Britain's African Institution.

The first passage establishes the trope of Brazil as a more lenient slave-owning society, and the second could be seen as indulging in the myth of miscegenation as a Portuguese inclination:

> The general equity of the laws regarding free persons of colour in the Portuguese South-American possessions has been, to a certain degree, extended to that portion of the population which is in a state of slavery; and the lives of the slaves of Brazil have been rendered less hard and less intolerable than those of the degraded beings who drag on their cheerless existence under the dominion of other nations. . . . (227)

> Thus has Portugal, of late years from policy, continued that system into which she was led by her peculiar circumstances in former times. Some of the wealthy planters of Pernambuco, and of the rich inhabitants of Recife, are men of colour. The major part of the best mechanics are also of mixed blood. (212)

Both in *Travels in Brazil* and in his pamphlet "On the Amelioration of Slavery," Koster makes the case for the progressive abolition of the slave trade and of the institution of slavery (which, according to him, would be a longer process), based on both the information obtained in archival research and his experience as an eyewitness, at a time when he could still claim the privilege of being one of the first foreigners to have unfettered access to the interior of Brazil, as the Treaty of Commerce and Navigation was signed between Portugal and Great Britain in 1810.[11] The arguments in support of his case are varied, but subsumable under the two main ideas found in the passages above. First, "the general equity of the laws" applies equally to free persons of color and to enslaved persons, in the ecclesiastical as well as civil domains. Second, miscegenation in Brazil at the time he writes derives from what he sees as a more equitable racial policy that in its turn stems from the "peculiar" historical circumstances that forced the Portuguese to rely on native and African women for the effort of settling the immense territory. This idea is further developed in a different passage that brings to mind the concluding paragraphs in Charles Boxer's *Race Relations in the Portuguese Empire, 1415–1825*:

> In the Portuguese South American dominions, circumstances have directed that there should be no division of casts [*sic*], and very few of those degrading and most galling distinctions which have been made by all other nations in the management of their colonies. That this was not intended by the mother country, but was rather submitted to from necessity, is to be discovered in some few regulations, which plainly show, that if Portugal could have preserved the superiority of the whites, she would, as well as her neighbors, have established laws for this purpose. The rulers of Portugal wished to colonize to an unlimited extent; but their country did not possess a population sufficiently numerous for their magnificent plans. (Koster 1816, 385)

Koster's arguments here are of a historical rather than exceptionalist nature, positing demographic deficit instead of official policy or natural character as the explanation for the presumed lack of racial prejudice in Brazilian colonial society. He maintains this critical line of reasoning when, in the following two passages, he comments on the attempts made by advocates of slavery to turn individual cases of humane treatment of slaves in Brazil into a generalized principle of justification of the institution:

> When the advocates of slavery relate such stories as these, they give them as tending to prove that slaves in general are happy. Anecdotes of this kind demonstrate individual goodness in the master and individual gratitude in the slave, but they prove nothing generally; they do not affect the great

> question; *that* is rested upon grounds which are too deeply fixed to be moved by single instances of evil or of good. (418)

> To the planters I fear that scarcely any arguments would be of any avail; they imagine that without slaves their estates must decay, and therefore they fortify themselves under the notion of the humanity of the trade by which they obtain their supplies. (445)

The philosophical principle that informs these statements is that slavery is abhorrent to human nature and therefore could not be tolerated in any latitude or social landscape. This is what transpires in both of Koster's known writings, sometimes in contradiction with his premise that historical circumstances—demography and religion—had made Brazil a colonial experiment that had yielded policies worth considering as a model for the reforms that would have to be implemented in slave-owning societies under British rule if they were to follow the path to ultimate freedom. Even though Koster's discriminating appraisal of the specificities of Portuguese colonial rule in Brazil is generally persuasive, it was the authority of his testimony as an eyewitness to daily life in northeastern Brazil that made *Travels in Brazil* such a popular publication, with two consecutive English editions immediately followed by American, French, and German editions. As Manuela Carneiro da Cunha suggests, it was to capitalize on the rhetorical advantages of the testimonial that Koster decided to publish his pamphlet "On the Amelioration of Slavery" shortly after *Travels in Brazil*, so that the book could be seen as an independent source (1990, 368). Yet, and despite the widely recognized rigor of his observations of the flora and fauna of northeastern Brazil, as well as of its social and cultural institutions, which granted him the nickname "accurate Koster" coined by the English explorer Richard Burton (1869, 3), Koster seems to have excessively relied on the power of testimony. In terms of ecclesiastical policy, he presents the case of Benedictine plantations as an example of more humane treatment of slaves, but Stuart Schwartz has shown that the humane policies implemented in the plantations owned by the order of St. Benedict had profit and good business as an ulterior goal (1982, 22). More important, because it directly relates to the idea that came to form the core of Hegel's reference to the "English writer" in *The Philosophy of World History*, whose textual history I revisit in this article, is Koster's argument about manumission and why it was easier to obtain for enslaved persons in Brazil than anywhere else in the hemisphere. Historians such as Frank Tannenbaum and Stanley

Elkins have written about the mediation that the State and the Church provided in the relations between master and slave as the reason behind Brazil's alleged more lenient treatment of slaves, but it was Cunha who located the source of this common view in Koster, whom she sees as the originator of a misperception. Koster dedicates almost one hundred pages of *Travels in Brazil* to the direct discussion of the issues of slavery and free persons of color in colonial Brazilian society, and further references to those topics are interspersed elsewhere throughout the book, which shows the centrality of slavery in the life of the colony and what was then the United Kingdom of Portugal, Brazil, and the Algarves.[12] The key passages related to the issue of manumission merit a closer look:

> The slave can oblige his master to manumit him, on tendering to him the sum for which he was first purchased, or the price for which he might be sold, if that price is higher than what the slave was worth at the time he was first bought. This regulation, like every one that is framed in favour of slaves, is liable to be evaded, and the master sometimes does refuse to manumit a valuable slave; and no appeal is made by the sufferer owing to the state of law in the country, which renders it almost impossible for a slave to gain a hearing. (Koster 1816, 404)

Koster comes across as being well informed about colonial Brazilian institutions, and how regulations could fairly easily be circumvented by plantation owners, or in any case about how enslaved Brazilians could not expect much from the justice system if their masters refused to manumit them. Of course, the passage also shows that Koster knew why manumission did seem to be easier to obtain in Brazil than elsewhere, as he discusses amply in both of his publications: over time, the ability to work on their own on Sundays and holidays allowed enslaved Brazilians to accumulate the amount necessary to purchase their freedom. The problem with the scenario that he lays out in *Travels in Brazil* is that, as Cunha has analyzed, there was never in Brazil a codified law for the custom he describes in the passage above. It is difficult to doubt Koster's word, not only because he is well informed about colonial Brazilian institutions (or because he shares a treasure trove of information framed as eyewitness testimony at a time when that was a privileged position), but also because he is indeed sincere. The widespread custom, along with the testimony he obtained from his interlocutors—slave owners themselves or their dependents—did not allow him to pursue with enough scrutiny the validity of the information that the veil of customary social practices made out to be credible. This much becomes evident in the footnote that he adds to the above passage:

> This instance of refusal, and some others of which I have heard, would make me very doubtful of the foundation upon which the custom of manumitting is placed, if I did not know how easily the laws relating to many other important points are evaded through the influence of wealth and power. I did not see a copy of the law or regulation on the subject, but I never met with anyone who doubted that the slave had a right to appeal, if he thought proper; whether he would be heard or not was another question. (quoted in Cunha 1985, 428)

As it turns out, the very same wealth and power, associated with the cogency of Koster's bearing witness to the power of its influence, is what ends up convincing him that a law was codified to provide a legal framework to the practice of manumission at that time. I cannot follow Cunha's discussion to its full extent here, which includes a list of the many historians who have reproduced Koster's error up to the modern times, but, as she points out, "this right had no basis in law until 1871, that is, until the 'Free Womb' Law; and significantly this Law, which laid down that all children thereafter born to slaves would be free, heralded the beginning of the official dismantling of slavery" (1985, 429). In other words, the practice of manumission never affected slave owners negatively, or manumission requests were rejected when it did. In any case, the practice never threatened the institution of slavery, slave owners had the sole power to accept or reject manumission requests from their slaves, and the state only intervened when its own interest was in play (Cunha 1985, 430). What this means is that, contrary to what Koster asserts, manumission was a quintessential example of customary law; the absence of manumission codes from the books was deliberate, not an omission; and it had one purpose: to maintain moral ties between master and former slave as a way to ensure relations of dependence between freedmen and their former enslavers, as the possibility of reversal of manumission existed for cases of ingratitude, which was broadly defined to include verbal ingratitude (Cunha 1985, 438). The coexistence of customary law and written law helps to conjure up a polity in which the former serves to create an international image for the system that domestically works in different ways:

> The true society of 19th century Brazil is this complex of written and unwritten laws which do not intersect, one affirming relations without privilege between

> equivalent citizens, the other dealing with private relations of dependence and power. They coexist without hindrance because, as allies, they carve out basically distinct fields of application for themselves: the law, essentially, is for the free poor; customary law is for the powerful, their slaves and their dependent clients. The former is also the external face—international, but not necessarily false—of a system which, domestically, is something else. (Cunha 1985, 441)

What Koster and so many after him saw as an example of "humane colonialism" was in fact one cornerstone of a system of personal dependence that for two hundred years has had the capacity to build itself as a benevolent façade for a society that was utterly dependent on enslaved labor for its survival. Koster's readers, including Hegel (and Cortesão through him), may have read him at face value, and that explains to a great extent why the idea of "humane colonialism" had had currency for so long before it was actually enlisted in the service of official Portuguese discourse from the 1950s onwards. But more instructive of its enduring power of persuasion is Koster's trusting that the testimony obtained from slave owners and/or their dependents about manumission in colonial Brazil was sufficient to confirm the existence on the books of a law that was never codified before 1871. It is as if the tangible benevolence that he himself received from his hosts could come to define a society that had managed to render the utter violence of its labor system intangible to those observing from a relative distance. When Hegel, emulating Koster, celebrated the high number of freedmen in Brazil's coastal cities, he couldn't know that he was actually celebrating the endurance of servitude in freedom.

Henri Grégoire and the Intangible Source of Benevolent Brotherhood

Pierre-Franklin Tavares had reason to identify Abbé Henri Grégoire (1750–1831) as Hegel's likely source in the passage from *The Philosophy of World History*. We know that the attribution is incorrect because, among the many uncertainties regarding the production of Hegel's text, we do know the philosopher mentions "an English writer." But if we are right to identify Henry Koster as that writer, then Grégoire is a more than plausible influence, since Koster is likely to have read him in Robert Southey's library, and even discussed his books with William Wilberforce and other British abolitionists who had been inspired by Grégoire.

Contrary to what Manuela Carneiro da Cunha suggests in the article about Koster's pamphlet "On the Amelioration of Slavery," the English writer was not the inventor of comparative slavery regimes, nor even of basing such comparisons on ethical criteria. Although I cannot categorically attribute this role to Grégoire, it is important to recognize that he anticipates Koster in that domain. Published in 1808, his book *De la littérature des nègres* (published in English two years later as *An Enquiry Concerning the Intellectual and Moral Faculties, and Literature of the Negroes*) vigorously promotes the rehabilitation of the image of Africans and their descendants in Europe and the New World by arguing for the preeminence of African history and civilization and the dignity of Black intellectual production, and by questioning, through the lens of Scripture, the assumptions of coeval European racialist discourse in what constitutes a pioneering effort to ground equality. Interestingly, of the inventory of writers of different nationalities that to his day had defended the cause of Black and mixed-race peoples and to whom he dedicates his book, Portuguese writers are entirely absent. More interesting still is how the former Constitutional bishop of Blois rationalizes that absence. This becomes apparent in two passages from Grégoire's book, which bring to light the contradiction inherent to the idea of "humane colonialism" from a different angle.

After listing intellectuals from all the European countries that had direct or indirect involvement in the transatlantic slave trade, and who had written in defense of the interests of enslaved Africans and their descendants, Grégoire refers to the Spanish and Portuguese cases:

> One should not be surprised not to find here any Spanish or Portuguese author (with the exception of Avendano); beyond the Pyrenees, those rights and duties were never a problem; and who would they need to defend, if there is no aggressor? . . . Only in our time, through unconvincing efforts, has a Portuguese tried to justify colonial slavery, so different from that which, with the Hebrews, was like a type of domesticity; but Azeredo's brochure went from the book shop to oblivion. (Grégoire 10–11)[13]

This is an interesting passage: already in the early nineteenth century, when antiquity was tapped for references about slavery to inform anticolonial sentiment among North American slave owners such as Thomas Jefferson, Grégoire points out the difference between ancient slavery and early-modern colonial slavery, a point of contention in conservative positions in today's debate about the legacies of slavery in Portugal. On the other hand, and more to the point, he predicates the absence of abolitionist discourse in Spanish and Portuguese on the supposed absence of grievances of Africans living under Spanish and especially Portuguese rule in comparison to those living under other European colonial regimes. Further ahead, Grégoire adds:

> In general, in the Spanish and Portuguese domains, Negroes are seen as brothers of a different color. The Christian religion that purifies joy, wipes tears, and whose hand is always ready to spread benefits, this religion mediates between the slaves and their masters in order to sweeten the rigors of authority and the burden of obedience. Thus, in these two colonial domains, nobody wrote useless defenses of the Negroes. . . . ([1808] 1991, 12–13)

The issue of the role of the Catholic Church as a mediator between masters and slaves in colonial Brazil is a historiographical subfield in itself, and the bibliography is growing. The details of this discussion are not my concern here. Irrespective of the validity of Grégoire's claims (and of the fact that, although his sources are usually documented throughout the book, it is unclear who he is thinking of specifically in these passages), what stands out is that he reproduces eighteenth-century Portuguese ecclesiastical discourse about slavery, resonating particularly with Manuel Ribeiro Rocha's *Etíope resgatado* (1758). The problem with emulating this source is that it fundamentally contradicts Grégoire's fierce abolitionist advocacy, since what Rocha defended in his book was the need for a more humane treatment of slaves, a concern that, despite its humanitarian overtones, aligned perfectly with the more pragmatic goal of ensuring a smooth operation in the daily management of forced labor for the plantation owners of Brazil. In other words, what Grégoire may have seen as the advocacy for the interests of enslaved Brazilians—the kind of document he asserts does not exist in Portuguese because it is not necessary—was also a defense of the system of personal dependence that Cunha scrutinizes in her reading of Koster's involuntarily blind defense of Portuguese racial exceptionalism, and that ensured the long-term survival of forced labor in Brazil and in Portugal's African colonies. Koster's unfounded belief in the existence of a codified law managing the state's mediation in cases of manumission may as well have been structured around his reading of Grégoire's advocacy book. He does not, however, mention Grégoire a single time in either of his publications. Truly important sources, in the case of one writer or the other, go unmentioned. It is not so much that they are intangible, but that their intangibility, as in the issue of "humane colonialism," begs the question: the more we look for sources the more intangible it becomes, in the reverse proportion that the social system that it made possible becomes ever more tangible—and unsettling.

I believe this revision, by almost two centuries, in the chronology of Lusotropicalism's genealogy sheds some light on the sentiment of guarded appreciation that Cortesão reserves for the figure of Freyre in the first excerpt from the interview quoted earlier in this article. The growing enthusiasm for Lusotropicalism that was visible in Portugal during the 1950s must have been puzzling for someone who had already found its vindication in an early-nineteenth-century collection of lectures by one of that century's most acclaimed philosophers. Yet the study of the sources of Cortesão's alternative genealogy of Lusotropicalism need not lead to an elusive quest for origins, or even to a transatlantic dispute about scholarly preeminence. Rather, such study is instructive to the extent that it allows us to establish a textual history that spans at least three continents and different cultures and linguistic registers, and is characterized by the periodical reiteration of exceptionalist tropes that will be appropriated by Brazilian and Portuguese intellectuals alike, in their efforts to come to terms with their countries' hegemonic discourses of nationalism.

It is likewise enlightening to realize that Portuguese racial exceptionalism has also been reproduced by scholars outside of the Lusophone sphere with purposes that do not immediately or necessarily align with Portuguese and/or Brazilian interests. That is how, before an abolitionist debate took shape in the colonial Portuguese world, Grégoire could have invoked Portuguese racial exceptionalism to advocate for total abolition, something that, in the Portuguese-speaking world, would take the better part of the nineteenth century to accomplish, and that, when it finally happened, did not come close to matching Grégoire's sense of dignity among equals. After all, African history is not a subject routinely made available to students going through the Portuguese educational system to this day. Conversely, and as we have seen, these nationalistic appropriations do not exist without substantive foreign mediations—German, British, and French—giving shape to what Robert Stam and Ella Shohat have recently called "intercolonial narcissism" (2014, 387). Long in the making, such discursive mode eloquently confirms that, as the epigraph from Pierre-Franklin Tavares proposes, sources are always about something else.

NOTES

1. This and all remaining translations are my own, unless otherwise noted. Research for this essay was made possible by two grants from FLAD (Fundação Luso-Americana para o Desenvolvimento) and one grant from the Ohio State University's College of Arts and Sciences that allowed me to conduct research in the Jaime Cortesão archives at the National Library of Portugal, the Sociedade de Geografia, and the Academia das Ciências in Lisbon. I would like to acknowledge the valuable feedback I received for different versions of this manuscript from Joan Ramón Resina, Vincent Barletta, and Marília Librandi Rocha at Stanford; Devin Fergus and all the colleagues in the Department of African American and African Studies at OSU; Joe Blackmore at Harvard; and Cláudia Castelo and Cristiana Bastos at the CIEA9 conference in Coimbra, Portugal. This essay would not have been written without the invitation to speak at the Iberian and Latin American Transatlantic Symposium at the University of Oregon in fall of 2013. I am indebted to Pedro García-Caro, Cecília Enjuto Rangel, Robert Newcomb, and Sebastiaan Faber for a great weekend of reflection and debate; I am just as grateful to Anna Klobucka and Miguel Bandeira Jerónimo for the opportunity to speak at the colloquium on Heritages(s) of Portuguese Influence: Histories, Spaces, Texts, and Objects at the University of Massachusetts Dartmouth in April 2019 and to share the new insights I have gained from this longstanding research project.

2. Ownership of slaves was abolished in metropolitan Portugal by Sebastião José de Carvalho e Melo, the Marquis of Pombal, in 1761. The purpose of the decree was to curtail competition with the colonies and to divert the slave trade towards Brazil, where demand for enslaved labor grew throughout the eighteenth century in response to the discovery of significant mineral deposits in what is now the state of Minas Gerais. Portugal's president used the date of 1761 as a marker of the effective abolition of slavery, which in fact happened only in 1869. The presidential remarks in Senegal prompted a sizable group of international scholars to sign an open letter, published in the Portuguese newspaper *Diário de Notícias* (Câncio 2017).

3. The lawyer and former conservative party leader José Ribeiro e Castro wrote in an op-ed in the daily newspaper *Público* that "O Luso-tropicalismo não é somente narrativa do que vemos, acreditamos e concluímos, mas, acima de tudo, um programa do que queremos, o programa" (Lusotropicalism is not just the narrative about what we see, believe, and conclude, but, above all, a program for what we want, the program") (Castro 2020).

4. About the controversy following the publication of Boxer's *Race Relations in the Portuguese Colonial Empire*, see Cummins and Rebelo (2001).

5. See Anderson, Roque, and Santos (2019). The journal *Lusotopie* devoted an entire issue to the topic in 1997 ("Luso-tropicalisme: Idéologie coloniales et identités nationale dans les mondes lusophones").

6. To be sure, wholesale associations of a generic Lusotropicalist discourse with Freyre are in themselves problematic, as they tend to conflate the ideas expounded in Freyre's post-1950 writings with his 1933 magnum opus *Casa-grande & senzala* (The Masters and the Slaves).

7. Robert Bernasconi, (1998, 300) in his "Hegel at the Court of the Ashanti," reminds us that "the travel literature of the seventeenth and eighteenth centuries was transformed by academicians into a discourse of race that, when tied to the philosophy of history, was used to legitimate the violent and destructive character of nineteenth-century colonialism."

8. About Lusofonia as a myth, see Margarido (2000) and Martins (2006).

9. For instance, the reference to a certain "Dr. Kingera," a Black man said to supposedly have discovered quinine in colonial Brazil, whose existence is not recorded anywhere else.

10. Knowledge of Koster's and Southey's acquaintance was not always immediately available in the twentieth century. As recently as 1966 the historian C. Harvey Gardiner, who prepared and prefaced an abridged edition of *Travels in Brazil* for Southern Illinois University Press, wrote: "When Southey and Koster first met is not known. Perhaps they were acquainted before Henry's initial departure for Brazil. . . . Southey's own travels in Portugal might have led to his meeting the Koster family" (Gardiner 1966, x–xi).

11. Koster dedicates a long appendix to the treaty in *Travels in Brazil* (1817, 2:463–74).

12. The United Kingdom of Portugal, Brazil, and the Algarves was a pluricontinental monarchy formed in 1815 and dissolved in 1822 with the independence of Brasil.

13. Brazilian-born José Joaquim da Cunha Azeredo Coutinho (1742–1821) was a bishop and the last inquisitor-general of the kingdom. He remains known as a defender of slavery and of the continuation of the slave trade from the Portuguese territories in West and West-Central Africa.

WORKS CITED

Alexandre, Valentim. 1973. "Le colonialisme portugais—realité et mythe." In *Suisse-Portugal, de l'Europe à l'Afrique*, edited by Carlos Almeida et al., 7–27. Genève: Éditions CETIM.

———. 1979. *Origens do colonialismo português moderno (1822–1891)*. Lisboa: Sá da Costa.

———. 1999. "Prefácio." In *"O modo português de estar no mundo": Luso-tropicalismo e ideologia colonial portuguesa (1933-1961)* by Cláudia Castelo, 5–6. Porto: Afrontamento.

Almeida, Miguel Vale de. 2004. *An Earth-Colored Sea: "Race," Culture, and the Politics of Identity in the Postcolonial Portuguese-Speaking World*. New York: Berghahn Books.

Anderson, Warwick, Ricardo Roque, and Ricardo Ventura Santos. 2019. *Luso-Tropicalism and Its Discontents: The Making and Unmaking of Racial Exceptionalism*. New York: Berghahn Books.

Bastos, Cristiana. 2019. "Luso-Tropicalism Debunked, Again: Race, Racism, and Racialism in Three Portuguese-Speaking Societies." In Anderson, *Luso-Tropicalism and Its Discontents*, 243–64.

———. 1998. "Tristes trópicos e alegres luso-tropicalismos: Das notas de viagem em Lévi-Strauss e Gilberto Freyre." *Análise Social*, no. 33, 415–32.

Bernasconi, Robert. 1998. "Hegel at the Court of the Ashanti." In *Hegel after Derrida*, edited by Stuart Barnett, 41–63. London: Routledge.

Bethell, Leslie. 2003. *Brazil by British and Irish Authors*. Oxford: Centre for Brazilian Studies, University of Oxford.

Burton, Richard Francis. 1869. *Explorations of the Highlands of the Brazil. With a Full Account of the Gold and Diamond Mines*. Vol. 1. London: Tinsley Brothers.

Câncio, Fernanda. 2017. "'Marcelo lançou finalmente o debate público sobre a escravatura.'" *Diário de Notícias*, April 19, 2017. https://www.dn.pt/portugal/marcelo-lancou-finalmente-o-debate-publico-sobre-a-escravatura-6228783.html.

Castelo, Cláudia. 1999. "Gilberto Freyre's View of Miscegenation and Its Circulation in the Portuguese Empire, 1930s–1960s." In Anderson, *Luso-Tropicalism and Its Discontents*, 23–44.

———. 1998. *"O modo português de estar no mundo": Luso-tropicalismo e ideologia colonial portuguesa (1933–1961)*. Porto: Afrontamento.

Castro, José Ribeiro e. 2020. "Somos bonzinhos, mas burros e preguiçosos!" *Público*, February 15, 2021. https://www.publico.pt/2020/02/15/sociedade/opiniao/bonzinhos-burros-preguicosos-1903247.

Cortesão, Jaime. 1941. "O carácter Lusitano do descobrimento do Brasil." *Ocidente* 14:93.

———. 1959. "Existe um grande número de bons escritores." *Diálogo: Artes, Letras, Espectáculos* (suplemento do *Diário Ilustrado*), no. 32 (August 8).

Cummins, J. S., and L. de Sousa Rebelo. 2001. "The Controversy over Charles Boxer's 'Race Relations in the Portuguese Colonial Empire 1415–1825.'" *Portuguese Studies*, no. 17, 233–46.

Cunha, Manuela Carneiro da. 1990. "'On the Amelioration of Slavery' by Henry Koster." *Slavery & Abolition* 11 (3): 368–98.

———. 1985. "Silences of the Law: Customary Law and Positive Law on the Manumission of Slaves in 19th Century Brazil." *History and Anthropology* 1 (2): 427–43.

Fele, Buanga. 1955. "Qu'est-ce que le 'luso tropicalismo'?" *Présence africaine*, no. 4, 24–35.

Freyre, Gilberto. 2002. *Casa-grande & senzala*. Edited by Guillermo Giucci, Enrique Rodríguez Larreta, and Edson Nery da Fonseca. Madrid: Allca XX.

Gardiner, C. Harvey. 1966. Introduction to *Travels in Brazil*, by Henry Koster, vii–xvi. Carbondale: Southern Illinois University Press. VII-XVI.

Grégoire, Henri. (1808) 1991. *De la littérature des nègres*, ou, Recherches sur leurs facultés intellectuelles, leurs qualités morales et leur littérature: *Suivies de notices sur la vie et les ouvrages des* nègres qui se sont distingués dans les sciences, les lettres et les arts. Paris: Perrin.

Grin, Monica. 2012. "Mitos de excepcionalidade: Versões do Império português e da nação miscigenada brasileira." In *Memória, escrita da História e cultura política no mundo luso-brasileiro*, edited by Jacqueline Hermann, Francisca L. Nogueira de Azevedo, and Fernando Catroga, 285–326. Rio de Janeiro: FGV Editora.

Hegel, Georg Wilhelm Friedrich. 1975. *Lectures on the Philosophy of World History. Introduction: Reason in History*. Translated by H. B. Nisbet, with an introduction by Duncan Forbes. Cambridge: Cambridge University Press.

Klein, Herbert S. 2012. "The Free Afro-Brazilians in a Slave Society." In *Racism and Ethnic Relations in the Portuguese-Speaking World*, edited by Francisco Bethencourt and Adrian J. Pearce, 227–54. Oxford: Oxford University Press.

Klobucka, Anna. 2002. "Lusotropical Romance: Camões, Gilberto Freyre, and the Isle of Love." *Portuguese Literary & Cultural Studies*, no. 9, 121–36.

Koster, Henry. 1816. *Travels in Brazil*. 1st ed. London: Longman.

———. 1966. *Travels in Brazil*. Carbondale: Southern Illinois University Press.

———. 1942. *Viagens ao Nordeste do Brasil*. São Paulo: Companhia Editora Nacional.

Lourenço, Eduardo. (1961) 1984. "A propósito de Freyre (Gilberto)." In *Ocasionais I*, 105–12. Lisboa: A Regra do Jogo.

———. 2014. *O colonialismo como nosso impensado*. Lisboa: Gradiva.

Margarido, Alfredo. 2000. *A Lusofonia e os lusófonos: Novos mitos portugueses*. Lisboa: Edições Universitárias Lusófonas.

Martins, Moisés Lemos. 2006. "Lusofonia e luso-tropicalismo: Equívocos e possibilidades de dois conceitos hiper-identitários." In *Língua portuguesa: reflexões lusófonas*, edited by Neusa Barbosa Bastos, 49–62. São Paulo: Editora PUCSP/EDUC.

Pereira, Pedro Schacht. 2009. "Fermento da República, bolor do Império: Civilização Ibérica, excepcionalismo e o legado luso-brasileiro do lusotropicalismo." *Estudios Portugueses*, no. 9, 151–70.

Rocha, Manuel Ribeiro. 1758. *Ethiope resgatado, empenhado, sustentado, corregido, instruido, e libertado: Discurso Theologico-Juridico* [. . .]. Lisboa: Officina Patriarcal de Francisco Luiz Ameno.

Santos, Boaventura de Sousa. 2002. "Between Prospero and Caliban: Colonialism, Postcolonialism, and Inter-Identity." *Luso-Brazilian Review* 39 (2): 9–43.

Southey, Robert. 1856. *Selections from the Letters of Robert Southey*. Edited by John W. Warter. Vol. 1. London: Longman, Brown, Green, and Longmans.

Schwartz, Stuart. 1982. "The Plantations of St. Benedict: The Benedictine Sugar Mills of Colonial Brazil." *The Americas* 39 (1): 1–22.

Stam, Robert, and Ella Shohat. 2014. *Unthinking Eurocentrism: Multiculturalism and the Media*. New York: Routledge.

Tavares, Pierre-Franklin. 1993. "Hegel et l'abbé Grégoire ou Question Noire et Révolution Française." In *Révolution aux colonies: Publication des Annales Historiques de la Révolution Française*, 491–509. Paris: Societé des Études Robespierristes.

Trouillot, Michel-Rolph. 1995. *Silencing the Past: Power and the Production of History*. Boston: Beacon Press.

PEDRO SCHACHT PEREIRA is associate professor of Portuguese and Iberian Studies at the Ohio State University. He has a PhD in Luso-Brazilian Studies from Brown University (2005) and was a postdoctoral fellow at the University of Chicago between 2005-2008. His research interests include nineteenth, twentieth and twenty-first century Portuguese literature and culture, with a special focus on the literary production of/about Afrodescendant authors and their connections with other African diasporic subjects.

WALTER ROSSA

Myth as the Catalyst of a Cultural Heritage-Building Process: The Case of Goa

ABSTRACT: In the 1530s, Goa, conquered in 1510, became the center of the Portuguese Estado da Índia. It was an unprecedented situation, which made planning impossible. A century later, Goa's unexpected urban expansion revealed the site's adverse conditions, causing its residents and public servants to gradually begin abandoning the city. At the same time, however, Goa's Catholic institutions were engaged in an intense enterprise of building and reconstruction, which led them to resist any call to change or relocation until their expulsion from the Portuguese Empire in 1834. The continuing decay of Goa's urban fabric was finally acknowledged by the Portuguese Crown in 1843 with the move of the capital to Panjim. All the while, the magnetic attraction of St. Francis Xavier's relics continued to be capitalized on by the Catholic elites, reinforcing the myth of the "Golden Goa" and "Rome of the East." Forced integration of Goa into the Republic of India in 1961 did not interrupt the process of heritage building. In 1986, as a result of a formal proposal by India's central government, the "churches and convents of Goa" were added to UNESCO's World Heritage List. Goa's landscape is a dramatic expression of this immaterial process of cultural-heritage construction.

KEYWORDS: myth of St. Francis Xavier, Goa, cultural heritage, Portuguese Estado da Índia, capital city

RESUMO: Na década de 1530 Goa, conquistada em 1510, transformou-se no centro do Estado da Índia Portuguesa. Era uma situação inusitada e por isso impossível de planear. Um século depois, a sua inesperada explosão urbana revelou as condições adversas do local, levando a que os habitantes e funcionários públicos lentamente a fossem abandonando. Porém, as instituições católicas estavam então no auge de uma enorme campanha de construções e renovações, o que as levou a resistir a qualquer ímpeto de abandono ou mudança até serem expulsas de todo o universo português em 1834. A urbanidade de Goa foi assim agonizando, até que em 1843 a Coroa o reconheceu e investiu em Panjim como nova capital. No meio de tudo isso, o magnete constituído pelos restos mortais de São Francisco Xavier, foi sendo desenvolvido pela elites católicas do território, que com isso reforçaram o mito da *Goa Dourada* e *Roma do Oriente*. A integração forçada na República da Índia em 1961 não interrompeu esse processo de patrimonialização, e em 1986, necessariamente sob proposta do Governo da República, as Igrejas de Conventos de Goa foram inscritos na Lista do Património Mundial da UNESCO. A paisagem de Goa é uma dramática expressão desse constructo imaterial de património cultural.

PALAVRAS-CHAVE: mito de São Francisco Xavier, Goa, património cultural, Estado da Índia Portuguesa, cidade capital

---

Introduction

Goa is the unimposing name of the smallest state in India, with one of the highest per capita levels of income and standards of living in the country. These are three of the many measurable attributes that characterize the state's development, including in the postcolonial era. In stark contrast to these objective facts is the particular historical path Goa has forged, which has made its name a myth, a mantra even, and which goes far beyond its territorial, statistical, and administrative dimensions. The reasons for this are many, from the great variety of territories and forms of presence and governance over which it presided as the capital of the Portuguese Estado da Índia (State of India) to the influence of the Goan diaspora caused by the city's decline. In the center of the vortex of the state of Goa is the eponymous city, which today, like Velha Goa (Old Goa), is an oasis of coconut trees threatened by unpleasant new urban development. From this landscape emerge a number of whitewashed churches and convents, a pale reflection of the fleeting urban settlement that was once the seat of the first and longest-lasting European colonial presence in Asia. As one of the leading centers for Catholic worship, Goa nevertheless endures as a capital city of sorts, with the tomb of St. Francis Xavier, the "Apostle of the East," acting as a magnet for the faithful.[1] In an interpretation as immediate and generalized as it is simplistic, it can be said that Goa's urban development arose in parallel to that of its State (of Portuguese India) in the late sixteenth and early seventeenth centuries, an authentic golden century or age. It was an unlikely state, as it was discontinuous and took on distinct forms and expressions, which spread throughout the Indian Ocean and a small part of the Pacific. It was the century of mythical "Golden Goa" or "Rome of the East." When this state came to have jurisdiction over little more than the territory that would become the present-day state of Goa in the

Fig. 1. The view of Goa from the Lady of the Mount Hill, 2017.

Republic of India, Panjim, eight kilometers down the Mandovi River, emerged as the new center of power.

This emergence was not merely a change of the capital's location but also a paradigm shift in the relationship between the capital and the territory, and it occurred over centuries rather than decades, with a mixture of pain and nonconformity. The administrative act in which this change was embodied in 1843 was in itself significant: it created a new administrative unit, Nova Goa (New Goa), which joined the old capital to Panjim (on the insistence of its residents, Panjim ended up being the effective center) and to what lay in between, Panelim and Ribandar, always along the south riverbank of the Mandovi. Goa became Velha Goa since it now included Nova Goa, a name that, in a kind of official euphemism, was no more than the last of the reluctant gestures with which the Portuguese authorities always faced the decadence of the city. In other words, its status was transformed definitively from an administrative capital city into a myth. Paradoxically, Nova Goa no longer exists today while Velha Goa does, and therefore from now on I will be referring to the latter simply as Goa.

These are the main reasons why Goa has always seemed to be the most particular and extreme case among the former capital cities of the Portuguese Empire.[2] Its urban fabric contains various eras and places that represent critical points in the history of the empire and the State of India. On the other hand, Goa was always, among the various Portuguese areas of influence, the place that contained the most significant cultural, ethnic, and religious variety, density, and complexity. This diversity of contexts and contents has also caused most of the elements of Goa's urban development to disappear, so that their symbolic aspects became tangled up, only helping to develop the myth. In my study of

Goa, I have separated the stages of this process as follows: a) Portuguese establishment and rise; b) decline and creation of the myth; c) the ephemeral shift to Mormugao; d) conflict between the Pombaline Enlightenment reformism (so-called Restoration of the Estado da Índia) and the pragmatism of the residents, which ended imposing Panjim as the new center; e) Liberal era's resolution, with the euphemism of Nova Goa, which confirmed and accommodated Panjim; and f) turning Goa into cultural heritage.

In short, an exploration of the urban trends and expressions of the capital cities of Goa during Portuguese rule over the territory implies studying the hesitations between three different sites, two of which need to be observed in much greater detail, over the period of 450 years. This text will focus mainly on Goa, and therefore on stages a, b, and f. My aim is to produce a summary of the expressions, evolution, and ruptures in the urban development of Goa's capital, in contrast to the myth that surrounds it. I do not present any new facts, but I do offer an interpretation of the phenomenon over a long span of time, giving relevance to the process and its meanings, to the building of this heritage asset. The long process of turning Goa into cultural heritage is a sui generis affair that became crucial not only in itself but also to Goa's survival as a mythical capital city, one of a number of such sites in South Asia.[3]

The Push for a Capital City

Along the west coast of South India, Goa offers one of the most privileged gates to the Decan. The two basins of the rivers Mandovi and Zuari converge in an almost shared bar, separated only by the island of Tiswadi. Before that point on the seashore, the rivers communicate by a system of channels that are now becoming silted, likely due to climate change.

The hesitation about the island of Tiswadi as the right place for a capital city was a permanent, even chronic, element in the decision-making process around the location of Goa's capital. Before the late-seventeenth-century attempt to move the capital to Mormugao (a small peninsula on the opposite bank of the Zuari), and its effective relocation to Panjim in the nineteenth century (on the south bank of the Mandovi, near its mouth), this hesitation accompanied the settling on the site of Goa; firstly, by the shifting of locales occupied by the previous rulers, which I will address further on; and, secondly, in the framework of the initial strategic definitions of the Portuguese presence in Asia, as I will now summarize.

Fig. 2. Goa and Tiswadi Island's geographic shape and defensive system (in Rossa and Mendirata, "A cerca adormecida," 2012).

Cochin, whose authorization for the establishment of a Portuguese city was given by the local sovereign in 1503, only five years after the arrival of the Portuguese ships in the Indian Ocean, was almost a natural choice for the settling of the main Portuguese base. Even so, the decision was not immediate. It should be noted, for example, that in 1506 the king wrote to the Viceroy Francisco de Almeida, ordering him to decide on that "main base" and suggesting its location in Sri Lanka, as the island was "at the center of all the fortresses and things we own there" (Santos 1999, 90; my translation). Even before being seized in 1510 from the Sultanate of Bijapur, under the command of Afonso de Albuquerque, Goa emerged as a possibility in that discussion. The strategic context that influenced the decision and subsequent military actions led by that eminent Portuguese viceroy (1509–15) is well known, basically consisting in the opportunity to control Indian Ocean routes and trade by taking possession of the main ports of Goa, Ormuz, and Malacca, along with a few of secondary importance.[5]

But Albuquerque's strategy was questioned after his death, and the vagueness of Goa's rise as the Portuguese center in Asia is as complicated as it is well known. For example, one of its usually referenced highlights is the conflict between Governors Pedro de Mascarenhas and Lopo Vaz de Sampaio in the 1520s about the location of the central base, which ended with the arrival of Nuno da Cunha in 1529 with orders to shift the capital away from Cochin. Goa was then assumed to be the capital city of a state for which territory was sought not only around it but, more successfully, in what became the Província do Norte (Northern Province).

As early as 1530, Goa and its viceroy (at times only governor) received the respective functions and attributes (regalia) from the central government thus far established in Cochin, and later other symbols and the ceremonial court, hitherto the exclusive prerogative of the monarch in Lisbon. It was necessary to legitimize as a (vice)royal sovereign someone who was not the king. These decisions have to be read in the context of the strategic rearrangement of the entire Portuguese expansion, with its emphasis on North Africa/Morocco and especially on America. It is only from there that the beginning of the colonization of Brazil was considered. This rearrangement occurred under the apparent intensification of religious proselytizing provoked by the Reformation (1517) and the inevitable Catholic reaction, the Counter-Reformation (1545).

Location and a Glance at the Urban Landscape

At around 20 hectares, Goa Bijapuri was small, around two-thirds the size of other Portuguese cities in Hindustan, except Cochin, which was well above the average. It was also a young, disordered, and sparsely populated city. The houses were constructed poorly, as were government buildings, to which I will return. With regard to urban structures in general (as distinct from the architecture), in 1617, Silva y Figueroa put it plainly in one of his *Comentários*: "the city is all disorganized, scattered and spaced out, especially at its extremities, with many palms and other trees between the buildings; most streets are very crooked, without any policy or design, so that except for the few that are included within its old walls, the rest give more the impression of large overcrowded houses among trees than that of an ordered city" ([1617] 1903–5, 121; my translation).

Until its capture from the Hindus of Vijayanagar by the Muslims of the Bahmani Sultanate in 1469, the capital of the territory was a city on the south side of the island, on the north bank of the Zuari, a place known as Goa Velha.[4] The Muslims moved the capital to the opposite extreme of the island, on the south bank of the Mandovi. Shortly afterward, the potentate fragmented into several sultanates, one of which, Bijapur (today Vijayapur), continued to rule

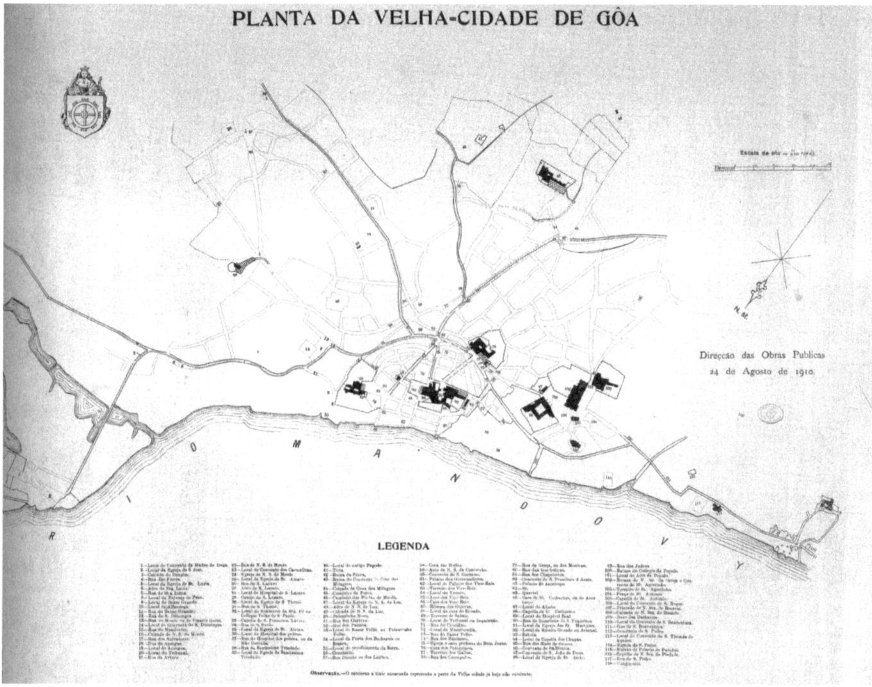

Fig. 3. *Planta da Velha-Cidade de Gôa* (Plan of the Old City of Goa). Goa: Direcção das Obras Públicas, 14 August 1910, lithograph.

over Goa. Only four decades before the conquest under the command of Afonso de Albuquerque, the territory got a new capital city, "which was entirely walled, with large slabs on the outside, and a large moat full of water" (Correia [1560] 1975, 2:60), with its center marked by an imposing square with a mosque and a palace, and a castle controlling the primary access to the city and the port area. It was Bijapur's second city and the commercial port connecting it to the outside world, and until the sultanate's total absorption by the Mughal Empire in 1686, there were repeated attempts to recapture it. Hence the constant need for defense, which led not only to the construction of an 18.5 km peripheral wall, enclosing 1,933 hectares (Rossa and Mendiratta 2012), but also to the rise of a complementary defensive system, whose most significant remnants are the forts such as the Aguada and Reis Magos, as well as what little is left of Rachol's perimeter and the impressive Colvale-Tivim wall.[5]

The choice of location for a small Bijapur port city in the late 1460s is understandable, but its adoption as the center of Portuguese operations in Asia some six decades later can only be explained by its convenience. However, there was no idea yet of what these operations would become, nor their scale, and the choice violated the most elementary principles of location then habitually followed overseas by the Portuguese, who sought sites surrounded by the sea (islands, peninsulas), well defended from the preferably narrow landside, and with a good port and health conditions. But those factors were considered when choosing a site to establish a settlement, sometimes near and under the authority of preexisting cities, such as Cochin and Chaul. In Goa, the occupation occurred through conquest, which made a city and its territory available, without prior knowledge of its pernicious potential for health problems, its sturdy defense, the silting up of the river, or the impossible navigation of its mouth during the monsoon season. As the future demonstrated, the Zuari River option, as that previous to the Bahamani Sultanate conquest, would not have produced these problems.

There are numerous documents, reports, and accounts providing evidence of how poor the choice of Goa's location was, such as Silva y Figueroa's straightforward commentary in 1617: "time and experience have clearly shown how bad their [the Muslims'] choice was in leaving the gentle and healthy location of Goa Velha" ([1617] 1903–5, 122; my translation). In the late sixteenth century, six decades after the decision to make Goa the Portuguese base in Asia, it was already clear that it would not be sustainable as the capital city of the Estado da India, even as it was being transformed precisely then into a large construction site, with the almost simultaneous building of several religious complexes.

Structure and Form

It is not the purpose of this article to discuss the establishment of Goa's new society under Portuguese rule and its progression during the so-called Classical Age,[6] or its urban development during the same period, which has been well documented in numerous studies, including some old engravings and more recent reconstitution drawings, especially relevant to the understanding of Goa's complex orography and organic urbanistic pattern (both impossible to describe here).[7] I will only draw attention to some less-understood aspects, particularly the linkage between the cities of Goa and Lisbon, expressed by the adage "Quem viu Goa escusa de ver Lisboa" ("He who has seen Goa need not see Lisbon") and by a forced vision of each city's seven hills, likening them to Rome. The rationale for this linkage was essentially political and ideological, boiling down to the fact that it was necessary to delegate real power and dignity to the role played by the

Fig. 4. Archbishop's Palace, 2017; Model of the Viceroy's Palace, Fundação Oriente Museum, Lisbon.

governors or viceroys and to make the city rhetorically worthy of its status as a Portuguese political, religious, and (essentially) trading capital city in Asia. And, to be clear, like Lisbon and contrary to what is commonly asserted, except for its churches Goa was not a city of monumental or even high-quality architecture. The same applies to its town planning and infrastructure (Rossa 2018).

The truth is that, in Goa, the adaptation of the preexisting city undertaken by the Portuguese displaced the palatine function of the central square. Here, the parish was first established and later the cathedral, Archbishop's Palace, the Inquisition (1560), and the council chamber, while the old castle was renovated in 1554 as the Viceroy's Palace, which dominated a square that on its north side opened toward the Mandovi River and served as the focal point for a series of functions, spaces, and buildings along the riverfront. This arrangement also occurred in Lisbon and, with compelling similarity, in other capital cities of the empire, particularly in Salvador, Rio do Janeiro, a little later in Luanda, and later still in one Enlightenment project for Panjim.[8] An urban riverside settlement with a riverine square mediating the relationship between the city, the palace, and the water, and used for ceremonies and festivals to celebrate kings, viceroys or governors, was one of the most important constants in the capital cities of the first Portuguese Empire. Among them, Goa is the only case that did not include any building that functioned as the palatine chapel.

Except for the first to arrive, the Franciscans, all Catholic orders and congregations established themselves beyond the perimeter of the Islamic city. Like the Franciscans, the Jesuits built their church over a mosque, but like the other religious orders they helped to encourage urban expansion beyond the original city wall. Within the walls, these processes of adaptation were slow and stretched over time, and they generally respected the street layout and structure of existing public spaces. In fact, and almost invariably, the destruction brought about by the conquest and adaptations led by Afonso de Albuquerque affected individual buildings, not the urban structure. On the other hand, renovations and, even more so, the creation of monuments resulted from a series of modifications that were never part of an overall or even partial plan. Significant examples include the two versions of the Franciscan monastery (the original Manueline and the surviving one);[9] the beginning, in 1562, of the slow construction of the imposing cathedral on the early parish church; and the transformation of two doors in the old Islamic wall, which practically merges into the Arches of Our Lady of Conception and the Viceroy's Arch, the memorial marking the centenary of Vasco da Gama's first voyage, which opened the sea route to India (Moreira 1987).

Together with the Archbishop's Palace, these arches are notably the only surviving examples of civil or even military architecture. I suspect the reason for this is not so much the systematic, and for some uncontrolled, dismantling of civic buildings to use their materials for houses in Panjim, but the fact that they were of little relevance in architectural, monumental, and construction terms. If this is not the case, why are there no decorative features among the reused materials in the houses of Panjim? Why do their descriptions say little about them apart from their size? If we examine drawings from the surveys of the most relevant buildings in Goa that were carried out in the 1770s—the Viceroy's Palace, built inside the former Islamic castle, and the Palace of the Inquisition, the 1554 adaptation of the former Viceroy's Palace, which in the early decades was within the old sultan's palace—and the model of the former based on these drawings, we can see that the buildings were much more modest than contemporary and later narratives made them out to be. Indeed, the Archbishop's Palace is an excellent example of this. There are no written records or plans to allow us to judge the architectural quality of other buildings, such as the notorious hospital or customs house, which seem to have been of even lower value as monuments, although they were large in scale.

As in Lisbon, rather than systematic organization of new urban dwellings or their renovation, it was the gradual standardization of current architecture, now totally disappeared, that gave Goa the urban unity described by some travelers, along with its monumental religious buildings and, in particular, the cosmopolitan bustle that perhaps corresponds to what we may glimpse today if we half-close our eyes in the more authentic Indian bazaars. As I observed elsewhere:

> The city continued to change, crystallizing a synthesis of the cultures present into everyday architecture. According to descriptions and iconography, the typical house had two floors, and a yard was built of mortar, covered with a tiled roof, and often painted with water-based paints in tones of red and white. The fronts had windows protected by railings and jalousies;[10] polished oyster shells (*carepas*) fulfilled the role of glass. (Rossa 1997, 46)

The famous Rua dos Leilões (Auctions Street), which linked the main squares of the city, corresponds precisely to this description. Some of these elements, such as tiles and the lime required for mortar, were introduced by the Portuguese, while the bright colors and *carepas* were not, and *muxarabi* was common from the Iberian Peninsula to Southeast Asia. Otherwise, regarding architecture and urbanism, the descriptions are laconic, and the design elements are unknown or even nonexistent. On civil architecture, therefore, nothing relevant can be added here.

Decay

The plans for the attempted Pombaline "Restoration of the State of India" from 1774 to 1777,[11] approximately halfway between Albuquerque's conquest and the present day, show how remarkably swift the decline of the "civil city" was. Residents, including the holders of the highest offices of the Crown and even archbishops themselves, had settled along the road that followed the south bank of the river to Ribandar. Except for Rua dos Leilões, the port, and Army and Navy facilities, only religious buildings were depicted in the plans. The Arsenal would only be removed in 1856, thirteen years after the official designation of Panjim as the new capital city.

The large influx of people who quickly settled in Goa in the mid-sixteenth century led to an explosive growth of the city, which was unregulated and lacked accompanying infrastructure. The location, besides being unbearably hot, proved unhealthy. The situation was not helped by a lake of stagnant water inside the walls (to the southeast), no collection system for the sewage, which was dumped everywhere, and the inevitable contamination of water from the wells, the only source available for consumption.[12] For its part, the Mandovi was not navigable during the monsoon and silted up with the increasing drafts of the boats, making navigation difficult.

At the end of the century, the inhabitants began to look for places more favored by sea breezes. The viceroys themselves had modifications made to their residence at what became known as the Idalcao Palace in Panjim, and soon they built the palace at Panelim that later became the Gunpowder House and Military Hospital, of which there is no trace today. The construction, in 1633, of the 3,150-meter causeway named Conde de Linhares Bridge, connecting Goa and Panjim, further accelerated this process. Only periods of insecurity in the face of external attacks mobilized the return of the Goans from the first diaspora to the city, even though the large peripheral wall and steps continued to be maintained and reinforced.

Between the 1670s and the first decade of the eighteenth century (in fact, significantly, during the entire regency and reign of King Pedro II), the capital was moved to Mormugao while building work was carried out (Rivara 1866–67; Martins 1910). At the time, various forces conspired to prevent the success of the enterprise, demonstrating, once again, the proverbial hesitation about the Portuguese strategic options in Asia. In this case, however, the decisive factor was no longer a hesitant approach by the powers in Lisbon but the disobedience of distant subjects in Goa, so that the next initiative, the Restoration of the State of India planned and promulgated by the Marquis of Pombal between 1774 and 1777, also failed to move forward (Barbuda 1841).

As I have already noted, progress in the first decades of the Portuguese presence in the Indian Ocean was unprecedented, and thus total experimentation was the rule. There was, therefore, no expectation of planning for what could not be known or foreseen, namely the capital city of an unlikely state, the continental seat of a religious creed of enormous proselytizing potential. Despite all this, and primarily as a European colonial capital functioning as the center of a field of intensive intercultural relations, Goa for nearly a century represented the phenomenon of a capital city that was absolutely new, fascinating, but ultimately unsustainable. Indeed, in another form, it has remained so to this day.

The Rise of the Myth

Instead of a process of civil decay, the commitment to Catholic evangelizing that underlay the Portuguese patronage system in the East played a decisive role in monumentalizing Goa and, concomitantly, in constructing the myth of "Golden Goa" or "Rome of the East," as well as in maintaining it over time.[13] Of course, the repression and proselytism within the Counter-Reformation played a part. To give some idea of the powerful escalation of this phenomenon, it is noteworthy how, in four decades, the Padroado made Goa into the "New Rome" of the Counter-Reformation: diocese in 1533/34; metropolitan archbishopric in 1557

Fig. 5. Goa cathedral's crossing vault, 2013.

Fig. 6. St. Francis Xavier's casket at the Bom Jesus Church in Goa, 2017

(ruling over the bishoprics of Cochin and Malacca immediately, and later on those of Macau, Funai, Cranganore, Meliapor, Nanking, Peking, Mozambique, and Daman); Inquisition in 1560; Primate of the East in 1572. Already famous for its monumentality, but undergoing the process of its civil decline, Goa was crowned the Catholic magnet of Asia with the beatification of St. Francis Xavier (1506–1552) in 1619 and his subsequent canonization in 1622. Francis Xavier was a Navarrese Jesuit saint who worked hard within the Portuguese Padroado long before the Iberian Union (1580–1640).

In contrast to everything else (integration of the Iberian empires, the shift of the Portuguese Empire's focus toward Brazil, sanitary problems, decay, and depopulation), as a Catholic capital Goa grew precipitously. All the religious orders sought to have a house in the city. In addition to the new buildings, among those erected since 1510 only the Church of the Priorado do Rosário and the Chapel of Santa Catarina were not replaced by more imposing structures. This resulted in a landscape-urbanistic free-for-all, along Baroque lines, in the capital city of the Estado da Índia. As in the European territory, but here with features and dimensions never reached elsewhere in the Portuguese Empire, the increase in the scale and splendor of religious architecture was understood as an essential element in the fight against heresy, as associated with Hindu and Muslim architecture of significant impact and quality. However, while the capital city of the Estado da Índia had disappeared, the capital of the Portuguese Patronage, with its tomb of the Apostle of the East, had not. Francis Xavier canonized Goa.

The creation of Nova Goa in 1843, which entailed recognizing Panjim as the colony's capital, was simultaneously a recognition of the end of Goa's urbanity. This shift had already been foreseen a few years earlier, when in 1834 one of the most far-reaching measures was taken by the new liberal regime: the abolition of religious orders. For Goa, this was decisive because it deprived it of its purpose and of its remaining residents. In other words, the post-ancien régime liberal background against which both events took place was only the most immediate factor in the structural paradigm change that unleashed the building of heritage in what remained of the city, its myth enshrined in Catholicism. The city's gradual abandonment by civilians from the second quarter of the seventeenth century onward was followed by the legally authorized and systematic dismantling of Goa that began in the mid-nineteenth century. What also followed was the ruin of much of what remains, except for some churches and a few convents, which are now the material core of Goa's World Heritage listed assets.

The systematic creation of the concept of cultural heritage and its public awareness were the fruit of the Industrial Age. The process gathered momentum at the end of the nineteenth century and was consolidated as a discipline and a cause around which social forces could be mobilized throughout the next century. Goa is an excellent example to follow along this path, but that is not within my scope in this essay. There are, however, a few facts that I need to introduce for a basic understanding of Goa's development as a heritage asset. They are listed here selectively and in chronological order:[14]

1859 The first exhibition of the century, of the relics of St. Francis Xavier on the anniversary of his death (December 3), led to the repair of some buildings but also to demolition of ruins. This practice would be repeated often.

1892 Among the rubble produced by the 1859 crumbling of the church of Nossa Senhora da Serra, the empty original sarcophagus of Afonso de Albuquerque was discovered.

1895 The discovery of Albuquerque's sarcophagus eventually led to the creation of the Permanent Commission of Archaeology and, in 1896, of the Royal Museum of Portuguese India.

1910 The first scientific cartographic survey of Goa, one of the heritage initiatives generated by cyclical public exhibitions of St. Francis Xavier's relics.

1930s Beginning of the inventory and classification of Goa's cultural heritage.

1947 Following the end of the Second World War, the independence of India triggered Portuguese reformism in the colonies. Scientific missions were promoted, including a 1951 project focused on history and art, led by Mário Tavares Chicó, and reports and books about the so-called Indo-Portuguese art, architecture, and urbanism were published.

1950 Abolition of the Permanent Commission of Archaeology and arrival of Baltazar de Castro, an experienced architect from the Portuguese General Directorate of National Buildings and Monuments (Direcção-Geral dos Edifícios e Monumentos Nacionais, DGEMN).

1952 Under Castro's supervision and in the framework of the fourth centenary of the death of St. Francis Xavier, a few far-reaching restoration works were inaugurated, namely on the Viceroy's Arch, the Chapel of Santa Catarina, and the Church of Bom Jesus.[15]

1960 In the context of *Comemorações Henriquinas* (celebrations of the fifth centenary of the death of Henry the Navigator), a plan for the "Reintegration of the City of Velha Goa in its Historical, Archaeological, Monastic, and Religious Setting" was launched.

It has become clear by this point that the great *worker* behind the development of Goa's cultural heritage and its recognition is St. Francis Xavier himself.

The "Reintegration of the City of Velha Goa" plan was drawn up in 1959 by a commission presided over by Ismael Gracias, who stated in his presentation that the idea was to reestablish the Old City of Goa as a "beacon of Portuguese spirituality."[16] This phrase is the cornerstone, almost an ideological summary, of the whole process. Still, Gracias's pompous statement had surely been inspired by the Portuguese governor's dispatch, which envisioned "Old Goa, the dead city, revived; not resurrected but reborn, transformed into a monastic city, spiritual city, silent but filled with life, in homage and respect to its glorious legacy of which we should be proud."[17] There is no doubt that this sequence of events and statements adds up to a clear example of what today we identify as a "heritage-building process," implemented by Goa's Catholic elites with the support of Portuguese colonial administration.

The Myth as World Heritage

Work on the "reintegration" project had barely begun when, in December 1961, Goa ceased to be a Portuguese colony. The project was, however, resumed shortly afterward, under the direction of the Republic of India's central authorities and according to the Gracias plan. The new urban design ignored the urban structure and memory of the obliterated city, opening up entirely novel spatial relationships, particularly the new central promenade. Thus, a renewed body, a new asset, emerged, supporting what in 1986 was inscribed by UNESCO in the World Heritage List under the designation "Churches and Convents of Goa."[18] It was the recognition, at the highest national and international levels, of Goa's myth; at the same time, it spelled out a declaration, both implicit and unconscious, that the urbanism of the capital city of Goa was irrelevant in its overall quality, sealing its effective loss of urbanistic value.

The UNESCO declaration refers directly to seven churches and convents, excluding any other assets, except for "the tomb of the apostle of India and Japan [that] symbolizes an event of the universal significance of the influence

Fig. 7. Goa World Heritage promenade. Courtesy of Tripraja (https://tripraja.com).

of the Catholic religion in the Asian world in the modern period." Clearly, the declaration values the spiritual presence of the saint over Goa's material assets. Complementing this statement, the argument foregrounding the spread of Catholicism in Asia is reinforced in other parts of the declaration, e.g., "The monuments of Goa, 'Rome of the Orient,' exerted great influence from the 16th to the 18th century on the development of architecture, sculpture and painting . . . throughout the countries of Asia where Catholic missions were established." These monuments are also said to be "an outstanding example of an architectural ensemble which illustrates the work of missionaries in Asia." This wording had necessarily come out from the proposal submitted to UNESCO by the Republic of India's government.[19]

A year later, in 1987, Goa became the twenty-fifth state of the Republic of India.[20] Its World Heritage listing cannot have been unrelated to that milestone advance in administrative autonomy. In the 1980s the world was changing swiftly, and India was becoming more actively involved in the process of economic globalization. In this context, Goa had enormous potential, ranging from mineral resources to tourism. It was also the right place to substantiate the rhetoric of multiethnic, multiracial, and multireligious coexistence that had nourished India's politics from independence till the end of the second millennium. The recognition of Goa's Catholic centrality within Asia and, implicitly, of its relevance as the only non-British ex-colonial enclave, factored in this trend.[21] A breeze of reconciliation blows from this 1980s action of India's central administration.

A visit to Goa today makes it easy to realize how these stated expectations were in the end set aside, to the point that everything intended to be safeguarded is now at risk. The territory's coastal strip is a site of frenetic commercial, industrial, and leisure activity, where intense real-estate development brings with it the usual problems. A significant part of this business frenzy is carried out by outside investors and migrant workers from poorer Indian states, who cannot be expected to recognize the value of Goan cultural heritage (Waterson and Smith 2010), especially insofar as much of it is directly identified with a religion other than Hinduism (today Goa is twenty-five percent Catholic and sixty-six percent Hindu).[22] Gentrification has walked hand in hand with harm to cultural assets and landscape disruption.

Let us examine just three clear indicators specifically regarding the World Heritage-listed site: the abandoned old capital city precinct is being urbanized; the new route of the Panjim-Belgão highway (National Highway 4), passes only 175 meters away from the Basilica of Bom Jesus; the last "state of conservation report" submitted to UNESCO dates from 1999, and no management plan or equivalent currently exists.[23] It seems that, with the comfort assured by the notoriously mild UNESCO management practices, the World Heritage List recognition has been taken for granted. On a broader scale, Goa's balance of economic, social, ethnic, and religious forces is now very different than in the past, and the scope of Indian administration's practice of tolerance has narrowed considerably in recent years.

The process of the international recognition of Goa's cultural relevance is a good example of how borderline boundary facts can be transformed into pivotal aspirational realities by using cultural heritage as a tool. The monumentality of Goa's remains is far more potent now than what the city had ever been in the past. Therefore, in terms of cultural heritage, the "Churches and Convents of Goa" are a construction, the result of a pact between Goan Catholic elites and the Republic of India.[24] But pacts are not immortal, even when negotiated over the remains of a saint. Today, the construct of Goa's cultural heritage inscribed in the World Heritage List should be recognized as being under threat. As in many other cases and contexts, it could be discussed whether the relevant concept is *contested heritage*, *heritage in conflict*, *heritage at risk*, or any other keyword that scholars invent and debate at random, but that matters little. It will be more important to bring up to date the awareness of the significance of its value for the communities of Goa and India, as well as for others, namely Catholics in Asia and worldwide. What is at stake, again, is the question of what is or what will be understood by "world heritage" and how to engage with the sovereign powers that hold control over heritage assets.

Myths gain a hold and thrive when they are preferable to and seem more powerful than the reality we are familiar with. They go up in smoke when what is revealed again transcends them; they are confirmed when disfigured. The myth of Goa has hidden and will continue to hide the perception that history has produced for many of its essential dimensions, undoubtedly because the reality that is being historicized is no more interesting than that narrated by the myth. That is an unconscious collective option that should not hinder the development of knowledge, because it is the only way to offer the opportunity to choose between myth and reality while also taking into account the endless seductive nuances between the two. I also prefer the urban myth of "Golden Goa" to what I have described as the real Goa.

NOTES

1. The presence of St. Francis Xavier, through his tomb in Goa, is a crucial issue in this text. For a comprehensive discussion, see Pamila Gupta, *The Relic State*. I draw on Gupta's work throughout the essay without citing it directly in every instance.

2. Among the vast bibliography on the subject, three studies stand out as genuinely essential and complementary—Dias, *De Goa a Pangim* (2005); Faria, *Architecture Coloniale Portugaise à Goa* (2014); and Santos, *"Goa é a chave de toda a Índia"* (1999)—although travel literature, editions of primary sources, and other research publications are equally important. As was customary in Portuguese culture at the time when Goa was an authentic city, in terms of reconstructing urban morphology and its development, cartography, illumination, paintings, and engravings are of minimal use, having led to misconceptions. The first accurate designs dated from the attempted Pombaline reconstruction of the 1770s (see note 13). For a comprehensive commented list of those texts, image sources, and contexts, see Rossa, "A capitalidade de Goa" (2020).

3. Beginning with the "seven cities of Delhi"; among the vast bibliography on the subject, the classic study by Gordon Risley Hearn, *The Seven Cities of Delhi* (1906), remains as the main reference.

4. The change of word order from Goa Velha to Velha Goa produces a subtle semantic effect in Portuguese that has no correspondence in English. While the meaning of "velha" in Goa Velha suggests something disposable, in Velha Goa the adjective connotes deference and respect.

5. Nuno Lopes's *The Heritage of Defence* (forthcoming), with its survey and systematization of available evidence, is a precious and revealing source of data on the fortification of Goa's territory.

6. On this subject see, among others, Lopes, *Goa setecentista, tradição e modernidade* (1999); Xavier, *A invenção de Goa* (2008); and Carreira, *Globalising Goa* (2014).

7. For example, this and the previous sections draw on the following in-depth urbanistic studies: Rossa, *Indo-Portuguese Cities*, (1997, 40–53, 92–111); Rossa, "Goa" (2010).

8. José de Morais Antas Machado, "*Projecto para a nova Cidade de Gôa se erigir no sítio de Pangim, que por ordem do Ill.mo e Ex.mo Sñr. D. Jozé Pedro da Camara Governador, e Cappitão General da Índia fêz e desenhou* [...] *em Março de 1776*", man., Goa, Gabinete de Estudos Arqueológicos da Engenharia Militar, 1236/2A-24A-111, dim. (mm) 1175x671.

9. The so-called Manueline "style" consists of a mainly decorative late medieval/Gothic architectural repertoire, assembled and used by the Portuguese in the late fifteenth and the first decades of the sixteenth century. It is widely referred to as a style, which it is not, even for those who still use the concept.

10. The upper-story balconies, completely enclosed by jalousies, were described as built in *muxarabi* manner.

11. Joze de Moraes d'Antas Machado, *Projecto para a nova Cidade de Gôa por…, Sargento Mor de Infantaria com exercício de engenheiro*, man., Goa, (w/d), Gabinete de Estudos Arqueológicos da Engenharia Militar 1241/2A-24A-111, dim. (mm) 1605x695; Joze de Morais d'Antas Machado, *Projecto da Cidade de Gôa por… Sargento Mor de Infantaria com exercício de Engenheiro, em* 1775, man., Goa, 1775, Gabinete de Estudos Arqueológicos da Engenharia Militar 1237/2A-24A-111, dim. (mm) 1467x470; João António Aguiar Sarmento, *P. Principe pella Fê P. Pátria Projecto para a nova Cidade de Goa feito por ordem do Ilustrissimo, e Excellentissimo Senhor Dom Joze Pedro da Camera Governador e Capitão General da India – Por … Capitão de Infantaria cõ exercicio de Engenheiro em MDCCLXXVII. Janeiro de 1777.*, man., Goa, 1777, Gabinete de Estudos Arqueológicos da Engenharia Militar 1240/2A-24A-111, dim. (mm) 1702x424.

12. Alberto Correia's *La Vieille Goa* (1931) is a shocking study of the mortality caused by frequent epidemics of cholera and smallpox, which killed many viceroys, inquisitors, archbishops, and other high officials and nobles.

13. The Portuguese Padroado (Patronage) consisted of a series of exclusive privileges, rights, and duties that had been gradually granted by popes to Portuguese monarchs

through a series of bulls and papal letters, the first of which was *Inter Caetera* (1456). Because they were absorbed with simmering problems in Europe, the popes delegated to Portugal the patronage of the Roman Catholic missions in the vast overseas regions the Portuguese dominated. When that delegation started in the fifteenth century, no one could have had the slightest idea of the scale the Padroado would reach. Irrespective of their nationality, priests who worked in these territories were sustained by the Crown and owed obedience to the king of Portugal, like the Navarrese Francis Xavier. For various reasons, its most relevant expression was achieved precisely in Asia, with Goa at the forefront. For a comprehensive and updated view, see Xavier and Olival, "O padroado da coroa de Portugal: Fundamentos e práticas" (2018) and Paiva, "Uma religião para o mundo: Padroado régio e uma diocese pluricontinental" (2020).

14. For more information, see Santos and Mendiratta, "'Visiono Velha Goa, a cidade morta, reanimar-se'" (2012) and Santos, "Reinstalling the Old City of Goa as an Eternal Light of Portuguese Spirituality" (2018).

15. Commemoration of the anniversary of St. Francis Xavier's death made the December 3 the annual climax of his and Asia's Catholic faith's cult. Round anniversaries, in 1952 (the 400th) and 2002 (the 450th), were of course most intensely celebrated. See Gupta, "The corporeal and the carnivalesque" (2017).

16. Gracias, *Goa, fanal da espiritualidade portuguesa* (1960). In translating this title, I opted for "beacon" instead of "lighthouse," a more direct translation of the Portuguese word "fanal" (an old and very seldom used form of "farol").

17. Dispatch dated 19 May 1959, in *Boletim Oficial do Governo do Estado da Índia* 22, II série, 29 May.

18. The proposal was part of India's first set of submissions, together with Ajanta Caves, Ellora Caves, Agra Fort, and Taj Mahal. All were accepted for listing by the World Heritage Committee Ordinary Session in 1983, except Goa, on which the decision was deferred due to the lack of some information. Between 1983 and 1986, two other Indian assets were listed (the Group of Monuments at Mahabalipuram and the Sun Temple in Konârak). In the end, Goa turned out to be the seventh Indian site included, ahead of other well-known jewels. Despite the delay in the proposal's acceptance, it seems clear that Goa's listing it has been a Union Government priority.

19. The inclusion in UNESCO's World Heritage List requires an application with a proposal dossier, presented by a state institution. Excerpts quoted in this paragraph were the respective justifications for the use of the sixth, second, and fourth criteria of the *World Heritage Convention* and its *Operative Guidelines* (UNESCO World Heritage Committee 2019, 5).

20. From its annexation in 1961 until 1987, Goa was, together with Daman and Diu, a territory of the state of India, administered directly by the central government.

21. There are many official statements to this effect, but I like to quote Vinay Sheel Oberoi, India's ambassador at UNESCO 37th session of the World Heritage Committee (Phnom Penh,

22 June 2013), who stated (while commenting on the candidacy of the University of Coimbra to the World Heritage List): "I think you have to be Indian, and not necessarily from Goa, to understand the significance of this. . . . Over almost five hundred years there has been this interface. . . . You must remember [Goa] was an enclave, the only non-English speaking enclave with any significance in India. The French and the Danes didn't really develop that, but it was here [Goa] that it has been established, it was here that this link has been sustained." https://whc.unesco.org/en/sessions/37COM/records/?day=2013-06-22#t2jmdjT97SIE0 (2:06.50)

22. Even within Hinduism, problems are arising. Like Catholic churches, Hindu temples in Goa had a specific architectural expression that emerged throughout the seventeenth century, but in recent years they have been systematically reformed or substituted with solutions similar to those in surrounding states. See Kanekar, "The Politics of Renovation" (2017); Kowal, "The Hindu Temples of Seventeenth and Eighteenth century Goa" (2001); and Gupta, "Indo-European Temples of Goa" (1991–92).

23. UNESCO's general *Operational Guidelines* establish the requirement, but the "Protection and management requirements" clause of the site-specific document (UNESCO World Heritage Committee, "Goa" [2019]) makes clear the weakness of the asset-management system.

24. Over the last decades, debates on cultural heritage have underlined its "ephemeral" character, dependent on its recognition *as* heritage. Among many worthy contributions to this discussion, see in particular Smith, *The Uses of Heritage* (2006) and Harvey, "Heritage Pasts and Heritage Presents" (2001).

WORKS CITED

Barbuda, Claudio Lagrange Monteiro de. (1841) 1903. Instrucções com que El-Rei D. José I mandou passar ao Estado da Índia o Governador e Capitão General e o Arcebispo Primaz do Oriente no anno de 1774. Pangim: Typographia Nacional.

Carreira, Ernestine. 2014. Globalising Goa (1660-1820): Change and Exchange in a Former Capital of Empire. Goa: Goa 1556.

Correia, Alberto Carlos Germano da Silva. 1931. *La vieille Goa*. Bastora: Jaime Rangel.

Correia, Gaspar. (1560) 1975. *Lendas da Índia*, 4 vols. Lisboa: Lello & Irmão.

Dias, Pedro. 2005. De Goa a Pangim. Memórias tangíveis do Estado da Índia Portuguesa. Lisboa: Santander Totta.

Faria, Alice Santiago. 2014. Architecture coloniale Portugaise à Goa: Le Département des Travaux Publics, 1840–1926. Saarbrüchen: Presses académiques francophones.

Gracias, José António Ismael. 1960. *Goa, fanal da espiritualidade portuguesa*. Goa: Imprensa Nacional.

Gupta, Pamila. 2017. "The Corporeal and the Carnivalesque: The 2004 Exposition of St. Francis Xavier and the Consumption of History in Postcolonial Goa." *Etnográfica* 21 (1): 107–24. http://journals.openedition.org/etnografica/4840.

———. 2014. The Relic State: St. Francis Xavier and the Politics of Ritual in Portuguese India. Manchester: Manchester University Press.

Gupta, Samita. 1991–92. "Indo-European Temples of Goa." *Bulletin of the Deccan College Post-Graduate and Research Institute*, no. 51–52, 479–88.

Harvey, David C. 2001. "Heritage Pasts and Heritage Presents: Temporality, Meaning and the Scope of Heritage Studies." *International Journal of Heritage Studies* 7 (4): 319–38.

Kanekar, Amita. 2017. "The Politics of Renovation: The Disappearing Architecture of Goa's Old Brahmanical Temples." In *Preserving Transcultural Heritage: Your Way or My Way?*, edited by Joaquim Rodrigues dos Santos, 253–63. Lisboa: Caleidoscópio.

Kowal, David M. 2001. "The Hindu Temples of Seventeenth and Eighteenth Century Goa: The Maintenance of a Sacred Integrity and the Process of East-West Cross-Fertilization." *Portuguese Studies Review* 9 (1–2): 398–434.

Lopes, Maria de Jesus dos Mártires. 1999. *Goa setecentista, tradição e modernidade* (1750–1800). Lisboa: Universidade Católica Portuguesa.

Lopes, Nuno. Forthcoming. *The Heritage of Defence: Goa 1510–1660*. Goa: Goa 1556.

Martins, J. F. Ferreira. 1910. "Mudança da cidade de Goa para Mormugão." *O Oriente Português* 7 (1): 34–42 and 7 (4): 89–100.

Moreira, Rafael. 1987. "A primeira comemoração: O Arco dos Vice-Reis." *Oceanos*, no. 19/20, 156–60.

Paiva, José Pedro. 2020. "Uma religião para o mundo: Padroado régio e uma diocese pluricontinental." In *História Global de Portugal*, edited by Carlos Fiolhais, José Eduardo Franco, and José Pedro Paiva, 353–59. Lisboa: Temas e Debates.

Reintegração da Cidade de Velha Goa no seu ambiente histórico, arqueológico, monástico e religioso. 1960. Relatório da Comissão nomeada por despacho de S. Ex.ª o Governador-Geral de 19 de Maio de 1959. Goa: Imprensa Nacional.

Rivara, Joaquim Heliodoro da Cunha. 1866–67. "Tentativa de mudança da cidade de Goa para Mormugão." *O Chronista de Tissuary* 1–2 (5–13).

Rossa, Walter. 2020. "A capitalidade de Goa: Expressão urbanística do mito e da legitimização colonial." *Os portugueses e a Ásia Marítima: trocas científicas, técnicas e sócio-culturais (séculos XVI-XVIII)*, 301-327. Lisboa: Academia de Marinha.

———. 2010. "Goa." In *Portuguese Heritage around the World: Architecture and Urbanism; Asia and Oceania*, edited by José Mattoso, 230–40. Lisboa: Fundação Calouste Gulbenkian.

———. 1997. Indo-Portuguese Cities: A Contribution to the Study of Portuguese Urbanism in the Western Hindustan/Cidades Indo-Portuguesas: Contribuição para o estudo do urbanismo português no Hindustão Ocidental. Lisboa: Comissão Nacional para as Comemorações dos Descobrimentos Portugueses.

———. 2018. "Lisboa Moderna: da utopia de uma imagem de capital ribeirinha." In *Projecções de Lisboa: Utopias e estratégias para uma cidade em movimento perpétuo*, edited by João Seixas, 42–59. Casal de Cambra: Caleidoscópio.

Rossa, Walter, and Sidh Mendiratta. 2012. "A cerca adormecida: Recuperação histórico-cartográfica da muralha poruguesa de Goa." In *Goa passado e presente: Atas do Congresso*, vol. 1, 413–23. Lisboa: CEPCEP/Universidade Católica Portuguesa & CHAM/Universidade Nova de Lisboa.

Santos, Catarina Madeira. 1999."*Goa é a chave de toda a Índia": Perfil político da capital do Estado da Índia (1505–1570)*. Lisboa: Comissão Nacional para as Comemorações dos Descobrimentos Portugueses.

Santos, Joaquim Rodrigues dos. 2016. "'Reinstalling the Old City of Goa as an Eternal Light of Portuguese Spirituality': The Plan for the Reintegration of Old Goa at the End of the Colonial Period." *Architectural Histories* 4 (1): 1–21. http://doi.org/10.5334/ah.58.

Santos, Joaquim Rodrigues dos, and Sidh Mendiratta. 2012. "'Visiono Velha Goa, a cidade morta, reanimar-se': O plano de intenções de 1960 para a musealização de Velha Goa." In *Goa: Passado e presente*, edited by Artur Teodoro de Matos and João Manuel Teles e Cunha, vol. 1, 425–42. Lisboa: CEPCEP/Universidade Católica Portuguesa & CHAM/Universidade Nova de Lisboa.

Silva y Figueroa, Garcia. (1617) 1903–5. *Comentários [...] de la embajada que de parte del rey de España Don Filipe III hizo al rey Xa Abas de Pérsia*, edited by Manuel Serrano y Sanz. Madrid: Sociedad de Bibliófilos Españoles.

Smith, Laurajane. 2006. *The Uses of Heritage*. London: Routledge.

UNESCO World Heritage Committee. 2019. "Goa." *Adoption of Retrospective Statements of Outstanding Universal Value. WHC/19/43.COM/8E*, 5–6. Paris: UNESCO. https://whc.unesco.org/archive/2019/whc19-43com-8E-en.pdf.

UNESCO. 2019. Operational Guidelines for the Implementation of the World Heritage Convention. Paris: UNESCO. https://whc.unesco.org/en/guidelines/.

Waterton, Emma, and Laurajane Smith. 2010. "The Recognition and Misrecognition of Community Heritage." *International Journal of Heritage Studies* 16 (1/2): 4–15.

Xavier, Ângela Barreto. 2008. A invenção de Goa: Poder imperial e conversões culturais nos séculos XVI e XVII. Lisboa: Imprensa de Ciências Sociais.

Xavier, Ângela Barreto, and Fernanda Olival. 2018. "O padroado da coroa de Portugal: Fundamentos e práticas." In *Monarquias ibéricas em perspectiva comparada (séculos XVI-XVIII): Dinâmicas imperiais e circulação de modelos administrativos*, edited by Ângela Barreto Xavier, Federico Palomo, and Roberta Stumpf, 123–60. Lisboa: Imprensa de Ciências Sociais.

WALTER ROSSA holds a PhD in Architecture and an MA in Art History. He is Professor in the Department of Architecture, a researcher at the Center for the History of Society and Culture, and UNESCO Chair in Intercultural Dialogue in Heritages of Portuguese Influence at the University of Coimbra. He also co-shares the Cunha Rivara Chair at Goa University. Rossa researches the theory and history of architecture and urbanism, especially on town planning, the landscape, and the cultural heritage of the former Portuguese colonial universe. He has dedicated his recent academic efforts to cooperation and the operative relation between heritage, history, planning, and development to establish interactions between his academic activity and development actions.

Heritage Policies and Sensitive Pasts: Between Ambiguities and Rights from Global to Local[1]

ABSTRACT: This article analyzes the cultural heritage policies and the uses of the past in Brazil to reflect on the social function of cultural heritage, which will be done on three scales of observation. On the smaller scale, I will examine UNESCO and the presence of Brazil in its lists of World Heritage and Heritage of Humanity, both material and intangible. The intermediate scale will offer a reading of the heritage policies in Brazil, implemented by the National Historical and Artistic Heritage Institute, which will seek to identify their conceptual roots that reverberate in the country's global image. On the third scale, I will observe the heritagization of the Ruins of São Miguel das Missões in Brazil, reflecting on new paradigms in dispute in this process. The state, understood through the extended perspective of Antonio Gramsci, and the specialist, in the relational perspective of Pierre Bourdieu, are the key categories for analyzing how classification struggles operate in this cultural arena.

KEYWORDS: World Heritage and Heritage of Humanity, UNESCO, Brazil, material and immaterial cultural heritage, São Miguel das Missões/Tava Guarani, scales.

RESUMO: Esse artigo analisa as políticas de patrimônio cultural e os usos do passado no Brasil para refletir sobre a função social do patrimônio cultural, o que será feito em três escalas de observação. Na escala menor, será observada a UNESCO e o Brasil nas Listas de Patrimônio Mundial e Patrimônio da Humanidade—de natureza material e imaterial. A escala intermediária servirá para uma leitura das políticas de patrimônio no Brasil, implementadas pelo Instituto do Patrimônio Histórico e Artístico Nacional, buscando raízes conceituais que reverberam na imagem global. A terceira escala observa a patrimonialização das Ruínas de São Miguel das Missões, no Brasil, refletindo sobre novos paradigmas em disputa. O Estado, entendido na perspectiva ampliada de Antonio Gramsci, e o especialista, na perspectiva relacional de Pierre Bourdieu, são as categorias chave para analisar como as lutas de classificação operam nessa arena cultural.

PALAVRAS-CHAVE: Patrimônio Mundial e Patrimônio da Humanidade, UNESCO, Brasil, patrimônio cultural material e imaterial, São Miguel das Missões/Tava Guarani, escalas

Introduction

The growth of competition around the World Heritage designation, within the framework of the 1972 Convention on World Cultural and Natural Heritage of the United Nations Educational, Scientific, and Cultural Organization (UNESCO), unequivocally demonstrates the expansion of the field of heritage in its global definition as well as in the arena of symbolic and material disputes that surround it. The same can be said about the 2003 Convention for the Safeguarding of the Intangible Cultural Heritage of Humanity.

According to Chiara Bortolotto (2010), the paradigms governing the two conventions differ substantially, due to the criticisms the former convention attracted in the wake of its practical application and due to new demands for change in the field of heritage. The Convention for the Safeguarding of the Intangible Cultural Heritage of Humanity adopted a culturally relativistic perspective, conveying a critical stance toward the modern universalism that underlies the World Heritage Convention and UNESCO itself. For Bortolotto, the major distinction of the 2003 Convention is the requirement that assets to be included in the list must be established by their bearers in dialogue with specialists. This requirement legitimates the presence of new subjects entrusted with the attribution of value in the processes of heritagization implemented by various states, whereas according to the norm established by the World Heritage Convention such attribution is solely the responsibility of specialists.

This article aims to analyze heritage policies and the uses of the past in Brazil to contribute to a reflection on the social function of cultural heritage in global terms, carried out at three levels of observation. For the initial level, I have selected the collection of assets that became World Heritage and Heritage of Humanity in Brazil, respectively material and immaterial. Two reasons guided this selection: Firstly, I intend to illuminate the hegemonic thinking that guides the heritage policies in Brazil, as reflected in the World Heritage List with its established and recognizable image. Secondly, it is interesting to reflect on the action of the state, which outlines strategies for participation in the politics of world heritage, a forum in which an image of Brazil is defined for itself and for the world.

In making this selection, I do not intend to erase the specificities of heritage policies at the national level, as opposed to those involving UNESCO, but to connect the two spheres so as to give agency to the local. For this reason, the article's second part, which operates on an intermediate scale of national scope, will offer a reading of the heritage policies in Brazil implemented by the National Historical and Artistic Heritage Institute (IPHAN—Instituto do Patrimônio Histórico e Artístico Nacional) in order to understand its conceptual roots, reproduced in the image of Brazil's heritage that reverberates globally.

In the third part, observation will be local. On a larger scale, the process of heritagization carried out by the Brazilian state, through IPHAN, will be observed in order to understand and reflect on new paradigms in dispute that come into play in specific empirical situations. The notion of classification struggles proposed by Pierre Bourdieu (2011) is operational here for the understanding of these disputes as a form of competition, since it situates the issue of heritage in a field of power struggle. In this case, the focus is on submerged identities and sensitive pasts, with the intent to determine the ways in which groups operate their identities and their ability to decenter dominant narratives. With this objective in mind, I will analyze the emblematic case of heritagization of the Ruins of São Miguel das Missões, which underwent significant modifications since the first action in 1937 until becoming Tava, Place of Reference for the Guarani People (Tava, Lugar de Referência para o Povo Guarani), in 2014. This third scale of analysis is based on the following assumptions. In order to understand the politics of heritage, one must focus on the processes of attributing value and meanings to assets, as well as on the subjects who act in these processes, so that the tensions and disputes waged in the course of heritagization may become visible. Thus heritage ceases to be seen as something given a priori and, at the same time, different meanings, values, and feelings are revealed in relation to the same cultural asset, which can then be compared with those produced on the previously examined scale of World Heritage.

This analysis relies on two key categories. The state is understood, based on Antonio Gramsci's theorization, as produced by the interrelation between the civil society and the political society. The former relates to the notion of legitimacy and the latter to the notion of coercion, with dynamics and disputes for hegemony and consensus, seeking consent and adherence through cultural means (Gramsci 1978). As theorized by Norbert Elias (1993), national states are the result of integration efforts towards more intertwined societies. Such efforts proceed through structural conflicts and tensions, and through struggles for the balance of power. The Brazilian state has constitutional obligations to protect the Brazilian cultural heritage. To ensure correct application of preservation measures, it can rely on its political power, thus acting through coercion. At the same time, the participation of different agents and entities of civil society in official positions, serving as experts on advisory boards or in technical capacity, among others, confers legitimacy on public policies (Chuva 2009).

The other key category, that of specialist, is here understood from the perspective of Pierre Bourdieu. In his relational view of the social world, Bourdieu refers to the formation of networks of material and symbolic ties in which social agents act. These relationship networks exist in the form of objective positions that people occupy institutionally, which shape their perceptions and actions, and in incorporated form, which relates to the notion of *habitus*, as embodied acquired attitudes or habitual ways of being (Bourdieu 1983). The heritage specialists possess a habitus acquired through formal education and the heritage field in which they work, engaging with its mechanisms of prestige and promotion. They participate in the field through the formulation of discourses and practices of recognition, belonging, and exclusion. They occupy positions of distinction that correspond to their legitimacy, and they labor to impose a social view of the world aligned with their interests (Bourdieu 2011).

The decision to analyze the heritagization practices of the state does not imply that this is the only way in which heritage is constituted, as different groups develop their own narratives of identity and belonging that materialize in cultural assets (objects or practices) recognized by the whole group. However, this reflection focuses on public heritage policies whereby the state, through its agency and its specialists, maintains a monopoly on the definition of cultural assets that will receive its seal of approval. The same procedure is repeated on a global scale. What makes this approach fruitful is the analysis of the ways in which this monopoly operates to construe the legitimacy of its specialists, through its interaction with civil society, as well as of its resonance, as explored by Stephen Greenblatt (1991): not as a stable and fixed social background but as a network of social forces that often find themselves in conflict.

1. UNESCO and the Brazilian Lists of World Heritage and Heritage of Humanity

UNESCO, created within the United Nations after the Second World War, is the agency responsible for the establishment and coordination of an international heritage system, which has played an important role in shaping a global

Table 1. List of Brazilian World Heritage

Name	Registered by UNESCO	Registered by IPHAN	Notes
Historic Town of Ouro Preto, Minas Gerais	1980	1938	
Historic Center of Olinda, Pernambuco	1982	1968	
Jesuit Missions of the Guaranis (in Brazil, Ruínas de São Miguel das Missões, Rio Grande do Sul)	1983	1938	The same UNESCO asset registration includes San Ignacio Mini, Argentina.
Historic Center of Salvador de Bahia	1984	1985	
Sanctuary of Bom Jesus do Congonhas, Minas Gerais	1985	1939	
Brasília, Federal District	1987	1990	
Serra da Capivara National Park, Piauí	1991	1993	
Historic Center of São Luís, Maranhão	1997	1974	
Historic Center of the Town of Diamantina, Minas Gerais	1999	1938	
Historic Center of the Town of Goiás, Goiás	2001	1978	
São Francisco Square in the Town of São Cristóvão, Sergipe	2010	1967	
Rio de Janeiro: Carioca Landscapes between the Mountain and the Sea	2012	from 1938	IPHAN protection applies to several isolated assets plus a small cluster.
Pampulha Modern Ensemble, Belo Horizonte, Minas Gerais	2016	1948–97	IPHAN protection: 1948, Church of São Francisco da Pampulha; 1997, Pampulha Ensemble.
Valongo Wharf Archeological Site, Rio de Janeiro	2017	—	
Paraty and Ilha Grande—Culture and Biodiversity	2019	1958–74	IPHAN protection applied in 1958 to the town center of Paraty, in 1974 to the entire county.

perspective on cultural heritage (Abreu and Peixoto 2014). The agency has achieved a high level of popularity worldwide, although its operations are based on a series of ambiguities, three of which I will identify here. The first ambiguity has to do with UNESCO's role in globalization. According to Marc Askew (2010), for a long time UNESCO held that its cultural programs aimed to mitigate the destructive effects of cultural globalization, represented by the culturally homogenizing industries of capitalism, with the organization turning its practices towards compensatory forms of globalization and positioning it outside of the harmful globalizing processes. But is it even possible to clearly distinguish between good and bad globalization, without considering the intricate networking and the nuances of such processes (Labadi and Long 2010)?

Another aspect of UNESCO's ambiguity concerns the technical legitimacy on which its practices are based. The power of the technical discourse enunciated by the specialist silences, in most cases, any other possibility of knowledge production in different sites, while it also imposes a Eurocentric and West-centric scientific logic, from which the agency has struggled to disassociate itself. For Labadi and Long (2010), this is because the agency presents as canonical the technical and symbolic legitimacy of its World Heritage List and, more recently, of its Representative List of the Intangible Cultural Heritage of Humanity. UNESCO professionals and consultants, referred to here as specialists, are its greatest apologists, as they reproduce their own status, identity, and legitimacy in the technical order of their work in the field of conservation while at the same time enshrining the agency.

Therefore, if on the one hand UNESCO has tried to move away from a Eurocentric conception of culture and cultural heritage toward a perspective that effectively promotes the diversity of the world's cultures through the Convention for the Safeguarding of the Intangible Cultural Heritage, on the other hand, as Bortolotto (2010) suggests, the very nature of the UN system gives national states the power to determine their representative cultural expressions, thus limiting the perception of cultural diversity to the lenses of state agents and agencies. According to Bortolotto, this generates a tense relation with the determination to involve local communities in the nomination process for inclusion in the UNESCO list, with which member states must deal.

The third ambiguity lies precisely in the fact that UNESCO's popularity comes from its support by nation-states, even though the agency imposes technical and formal standards to which they must conform, which makes the members' support for this supranational body seem surprising. Askew (2010) believes that this can be explained by the use of the universalism of the World Heritage Convention for the member states' own domestic agendas of cultural hegemony (Santos 2002).

1.1 The Brazilian World Cultural Heritage

The 1972 World Cultural and Natural Heritage Convention has been extremely popular, with the participation of 193 states (Londoño 2017). Brazil is a member of this group, actively participating in the forum, with fifteen assets registered in the cultural or mixed category, from 1980 until its latest registration in 2019.[2]

Analyzing the Brazilian presence in the UNESCO World Heritage List yields a very homogeneous image of Brazil. Of the fifteen registered assets, ten relate to the Portuguese colonial period (from 1500 to 1822), European civilization, the Catholic faith and/or related Baroque art; two are examples of modern Brazilian architecture;[3] and two are archeological sites: the National Park Serra da Capivara (with pre-Cabraline, i.e., pre-sixteenth-century, rock inscriptions) and the Valongo Wharf Archeological Site, a site of sensitive memory. Finally, the city of Rio de Janeiro is registered in the Cultural Landscape category. Table 1 lists the fifteen Brazilian assets.

In this listing, the white Portuguese heritage is clearly predominant. What we see represented on the global level, therefore, is a particular type of Brazilian asset, continuously guided by Western civilizing narratives, with an emphasis on its aesthetic attributes. This reading is confirmed (more or less subtly) in the entries describing each of these assets on the website of IPHAN, the body responsible for the preparation and submission of world heritage dossiers to UNESCO (IPHAN 2014).

Brazilian UNESCO registrations have occurred with some regularity over time, the first in 1980 and the latest in 2019. Their predominantly colonial origin has given them homogeneity, maintaining the same aesthetic pattern that suggests the hegemony of a national imagination that was first outlined in the 1930s within the scope of heritage policies, and has been continually updated and reaffirmed. This selection is obviously inadequate to present an image of the plurality of the nation or represent the diversity that exists within Brazilian borders. From the first to the most recent registration, Brazil's activity within the scope of UNESCO's 1972 World Heritage Convention has spanned forty-one years, with the last registered asset being the town of Paraty. The image of Paraty posted on

IPHAN's website shows the oceanfront of a historic, colonial coastal city and has a strong aesthetic appeal. It should be noted, however, that the arguments for its inclusion in the UNESCO list as a mixed (cultural and natural) asset have changed significantly, as can be seen in its official description (IPHAN 2014b).[4]

1.2 The Intangible Cultural Heritage of Humanity in Brazil

Affirming the popularity of the previous convention, 174 countries ratified UNESCO's Convention for the Safeguarding of the Intangible Cultural Heritage of Humanity (Lodoño 2017). The following analysis of the Brazilian cultural assets included in the list of Intangible Cultural Heritage of Humanity sought to determine whether this selection might address the gaps in the representation of Brazilian cultural diversity mentioned above.[5] Table 2 below lists assets registered by IPHAN and UNESCO.

Table 2. Representative List of the Intangible Cultural Heritage of Humanity in Brazil.

Name	Registered by UNESCO	Registered by IPHAN[6]
Oral and graphic expressions of the Wajapi	2003	Forms of Expression 2002
Samba de Roda of the Recôncavo Baiano	2005	Forms of Expression 2004
Frevo, performing arts of the Carnival of Recife	2012	Forms of Expression 2007
Círio de Nazaré (The Taper of Our Lady of Nazareth) in the city of Belém, Pará	2013	Celebrations 2004
Capoeira circle	2014	Forms of Expression 2008
Yaokwa, the Enawene Nawe people's ritual for the maintenance of social and cosmic order[7]	2011	Celebrations 2010
Cultural Complex of Bumba-meu-boi in Maranhão	2019	Celebrations 2011

Brazilian registration of these assets took place between 2003 and 2019. At first glance, the realm that appears here might as well be from another country. On this scale of observation, the two UNESCO lists, taken in their totality, reveal very different images of Brazil. One explanation for this would be that the recognition of this intangible heritage is directed by a Eurocentric vision, as if these assets were the remains of an exotic people in the twenty-first century. However, the fact that many assets included in the two lists were registered in the same time period, and within the same institution, but with no apparent interaction and a total lack of intersection between the two sets, leads me to formulate another hypothesis. The parallel lists may be the evidence of struggles about classification in the Brazilian heritage field within the same state agency, that is, of different and possibly competing conceptions of heritage, indicating the existence of disputes between worldviews within the field and the agency itself (Bourdieu 2011).

Conflicts over the meanings of the past for Brazilian society are, in fact, outside UNESCO's purview, and therefore to attempt to understand these conflicts by focusing the research only on the assets listed as World Heritage may not fully capture the range of tensions and confrontations in the field (Askew 2010). Thus, although these lists function as significant indices, other scales of analysis may point out singular aspects of these practices and struggles that have not been clarified from the viewpoint adopted thus far in this paper.

2. Imagining the Nation: The Intermediate Scale

The convergence that took place in so many Western countries between the writing of the nation's genealogy and the establishment of legal protections for national heritage also occurred in Brazil. The 1930s saw the creation of the National Historical and Artistic Heritage Service (SPHAN, now IPHAN) and the implementation of the Decree-Law 25, in 1937, which organized the protection of public and private material assets, imposing limitations on the right to property, with the introduction of the legal and administrative instrument of asset registration.[8] The legislation remains in force today and gives the institution relative autonomy to define what it selects as representative of the Brazilian nation. A group of intellectuals linked to one of the directions of the literary modernist movement, such as Mário de Andrade, Carlos Drummond de Andrade, and Rodrigo Melo Franco de Andrade, as well as Lucio Costa, who led the modernist movement in architecture, held positions at the institution, bringing in a select group of architects and becoming the principal mentors of Brazilian heritage. They positioned themselves as the experts who would reveal Brazil's identity to the nation. The nation's origins became materialized in Baroque art and colonial architecture, with a strong Catholic accent, seen as pure and genuinely Brazilian and free from the foreign influences introduced in the late nineteenth and early twentieth centuries. In this form of the nation's genealogy, modernist architecture was elevated as the legitimate heir to the Baroque colonial architecture originally produced in Brazil. This vision, which favors aesthetic and formal values, was realized through asset registrations of the 1930s and 40s—almost a third of the total number of assets registered by IPHAN until today—and enshrined its particular image of the nation, whose resonance retroactively continues to nurture heritage policies in Brazil (Chuva 2009).

Several studies have pointed to this emphasis on architectural assets from the colonial period. Portuguese roots, especially evident in Catholic religious buildings, had the privilege of protection (see Chuva 2009, Fonseca 1997, Rubino 1996, and Marins 2016, among others). Such studies have also abundantly demonstrated that a certain kind of modernist architectural production, championed by Costa and its main practitioner, Oscar Niemeyer, had two objects registered as heritage assets as soon as they were built—the building of the Ministry of Education and Health, today called Gustavo Capanema Palace, in Rio de Janeiro, and the Church of São Francisco da Pampulha, in Belo Horizonte—owing to Costa's intellectual leadership of the federal agency.

This interpretation of the nation's origins was in tune with the ideas of racial democracy forged by the sociologist Gilberto Freyre, beginning with the publication of *Casa-grande & senzala* in 1933, which were dominant in Brazilian social thought during the first half of the twentieth century and still resonate in the present. According to this view, the miscegenation between the Portuguese, Africans, and Brazilian natives, with the predominance of European whites, produced a genuinely mixed population and a country without racism. It can be said that this interpretation was, at the same time, certified by the absence of explicitly segregationist laws in Brazil and, perversely, justified the absence of laws that could have favored processes of inclusion of formerly enslaved people and their descendants in the Brazilian society. In the same period, the policy implemented through the Indian Protection Service (SPI), created in 1910, placed Indigenous Brazilians under the guardianship of the state, which became responsible for their protection until their incorporation into society as national workers (Souza Lima 1995).[9]

Public policies for the protection of heritage, founded on the same interpretative matrix of Brazilian society, also contributed to camouflaging the contradictions of a country that had recently emerged from slavery and barely knew how to deal with its material and symbolic estate. The homogeneous image construed by patrimonial policies—although not only by them—contributed to obscure other ethnic groups present within national borders. It is a fact that, in Brazil, in relation to the rights of memory and the uses of the past, processes of exclusion, silencing, or erasure cannot be dissociated from skin color. The structural racism that still prevails in Brazilian society affects Afro-descendants and Indigenous people, treating them as incapable or primitive. Until the 1980s, the inclusion of elements of Black, Indigenous, or immigrant cultures among the assets protected as national heritage would have been unlikely.

Since the second half of the 1970s, urban social movements and residents' associations in Rio de Janeiro have appropriated asset registration as a tool in their struggle for rights, especially the right to quality of life in the city (Nascimento 2016). Some Black movement activists also demanded the registration of the Terreiro da Casa Branca, in Salvador, which took place in 1984, in a struggle for the right to diverse cultural expression and the right to memory and identity, and as a result managed to guarantee their continuing occupation of the site when threatened with eviction (Fonseca 2003; Chuva 2017). In 1988, the high point of the redemocratization process after twenty-four years of military dictatorship in Brazil was the new legal framework consolidated with the promulgation of the new Brazilian Federal Constitution, which condensed earlier reflections and struggles.

Brazilian cultural diversity has become the predominant value since this landmark document, which created the state's obligation to safeguard Brazilian cultural expressions, guaranteeing the full exercise of cultural rights, including by Indigenous and Afro-descendant communities. In article 216 of the Constitution, three points stand out: the reference to the different groups that form Brazilian society, the mention of material and immaterial cultural assets, and the community's participation in the definition of its heritage. These provisions created an opening for changes in the heritage sector's public policies, which have progressively moved closed to the field of human and civil rights. The expansion of the notion of heritage did not only imply the inclusion of assets that had previously been neglected; it also meant the recognition of new subjects determining the attribution of value. In this way, the aesthetic and stylistic perspective—educated, cultivated, civilized—that saw intrinsic value in colonial Baroque art, considered the expression of the nation's origins, would have to coexist with other logics that were starting to operate in the world of heritage.

The new Brazilian Constitution also had unexpected effects, for example in relation to the characteristics of the Brazilian population. Some recent population data show interesting evidence of this: according to claims of self-identification gathered by the population census, the numbers of Indigenous, mixed-race (*pardo*), and Black people have been growing since the 2000s. The Brazilian census revealed a growth of the indigenous population well above expectations; this increase has not been due to demographic growth but to the increase in the number of people who recognize themselves as Indigenous, mainly in urban areas of the country, currently representing 0.4% of the total. Similar growth can be seen in the Black population. 2010 census data showed that 50.7% of the Brazilian population declared themselves mixed-race or Black, a higher percentage than registered in previous decades (IBGE 2021). The reasons for this are complex and varied. It is possible that they are related to cultural inclusion programs that have empowered populations hitherto silenced, such as quotas for Black students in public universities and the existence of higher education institutions serving Indigenous peoples, and may have produced these changes in self-identification.[10]

New heritage policies in Brazil began to be formulated in order to meet the new constitutional requirements. In the year 2000, Decree 3551 implemented the instrument named Registration of Cultural Assets of Immaterial Nature with the aim to safeguard these assets. The methodology of the National Inventory of Cultural References (INRC) aimed to map cultural assets, supporting proposals for inclusion in the registry of immaterial assets.[11] As we have seen, this Brazilian legislation predated the UNESCO Intangible Cultural Heritage Convention of 2003, including some elements present in the Brazilian laws, such as the direct participation of the relevant community in the preparation of the registration application, which is also featured in the convention. This item was crucial for the inclusion of new legal subjects into the process of the attribution of heritage value, as we will see in part three of this article.

In Brazil, although the hegemonic narratives impose themselves even today, themes that fall under the category of "sensitive pasts" have been brought into the patrimonial debate by social movements demanding that the state take a position on such issues and summoning it to act in this delicate area. As already noted, the state and its agency are not cohesive and monolithic blocks but are constituted by the interaction between political and civil society, and initiatives of this nature may take off due to loopholes or more or less casual opportunities. This was the case of the archaeological site of Cais do Valongo, which was discovered during major reconstruction works in the port area of Rio de Janeiro. Initially, the municipal government considered burying the site after the archeology team concluded its work. However, the immense resistance from researchers and the Black movement led the city to revise its plans, resulting in the inclusion of Black heritage among the tourist attractions of the Porto Maravilha project.

The next step was the struggle to nominate the archaeological site for the World Heritage List. Among the various controversies surrounding this process, I will highlight two to illustrate its main tensions. Firstly, the site revealed the Valongo Wharf, built in 1811, at its deepest level of excavation. On top of it was the Empress's Pier, built in 1843 to receive the future Empress of Brazil, Princess Tereza Cristina. The controversy was about which name would be put forward for UNESCO candidacy and how the object would be presented. In the midst of intense disputes, the name Valongo Wharf prevailed and the justification of its recognition classified it as a "historic site of sensitive memory," in reference to the fact that almost one million enslaved Africans entered Brazil through this pier, brought in slave ships between 1811 and 1831, the year in which the traffic became illegal (Honorato 2008; IPHAN 2017).

As for "sensitive memories" of the military dictatorship, there are movements in Brazil and also in other countries, such as Chile, that demand preservation of buildings used as political prisons known for practicing torture. Such sites are called Memorials of the Resistance, as in the case of the old DEOPS building in São Paulo (Almeida 2017).[12] The Indigenous sites may also be framed as heritage in the category of sensitive memory, as we will see in part three of this article. In this last section, with the intention of reflecting on the social function of heritage, I will explore a particular case of heritagization in Brazil, seeking to understand the subjects who are legally entitled to attribute patrimonial value. I propose a reflection at the local level as a contribution to deconstructing the false idea that heritage value exists in and of itself, that it is fixed and determined, and that it must be discovered or revealed by the specialist who has studied to attain this competence. In this way, I intend to demonstrate how submerged identities and sensitive pasts can decentralize dominant discourses and to identify how the state (in Gramsci's amplified perspective) operates in such a process.

Fig. 1. Indigenous people selling handicrafts on the balcony of the Missions Museum in 2017. In the background, Tava, the ruins of the Church of São Miguel das Missões. Photo by Leandro Kibisz, Wikimedia Commons.

3. Tava, a Place of Reference for the Guarani People in Southern Brazil

Population estimates indicate that there were about five million Indigenous people living on Portuguese-occupied lands in America in the sixteenth century. Much of this population was killed when the territory was occupied. According to the population census conducted in 2010, the Indigenous population of Brazil currently counts around 800 thousand. Of this total, about fifty thousand Guarani natives live in southern Brazil, making them the largest native ethnic group in the country. The Guarani people also live in the neighboring countries of Paraguay, Bolivia, and Argentina.

Tava, a Place of Reference for the Guarani People, was registered as belonging to Brazilian intangible cultural heritage in 2014, following demands issued by representatives of the Guarani community.[13] Surprisingly, Tava is materially the same asset that was registered in 1938 by SPHAN as the Ruins of the Church of São Miguel das Missões and included under this name in the UNESCO World Heritage List in 1983.

Tava's registration was not foreseen when IPHAN started working on the INRC of the Mbyá-Guaranis in the region. According to testimony by Beatriz Muniz Freire, an anthropologist from IPHAN who works in Rio Grande do Sul,

INRC started in 2004 because a group of specialists from the agency criticized the way in which the history of the Missions was told and reproduced through institutional actions (Weissheimer 2017). They then initiated historical research, which took the researchers to the indigenous Guarani who since the 1990s have sold handicrafts at the door of the Museum of the Missions. It is worth mentioning that the museum was designed by Lucio Costa in 1938 and soon afterwards built by SPHAN next to the ruins.[14]

For anthropologist Rodrigo Lacerda (2019), who carried out an ethnographic study on the heritagization of Tava, the Indigenous people realized that by collaborating with the researchers they could open a negotiation channel with a view to finding solutions to the land problems they faced. Several meetings were organized during the Inventory, with the intention of understanding whether the place had any symbolic meaning for the Guarani. It was in this way that the specialists responsible for the execution of the INRC learned, at a meeting held in 2006, that the ruins were called Tava Miri, Miri meaning perfect and heavenly, in reference to those who arrived on Earth without evil. According to Lacerda, among several proposals for cultural assets subject to heritage recognition, the ruins emerged "as a synthesis, not of a culture, but of a past and present colonial situation understood through Guarani metaphysics" (2019, 155) because they condensed the most sensitive aspects of the Guarani's existence: the ever-present colonial violence, their expulsion from their territory, and past and present racism, along with the difficulties in demarcating their lands.

The Advisory Council of IPHAN, the highest decision-making body on applications for registration and protected status, chaired by the president of IPHAN, met in 2014 to analyze the application for registering the ruins of São Miguel das Missões as Tava and approved it unanimously.[15] Attending the meeting were the representatives of IPHAN in Rio Grande do Sul along with Ariel Ortega, Patrícia Ferreira, and other Mbyá-Guarani representatives. The minutes of the meeting contain Ortega's explanation of the land issue that affects the community:

> [T]oday we only have 234 hectares in São Miguel das Missões, when before this vast territory was all ours. I am very grateful to Nhanderu for this moment, for enlightening each one of you on the council. I am sure that all Caraís, spiritual leaders, were also meditating to make this moment happen. So I want to thank you for this moment, thank you. (IPHAN 2014a, 74).[16]

The Guarani people believe that their ancestors left their marks on the stones of the ruins of the São Miguel das Missões Jesuit church, which they worked hard to build in the eighteenth century. These marks incorporated their ancestors and made them immortal, allowing them to reach the Earth without evil. Tava demonstrates the way in which contemporary Guarani people interpret the historical events of the Jesuit Guarani missions of the past by incorporating their own narratives of ancestral wisdom. During the INRC, the Indigenous people were consulted about their interest in having a reference asset for them registered as a Brazilian cultural heritage site and asked what they would like to be recognized and certified by the state in this category. In response, they brought to the table their knowledge of their own cosmogony and elected Tava because that was the place chosen by Nhanderu for his people to live.

Lacerda calls attention to an essential aspect in reference to the reflections of Rodney Harrison (2013), who defends the constitution of "hybrid forums" in thinking about expanding the concept of participation. In the case of Tava's heritagization, Lacerda claims that it involved the creation of a hybrid forum, in which human and nonhuman beings (such as Nhanderu) as well as material objects (such as the ruins) participated in the process of choosing the ruins as an asset to be registered, producing "a more dialogical democracy that takes into account different ways of building the world" (Lacerda 2019, 160).

Thus, the well-known Jesuit processes of civilizing and evangelizing the Guarani people, enshrined since 1938 by Brazilian heritage policies as a glorious past event that represents one of the most important symbols of Western civilization in Brazil, took on a new meaning through the lens of the Guarani in the present—as a present problem. Not a past that was left behind, well-defined and distant, but indeed a present reality. Until then, the protection of the ruins ignored the Indigenous people as if they too belonged to a distant past. However, even in the 1930s, the natives were there, albeit regarded as invisible. They were present all the time, traveling around the region, as is the custom among the Guarani. Not to mention that they have been selling handicrafts on the terraces of the Museum of the Missions, in search of resources to survive, since at least the 1990s. These individuals have found an opportunity there to make use of public policy-building tools in their search for affirmative policies that would recognize them as part of a whole. They understand, as can be inferred from Ortega's words, that the inclusion of diverse cultural identities in nationally consecrated spaces is perhaps one of the first steps towards other demands, such as the demarcation of their lands. Undoubtedly, this case contributes to the deconstruction of canons forged in the modern paradigm of Western Europe (which subordinates other epistemic models) and to the recognition of different types of knowledge without a governing hierarchy.

Although it has not become the dominant rule in institutional practices, it was possible to observe in this case a process of decolonization of heritage, brought about by legitimate agents, through relationships between specialists and Indigenous people, by way of new meanings attributed to material heritage. That is, in the ruins of the church of São Miguel das Missões, sensitive pasts are on stage as narratives in dispute, facing different meanings, agents, and public policies implemented for the same asset. It is a complex case, a continuing and disputed process of heritage management, in which new subjects presented themselves legitimately and new meanings were attributed to a consecrated material asset, producing unexpected effects on patrimonial policies.

Final Considerations

Can heritage in its different modalities and scales be used to deal with sensitive pasts and heal historical wounds in communities marked by secular violence and the lack of broader strategies for security, protection, and reparation? The main critics of World Heritage condemn its agents and authorized global experts (UNESCO in particular) for being part of a regime of power.[17] In fact, it is necessary to explain that heritage work is forged by cultural practices in the present, which, as seen in this study, do not reflect a consensus or a hegemonic understanding. Such criticism has been widely shared since the seminal works of Eric Hobsbawm, David Lowenthal, and Pierre Nora, in the 1980s, who understood heritage as a process of political and cultural construction being worked out in the present. For this reason, the persistence of practices that deal with heritage as a given, relative to the past but with intrinsic value in the present, is surprising and must be questioned. Therefore, a possible answer to this has to do with the network of power relations that involves heritage agents and specialists, who prefer to remain in their safe and recognized spaces.[18]

As this article has sought to demonstrate, World Heritage is formed through the power granted to national states in the global order that is still formed by them; therefore, the critical organizational level on which heritage policies and discourses are framed is still the national, with the practical and symbolic consequences being discussed among members of national bureaucracies. UNESCO ratifies this arrangement by requiring asset nominations to be presented by the state because as a supranational agency it could not disrespect national sovereignties, and it legitimizes the entire path of recognition and enshrinement through its specialists.

The social function of heritage, in the perspective advocated in this article, in global terms concerns the overcoming of sensitive pasts, symbolically and socially, creating conditions of possibility for the conquest of other rights. The demands that connect sensitive pasts and heritage come from several fronts. In Brazil, they involve Indigenous peoples who demand intergroup dialogues, as seen in the case presented here, but also the descendants of Africans, who have suffered from the symbolic violence present since the abolition of slavery and its perverse effects. Until the 1980s, public heritage policies in Brazil seemed unaware of this issue and did not regard it as their concern. Contributing to change this scene, social movements have sought recognition using normative instruments in the field of heritage for the production of counterhegemonic actions through which they have gained rights. These struggles also employ tactics to combat structural racism present in institutional practices. Thus, when illuminating the ambiguities that constitute the field of heritage, perceptible on the three scales of observation, I have sought to highlight real, and not ideal, dynamics, movements, gaps, and spaces of action.

Considering what was examined for this article, popular movements will have a chance to occur and even to reach the global level only if they are built locally. Such limits frame heritage on the side of order, obedience, strategies. Once again, however, if the intention is to expand rights based on public heritage policies, the forum for this must be the democratic rule of law from the vantage point of the interrelationships between political and civil society and the heritage classification struggles that take place within them, in the context of these relationships and at the different levels analyzed here. It remains to guarantee the rule of law, in which civil society can find openings to act.

The modern paradigm gave specialists the task of revealing to everyone their heritage, which in this configuration has a static and intrinsic value in relation to assets, maintaining nostalgic practices to deal with the past in the illusion of being able to integrate the civilized Western European world. As long as national heritage policies and their global counterparts through UNESCO do not overcome this paradigm, progress in the direction of inclusion, participation, reparation, and paths for dialogue between different fields of knowledge with the aim of creating practical provisions for living with difference will be limited. For this reason, it is necessary to confront what Aníbal Quijano (2005) has termed the coloniality of knowledge to produce a conceptual revision of the field of heritage. The sacred quality conferred on the specialist's utterances, constituted within the modern scientific epistemology, as seen in the procedures of UNESCO and also of IPHAN, needs to be put in check. The specialist integrated into the world of order accepts a series of divisions in a naturalized way: between practice and theory, subject and object, technique and politics. The requirements of the present time are the construction of bridges to deal with other forms of knowledge and other, nonhierarchical epistemologies, as the hybrid forum that harbored the registration of Tava sought and managed to accomplish.

NOTES

1. This article is part of the project ECHOES—European Colonial Heritage Modalities in Entangled Cities that has received funding from the European Union's Horizon 2020 research and innovation program under grant agreement no. 770248.

2. The additional seven Brazilian assets registered as natural heritage will not be discussed here.

3. In part two, the heritage of modernist architecture will be briefly discussed.

4. I have drawn on this source because it functions as the institutional showcase, which communicates to the public IPHAN's official values, principles, and mission. Several earlier proposals for Paraty's inclusion in the World Heritage List had been presented and failed. Only in 2019, with the dossier submitted by IPHAN to UNESCO renamed as "Paraty and Ilha Grande: Culture and Biodiversity" (thus fitting into the category of a "mixed" site—cultural and natural), was a new approach that formulated a broader view of the region, encompassing a wider area besides the historic town center, which may be an indication of evolving heritage management perspectives. It was an innovative proposal, describing a territorial culture that encompasses areas and assets that integrate the region's natural and cultural heritage. It covered the entire municipality of Paraty and an important part of Angra dos Reis, as well as small portions of neighboring towns, on the margins of protected natural areas such as parks and environmental conservation units.

5. For an institutional perspective on this subject, see Fonseca (2013). For images and descriptions of the assets, see IPHAN (2014c).

6. The Decree 3551/2000, which created the registration instrument, organizes the safeguarding of Brazil's intangible cultural heritage in four registers: Celebrations, Forms of Expression, Knowledges, and Places.

7. The treatment given to this asset differs from the others, since its registration was made only on the UNESCO's List of Intangible Cultural Heritage in Need of Urgent Safeguarding.

8. As defined in the Decree-Law 25/1937, *tombamento*, or asset registration, is the term adopted in Brazil for the legal and administrative instrument for the protection of heritage, similar to "classification" used in other countries, such as France and Portugal. It is applicable to any material property and prohibits the destruction of the protected property. Before any modification to the property can be made, the heritage agency must be consulted. The institution has a supervisory duty and, as such, may use its policing power to embargo illegal works (Chuva 2009).

9. In 1967, the former SPI was replaced by the National Indian Foundation (FUNAI), as an indigenous body responsible for the guardianship, protection, and demarcation of indigenous lands.

10. These programs are threatened by the setbacks in the current political context in Brazil, with the Indigenous populations being targeted as victims by the government and agribusiness's neoliberal, fascist, and racist politics.

11. The methodology of INRC (National Inventory of Cultural References) was developed and tested in 2000, in the Porto Seguro region in Bahia, through a partnership between IPHAN and anthropologist Antonio Augusto Arantes. It is organized into three successive stages—preliminary, identification, and documentation—and proposes to map cultural references related to groups, based on cultural practices or defined territories. For more information, see Arantes (2009).

12. DEOPS (Department of Public and Social Order of the state of São Paulo) was an institution created during the Brazilian military dictatorship (1964–85) to carry out social control, censorship, imprisonment, and torture of the regime's opponents.

13. The meaning of community for the Guarani, according to Lacerda (2019), encompasses all individuals and villages spread throughout different regions of the South and Southeast of Brazil. In this case, I'm using the term "community" as it appears in the Brazilian legislation and the registration dossier of Tava (IPHAN 2014a), with a Western meaning, restricted to the group with which the INRC was negotiated, which lives and circulates in the territory of the Missions. See also Souza et al. (2007).

14. For more on the Museum of the Missions, see Chuva (2014). Lucio Costa produced a report, dated 12/20/1937, about his trip to the region of the Seven Peoples of the Missions, in Rio Grande do Sul, his first assignment for SPHAN. The report is reproduced in Pessoa (1999).

15. The Advisory Council for Cultural Heritage was created in 1937 as a deliberative body responsible for the final decision on all the registrations made by IPHAN. The institute's website (http://portal.iphan.gov.br) archives the minutes of all the Council's meetings.

16. In May 2015, the Jesuit missions of Guarani, Moxos, and Chiquitos were declared Cultural Heritage of Mercosul (PCM). This category, created in 2012, aims to strengthen the Mercosul countries' cooperation and integration. At the XVII Meeting of the Mercosul Cultural Heritage Commission, in 2018, in response to the demands of Guarani representatives, Tava was recognized as Mercosul Cultural Heritage (Tagarro 2019).

17. According to Labadi and Long (2010), Laurajane Smith and, before her, Barbara Kirshenblatt-Gimblett have been the main critics of World Heritage and its power system. See also Smith (2007).

18. David Lowenthal published *The Past is a Foreign Country* in 1985; the Brazilian edition dates from 1989. Eric Hobsbawm and Terence Ranger's *The Invention of Tradition* (1983) was published in Brazil in 1984. Pierre Nora's provocative *Between Memory and History: The Problematics of Places*, published in 1992, was translated in Brazil in 1993.

WORKS CITED

Abreu, Regina, and Paulo Peixoto, eds. 2014. "Construindo políticas patrimoniais: Reflexões em torno dos 10 anos da Convenção do Património Cultural Imaterial." *e-cadernos CES*, no. 21, 3–13.

Almeida, Priscila Cabral. 2014. "Lugar de memória da resistência: Verdade e negociação no processo de tombamento do prédio do DEOPS/SP." In *Documentos sensíveis: Informação, arquivo e verdade na Ditadura de 1964*, edited by Icleia Thiesen, 269–88. Rio de Janeiro: 7 Letras.

Anderson, Benedict. 2008. *Comunidades imaginadas*. 2nd ed. São Paulo: Companhia das Letras.

Arantes, Antonio Augusto. 2009. "Sobre inventários e outros instrumentos de salvaguarda do patrimônio cultural intangível: Ensaio de antropologia pública." *Anuário antropológico* 1 (1): 173–222.

Askew, Marc. 2010. "The Magic List of Global Status: UNESCO, World Heritage and the Agendas of States." In Labadi and Long, *Heritage and Globalisation*, 19–44.

Bortolotto, Chiara. 2010. "Globalising Intangible Cultural Heritage? Between International Arenas and Local Appropriations." In Labadi and Long, *Heritage and Globalisation*, 97–114.

Bourdieu, Pierre. 2011. *A distinção: Crítica social do julgamento*. Porto Alegre: Zouk.

———. 1983. *Questões de sociologia*. Rio de Janeiro: Marco Zero.

Chuva, Márcia. 2009. *Os arquitetos da memória: Sociogênese das práticas de preservação do patrimônio cultural no Brasil (1930–1940)*. Rio de Janeiro: UFRJ.

———. 2013. "Para descolonizar museus e patrimônio: Refletindo sobre a preservação cultural no Brasil." In *90 anos do Museu Histórico Nacional: Em debate (1922–2012)*, edited by Aline Montenegro Magalhães and Rafael Zamorano Bezerra, 195–208. Rio de Janeiro: Museu Histórico Nacional.

———. 2017. "Possíveis narrativas sobre duas décadas de patrimônio: De 1982 a 2002." *Revista do patrimônio histórico e artístico nacional*, no. 36, 79–103.

Elias, Norbert. 1993. *O processo civilizador: Formação do estado e civilização*. Rio de Janeiro: Jorge Zahar.

Fonseca, Maria Cecília Londres. 2003. "Para além da pedra e cal: Por uma concepção ampla de patrimônio cultural." In *Memória e patrimônio: Ensaios contemporâneos*, edited by Regina Abreu and Mário Chagas, 59–79. Rio de Janeiro: DP&A.

———. 2013. "O patrimônio cultural imaterial inscrito nas listas da Convenção de 2003 da UNESCO: Observações preliminares." *Políticas culturais em revista* 2 (6): 1–13.

———. 1997. *O patrimônio em processo*. Rio de Janeiro: UFRJ/IPHAN.

Freyre, Gilberto. 1933. *Casa-grande & senzala*. Rio de Janeiro: José Olympio.

Gramsci, Antonio. 1978. *Maquiavel, a política e o Estado Moderno*. Rio de Janeiro: Civilização Brasileira.

Greenblatt, Stephen. 1991. "O novo historicismo: ressonância e encantamento." *Estudos históricos* 4 (8): 244–61.

Harrison, Rodney. 2013, *Heritage: Critical Approaches*. New York: Routledge.

Hobsbawm, Eric, and Terence Ranger. 1984. *A invenção das tradições*. São Paulo: Paz e Terra.

Honorato, Cláudio de Paula. 2008. "Valongo: O mercado de escravos do Rio de Janeiro, 1758 a 1831." Master's thesis, Universidade Federal Fluminense.

IBGE (Instituto Brasileiro de Geografia e Estatística). 2021. "Censo 2010." https://censo2010.ibge.gov.br/.

IPHAN. 2014a. "Ata da 77ª reunião do Conselho Consultivo do Patrimônio Cultural." Brasília, December 3–4, 2014. http://portal.iphan.gov.br/uploads/atas/ATA__77_Reuniao_Conselho_Consultivo__03_e_04122014.pdf.

———. 2014b. "Paraty e Ilha Grande (RJ): Cultura e Biodiversidade." http://portal.iphan.gov.br/pagina/detalhes/819.

———. 2014c. "Patrimônio Cultural Imaterial da Humanidade." http://portal.iphan.gov.br/pagina/detalhes/71.

———. 2014d. "Patrimônio Mundial." http://portal.iphan.gov.br/pagina/detalhes/24.

Labadi, Sophia, and Colin Long. 2010. *Heritage and Globalisation*. Oxon: Routledge.

Lacerda, Rodrigo. 2019. "Participação e património cultural imaterial: O estudo de caso de 'Tava, lugar de referência para o povo Guarani.'" *Comunicação e sociedade*, no. 36, 143–62.

Londoño, Juan Luiz Isaza. 2017. "Uma ordem imaginada." *Revista do patrimônio histórico e artístico nacional*, no. 36, 13–22.

Lowenthal, David. 1989. "Como conhecermos o passado." *Projeto História*, no. 17, 63–201.

———. 1985. *The Past is a Foreign Country*. Cambridge: Cambridge University Press.

Marins, Paulo. 2016. "Novos patrimônios: Um novo Brasil? Um balanço das políticas patrimoniais federais após a década de 1980." *Estudos históricos* 29 (57): 9–28.

Nascimento, Flávia Brito do. 2016. "Patrimônio Cultural e escrita da história: A hipótese do documento na prática do IPHAN nos anos 1980." *Anais do Museu Paulista: História e cultura material*, no. 24, 121–47.

Nora, Pierre. 1993. "Entre Memória e História: A problemática dos lugares." *Projeto História*, no. 10, 7–28.

Pessoa, José, ed. 1999. *Lucio Costa: Documentos de trabalho*. Rio de Janeiro: IPHAN.

Quijano, Aníbal. 2005. "Colonialidade do poder, eurocentrismo e América Latina." In *A colonialidade do saber: Eurocentrismo e ciências sociais; Perspectivas latinoamericanas*, edited by Edgardo Lander, 107–30. Buenos Aires: CLACSO.

Rubino, Silvana. 1996. "O mapa do Brasil passado." *Revista do patrimônio histórico e artístico nacional*, no. 24, 97–105.

Santos, Boaventura de Sousa. 2002. "Para uma sociologia das ausências e uma sociologia das emergências." *Revista crítica de ciências sociais*, no. 63, 237–80.

Smith, Laurajane. 2006. *Uses of Heritage*. New York: Routledge.

Souza, José Otávio Catafesto de, Daniele de Menezes Pires, Carlos Eduardo Neves de Moraes, Mônica Arnt, and J. C. P. Morinico. 2007. *Tava Miri São Miguel Arcanjo, Sagrada Aldeia de Pedra: Os Mbyá-Guarani nas Missões*. Porto Alegre: IPHAN.

Souza Lima, Antonio Carlos de. 1995. *Um grande cerco de paz: Poder tutelar e indianidade na formação do Estado brasileiro*. Petrópolis: Vozes.

Tagarro, Helena Amanda Faller. 2019. "Tava Guarani: De lugar simbólico a Patrimônio Cultural do MERCOSUL." *Caderno de geografia* 29 (2): 298–310.

Weissheimer, Marcus. 2017. "Tava Guarani, moradas de Nhanderu e Porongos: O patrimônio imaterial desconhecido do RS." *Sul 21*, August 19, 2017. https://www.sul21.com.br/ultimas-noticias/geral/2017/08/tava-guarani-moradas-de-nhanderu-e-porongos-o-patrimonio-imaterial-desconhecido-do-rs/.

MÁRCIA CHUVA is an Associate Professor at the Federal University of the State of Rio de Janeiro (UNIRIO) in Rio de Janeiro, Brazil. She is also a professor in the Professional Master's program in Cultural Heritage at IPHAN (National Institute of Historical and Artistic Heritage) and a researcher for CNPq (National Council for Scientific and Technological Development). Chuva holds a PhD in History from Fluminense Federal University (UFF) (1998) and has twice held the position of visiting research fellow at the University of Coimbra, in 2014 and 2019.

ABEL DJASSI AMADO

The União Nacional in Cabo Verde, 1937-1945: Local Politics in an Imperial Political Party

ABSTRACT: The literature on the União Nacional (National Union), the political party supporting the Portuguese dictatorial regime of Estado Novo (1933–74), is rich and abundant. Yet scholars and researchers have given scant attention to the ramifications of the party in the Portuguese colonial empire. To fill this void, this paper sheds light on the imperial history of the União Nacional. To such desideratum, a focus is placed on the complex and intricate process of establishing and developing a branch of the União Nacional in Cabo Verde, in the second half of the 1930s. As it linked local politics to metropolitan politics, the local branch of the União Nacional functioned as a nursery of regional political ideas and ideologies. Thus, the paper further argues that the local branch of this party assisted in the politicization, publicizing, and normalization of colonial and regional ideas and ideologies.

KEYWORDS: União Nacional, Commission of Colonies, União Nacional Colonial Commission of Cabo Verde, nativism, metropolitanism

RESUMO: A literatura sobre a União Nacional, partido político de apoio ao regime ditatorial português do Estado Novo (1933–74), é rica e abundante. No entanto, estudiosos e pesquisadores têm dado relativamente pouca atenção às ramificações da União Nacional no contexto do império colonial português. Para preencher essa lacuna, este trabalho lança luz sobre a história imperial da União Nacional. Para tal desiderato, destaca-se o complexo e intrincado processo de constituição e desenvolvimento de uma sucursal da União Nacional em Cabo Verde, na segunda metade da década de 1930. Por vincular a política local à política metropolitana, o braço local da União Nacional funcionou como um viveiro de ideias e ideologias políticas regionais. Assim, o artigo argumenta ainda que o braço local desse partido ajudou na politização, divulgação e normalização das ideias e ideologias coloniais e regionais.

PALAVRAS-CHAVE: União Nacional, Comissão de Colónias, Comissão de Colónia da União Nacional de Cabo Verde, nativismo, metropolitanismo

Introduction[1]

In the past three decades, the scholarship on the União Nacional (National Union), the political party of the dictatorial regime in Portugal from 1930 to 1974, has experienced a significant boom.[2] A number of studies published on the topic have helped to elucidate different aspects of the organization's political life and culture (Leal 1998; Costa Pinto 1992, 2015; Caldeira 1986; Cruz 1988; Caetano 1977). Despite the breadth of knowledge on the União Nacional, which has shed some light on how the political regime operated, scholars have given little attention to the processes and operations of this political party in the Portuguese colonial empire. By the end of the 1930s, however, the União Nacional had a local branch in each of the Portuguese colonies in Africa and Asia.

The literature on the União Nacional has yet to include an analysis of the origins, development, and political processes of this political party in the colonies. Against this backdrop, this paper fills a void in the literature by analyzing the sociopolitical processes through which the União Nacional was established in the then-colony of Cabo Verde and by engaging critically with the new literature on the Portuguese colonial empire. A new stream of Portuguese imperial studies has connected the development of colonial institutions and ideology with supranational agents and organizations as well as with local actors (that is, in the colonies) (Jerónimo 2015; Jerónimo and Monteiro 2014).

Connecting with this body of literature, my analysis centers on understanding the basis and development of political institutions in the colonies. The central argument of this paper is that the implantation of the branch of the União Nacional in Cabo Verde was not simply reflective of metropolitan politics. On the contrary, local political actors, acting autonomously and pursuing their own interests, greatly contributed to the União Nacional's presence in the colonies. Local actors, pursuing their own socioeconomic and political goals, negotiated with metropolitan actors and colonial administrators to imprint their views and to embed their interests in the institutions under construction. Colonial institutional development cannot merely imitate metropolitan politics. Rather, the concurrence of sociopolitical actors is ubiquitous in the colonial policies implemented in the colonies—and, by extension, in many of the political institutions established and constructed in the colonial context (Rodrigues 2003).

In the next section, I discuss the União Nacional as an imperial political party, and not simply a national political organization. Organizationally, the União Nacional spread its tentacles across the empire to assist in the double tasks of legitimizing the regime and quelling political dissent. From this macroanalysis, the paper then delves into local politics and the formation of the branch of the União Nacional in Cabo Verde. The paper suggests that the União Nacional was an arena of political disputes involving local elite factions predicated on different ideologies. The study of the branch of the União Nacional in Cabo Verde exposes the impact and influence of the local elites in "nativizing" a metropolitan political institution and permits us to learn about the processes of exporting European political parties and party structures to colonial Africa. My concluding remarks critically restate my key points and indicate directions for future research.

The União Nacional as an Imperial Political Party

On May 26, 1926, the liberal democratic experience in Portugal came to a halt, with the military assuming power after a coup d'état. For the next fifty years, Portugal and its colonies in Africa and Asia lived under an unbending right-wing authoritarian regime, first as a typical praetorian regime (1926–32) and then as a civilian-led dictatorship, self-labeled as the "Estado Novo," the New State (1933–74). Like its European counterparts of the 1930s, the Estado Novo was a one-party state; the formal structures of power were closely associated with the União Nacional, the only legally sanctioned political party.

The origins of the União Nacional date to the late 1920s, right after the institution of the military dictatorship (Caldeira 1986). On July 30, 1930, the military regime announced the establishment of a political organization labeled União Nacional. The regime initially avoided the construction of a political party, aiming for a no-party system. The function of the União Nacional was essentially to assist the regime in its quest for further legitimation. The status of the organization changed in 1932, with the rise of António de Oliveira Salazar, a conservative university professor, to the position of head of government. On August 20, 1932, through a decree, the government approved the bylaws of the União Nacional, formalizing it as the political arm of the civilian rule. Thus, the União Nacional's founding can be understood in two distinct phases: the formal announcement under the military dictatorship in July 1930; and the statutory foundation when the organization's bylaws were approved by the civilian-led government in August 1932.

Salazar inherited a party that was institutionally weak but had significant national presence. By the end of 1931, still under the military regime, the União Nacional had created branches across continental Portugal and, in the following years, in the adjacent islands of the Azores and Madeira. Like his military predecessors, Salazar used the political party to advance his own agenda and interests; the União Nacional became a key tool in garnering and mobilizing political support (Caetano 1977). The União Nacional was initially founded as a "patriotic league," tasked with buttressing support for the military regime. Upon assuming power in 1932, Salazar reengineered the party to his ideological and political image to stand on the twin pillars of ultranationalism and corporativism. The first ideological principle, that of ultranationalism, entailed an ostentatious celebration and promotion of the empire as well as the institution of a strong state that fully controlled and dominated society. Under the banner of corporativism, the União Nacional assisted in constructing a society based on class cooperation and free of class conflict. Its main political activities consisted of mass rallies in support of the regime, electoral mobilization, and recruitment of local elites in Portugal and throughout the empire.

The process of "Salazar-ization" of the União Nacional led to the personalization of power and authority within the structures of the party. The ultimate authority rested in the hands of Salazar, who had the power to oversee as well as to appoint leadership to key organisms and bodies of the party. At the same time, with Salazar at its helm, the party went through a complex process of institutionalization and bureaucratization; new core bodies were either established or renovated to facilitate internal communications, processes, procedures, and operations of power.

In its internal documents and in major works written by its leaders and ideologues, the União Nacional eschewed the "party" label. The party's first main document, *Manifesto da União Nacional* (1930) identifies it as a "patriotic league" (União Nacional 1930, 10). The 1932 bylaws characterized the União Nacional as an "association without the character of a [political] party" ("Estatutos" 1932, 1753). The non-party character of the União Nacional was forcefully promoted by its key leaders. A leaflet produced by the branch of the organization in Leiria categorically declared that "the União Nacional is not a political party."[3] Marcelo Caetano, a noted leader of the organization and one of its chief architects, argued that the União Nacional amounted to the opposite of a political party, an "anti-party" (Caldeira 1986, 972). For the intellectuals of the regime, the notion of political party was a core feature of parliamentary democracy, a system that many saw as the culprit of the social and political decay in the country. Despite this characterization, the União Nacional, in its structures, operations, procedures, and processes, was indeed a political party (Costa Pinto 1992).

According to its 1932 statutes, "The União Nacional has its headquarters in Lisbon, and can establish in all national territory of the continent, adjacent islands and colonies of the Portuguese Empire and may have dependencies in foreign countries where there is important Portuguese presence, if the local laws allows" (União Nacional 1932, 1753). The article in question points to the tridimensionality of the União Nacional as a national, imperial, and diasporic organization. Under Salazar's tight control, the União Nacional, originally national in scope, transmuted into an imperial political party, that is, a political organization with tentacles stretching from Lisbon to all corners of the colonial empire through the establishment or reorganization of local party branches. In other words, local branches were either created or, for those that already existed, put under central authority control (as was the case in Angola and Mozambique).

In Angola and Mozambique, the two settlement colonies, the establishment of the branches of the União Nacional anteceded the statutory foundation of the organization. The Angolan branch of the party was founded in December 1931 ("União Nacional" 1932; "União Nacional em Angola" 1932, 2). The formation of the branch (União Nacional de Angola) was independent from the Portuguese state authorities, namely the Minister of the Interior, who, at the time, was the chief executive of the party. In this case, the leadership of the branch was not appointed by the minister or his interlocutors, as was the norm in Portugal, but through autonomous vote by the branch's membership. In the other colonies in Africa and Asia (Cabo Verde, Guinea, São Tome and Principe, Timor, Macao, and Estado da Índia), it was only in the second half of the 1930s that local branches were instituted.

Nationalism and imperial mystique, the two main features of the regime in the 1930s, were also the two political forces that sustained the idea of expanding the structures of the União Nacional to the colonies. The União Nacional was not the first European political party with transnational and imperial pretensions. Its counterparts from Italy and Germany had developed party branches designed to mobilize their citizens residing abroad. For instance, Benito Mussolini's own National Fascist Party had the Fasci all'Estero, an office whose main function was to coordinate Italian fascist cells abroad (Baldoli 2003; Caprariis 2000). In Germany, the Nazi party had since 1931 organized a similar body, the Auslandsorganisation (NSDAP-AO), whose main task was to assist in the recruitment and coordination of German Nazi sympathizers residing outside Germany (McKale 1977).

To understand the process of the União Nacional's expansion to the colonies, it is important to consider that the leaders of Estado Novo sought to, and eventually did, construct what can be called a *conscription empire*. The concept of conscription empire, as interpreted here, is inspired by Gregory James Kasza (1995), who has advanced the notion of "conscription society," a regime with a number of mass organizations that recruit and mobilize social masses for the purposes of regime legitimacy and elimination of dissenting voices. Under the Estado Novo, colonialism entailed the deployment of mass organizations to the colonies, designed to conscript, recruit, and mobilize two publics: Portuguese natives residing in the empire and the assimilated, nonwhite natives of the colonies who had Portuguese citizenship. The União Nacional was one of these organizations deployed to the colonies. Other mass organizations included the male and female youth organizations (Mocidade Portuguesa and Mocidade Feminina Portuguesa) and the paramilitary organization Legião Portuguesa.

Organizationally, the União Nacional was an imperial political party; it was a political formation that extended throughout the colonies via the establishment of local representative branches, dependent on the central offices in the metropolis. The local branches of the União Nacional in the colonies had to adhere strictly to the directives emanating from the central offices, passed on via the Commission of Colonies. Through the Commission of Colonies, the various colonial commissions had access to the propaganda and political materials generated in the metropolis. Books, pamphlets, posters, documentaries, and other materials produced by the União Nacional in Lisbon were distributed to the colonies.

In order to coordinate the various branches of the União Nacional in the colonies, in 1934 the Central Commission of the União Nacional, the party's highest policy-making body, formed a subsidiary organism, the Commission of Colonies (Comissão de Colónias), which consisted of a president and three officers. Initially, Francisco Vieira Machado, a civilian and a member of the regime selectorate, led the Commission. With Machado's appointment to the government in late 1934, the presidency was entrusted to a military man, General Eduardo Augusto Marques ("Homenagem" 1944, 144). General Marques's tenure as the president of the body lasted until his death in 1944, when another army officer, Colonel António Lopes Mateus, a member of the body, was appointed by Salazar to assume the presidency ("Posse" 1944, 77).

The Commission of Colonies was not a standing committee of the União Nacional; the statutes of the organization do not refer to this body. The mission of the commission was to assist with disseminating information from Lisbon to the colonies, coordinate the actions of the various branches, and appoint leadership of the organization in the colonies. The Commission of Colonies functioned as the conduit between the central organs of the União Nacional and the various branches created across the Portuguese colonial empire. Political communications between the central offices of the União Nacional and the branches in the colonies followed a different pattern compared to exchanges between Lisbon and the various district commissions in Portugal and in the islands of Azores and Madeira. According to the organizational architecture, the local colonial branch of the União Nacional (called Comissão de Colónia) occupied the same institutional stratum as the district branch in Portugal (Comissão Districtal). In reality, however, the colonial branches were of a lower political significance vis-à-vis the district branches. The leaders of the various district commissions, i.e., party branches in Portugal, could communicate directly with the central offices, via the Secretary General. However, the colonial branches of the party had to go through the Commission of Colonies. This added structure created additional transaction costs and slowness in communication.

The União Nacional was created by the military regime in 1930 as a tool to assist in its own legitimation within Portuguese society. The rise of the civilian authority in 1932, with Salazar occupying the leadership of the government, did not alter the main mission of the União Nacional. If anything, Salazar assisted in the institutionalization of the political party through the approval of its bylaws while promoting the expansion of the party throughout the empire. In essence, by the end of the 1930s, the União Nacional was a de facto imperial political party, with appendages spreading from Lisbon to the different colonies that constituted the Portuguese empire.

The Implantation of the União Nacional Branch in Cabo Verde

By the end of 1937, Cabo Verde was the only Portuguese colony in Africa where the União Nacional had no institutional presence. Following its implantation throughout continental Portugal and the islands of Azores and Madeira in the early 1930s, the União Nacional went on to stretch throughout the Portuguese colonial empire. In the case of Cabo Verde, the process of founding the local branch had two distinct moments. First, characterized by the bottom-up approach, few individuals from Cabo Verde took the initiative to contact the central bodies of the União Nacional in Lisbon, namely its Secretariat General and the Central Commission, to request authorization to organize a branch of the party in the colony. In the second moment, the opposite pathway took place: the central offices, chiefly the president of the Commission of Colonies, General Marques, in conjunction with the governor of the colony, led the way in carrying out a top-down approach toward the establishment of a branch of the União Nacional in Cabo Verde. The fact that the idea to establish the branch came both from the locals and from metropolitan elites is an indication of the historical agency of the former and the complexity of colonial politics.

The political process of creating the branch of the União Nacional in Cabo Verde was an intricate one. Attention needs to be paid to the colonial elite in Cabo Verde in the 1930s, a social group that was far from being a monolithic entity, as it contained both Cabo Verdean and Portuguese elements. The Cabo Verdean elites had attained considerable levels of education and exercised positions of political and economic significance in the context of the colonial state and society. The members of this group included liberal professionals, businesspeople, teachers, and functionaries of the colonial state. The elite can be further subdivided in two distinct regional elites, those from the northern islands (or the Windward Islands) and those from the southern islands (the Leeward Islands). Additionally, a small number of Portuguese citizens worked at different levels of the colonial state and in the military. Portuguese citizens shared the same social space as the native elites, with whom they often competed for resources and prestige.

In the 1930s, there was a consensus within the native elite group about their Portuguese identity. They self-identified as Portuguese first; the idea of Cabo Verdean identity was perceived as a subset, or regional form, of Portuguese national identity. The idea of dual identification—or "cissiparidade pátrida" (fatherland duality), as Manuel Ferreira named it, had been a common dominator among local *culturati* since the early 1900s (Ferreira 1986, xli). As will be discussed later, this cultural identification with Portugal influenced and shaped the elite's political projects in the colony, namely the changing of the local and political status for Cabo Verde from a colony into an adjacent island.

The earliest case of the bottom-up approach to create a branch of the União Nacional in Cabo Verde came from Teófilo Vieira Barbosa, a native of the Brava Island, who wrote to the General Secretary of the União Nacional.[4] In the missive, Barbosa noted that he was already a member of the party, a status that he had arranged while he lived in Portugal years before moving back to his homeland. Barbosa's main objective was to assist in "the expansion of the current political institutions, chiefly in this colony, where public opinion is badly informed by political deportees." Barbosa referred to the fact that a number of Portuguese political exiles freely roamed in Cabo Verde, most of whom opposed and partook in activities against the regime in Lisbon (Barros 2009). Barbosa attached a petition signed by local notables, including the town administrator, João Maria Feijóo; the mayor of Brava, Augusto José de Azevedo; and many other public functionaries and property owners. The group indicated their intention to join the organization and their "unconditional support for the politics of Salazar," whom they recognized as the "supreme Chief." Ultimately, the group requested from the central offices that a "delegation of the União Nacional be created in this island."

Another case of the bottom-up approach was that of Manuel Ribeiro de Almeida, a native of the island of São Vicente and publisher of *Notícias de Cabo Verde*, the colony's major newspaper in the 1930s. Uninformed of the complex bureaucratic processes and institutional chain of command within the União Nacional, Almeida wrote directly to the party's Secretary General. Almeida was the figurehead of a group of fifteen people from the island of São Vicente who wished to join the União Nacional.[5] In the letter, he noted that the party did not have any representative or office in the colony and contended that an office or branch of the União Nacional in Cabo Verde would serve as tool for diffusion of the new ideas from the metropolis. Almeida offered to have *Notícias de Cabo Verde* function as an informal communicative channel for the party. Moreover, his letter included fifteen individual applications for membership in the organization. He ended his letter by noting that the colony possessed the necessary human capital to establish a branch of the União Nacional.

The two letters described above received replies from General Marques, the head of the Commission of Colonies.[6] In each case, Marques noted that the implantation of the União Nacional in the colony was underway. He further added that the authority to appoint new committees of the União Nacional in the colonies rested with the Commission of the Colonies. Marques's letter to Almeida included a demand, namely that the newspaper *Notícias de Cabo Verde* publicize the process of implanting the branch of the party in the colony. As a result, the December 1936 edition of *Notícias de Cabo Verde* featured, on its front page, the news that the branch of the União Nacional was in the process of being created ("A União" 1936).

Still, there was yet another bottom-up attempt to institute a branch of the União Nacional in Cabo Verde. In 1936, Horácio Afonso de Mesquita, a Portuguese-born high school teacher in São Vicente, wrote to the Central Commission of the União Nacional, noting that he was already a member of the party and describing himself as an enthusiastic partisan and a fervent nationalist defending the cause of the Estado Novo in the colony.[7] Mesquita further argued that the "the doctrines of the New Era have yet to be fully solidified and the Estado Novo, here in São Vicente, is challenged in a revolting, at will manner!" For Mesquita, the colony was yet to fully embrace the ideology and principles of the Estado Novo. In his view, there was a "total and complete lack of trust towards the Estado Novo; nobody believed in the Estado Novo or Salazar, particularly in the public offices." He presented himself as a man who could change this state of affairs: "I offer myself to found [the branch of the União Nacional in Cabo Verde], under orders and direction of your Excellency."

In December 1936, Mesquita sent a complaint to the Central Commission of the União Nacional to protest the publication of an article in *Notícias de Cabo Verde* regarding the formation of the branch of the União Nacional, arguing that the piece was "impolitic, very infelicitous, insulting, antipatriotic, untimely, and *nativist*."[8] For Mesquita, the newspaper represented everything that was against the Estado Novo and the empire. He noted that the "newspaper that labels itself as nationalist, *in partibus*, maintains in the header: 'independent regionalist organ.'" According to Mesquita, the *Notícias de Cabo Verde* and its affiliates represented an obstacle to the Estado Novo and the grandeur of the empire; they were "false nationalists." Mesquita argued that the local elites were nativists, seeking to promote local interests, at the expense—and in spite—of those of the Portuguese nation and empire at large. Mesquita's accusation of "nativists" was a calculated one. Earlier generations of Cabo Verdean public intellectuals, from the 1910s and 1920s, advocated for what they called "nativism," a political ideology that promoted the interests of people of Cabo Verde in the context of the empire (Guimarães 2006). Mesquita found that being nativist was antithetical to being a patriot or nationalist in the sense of defending and promoting the interests and the ideals of Portugal and its empire.

A few months later, Mesquita amplified his attacks against the supposed nativism of the Cabo Verdean elites. The local government of the municipality of São Vicente planned to celebrate the one hundredth birthday of Roberto Duarte Silva, a native of the island and a renowned chemist. As part of the commemoration, one of the major streets of the city, Rua de Lisboa, was to be renamed as Rua Roberto Duarte Silva. For Mesquita, the name change "filled with indignation all the good metropolitans, because it was seen as a blow to the head of the empire, in a pure act of nativism."[9] It was clear to Mesquita that local history and individualities were promoted at the expense of the empire and magnificence of the Portuguese nation. The change in the street name, from the capital city of the empire to the name of a local man, however famous, was an indication of the extent that local symbols and interests were trumping Portuguese national and imperial ones.

Many metropolitan citizens residing in Cabo Verde saw the constitution of the branch of the União Nacional as a suitable instrument for political purification against the infected ideologies and ideas that circulated in the colony. Ideologies of nativism and other political ideas brought to the colony by exiled Portuguese citizens went against the principles of the Estado Novo. For instance, Mesquita thought that a branch of the União Nacional was needed to completely purge the political discourses and/or attitudes that ran against the ideological lines of the Estado Novo.[10] Similarly, for Eurico José Teixeira, a Portuguese citizen residing in the island of São Nicolau, the União Nacional in Cabo Verde would constitute a powerful force against all the novel influences deriving from the Portuguese political deportees in the islands.[11]

Whether initiated by Cabo Verdean or by Portuguese citizens residing in Cabo Verde, these bottom-up approaches to assist in the constitution of a branch of the União Nacional yielded no practical results. The central authorities of the União Nacional did not want to relinquish their power of initiative in the colonies. Thus, all bottom-up requests to form the local branch in Cabo Verde were simply discarded. In 1937, the central offices of the União Nacional, through its Commission of Colonies, took steps to build a branch of the party in the colony.

The initial thrust that paved the way for the establishment of the União Nacional branch in Cabo Verde came from a request from the Secretariat of National Propaganda (SPN), the nerve center of the regime in what concerned propaganda and cultural policy, for a list of branches in the empire "for reasons related to propaganda."[12] The request, which went unfulfilled, forced the União Nacional leaders to reckon with the fact that the statutory ideal of having the party present across the empire was far from being realized. In fact, at the time there were only two effectively organized branches of the União Nacional in the empire, namely in Mozambique and in Estado da Índia, as the branch that existed in Angola had been disbanded. In the following months, the Commission of Colonies led the process of appointing the branches across the empire, and, by the end of 1938, there were outposts of the União Nacional in each of the colonies.

In the case of Cabo Verde, the process of creating a branch of the União Nacional started on a May 13, 1937, with a letter from General Marques, the president of the Commission of Colonies, to the Governor of Cabo Verde, Amadeu Gomes de Figueiredo.[13] The letter focused on two main points: on the one hand, Marques asked for assistance in the process of establishing the branch in Cabo Verde; on the other hand, he inquired about what had been done to further such a goal. The governor responded that the process had been rather difficult, marred by local politics. He reported the old social scuffles between the northern and southern islands, along with other factors such as the geography of the colony, were a major hindrance to the establishment of the party branch in Cabo Verde. There had been a history of clashing interests and ideological conflict between the local elites from the city of Mindelo, in the northern island of São Vicente, and those from the capital city of the colony, Praia, in the southern island of Santiago. Gomes de Figueiredo noted that the question of which commission should be dependent of the other proved difficult to answer. His proposed solution was to create a commission of the colony that included members from both islands.[14]

While the central offices of the party and the governor of Cabo Verde worked to implant the branch in 1937, the process was stalled by a sociopolitical crisis that impacted the colony. On October 27, 1937, the central government in Lisbon, through the Ministry of the Colonies, decreed the closing of the Liceu Central Infante D. Henrique in São Vicente, the colony's only secondary-education institution. For the local elite, the decree was tantamount to a betrayal and another potent piece of evidence of second-class condition of the people of Cabo Verde. Against this state of affairs, disinterest and apathy became the dominant response to the calls for the forming of a local branch of the União Nacional.[15] Following organized protests by the local elites, primarily from São Vicente, the central government in Lisbon ultimately overruled its previous decision and let the Liceu stand.

A few months later, on November 15, General Marques wrote again to the governor, asking him to suggest "names of people that Your Excellency considers suitable [for the position] and who are willing to accept this burden."[16] In the same letter, Marques noted that Cabo Verde was the only colony in Africa where the União Nacional had no institutional presence. After the resolution of the problem of the Liceu in São Vicente in early 1938, Gomes de Figueiredo appointed a three-member organizing commission of the branch in Cabo Verde under the leadership of Adriano Duarte Silva, a renowned teacher in the Liceu and a lawyer.[17] The organizing commission had instructions to contact the Commission of Colonies to formalize itself. In the commission's letter of introduction to the Commission of Colonies, Adriano Duarte Silva emphasized their dual commitment, purporting to serve, equally, "the Nation [that is, Portugal in its totality] and the land in which we were born [Cabo Verde]."[18] In other words, the group made explicit that they could reconcile two political ideologies, namely that of Lusitanian nationalism and Cabo Verdean regionalism.

Once the branch of the União Nacional in Cabo Verde became official, the Commission of Colonies issued the "Directrizes estabelecidas para a política do Estado Novo em Cabo Verde," a document that laid out the branch's social and political responsibilities in the colony.[19] The document created a mode of political relationship to be developed between the branch of the União Nacional and the different levels of instituted political authority in Cabo Verde (central and local governments). In this regard, the document emphasized the idea that the branch of the União Nacional should constitute "an organization independent of the State." Its independence, nonetheless, should not constitute an obstacle to cooperation with the local political authorities. The "Directrizes" call for the União Nacional to be "an element of constant and loyal cooperation" with the authorities. At the same time, the document reaffirms the principle of chain of command within the União Nacional: the local branch, reporting to the Commission of Colonies, had the authority to establish subterritorial branches, the town commissions (or Comissões Conselhias) of the party throughout the colony. In other words, the Commission of Colonies had the authority to appoint the members of the Comissão de Cabo Verde and the latter body, in turn, had power to appoint the members of the party's town branches.

Prospective candidates to the position of leadership in the local branches were to be morally and intellectually suitable and have social prestige in their respective communities. Furthermore, because one of the critical objectives of the União Nacional was to foment its penetration in society, the "Directrizes" emphasized that recruitment of new members should be extended beyond the official elements. Recruitment of the local leadership constituted a strategy of capturing the local elites. Thus, the recruitment of territorial and subterritorial branches of the União Nacional focused on members of the local commercial bourgeoisie, professional liberals, schoolteachers, and members of other social classes that enjoyed significant prestige and popularity among their community. Recruitment of the local elites constituted one of the main strategies of capturing the colonial society. Another strategy was to increase the União Nacional's social visibility through participation in social, political, and commemorative events in the colony. Given the emphasis on commemoration of the colonial Estado Novo, which extended to the colonies, representatives of the União Nacional conspicuously partook in different events designed to celebrate and commemorate dates and individuals of Portuguese history in Cabo Verde. By October 1940, the branch of the party in Cabo Verde had more than 650 members (or more than ten percent of the União Nacional membership in the entire colonial empire), making it the third largest in the empire (see Table 1).

Table 1. União Nacional Membership in the Colonies (October 1940)

Colony	Total Membership	Population (1940 Census) Total	White
Angola	2,582	3,222,015	58,098
Cabo Verde	659	174,403	7,017
Guinea	235	426,009	1,226
India	20	579,970	—
Macao	351	157,175	—
Mozambique	1,710	4,006,011	12,131
São Tomé and Príncipe	343	48,869	967
Timor	3	463,996	—
Total	5,903	9,081,448	90,439

Source: A União Nacional nas Colónias. Filiados. Setembro 1940 (PT-TT-UN-A-A-12-4-C0066]; Instituto Nacional de Estatística, *Anuário Estatístico de 1940* (Lisboa: Imprensa Nacional, 1941).

The "Directrizes" also entailed instructions on political activities of the branch, particularly in regard to electoral campaign activities, in order to prevent what the document called "abstencionismo" (voter nonparticipation). Additionally, the branch was responsible for maintaining collaboration with the public authorities, both at the central and at the local levels, and for the recruitment of new members. Regarding electoral activity, the "Directrizes" emphasized that, for the presidential and legislative elections, the branch of the party in Cabo Verde had to adhere strictly to the instructions coming from the central offices of the União Nacional. For the local elections, the local branch had to collaborate with public authorities (such as the governor and/or local mayoral authorities).

The implantation of the branch of the União Nacional in the colony of Cabo Verde was neither linear nor simple. Regional elites sought to accrue sociopolitical advantages by taking the initiative to contact the central offices of the party in Lisbon to create the branch. The archives of the União Nacional show that native elites from the southern and northern islands, as well as Portuguese citizens residing in the colony, wrote to Lisbon and volunteered themselves to set up the institutional presence of the party in the islands. However, the party's central authorities disregarded those initiatives and, in concert with the governor of the colony, managed to form the branch in 1938.

The Multilevel Political Game of the União Nacional Branch in Cabo Verde

While not formally a member of the colonial state, the leadership of the União Nacional branch in Cabo Verde, particularly its president, enjoyed several protocol privileges typically reserved for state officials. For instance, when the President of Portugal, Óscar Carmona, visited Cabo Verde during his tour of the empire, Adriano Duarte Silva, as the president of the party branch in Cabo Verde, was included in the presidential delegation that toured the colony.

The branch of the União Nacional in Cabo Verde became a site of political dispute between different social groups espousing diverse—and sometimes contradictory—ideologies about the role and position of Cabo Verde and its people within the context of the Portuguese colonial empire. Local and metropolitan actors, moved by their own interests, often sought to influence how political institutions operated in the colonies. Colonial systems were not only erected through the barrel of a gun; the consent extended to different sections of the local elite also helped stabilize colonial rule. Local social actors used their influence and social capital to shape colonial policies or their implementation processes. Ultimately, the establishment of political institutions resulted from a complex and intricate blend of local and metropolitan politics.

The institutionalization of Salazar's party is an indication of this pattern as it intensified a two-level political game that characterized the colony of Cabo Verde since the late nineteenth century. On the one hand, there was a regional conflict, characterized by a war of interests between southern and northern islands, represented respectively by the cities of Praia and Mindelo. On the other hand, there was a political clash between representatives of native and metropolitan interests, each of them advocating for the inherent primacy of their part.

Since the late nineteenth century, two competing elite subgroups had developed in Cabo Verde, one from Praia, the capital of the colony, and another from Mindelo, on the island of São Vicente (Gatlin 1990). Given its marvelous port and possession of Cabo Verde's only secondary-education institution, São Vicente was the cultural as well as economic center of the colony. By the 1930s, political antagonism between the two subgroups had escalated, each defending the political and economy primacy of its region within the colonial context. Initially, the governor of Cabo Verde sought to include representatives from both regions in the organizing commission of the União Nacional in Cabo Verde. However, the plan ended up not being feasible and the organizing commission became dominated by three men, all from São Vicente. The constitution of the União Nacional branch in Cabo Verde was a political victory for the northern elites. Unlike other cases in the empire, the União Nacional in Cabo Verde did not have its headquarters in the capital of the colony; rather, Mindelo became the seat of the branch.

Through political subterfuge, social networking, and direct access to the governor of the colony, the regional elites from the southern islands, in the capital city of Cabo Verde, nonetheless subverted the party's regional authority emanating from São Vicente. While the 1938 "Directrizes" explicitly stated that the main branch in the colony had authority over all subterritorial branches created in Cabo Verde, local elites from Praia activated their social capital and networks, particularly their direct contacts with the governor of the colony, to appoint themselves to the branch. Specifically, the local elites from Praia convinced the governor into appointing the leaders of the União Nacional's town branch of Praia. Thus, for the Town Commission in Praia, the agency of local elites from the city, and not the organization's chain of command, became the decisive factor. Duarte Silva, as the head of the party in Cabo Verde, reluctantly gave in to the governor's demand.[20] In his view, the appointed members of the Commission of the União Nacional of Praia were not fit for the position, since, according to the rules of the party, leadership of the organization was not to be placed in the hands of individuals who were part of what the regime intellectuals called "old politics," that is, the political establishment before the 1926 coup d'état.

Duarte Silva complained to General Marques, his direct superior in the party's chain of command, about the total lack of communication from the party's town commission in Praia. He further noted he had reliable information that the Praia commission had no intention of working with the headquarters in São Vicente and that it had plans to subvert the party hierarchy by preparing "an exhibition to send to Lisbon [to the central offices of the União Nacional]."[21] In other words, the town commission of Praia was subverting the authority of Duarte Silva by disregarding the bureaucratic chain of command. According to the "Directrizes," communications from any local commission of the União Nacional in Cabo Verde had to be channeled through the main branch.[22]

By 1942, the União Nacional in Cabo Verde had lost its political momentum and had ceased to figure as a significant organization in the political and social life of the colony. One major reason for this was the dispersion of the branch's leadership, with Ribeiro de Almeida moving to Portugal. The branch became practically equivalent to Duarte Silva himself. In fact, Duarte Silva seemed frustrated with the political role that the União Nacional should play in Cabo Verde. He protested to the president of the Commission of Colonies that appointments of the leadership of local governments in the colony often happened without any consultation with the local branch of the party.[23] Moreover, the fact that Portugal sent a contingent of expeditionary forces to Cabo Verde to protect the islands against a possible attack by either the allied forces or Germans, both of whom had plans to do so, complicated the matters of the local branch. Duarte Silva expressed his dissatisfaction that the branch had to give up its headquarters to house the expeditionary forces, a fact that in his view "much contributed to the paralysis of our activities."[24]

It is against this backdrop that Martins suggested to the president of the Commission of Colonies that "more impulse and more prestige" be given to the União Nacional in Cabo Verde.[25] The new branch would have Duarte Silva as its president, aided by two other members, a Portuguese military man stationed in Cabo Verde (Capitão Tenente Carlos Pinto Bastos Carneiro) and Manuel Ribeiro de Almeida; this plan was approved by the Commission of Colonies in a telegram of December 24 of the same year.

The height of conflict between southern and northern interests within the União Nacional in Cabo Verde was in 1942 when Duarte Silva appointed a new União Nacional town commission for Praia, led by Bento Levy, a lawyer native of Praia. Levy first declined, arguing that the party in Cabo Verde was politically dormant and that he disliked the idea of the organization's headquarters being in Mindelo. After some pressure from Martins, the colony's governor, Levy agreed to lead the União Nacional in Praia in May 1943.[26] Like his predecessors, Levy maintained no communication with his party superiors, and never submitted a letter or note to the headquarters of the party in São Vicente.[27]

Some sections of the elite from Praia distrusted Duarte Silva, whom they perceived to be against the interests of the capital. Tensions between the two regional elites reached a higher level when *Notícias de Cabo Verde*, a newspaper close to Duarte Silva, published a piece mentioning the nineteenth-century law that mandated the transference of the capital of the colony from Praia to Mindelo ("Efemérides" 1945, 2). Many in Praia interpreted the piece as a sign that the elites from Mindelo were seeking to alter the administrative architecture of the colony. Duarte Silva ultimately had to send a message to Praia to calm their anxieties, emphasizing that he had no intention of advocating for the change of the capital of the colony (Silva 1945, 4).

The elections of 1945, called abruptly by the regime, further increased political enmity between Duarte Silva and Levy, representatives of the two regional interests. Influenced by the wind of change that heralded the wave of liberal democracy in the aftermath of Second World War, the Estado Novo called for competitive elections. For the first time in the regime's history, the electoral law mandated territorial representation: each of the colonies would have at least one seat in the new National Assembly. Duarte Silva was the candidate for the União Nacional. The opposition, formed around the Movimento de Unidade Democrática, was allowed to compete in the elections. In Cabo Verde, the candidate for the opposition was Álvaro de Paiva Lereno, native of the Brava Island in the south. Lereno was an inspector within the Banco Nacional Ultramarino (BNU) and some of his key associates were also affiliated with the BNU. His electoral campaign manager was a high-level member of the BNU bureaucracy in Cabo Verde, and Levy, his campaign counselor, was an attorney for the bank. Duarte Silva reacted to what he perceived to have been a complot within the BNU in Cabo Verde and sought to activate the central offices of the União Nacional to intercede before the headquarters of the BNU in Lisbon.[28] When it became news that Duarte Silva was the candidate for the União Nacional, Levy, who was part of the legal team of the opposition candidate, sought to have Duarte Silva's candidacy impugned by the administrative court.[29] The court sided with Duarte Silva, who went on to win the elections.

The other type of conflict within the União Nacional in Cabo Verde pitted locals against metropolitans. Unlike other Portuguese colonies in Africa, leadership of the local branch of the União Nacional in Cabo Verde rested in the hands of the local elites. In contrast, Portuguese residents assumed the leadership of the party's local branches in Angola, Mozambique, Guinea-Bissau, and São Tome and Príncipe. Native elements in these colonies, including the creoles and assimilated Africans, were simply not included in the leadership of the party. There are two major explanations for the "nativization" of the União Nacional in Cabo Verde. The first had to do with the fact that many local elites were part of the colonial and/or imperial bureaucracy. Being a part of the colonial apparatuses afforded these Cabo Verdeans the opportunity to develop a strong social capital with high-echelon members of the imperial bureaucracy, chiefly the governor. In the case of Cabo Verde, the governor played an important role in identifying potential leaders for the branch of the União Nacional. Having a strong connection with the governor was indeed a valuable political asset.

The second explanation had to do with the ideological positions of the governor of Cabo Verde in the 1930s. Governor Amadeu Gomes de Figueiredo held sympathetic views toward Cabo Verdeans, whom he believed to have assimilated Portuguese values and, as such, to be of equal worth to the metropolitan Portuguese. On several occasions, Gomes de Figueiredo recognized what he called "Portuguesism" (*portuguesismo*) of Cabo Verdeans (Neto 2009).

Given the primacy of the native elements in local society and politics, the other political game that surrounded the União Nacional in Cabo Verde centered on the native-metropolitan divide. Nativism in Cabo Verde consisted of a political ideology with origins in the early twentieth century. The heyday of nativism in Cabo Verde took place during the First Republic (1910s and 1920s) and was characterized by a vibrant public sphere (Semedo 2006; Oliveira 1998). In the case of Cabo Verde, nativism did not imply xenophobia or hatred against foreign elements. Rather, the ideology centered on two key principles: legal political equality between the natives of Cabo Verde and those of the metropolis, and the notion that the people of Cabo Verde, through their social and cultural elites, should have a voice in the matter of policies created and implemented on their behalf.

On the other hand, metropolitanism was a social ideology and attitude that developed among the few Portuguese settlers and professionals in the colony. This ideology was based on the principle of inherent superiority of the European-born individuals (the metropolitans) over both African-born people of European descent and native Africans. Its central premise was the rejection of the socially and professionally subordinate condition of the European-born vis-à-vis the non-Europeans. Positions of leadership in the colonial state were to be given to the metropolitans. The Liceu teacher Horácio Afonso de Mesquita was one of the main proponents of the ideology of metropolitanism. Another proponent was Eurico José Teixeira, a Portuguese citizen residing on the island of São Nicolau. In a letter addressed to the Central Commission of the União Nacional, Teixeira rhetorically asked: "Does Your Excellence agree that whites should be subordinated to blacks?"[30] For the few Portuguese residents of Cabo Verde, it was not conceivable that the metropolitan citizens could be put under the leadership of the natives, whom they perceived to lack the nationalist fervor or mental and moral capacities necessary to lead.

The feeling of inferiority imposed on Cabo Verdeans by metropolitan citizens was a common phenomenon. Duarte Silva made this point eloquently in his letter to the president of the Commission of Colonies, in June 1939, where he complained that treating Cabo Verdeans as if they were the same as the "natives of other African colonies" might create "a malaise that could result in nothing useful."[31] Duarte Silva referred to the *indigenato* policy, a core element of the Portuguese colonial regime that classified Africans in the colonies into two distinct categories: the assimilated, who had Portuguese citizenship, and the overwhelming majority of *indígenas* (natives) who lacked social and political rights. Since the 1910s, the indigenato policy was not applicable to Cabo Verdeans, and theoretically all Cabo Verdeans were Portuguese citizens. Duarte Silva criticized metropolitanism by noting that some Portuguese citizens in Cabo Verde "strive to separate the European from the Cabo Verdean, accusing the latter of lack of patriotism."[32]

Duarte Silva also rejected what can be called *institutional metropolitanism*, that is, the preferential treatment given to metropolitan citizens by the state, its policies, and its laws. On May 20, 1939, the government reorganized the Liceu in Cabo Verde, distinguishing between the native and metropolitan faculty members of the institution. Duarte Silva argued that such a law penalized the inhabitants of Cabo Verde, calling it "a legally established inferiority." For that reason, he resigned from his position as the president of the local branch of the União Nacional.[33]

The presence of the Portuguese expeditionary forces in Cabo Verde, sent to the islands in 1942 to defend the colony during World War II, caused widespread dissatisfaction, as the troops took for themselves the meager resources available in the colony. In March 1942, general frustration reached higher levels when it became known that the troops intended to occupy the installations of the hospital and the Liceu. The branch of the União Nacional, allied with other social organizations such as the local government, the business association, the trade union, the sport federation, Grémio Mindelo, and the parents' association, sent a telegram to the Minister of Colonies and the head of government to protest such a decision.

In summary, the branch of the União Nacional in Cabo Verde was not immune to local political conflicts among different sectors of the local elites. Social groups used social capital and developed concrete ideological systems in the fight for leadership of the branch of the party in the colony. On the one hand, regional elites from the two centers of the colony (Praia and Mindelo) competed against each other for the control of the branch. Ultimately, while power officially rested in the hands of the elites in São Vicente, the town branch of the party in Praia never fully submitted to the party headquarters in São Vicente. On the other hand, an intense conflict developed between the local elites and the individuals from Portugal who resided in the colony. For the former, Cabo Verdeans, as de jure Portuguese citizens, were to enjoy all the rights the Portuguese citizenship conferred. For the metropolitans, it was not conceivable to have the natives of the colony in positions of authority over them. In the end, the branch of the União Nacional was fully controlled by local elements of São Vicente.

Conclusion

The União Nacional, the official political party of the Estado Novo—though not in name—was a central institution that assisted in legitimizing the regime as well as controlling societal dissent. By the mid-1930s, the União Nacional had become an imperial political party, with branches stretching from Lisbon to different corners of the Portuguese colonial empire. The presence of this political party, along with other mass organizations created by the regime, facilitated the construction of a conscripted empire. Many assimilated Africans and Portuguese settlers in the colonies were attracted to the spheres of the União Nacional.

This paper analyzed the processes and the ideological conflicts surrounding the establishment of the branch of the União Nacional in Cabo Verde in the 1930s. One aspect that the analysis shows is that there was an intensive local agency and willingness to form a branch of the Salazar's political party in the colony. Local elites, whether indigenous inhabitants or of Portuguese background, sought to assume the front seat in the process. Archival research has elucidated that the implementation of colonial policy cannot be assumed to have been a direct, top-down process; colonized elites indeed played a role in assisting in the promotion of colonial rule and policies—or, in this particular case, of a branch of the regime's party.

The paper also examined the União Nacional in Cabo Verde not as a neutral political arena but rather as a sphere of confrontation within the policies of Salazar's centralist Estado Novo. Fierce disputes took place between different sections of the elites, who mobilized resources and social capital to their side. Ultimately, the political party became a stage on which two ideological conflicts developed. On the one hand, different regional interests were represented by the two centers of the colony, namely Praia, the capital city, and Mindelo, the economic and cultural center of Cabo Verde. While Mindelo became the seat of the main branch of the União Nacional, Praia responded by not fully submitting to the authority in Mindelo.

On the other hand, the issue of control over União Nacional in Cabo Verde developed into an intense political conflict that pitted local indigenous elites against the metropolitan residents in the colony. Local elites espoused the ideology of nativism—though they eschewed the use of the term. For them, local interests ought to have primacy in the context of the Portuguese colonial empire. Portuguese citizens residing in the colony, for their part, developed what can be called metropolitanism, a political ideology that defended categorical supremacy of the metropolitan element in the colony. Ultimately, União Nacional in Cabo Verde represented a political victory of the native elites over the few—and powerless—metropolitan elements in the colony.

NOTES

1. The author would like to acknowledge Jeanne M. Penvenne, Michael Panzer, and an anonymous reviewer for their insightful comments on the draft of the paper. As usual, the author is solely responsible for all the words and conclusions of the paper.

2. In 1970, following Marcelo Caetano's ascension to power, the União Nacional was rebranded as the Acção Nacional Popular.

3. União Nacional, *Ao Paíz—Alusão ao 1 de Dezembro de 1640*, União Nacional/Organização da União Nacional, Comissões, PT-TT-AOS-D-M-38-1-2, Arquivo Torre do Tombo, Lisbon, Portugal.

4. Correspondence from Teófilo Vieira Barbosa to Secretary General of União Nacional, 18 May 1935, União Nacional/Correspondência com a Comissão de Província de Cabo Verde, 1935-1952, PT/TT/UN-A/A-12-02/1, Arquivo Torre do Tombo, Lisbon, Portugal.

5. Correspondence from Manuel Ribeiro de Almeida to the Secretary General of the União Nacional, 19 September 1936, União Nacional/Correspondência com a Comissão de Província de Cabo Verde, 1935-1952, PT/TT/UN-A/A-12-02/1, Arquivo Torre do Tombo, Lisbon, Portugal.

6. Correspondence from General Eduardo Marques, president of the Commission of Colonies, to Teófilo Vieira Barbosa, 17 November 1936, União Nacional/Correspondência com a Comissão de Província de Cabo Verde, 1935-1952, PT/TT/UN-A/A-12-02/1, Arquivo Torre do Tombo, Lisbon, Portugal; correspondence from General Eduardo Marques, president of the Commission of Colonies, to Manuel Ribeiro de Almeida, 17 November 1936, União Nacional/Correspondência com a Comissão de Província de Cabo Verde, 1935-1952, PT/TT/UN-A/A-12-02/1, Arquivo Torre do Tombo, Lisbon, Portugal.

7. Correspondence from Horacio Afonso de Mesquita to the Central Commission of the União Nacional, 13 June 13 1936, União Nacional/Correspondência com a Comissão de Província de Cabo Verde, 1935-1952, PT/TT/UN-A/A-12-02/1, Arquivo Torre do Tombo, Lisbon, Portugal.

8. Correspondence from Horacio Afonso de Mesquita to the Central Commission of the União Nacional, 17 December 1936, União Nacional/Correspondência com a Comissão de Província de Cabo Verde, 1935-1952, PT/TT/UN-A/A-12-02/1, Arquivo Torre do Tombo, Lisbon, Portugal (added emphasis).

9. Correspondence from Horacio Afonso de Mesquita to the Central Commission of the União Nacional, 5 March 1937, União Nacional/Correspondência com a Comissão de Província de Cabo Verde, 1935-1952, PT/TT/UN-A/A-12-02/1, Arquivo Torre do Tombo, Lisbon, Portugal.

10. Correspondence from Horacio Afonso de Mesquita to the Central Commission of the União Nacional, 17 December 1936, União Nacional/Correspondência com a Comissão de Província de Cabo Verde, 1935-1952, PT/TT/UN-A/A-12-02/1, Arquivo Torre do Tombo, Lisbon, Portugal.

11. Correspondence from Eurico José Teixeira to Ruy Morais Vaz, Secretary General of the União Nacional, 16 March 1939, União Nacional/Correspondência com a Comissão de Província de Cabo Verde, 1935-1952, PT/TT/UN-A/A-12-02/1, Arquivo Torre do Tombo, Lisbon, Portugal.

12. Correspondence from the President of the Central Commission of the União Nacional to the President of the Commission of Colonies, 26 February 1936, União Nacional/Correspondência com a Comissão de Província de Cabo Verde, 1935-1952, PT/TT/UN-A/A-12-02/1, Arquivo Torre do Tombo, Lisbon, Portugal.

13. Correspondence from Eduardo Marques to the Governor of Cabo Verde, 13 May 1937, União Nacional/Correspondência com a Comissão de Província de Cabo Verde, 1935-1952, PT/TT/UN-A/A-12-02/1, Arquivo Torre do Tombo, Lisbon, Portugal.

14. Correspondence from Governor Amadeu Gomes de Figueiredo to the Commission of Colonies of the União Nacional, 14 April 1937, União Nacional/Correspondência com a Comissão de Província de Cabo Verde, 1935-1952, PT/TT/UN-A/A-12-02/1, Arquivo Torre do Tombo, Lisbon, Portugal.

15. Correspondence from Governor Amadeu Gomes de Figueiredo to the Commission of Colonies of the União Nacional, 14 April 1937, União Nacional/Correspondência com a Comissão de Província de Cabo Verde, 1935-1952, PT/TT/UN-A/A-12-02/1, Arquivo Torre do Tombo, Lisbon, Portugal.

16. Correspondence from General Eduardo Marques to the Governor Amadeu Gomes de Figueiredo, 15 November 1937, União Nacional/Correspondência com a Comissão de Província de Cabo Verde, 1935-1952, PT/TT/UN-A/A-12-02/1, Arquivo Torre do Tombo, Lisbon, Portugal.

17. Adriano Duarte Silva was an influential member of the colonial society in Cabo Verde, particularly in his native São Vicente. As the teacher in the colony's only secondary-education institution, he was well known in the island and a fervent advocate of its interests. He became the first Cabo Verdean to be appointed as the rector of the Liceu. By the second half of the 1930s, Duarte Silva became one of the leading unofficial ideologues of the Estado Novo in Cabo Verde. In this capacity, at the start of the academic year 1937/38, he delivered a lecture before the student body and local community on the ideology of corporativism. See, among others, Adriano Duarte Silva, *O corporativismo e sua oportunidade histórica* (Praia: Imprensa Nacional, 1938) and Maria Adriana Sousa Carvalho, *O Liceu em Cabo Verde: Um imperativo de cidadania (1917-1975)* (Praia: Edições Uni-CV, 2011).

18. Correspondence from Adriano Duarte Silva, president of the Organizing Commission of the União Nacional in Cabo Verde, to the Commission of Colonies, 22 January 1938, União Nacional/Correspondência com a Comissão de Província de Cabo Verde, 1935-1952, PT/TT/UN-A/A-12-02/1, Arquivo Torre Tombo, Lisbon, Portugal.

19. Correspondence from General Eduardo Marques to Adriano Duarte Silva, 25 February 1938, União Nacional/Correspondência com a Comissão de Província de Cabo Verde, 1935-1952, PT/TT/UN-A/A-12-02/1, Arquivo Torre do Tombo, Lisbon, Portugal.

20. Correspondence from Adriano Duarte Silva to the Commission of Colonies, 29 November 1938, União Nacional/Correspondência com a Comissão de Província de Cabo Verde, 1935-1952, PT/TT/UN-A/A-12-02/1, Arquivo Torre do Tombo, Lisbon, Portugal.

21. Ibid.

22. Correspondence from Adriano Duarte Silva, president of the Commission of the União Nacional in Cabo Verde, to the Chefe de Repartição do Gabinete do Governador, 4 October 1949, União Nacional/Correspondência com a Comissão de Província de Cabo Verde, 1935-1952, PT/TT/UN-A/A-12-02/1, Arquivo Torre do Tombo, Lisbon, Portugal.

23. Correspondence from Adriano Duarte Silva, president of the Commission of the União Nacional in Cabo Verde, to the Commission of Colonies, 9 December 1942, União Nacional/Correspondência com a Comissão de Província de Cabo Verde, 1935-1952, PT/TT/UN-A/A-12-02/1, Arquivo Torre do Tombo, Lisbon, Portugal.

24. Ibid.

25. Correspondence from the Governor of the colony of Cabo Verde, José Diogo Ferreira Martins, to General Marques, 28 November 1942, União Nacional/Correspondência com a Comissão de Província de Cabo Verde, 1935-1952, PT/TT/UN-A/A-12-02/1, Arquivo Torre do Tombo, Lisbon, Portugal.

26. Correspondence from Adriano Duarte Silva, president of the Commission of the União Nacional in Cabo Verde, to the Chefe de Repartição do Gabinete do Governador, 4 October 1949, União Nacional/Correspondência com a Comissão de Província de Cabo Verde, 1935-1952, PT/TT/UN-A/A-12-02/1, Arquivo Torre do Tombo, Lisbon, Portugal.

27. Ibid.

28. Cable from Adriano Duarte Silva to the President of Commission of Colonies, Lopes Mateus, 1 November 1945, União Nacional/Correspondência com a Comissão de Província de Cabo Verde, 1935-1952, PT/TT/UN-A/A-12-02/1, Arquivo Torre do Tombo, Lisbon, Portugal.

29. Correspondence from Adriano Duarte Silva, president of the Commission of the União Nacional in Cabo Verde, to the Chefe de Repartição do Gabinete do Governador, 4 October 1949, União Nacional/Correspondência com a Comissão de Província de Cabo Verde, 1935-1952, PT/TT/UN-A/A-12-02/1, Arquivo Torre do Tombo, Lisbon, Portugal.

30. Correspondence from Eurico José Teixeira to Ruy Morais Vaz, Secretary General of the União Nacional, 16 March 1939, União Nacional/Correspondência com a Comissão de Província de Cabo Verde, 1935-1952, PT/TT/UN-A/A-12-02/1, Arquivo Torre do Tombo, Lisbon, Portugal.

31. Correspondence from Adriano Duarte Silva, president of the Commission of the União Nacional in Cabo Verde, to General Eduardo Marques, 3 June 1939, União Nacional/Correspondência com a Comissão de Província de Cabo Verde, 1935-1952, PT/TT/UN-A/A-12-02/1, Arquivo Torre do Tombo, Lisbon, Portugal.

32. Ibid.

33. Correspondence from Adriano Duarte Silva, president of the Commission of the União Nacional in Cabo Verde, to General Eduardo Marques, 1 August 1939, União Nacional/Correspondência com a Comissão de Província de Cabo Verde, 1935-1952, PT/TT/UN-A/A-12-02/1, Arquivo Torre do Tombo, Lisbon, Portugal.

WORKS CITED

Baldoli, Claudia. 2003. *Exporting Fascism: Italian Fascists and Britain's Italians in 1930s*. Oxford: Berg.

Barros, Victor. 2009. *Campos de concentração em Cabo Verde: As ilhas como espaços de deportação e de prisão no Estado Novo*. Coimbra: Imprensa da Universidade de Coimbra.

Caetano, Marcello. 1977. *Minhas memórias de Salazar*. Lisboa: Verbo.

Caldeira, Arlindo Manuel. 1986. "O partido de Salazar: Antecedentes, organização e funções da União Nacional." *Análise Social* 22 (94): 943–77.

Caprariis, Luca de. 2000. "'Fascism for Export'? The Rise and Eclipse of the Fasci Italiani All'Estero." *Journal of Contemporary History* 35 (2): 151–83.

Cruz, Manuel Braga da. 1988. *O partido do estado no salazarismo*. Lisboa: Presença, 1988.

"Efemérides Caboverdeanas." 1945. *Notícias de Cabo Verde*, October 13, 1945, 2.

"Estatutos da União Nacional." 1932. *Diário do governo*, 1st series, no. 195, 1753–56. August 20, 1932. https://dre.pt/application/conteudo/563063.

Ferreira, Manuel. 1986. "Prefácio: O fulgor e a esperança de uma nova idade." In *Claridade—Revista de artes e letras*, xix–xlv. Praia: ALAC.

Gatlin, Darryle John. 1990. "A Socioeconomic History of São Vicente de Cabo Verde, 1830–1970." PhD diss., University of California Los Angeles.

Guimarães, José Marques. 2006. *A difusão do nativismo em África: Cabo Verde e Angola; Séculos XIX e XX*. Lisboa: África Debate.

"Homenagem à memoria do Sr. General Eduardo Marques." 1944. *Boletim Geral das Colónias* 20 (229): 144.

Jerónimo, Miguel Bandeira. 2015. *The "Civilising Mission" of Portuguese Colonialism, 1870–1930*. Basingstoke: Palgrave Macmillan.

Jerónimo, Miguel Bandeira, and José Pedro Monteiro. 2014. "O império do trabalho: Portugal, as dinâmicas do internacionalismo e os mundos coloniais." In *Portugal e o fim do colonialismo: Dimensões internacionais*, edited by Miguel Bandeira Jerónimo and António Costa Pinto, 15–54. Lisboa: Edições 70.

Kasza, Gregory James. 1995. *The Conscription Society: Administered Mass Organizations*. New Haven, CT: Yale University Press.

Leal, Ernesto Castro. 1998. "A Cruzada Nacional D. Nuno Álvares Pereira e as origens do Estado Novo (1918–1938)." *Análise Social* 33 (148): 823–51.

McKale, Donald M. 1977. *The Swastika outside Germany*. Kent, OH: Kent State University Press.

Neto, Sérgio. 2009. *Colónia mártir, colónia modelo: Cabo Verde no pensamento ultramarino português (1925–1965)*. Coimbra: Imprensa da Universidade de Coimbra.

Oliveira, João Nobre de. 1998. *A imprensa cabo-verdiana 1820–1975*. Macau: Fundação Macau.

Pinto, António Costa. 2015. *Os camisas azuis e Salazar: Rolão Preto e o fascismo em Portugal*. Lisboa: Edições 70.

———. 2006. "'Chaos' and 'Order': Preto, Salazar, and Charismatic Appeal in Inter-War Portugal." *Totalitarian Movements and Political Religions* 7 (2): 589–610.

———. 1992. "As elites políticas e a consolidação do salazarismo: O nacional sindicalismo e a União Nacional." *Análise Social* 27 (116–17): 575–613.

"Posse do novo Presidente da Comissão de Colónias da União Nacional." 1944. *Boletim Geral das Colónias* 20 (233): 77.

Rodrigues, Isabel P. B. Fêo. 2003. "Islands of Sexuality: Theories and Histories of Creolization in Cape Verde." *International Journal of African Historical Studies* 36 (1): 83–103.

Semedo, Manuel Brito. 2006. *A construção da identidade nacional: Análise da imprensa entre 1877 e 1975*. Praia: Instituto da Biblioteca Nacional e do Livro.

Silva, Adriano Duarte. 1945. "Povo de Cabo Verde." *Notícias de Cabo Verde*, November 10, 1945, 4.

Tavares, Eugénio, and Félix Monteiro. 1997. *Pelos jornais*. Praia: Instituto Caboverdeano do Livro e do Disco.

União Nacional (Portugal). 1930. *Manifesto da União Nacional*. Lisboa: Papelaria e Tipografia Fernandes.

"União Nacional." 1932. *União Nacional* (Luanda), December 3, 1932, 2.

"União Nacional em Angola: Mudança de orientação?" 1932. *União Nacional* (Luanda), November 16, 1932.

"A União Nacional em Cabo Verde." 1936. *Notícias de Cabo Verde*, December 15, 1936, 1.

ABEL DJASSI AMADO is Assistant Professor of Political Science and International Relations at Simmons University. His research focuses on the late colonial state in Cabo Verde and other former Portuguese colonies in Africa, the politics of language, and the political and diplomatic history of national liberation in Africa. His articles have appeared in *Lusotopie*, *Journal of Cape Verdean Studies*, *Desafios*, and *Oxford Research Encyclopedia of African History*. He is currently working on a manuscript that examines the language and politics nexus in Cabo Verde from a historical and comparative perspective. He is presently the chair of the Lusophone African Studies Organization.

ELSA PERALTA

The Memorialization of Empire in Postcolonial Portugal: Identity Politics and the Commodification of History

ABSTRACT: The entire experience of modern imperialism has profoundly shaped European national identities in ways that continue to matter in postimperial times. This is also true of Portugal; as the first and the most enduring of the European colonial empires, its end did not erase the self-image of the country as an imperial nation. Although refashioned in a matter of style and content, major public representations of the nation's collective identity remain anchored in the memory of empire. This official memory combines a strong emphasis on the period of the "Maritime Discoveries" with the representation of Portugal as the pioneer of cultural dialogue on a global scale and of the Portuguese as "inventors" of the modern world. In this article, I will address some examples of the way in which Portugal's imperial history has been memorialized to convey the country's "brand image," for the purposes of both identity politics and the tourism industry.

KEYWORDS: public memory, Portuguese empire, nationalism, cosmopolitanism, commodification

RESUMO: Toda a experiência do imperialismo moderno moldou profundamente as identidades nacionais europeias de maneiras que continuam a ser importantes nos tempos pós-imperiais. Este também é o caso de Portugal: sendo o primeiro e o mais duradouro império colonial europeu, o seu fim não apagou a auto-imagem do país como nação imperial. Embora remodelada em termos de estilo e conteúdo, as principais representações públicas da identidade coletiva da nação permanecem ancoradas na memória do império. Esta memória oficial combina uma forte ênfase no período das "Descobertas Marítimas" com a representação de Portugal como pioneiro do diálogo cultural à escala global e dos portugueses como "inventores" do mundo moderno. Neste artigo, abordarei alguns casos através dos quais a história imperial de Portugal foi memorializada para transmitir uma "imagem de marca" de Portugal, tanto para as políticas da identidade quanto para a indústria do turismo.

PALAVRAS-CHAVE: memória pública, Império Português, nacionalismo, cosmopolitismo, comodificação

Introduction

At the opening ceremony of the Eleventh Web Summit in Lisbon, in early November 2019, the mayor of Lisbon, Fernando Medina, offered an astrolabe to Paddy Cosgrave, the founder of the technology and entrepreneurship conference. As an instrument used by the navigators during the so-called Portuguese "Discoveries," the astrolabe possessed a symbolism that Medina emphasized at the time:

> Lisbon was the capital of the world five centuries ago, this was the starting point for routes to discover new worlds, new people, new ideas. From Lisbon departed a great adventure that connected the human race. . . . Today it is you, the engineers, the entrepreneurs, the creators, the innovators, the start-ups, all the companies. (Lusa 2017c)[1]

In addition to establishing a line of continuity between the Lisbon of five hundred years ago and the Lisbon of today, calling it "a city of entrepreneurs and scientists," Medina also stressed the welcoming character of Lisbon and the Portuguese society as a whole, concluding that "the innovation that Lisbon went through 500 years ago was due to the fact that the city and Portugal have an open society" and that "freedom, tolerance, diversity, the ability to understand and talk to each other are the values of Lisbon and the values that we want to keep for the future" (Lusa 2017c).

This narrative serves as one example (among many others) of how, in postcolonial times, the memory of the Portuguese colonial empire has been reshaped by political agents and public cultural institutions. In this reformulation, an almost exclusive emphasis on the historical memory associated with what is conventionally called the Portuguese "Maritime Discoveries"—corresponding to the voyages of maritime exploration that began in the fifteenth century and to the "golden age" of national history—is combined with the image of a modern and cosmopolitan country. Accordingly, Portugal is portrayed as a pioneer of cultural dialogue on a global scale and the Portuguese as "discoverers" of the modern world, while forgetting the system of asymmetrical power relations that also characterized Portuguese colonialism.

This narrative started to be regenerated in the mid-1980s, on the basis of old imperial myths woven since nineteenth-century liberalism and the First Republic (1910–1926) and intensified during the Estado Novo (1933–1974), but more recently has become adapted to the new postcolonial languages and the symbolic demands of European integration (Peralta 2017). After the fall of the Estado Novo regime in 1974 and the swift decolonization that followed, in the public political discourses—then characterized by a revolutionary tone—the former empire was a no-name land. But as the young Portuguese democracy was being successfully implemented and the country was on its way toward eventually acceding to the European Economic Market in 1986, Portuguese national identity started to be reworked to fit into the new political and cultural context of liberal democracies. In this way, Portugal's imperial history began to serve once again as a chief rhetorical tool for locating Portugal in a new space of European identity, a space now dominated by notions of multiculturalism and cosmopolitanism.

This rehabilitation began in 1983 with the inclusion of the Jerónimos Monastery and the Belém Tower in UNESCO's World Heritage List. UNESCO justifies this classification with the observation that the two monuments "reflect the power, knowledge and courage of the Portuguese people at a time when they consolidated their presence and domain of intercontinental trade routes" and recall "the pioneer role the Portuguese had in the 15th and 16th centuries in creating contacts, dialogue and interchange among different cultures" (UNESCO, n.d.). Since UNESCO is an institution that represents a culture of peace, democracy, and coöperation in the world, this permanent classification bestowed lasting praise and prestige, legitimating Portugal's imperial past, regardless of the political configurations that modeled the action (Harrison and Hitchcock 2005). On 12 June 1985, the Treaty of Accession of Portugal to the European Economic Community (EEC) was signed at the Jerónimos Monastery.[2] In 1986, the National Commission for the Commemoration of Portuguese Discoveries was created and its activity continued until 2002, representing a huge state effort to revise the historical record and restore historiographical legitimacy to the period of Portuguese maritime expansion.[3] This endeavor would culminate in the commemoration of five hundred years of the "Discoveries" and the staging of the 1998 Lisbon World Exposition (Expo'98) with the theme "Oceans." From then on, two perspectives would be key in the composition of Portugal's memorial landscape with respect to the country's imperial past. First, a pedagogical perspective on the history of the nation, conveyed by the most diverse sectors of Portuguese society with an interest in signaling the full democratic inclusion of the country in the European context. Second, a perspective of commodification, in which the past gains an exchange value in the cultural and tourist consumption market.

In this article, I will focus on several examples that show how these ideas were capitalized in postcolonial times to create a brand image of Portugal, targeting external audiences but also functioning robustly as a mechanism for reproducing the former imperial myths for domestic audiences. I will look at Expo'98 ("Oceans"), an event that completely refurbished the geography of the city, and also at several acts of public culture that have converged in conceptualizing Lisbon as a "Global City." Drawing on these examples, I argue that memory narratives are malleable and adaptable constructions that can be reworked to suit new identity demands and changing circumstances. For this, I use the concept of "cosmopolitan mythscapes," to which I will now turn.

Cosmopolitan Mythscapes: European Memory, National Identity, and Empire

Empire was intrinsic to the construction of European nation-states; imperial projects are part of the history and memory of Europe, and the national and imperial categories remain deeply intertwined (MacKenzie 1986; Hall and Rose 2006). Even if it is particularly evident in countries that were former imperial centers, this condition has encompassed the whole of the continent because all European nations were complicit and involved in the imperial enterprise in several ways (Buettner 2018). Indeed, the making of modern Europe meant that countries that were not imperial powers were nonetheless shaped by continental histories of empire. Europe itself was formed through unequal geopolitical power relations woven by empire, with various instances of "internal colonization" (Peralta and Jensen 2017). Several countries without empires abroad embarked on campaigns to forcibly assimilate peoples and ethnic minorities within their borders, as happened with the indigenous Sámi of northern Sweden, Norway, and Finland (Loftsdóttir and Jensen 2012). Internal colonialism has also applied to unequal power relations between imperial European nation-states, as in the case of Portugal, which was a subordinate participant in the imperial system, particularly through its dependent position in relation to the British Empire. European colonialism thus established a series of interconnected processes that have impacted former imperial centers, the whole of Europe, and the world at large, with the establishment of an unswerving racialized dichotomy of relations and the institutionalization of the modern nation-state, which favors a division of labor critical for the expansion of capitalist economies.

These power relations were not severed by decolonization. Empires, as structures of power and influence that span vast geographical spaces, may formally come to an end, but they continue beyond colonial rule through practices, subjectivities, and discourses (Wolfe 1997). As such, past imperial experience is a key component of the mythscape of the old European power centers and, in fact, the whole of Europe.

The concept of "mythscape" that I use here is drawn from the formulation suggested by Duncan S. A. Bell in a paper entitled "Mythscapes: Memory, Mythology, and National Identity" (2003). Acknowledging the importance and centrality of national myths and memories in the construction of national identities and narratives (Smith 1999), Bell sets out to challenge the mainstream and sometimes abusive usage of the term "memory," considering that what scholars so often refer to as "memories" should be more accurately termed "governing myths" of the nation. Bell thus proposes the concept of mythscape, defining it as

> the temporally and spatially extended discursive realm wherein the struggle for control of peoples' memories and the formation of nationalist myths is debated, contested and subverted incessantly. The mythscape is the page upon which the multiple and often conflicting nationalist narratives are (re) written; it is the perpetually mutating repository for the presentation of the past for the purposes of the present. (Bell 2003, 66)

According to this reading, national identities are constructed, debated, negotiated, and contested in specific instances by resorting to a series of preestablished myths. The original foundational myth or system of myths is rewritten over time and continually updated as current circumstances change, even though it may maintain its vitality. This makes it possible for a relatively unchanging structure of national myths to retain its constitutive coherence as it is constantly reworked and adapted according to the identity needs and ever-changing meanings given to the past by each present circumstance (Koshar 2000).

In former European imperial countries, mythscapes are inevitably associated with their imperial experience, which has left indelible marks on European cultural and symbolic landscapes. But the past is reworked to meet the demands of the new postcolonial setting established after the demise of European colonial empires following World War II. Decolonization entailed the transformation of former European imperial powers into postimperial nation-states. Moreover, putting an end to empires and building the institutional architecture of the European Community were equally part of Western European politics after 1945. Not only did borders, previous economic relations, and citizenship rights have to be redesigned; the disappearance of the colonial empires also caused a large movement of people (former colonizers as well as formerly colonized people) to relocate to Europe, while the European integration project encouraged the movement of citizens within the Community (Laschi, Deplano, and Pes 2020). Furthermore, decolonization itself was the result of the affirmation of wider regional and transnational alliances after the 1960s—such as the Afro-Asian coalition under the framework of the United Nations (Oliveira 2017)—with their blunt condemnation of colonialism, along with their claims for indigenous peoples' right to self-determination. It was the opening of a new era, a time for taking into consideration the demands of the new identity politics of the "native," "aboriginal," and "tribal" peoples and their growing presence on the world stage. This presence became even more apparent in the 1990s and was reflected, among other things, in the protests against the Columbian Quincentenary and against the ceremonies celebrating the "finding" of Brazil. Finally, the aftermath of the Second World War was characterized by an unprecedented globalization that continuously reshaped the world through global flows of people, technological innovations, capital, information, and ideas (Appadurai 1990).

In this changing context, former European imperial centers had to be imagined anew and the whole European colonial history renegotiated. Most often, this negotiation was conducted on the basis of a memorial display, still putting empire at the center of national identity definitions (Buettner 2016), which also served as an instrument for the creation of new political constituencies from former imperial governance systems, such as the British Commonwealth, French Francophonie, and Portuguese Lusofonia. Here, the negative connotations associated with the exploitative nature of empires are reformulated to appear beneficial to both colonizers and colonized, and are usually articulated around ideas of cosmopolitanism, multiculturalism, and intercultural dialogue. These fit in tidily with both the cultural assertions of globalized indigenous movements and the liberal agendas of cultural recognition that have characterized contemporary forms of multicultural governance (Clifford 2007). It is against this general background that gestures such as French President Emmanuel Macron's 2018 Report on the Restitution of African Art must be viewed and considered.

Therefore, returning to Bell's contribution, I argue that Europe's original governing myth—which framed its entire imperial expansionist experience—is of Europe as the bearer of a progressive civilization, structured by notions of discovery and forward motion. As Jacques Derrida noted,

> In its physical geography, and in what has often been called . . . its spiritual geography, Europe has always recognized itself as a cape or headland . . . the point of departure for discovery, invention, and colonization . . . that of an advanced point . . . and thus, once again, with a heading for world civilization or human culture in general. (1992, 24)

The idea that Europe is an advanced space, radically superior to the rest of the world in all its forms of social and political organization, appeared in the sixteenth century when the European West imposed its interpretation of space and time on the world (Goody 2006). The recurrent axioms of Eurocentric diffusionism of Europe as innately superior, progressive, and innovating thus justified on moral grounds the civilizing mission of Europe's imperial enterprise by pushing forward the backward peoples and territories of the "rest" of the world to catch up with Europe's modernity (Blaut 1993). This European model of progressive civilization accommodates ideas of cosmopolitanism from ancient Greek philosophy and Immanuel Kant's reinvention of cosmopolitanism in the late 1700s as a utopian treatise for universal citizenship, as deriving from virtue and reason (Wood 1998, 69).[4]

I argue that today's specific European mythscape continues to be composed of a particular representation of Europe as cosmopolitan, modern, and civilized. However, because of the changing context imposed by the new world order post–World War II, this mythscape, while still maintaining its vitality, had to be reworked as a result of the new identity politics drawn in a context marked by complex interdependencies and everyday encounters with difference. Cosmopolitanism thus became reframed as a welcoming of difference, or, in Ulf Hannerz's words, "a willingness to engage with the other . . . an intellectual and aesthetic openness towards divergent cultural experiences" (1990, 239). This construct points toward both postcolonialism and neocolonialism. On the one hand, it allows for the transition of former European imperial centers to postcolonial nations, but without putting an end to their respective governing myths that stem from imperial history. On the other, it is shaped by paternalistic undertones as it reveals the ways in which colonial expansionist enterprises continue to inform contemporary debates on cultural and social diversity (Clifford 2007).

With this conceptual framework in mind, I now turn to the case of Portugal to explore continuities in the ways national identity and empire have been narrated in colonial and postcolonial times, and to analyze how these narratives are structured by a governing European mythology of discovery and forward motion.

Expo'98 and Postimperial Discourse

Portugal's image as the "country of the Discoveries" and pioneer of cultural contact on a global scale has been widely used by successive democratic governments and various public bodies to brand Portugal for both internal and external audiences. Through these actions, the depth of historical experience is combined with aspirations of modernity, thus claiming for Portugal a symbolic and geostrategic position that centers around, on the one hand, its full integration into the European context and, on the other, its demarcated pioneering vocation. The most definitive and paradigmatic action in terms of rehabilitating Portuguese imperial history in postcolonial times was the 1998 Lisbon World Exposition ("Oceans"), an event that would reconfigure the entire geography of the city.

Expo'98 took place in Lisbon from 22 May to 30 September 1998, and it lay within the legal framework governing international exhibitions established by the Bureau International des Expositions (BIE). Advertised as "the last exhibition of the twentieth century," Expo'98 focused on a specific theme: "The Oceans: A Heritage for the Future." As stated in the *Final Report of the Exhibition*,

> The idea to hold an international exhibition in Lisbon arose within the context of the work of the National Committee for the Commemoration of the Portuguese Discoveries, the objective of which was to organize a series of different events to commemorate the historical significance of the Portuguese Discoveries in the closing decades of the fifteenth century, which culminated in the first sea voyage to India, made by Vasco da Gama in 1498, and the commemoration of the arrival of Pedro Álvares Cabral in Brazil, in 1500. The historical relevance of Expo'98 therefore coincided with Vasco da Gama's sea voyage to India, where he arrived on 22 May 1498, thus opening up new perspectives for economic and commercial relations at that time, and promoting a process of intercultural exchange, which had major consequences for humankind. (Exposição Mundial de Lisboa 1999, 18)

This statement makes clear that the purpose of Expo'98 was to redeem the notion that Portugal's national history is linked to maritime expansion. But in order to legitimize this reworking, the exhibition updated earlier imperial discourse and dressed it in modern clothes by using oceans as thematic material and relating it to issues of sustainable management and environmental protection, which are the contemporary concerns of so-called modern, developed countries. Through this diplomatic endeavor around the global management of oceanographic resources, the designers of the exhibition were targeting the international promotion of the country and its image (Ferreira 2005). As António Mega Ferreira, former director of Expo'98, wrote in the *Official Guide to the Exhibition*,

> It was essential, when defining the concept, to understand that the Lisbon exhibition should distinguish itself from other recent events of the same type by the attention given to its main theme. Therefore, an ambitious thematic program was proposed, the aim of which was to place the oceans, their diversity and essential role in the equilibrium of the planet, at the center of the attention of the international community. . . . A strictly historical approach was therefore eschewed in favor of an orientation that approached the theme in terms of its future perspectives, by relating it to science, politics, technology, and art. The aim was to propose a new ethics regarding the relationship of humankind to the environment, a theme that seemed to us central to the political agenda of the twenty-first century. (Exposição Mundial de Lisboa 1999, 18)

Portugal was hereby represented, yet again, as leading the way to European and Western futures opened up by a reaffirmation of the faith in science, commerce, civilization, and modernity. By these means, Portuguese imperial discourses were reworked so the enhancement of the historical legacy of "Portuguese Discoveries" could be seen as a "gift to modernity," thus reclaiming a key position in the wider European identity construct in which Portugal was now placed. The whole exhibition was conceived to enhance and update this supposed gift, counteracting the secondary and peripheral role of Portugal within modern Europe. The thematic pavilions on the site included the Knowledge of the Seas Pavilion, the Oceans Pavilion, the Utopia Pavilion, the Pavilion of the Future, the Virtual Reality Pavilion (where visitors were given the virtual opportunity to travel to the depths of the ocean), and the Pavilion of Portugal. In addition, there were three "thematic areas": the Nautical Exhibition, the Garcia de Orta Gardens (named after the botanist who played a key role in generating knowledge through imperial expansion), and the Water Gardens. The exhibition also accommodated the pavilions of the various national and corporate participants, restaurants and shops, a new theater (Camões Theater), and a new metro station, Gare do Oriente, that opened into the main entrance to the exhibition site.

All in all, Expo'98 was an ambitious enterprise that embraced not only the mounting of an international exhibition but also the building of an entirely new area in the city of Lisbon. It comprised the urban regeneration of a rundown area covering nearly 340 hectares of eastern Lisbon on the bank of the Tagus River. This was previously an abandoned outlying area, characterized by insalubrious and dangerous premises, a sign of the decay that accompanies the transition from an industry-based to a service economy. Building the exhibition site in this area would bring it urban amenities, transport and communication infrastructure, and innovative systems and techniques for the provision of urban services. Together with the construction of architecturally appealing buildings in the area, this development would enhance the image of the city and the country in general to a level comparable with major European capitals, that is, modern, clean, orderly, cosmopolitan, and ecologically balanced. As noted by Patrícia Pereira (2018), the transformation of the urban fabric of the Portuguese capital wrought by Expo'98 is part of a global competition between port cities as they seek to assert themselves as vibrant European metropolises. Within this movement, waterfronts emerge as showcases for cities, contributing to their international recognition and helping to anchor new dynamics of tourism and gentrification, with an impact on the sectors of commerce, services, housing, culture, and leisure. The aesthetics of the world fair, the regeneration of the surrounding area, the construction of architecturally advanced homes and services, and the functional layout of the site were combined with powerful allusions to the country's seafaring and imperial past. Once the fair was over, the site was given the name Parque das Nações (literally, Park of Nations) and its streets were named after Portuguese navigators or entities alluding to the empire. The poetics of the space (with theaters, bridges, schools, and streets baptized with names taken from the theme of the "Discoveries") worked to establish a strong intimacy with the empire, embodied in the very experience of the space itself (Peralta and Domingos 2019).

The sea (or oceans) as the route to cultural encounters on a global scale and as a metaphor for a modern nation that is multifaceted and tolerant was converted into the chief rhetorical tool to locate Portugal in a new European identity space. This metaphor strategically publicizes an image of a modern and progressive country, one that is not stuck in its own past but that, then and now, is essentially expansionist, modern, and enterprising, a reading very accommodating to the neoliberal agendas with which the country's representatives were aiming to dialogue. Portugal was on show. The *Final Report of the Exhibition* is again instructive in this respect:

> A "Projection of Portugal in the World" and an urban regeneration and implementation of the exhibition in accordance with "the highest standards of quality and efficiency," which involves proving the modernity of the country and its capacity to plan and implement very complex projects: these are the primary strategic goals of the global project.
>
> These goals took form, in accordance with the program presented by the Expo'98 Commission, in November 1993, as the following seven objectives: 1) To evoke the pioneering and decisive contribution of the Portuguese Discoveries to the process of European expansion, in the fifteenth and sixteenth centuries, which led to an improved understanding of Man and the configuration of the planet, by projecting it into the future; 2) To reaffirm and give expression to the Portuguese vocation for peaceful and mutually beneficial encounters between different peoples and cultures; 3) To publicize the reality of a modern country, which is fully committed to the process of modernization and integration within a wider economic and institutional space; 4) To create an event with a worldwide projection, capable of creating a unique opportunity for the European Community to publicize and create a public awareness to the projects, activity and objectives of the Community in areas related to the exhibition theme; 5) To make a contribution to the affirmation of Lisbon as a great Atlantic city, by intervening in the renewal of its urban fabric in a creative and lasting manner; 6) To provide for the creation in Lisbon, in 1998, of a *forum* for the evaluation of the state of current knowledge about the oceans, thus contributing to the desirable creation of new systems to manage the planet's liquid mass and to preserve the ecological balance, by way of the rational use of marine resources; 7) To stimulate business activity in Portugal through the expansion of specific areas of the service and transport sectors and domestic industry and the creation of jobs. (Exposição Mundial de Lisboa 1999, 29–31)

Under the sign of the oceans, Expo'98 bridged the past—the Portuguese navigations and the maritime explorations—to the future: environmental concerns and oceanographic research. Adapted to globalizing languages, this image was fundamental to signal Portugal's position as an advanced service economy, as required by European integration itself. As Francisco Bethencourt notes,

> History is now used by the democratic power as a mere reference for cultural and tourist marketing, stripped as much as possible of its ideological burden, as it only serves as a way of drawing attention to a recognized past in other countries, making the ability of the Portuguese and their participation in building the future a central point. (1999, 450)

Expo'98 is thus a paradigmatic case of the way in which imperial discourses and earlier national mythologies were adapted to suit new identity needs in light of the challenges posed by Portugal's new European positioning. Cleansed of the previous associations with colonial institutions, the country's historical past was rehabilitated in the service of new identity negotiations. In those negotiations, the image of an imperialism without colonies emerges, picturing the country as having pioneered cultural encounters around the globe according to its new self-conceived position within a modern, democratic, multicultural, and cosmopolitan Europe (Neves 2019). To this end, the exhibition focused on the history of the Portuguese empire, particularly in the late fifteenth and early sixteenth centuries, searching in this past for the myths in which Portugueseness should be grounded at the end of the twentieth century, and thus articulating a postcolonial interpretation of the country's colonial past. The image of the country that Expo'98 projected, both nationally and internationally, was of Portugal as a European pioneer. As such, the country was overtly and intentionally reclaiming a high-ranking place in contemporary Europe, in spite of its peripheral geographic, political, and economic position. As noted by Marcus Power and James Sidaway, "In this spirit, Portugal has positioned itself as the exemplary European nation, insofar as it was the supposed pioneer exploration; the site of departure" (2005, 879).

Lisbon, Global City

Portugal's association with the ideas of leadership, discovery, and innovation, rewritten in accordance with the legacy of the "Discoveries," was successively capitalized, following the rhetorical reformulation carried out by Expo'98, through various public-culture initiatives and their branding of Portugueseness.[5] These initiatives conveyed an image of Portugal as an entrepreneurial, modern, and cosmopolitan country, together with the idea of an open and unbiased society, which is attractive to the tourism market and offers security to foreign investment. This was to be the happy result of a tolerant, nonracist, and hybridizing (imperial) history. The clear purpose of these operations was to place Portugal in the symbolic space of the West—modern, cosmopolitan, and enterprising—while using the country's imperial and maritime history and its supposed civilizational legacy as its foundation.

This representation finds its zenith in Lisbon; formerly the empire's capital, Lisbon is increasingly represented as the first global city in the history of the modern world, in line with the increasingly sustained interpretation of Portugal as the "pioneer of globalization" (Devezas and Rodrigues 2007). This is the favored representation reproduced in tour guides and websites geared to the touristic promotion of the country and of Lisbon in particular. For example, on the GoLisbon website, an online tourist information platform, Lisbon is presented to potential visitors through a semantics of tropes such as discovery, expansion, contact, and innovation. On the home page, two headings that read "Discovering the City of the Sea; The City of Explorers" and "Europe Starts Here—Welcome to Europe's West Coast!" are followed by a paragraph describing Lisbon as

> Europe's second-oldest capital (after Athens), once home to the world's greatest explorers, . . . becoming the first true world city, the capital of an empire spreading over all continents—from South America (Brazil) to Asia (Macao, China; Goa, India). (GoLisbon 2021)

This predominant representation of Lisbon as a global city was also used as a differentiating factor in the 2009 presentation of the *Carta Estratégica de Lisboa 2010/24* (Lisbon Strategic Charter 2010/24). In response to the fifth question posed in the charter—"How to Affirm the Identity of Lisbon in a Globalized World?"—Commissioner Simonetta Luz Afonso and her team proposed establishing a "Lisbon Brand" that would clearly identify the "Lisbon product" in a highly competitive tourism market. Her suggestion was that this brand should be sought in a renewed, "uncomplicated and modern," relationship with the national past:

> What would be the distinguishing proposal of Lisbon? Is it Lisbon the city of departures and arrivals? The city of travel? From the Discoveries to Bernardo Soares's disquiet, that great inner journey of Fernando Pessoa. Political discourse always tends to insist on modernity, which is certainly important, but

> don't those who visit us want to know more about our past? Wouldn't there be more visitors if we had an uncomplicated, modern discourse about the past? A past that has made Lisbon an exemplary city from the standpoint of tolerance. (Câmara Municipal de Lisboa 2009, 9)

As we can clearly infer from these words, the production of difference for the tourist consumer market involves the composition of a cosmopolitan memory, which, while maintaining or even strengthening national or local memory configurations, reshapes them in global terms. The modernizing discourse ends up fitting in syncretically with the depths of historical discourse to construct the image of a cosmopolitan, modern city that projects historical heritage as a differentiating asset for the future. The issues of national identity, once mobilized by ideological agendas, are now repositioned by reference to the demands of the consumer and leisure markets, especially tourism, increasingly compounding what Daniel Levy and Natan Sznaider (2002) have termed cosmopolitan memory cultures.

These discourses are strongly imprinted on the space of Lisbon itself, leaving their mark on both the territorialization of urban space and the processes of urban development and regeneration, often carried out in certain old and degraded neighborhoods in central Lisbon such as Mouraria and the squares of Martim Moniz and Intendente. Historically inhabited by poor and marginalized populations (Frangella 2013), which in recent years have been joined by various niches of immigrants, including Indian, Chinese, and Bangladeshi populations, these areas of the city have recently been the subject of a rehabilitation program initiated in 2010 by Lisbon's City Council. Like the models of multicultural governance of the main European capitals, the planned intervention in the urban space was not limited to upgrading buildings, but extended to an intervention in the field of local memory and related social representations whose main "leitmotif is diversity" (Oliveira 2013, 580). The performance of various cultural activities in the area, such as the Todos: Walk of Cultures Festival and the Fusion Market, seeks to create practical conditions and structures for the functioning of interculturality in the area, while at the same time mobilizing creative production, attracting gentrifiers, and capturing tourists who seek "authenticity." Intervention in this area of the city has thus been "built and grounded around diversity and interculturality as synonymous with cosmopolitanism and tolerance" (Oliveira 2013, 582), updating prevailing lusotropical myths inherited from earlier imperial ideologies

(Castelo 1999), which are now converted into economic and symbolic resources prone to encourage postmodern lifestyles and consumption patterns. In these instances, the destabilizing experiences of race, ethnicity, and class are read in the light of ideas such as multiculturalism and intercultural dialogue, which function as differentiating features in the market of global cities.

The same effect has been pursued through several acts of public culture. In this context, two exhibitions deserve special mention. Both took place at the National Museum of Ancient Art (MNAA) in Lisbon and conveyed an association of Portuguese imperial history with a globalizing enterprise. The first of these exhibitions was entitled *Encompassing the Globe: Portugal and the World in the Sixteenth and Seventeenth Centuries* and was featured at the MNAA between July and October 2009. This exhibition was originally produced by the Smithsonian Institution and displayed in the Smithsonian's Sackler Gallery in Washington, DC, between June and September 2007. In Portugal, the exhibition, which was sponsored by the Portuguese government, brought together 170 pieces, including some national treasures that had not been included in the original event.

The exhibition was structured around six geographical areas that followed the course of the Portuguese voyages of expansion. The first unit, focused on Portugal and sixteenth-century Europe, was followed by sections dedicated to Africa, India, China, Japan, and finally Brazil. Focusing on the first voyages of maritime expansion made by the Portuguese and the effect of these on the dissemination of knowledge about the world throughout Europe, the exhibition aimed to enhance the role of Portugal as the undisputed pioneer of the present globalization era. At the same time, it emphasized the beneficial contribution of the Portuguese voyages to establishing contacts and interaction between all peoples around the planet, thus creating the conditions for the cultivation of a markedly modern worldview. As stated by Aníbal Cavaco Silva, the President of the Portuguese Republic at the time of the opening of the exhibition, in the preface to the exhibition catalog,

> Portugal is one of the oldest states in Europe and the westernmost of the Old Continent. Since the beginning of its history, the sea has always been present, both as a source of natural resources and as an open frontier, stimulating the connection with the most diverse peoples, civilizations, and cultures. The voyages by Portugal's navigators that began in the fifteenth century, and which, in the words of poet Luís de Camões, gave "new worlds to

> the world," owe much to this experience gained by the people in maritime activities and the knowledge acquired in their contacts with other peoples. (Museu Nacional da Arte Antiga 2009, 5)

The second exhibition, titled *The Global City: Lisbon in the Renaissance* was on display at the MNAA between 24 February and 9 April 2017. It featured 249 pieces belonging to 77 Portuguese and foreign lenders, and was anchored by two paintings of unproven origin depicting Rua Nova dos Mercadores, "Lisbon's main trading artery in the fifteenth century, full of merchants, mummers, musicians, hawkers, knights, jewelry, silks, spices, exotic animals, and other wonders imported from Africa, Brazil, Asia" (Museu Nacional de Arte Antiga 2017). The purpose of the exhibition was, as stated on the MNAA website (2017), to "rebuild the heart of the most global city in Renaissance Europe," based on the argument that, in the transition from the fifteenth to the sixteenth century, Lisbon became a global city because objects and people from different origins and continents converged there. According to the exhibition's curators, Annemarie Jordan Gschwend and Kate Lowe (2015), there are five reasons for conceiving fifteenth-century Lisbon as a global city: the fact that it was at the center of the movement of commercial products; its population being a mixture of indigenous people (that is, Lisbon-born or Portuguese), other Europeans, and people from all over the globe; its "global consciousness"; its recognition by other cities as having this capability; and lastly, its position at the forefront of new forms of knowledge, technology, and communication.

Aside from these conceptualizations, the exhibition lacked a fuller contextualization of the curators' arguments and generated considerable criticism. Furthermore, the authenticity of the paintings of Rua Nova dos Mercadores was seriously called into question. The curators attributed their authorship to an unknown Flemish artist, who would have painted them sometime between 1570 and 1619, and contended that they belonged to the collection of the nineteenth-English painter Dante Gabriel Rossetti. However, several historians have questioned the paintings' provenance and authenticity: João Alves Dias, after having studied several elements of the paintings in detail, is certain that it is "a painting forged in the twentieth century to imitate the past"; for his part, Diogo Ramada Curto considers it impossible for the paintings to have belonged to Dante Gabriel Rossetti's collection and believes that their authenticity remains to be proven (Cadete, Carita, and Franco 2017). Even greater criticism was directed at the promoted interpretation of Lisbon as a global city in the fifteenth century. After all, who was depicted in the paintings? Barefoot Black people—most certainly slaves—occupied in menial tasks are the most noticeable facet of the many hierarchies of power that stand out in these works. Only very euphemistically could one consider them as proof that fifteenth-century Lisbon was a place for the meeting of cultures on a global scale. Ramada Curto again spearheaded this criticism in an article in the Portuguese weekly newspaper *Expresso*, which contested these interpretations, giving expression to a postcolonial critique that was beginning to take shape in Portuguese society at a time when the country was increasingly haunted by rampant national debt (Curto 2017).

Contesting Mythscapes and the Rewriting of History

Instead of being extinguished due to ruptures in the political and social order, national narratives are often updated and reconfigured to meet the demands and aspirations of each new present. In the case of Portugal, the imperial narrative that had structured national identity over several generations and successive regimes was renovated in the postcolonial period, either for reasons of internal identification or to respond to yearnings for political and economic affirmation on the international stage. As before, this narrative continues to revolve strongly around the early voyages of "discovery" and expansion, regarded as the "golden age" of national history. This focus on the idea and image of the empire closely approximates the phenomenon observed by Paul Gilroy in *Postcolonial Melancholia* (2005); as in the British case, so in Portugal there seems to be—notwithstanding the obvious differences between the two contexts—a refusal to accept the symbolic loss of the empire that had previously provided a sense of coherence to national culture. This image not only remains vivid in the national social fabric but is also deeply internalized by Portuguese of all social origins and generational strata (Cabecinhas and Cunha 2003). It even pervades the imagination of people visiting the country, who, subjected to Portugal's unequivocal representation as conveyed by the tourist information media, are seduced by a particular idea of history that is highly mythicized.

However, returning to the concept of "mythscape" suggested by Bell (2003), it should be noted that the governing myths of nations, whatever their stability, are incessantly subjected to debate, contestation, and subversion, in particular when a previously excluded national population forces its own writing upon history. The political mediation of the legacies of imperial power is conditioned by the migrant flow from the former colonies to Portugal and becomes prominent in the tensions and ambivalences that characterize the relationship between the white Portuguese population and the populations that came from Portugal's former colonies and their descendants. These are often perceived within the framework of the assimilationist model inherited from the colonial past, which conveys the idea of a cultural hybridism characterized by peaceful coexistence with racial and cultural difference. However, these assimilationist myths are usually in stark contrast to the pressing social marginality that often afflicts the descendants of migrants from former colonies and the neighborhoods in which they live, on the outskirts of Lisbon. As in other European capital cities that were formerly imperial power centers, ongoing material structures of inequality in Lisbon are significantly calling Portugal's governing myths into question. Embattled immigrant suburbs, together with the Euro deficit and the consequences of the financial crisis, are altering the image of Europe as a model of progressive civilization (Behr and Stivachtis 2015).

In this overall context, although there has been an increasing tendency toward the commodification of the national past (which contributes to a deflation of its ideological content), areas of contestation and articulation of counter-memories with regard to the legacy of the country's imperial past have also emerged, especially in recent years. Calls for a more problematizing representation of Portugal's colonial past reached unprecedented proportions in 2017. In that year, the *Testimonials of Slavery: African Memory* series of exhibitions was organized as part of the Lisbon 2017 Ibero-American Capital of Culture agenda (Lusa 2017b). This agenda also included the exhibition *Racism and Citizenship*, held in the Monument to the Discoveries (Padrão dos Descobrimentos 2017). At the same time, several associations of Afrodescendants active in the field of memory were created, such as the Djass Association, which in 2017 submitted a proposal to the Lisbon City Council's Participatory Budget to create a Memorial to the Victims of Slavery in Lisbon (Djass 2017). Several controversies arose with the emergence of divergent readings on the legacies of Portugal's imperial past. One of these disputes was triggered during the state visit of the President of the Portuguese Republic, Marcelo Rebelo de Sousa, to Senegal in April 2017. Specifically, at the end of his visit to a former slave-trading post on the island of Gorée, where Pope John Paul II had apologized for slavery, Marcelo Rebelo de Sousa stated that Portugal recognized the injustice of slavery when it abolished the institution in part of its territory "by the hand of the Marquis of Pombal in

1761" (Lusa 2017a). In response to these statements, an open letter was published in the newspaper *Diário de Notícias* on 19 April 2017, entitled "A Return to the Past in Gorée: Not in Our Name" and signed by numerous academics and intellectuals, who thus repudiated the "politics of memory advocated by the political powers in Portugal" in relation to the country's legacy of colonialism (*Diário de Notícias* 2017).

Another controversy that arose that year was associated with the inauguration of a statue in Largo Trindade Coelho, in Lisbon, to honor Father António Vieira—a distinguished Jesuit clergyman who was born in the Portuguese capital in 1608 and died in Bahia, Brazil, in 1697. At the inauguration ceremony, Fernando Medina, the mayor of Lisbon, considered it an essential tribute to "one of the greatest personalities of Portuguese thought," so far without "the proper expression of recognition" in the city (Barros 2017). The inauguration of the statue again provoked a protest, firstly because António Vieira accepted slavery, albeit selectively, and, secondly, because of the sculptural design chosen for the statue, which depicts the clergyman in a clear position of dominance over indigenous figures who are represented as children. The group Descolonizando (Decolonizing) called a demonstration to protest the statue.[6] However, the organization was unable to carry out the proposed action, scheduled for 5 October 2017, because of the presence of far-right groups on the site.

Still in 2017, a heated reaction met a proposal, included in Medina's electoral platform, for the City Council of Lisbon to create a Museum of the Discoveries (Silva 2020). More than one hundred academics, historians, and social scientists from national and foreign institutions signed and published an open letter in the *Expresso* newspaper, entitled "Why a Museum Dedicated to the Portuguese 'Expansion' and the Processes It Has Unleashed Cannot and Should Not Be Called 'Discoveries Museum.'" According to the letter, the term "discoveries" "crystallizes a historical inaccuracy," since the word "only refers to the perception of reality from the point of view of the European peoples," whereas "for the non-Europeans, the idea that they were 'discovered' is problematic." In conclusion, the letter's authors stated that, "at a time when debates on Portuguese colonial history intensify, . . . it is important that a new museum should also be a reflection of this problematizing richness" (Margato 2018).

All these initiatives were unprecedented in calling for a more problematic and critical memory of the long Portuguese imperial history that does not refer exclusively to the "golden age" of the "Discoveries." Thus, while the imperial past is still a memorial reference to national identity, these instances of countermemory have contributed to break the "dialogical forgetting" in relation to the imperial past in Portuguese society (Assmann 2010, 9–11). At the same time, countermemories add to the growing debate on identity politics that in recent years has become apparent in Portugal. It is difficult to predict how the governing myths of the Portuguese nation will adapt to this newly contested landscape. In today's overall scenario of global crisis, former imperial myths and mentalities seem to have gained a second life, often testifying to a grip on a nostalgic and biased version of the colonial past. However, this phenomenon sometimes helps to initiate a more complex debate on the legacies of colonialism, which still exert an influence on cultures and social relations, not only in former empires like Portugal, but also in Europe as a whole, which, as Benoit De L'Estoile (2008) has claimed, was shaped both objectively and subjectively by the imperial experience. As scholars, it is our task to continue to observe and analyze the unfolding of events that point to the renewed ways in which individuals and communities make sense of times past and present.

NOTES

1. All translations from Portuguese are mine.

2. The Jerónimos Monastery was also the venue for the signing of the Treaty of Lisbon on 13 December 2007.

3. For details of the activities of the Commission, see Oliveira 2003.

4. Cosmopolitanism is an ancient term with roots in the third century BC (e.g., the philosophy of the Stoics).

5. A good example of these initiatives was the national campaign launched in 2007, when the Treaty of Lisbon was signed at the Jerónimos Monastery. The campaign, called *Portugal: Europe's West Coast*, was sponsored by the Ministry of Economy and Innovation, Turismo de Portugal, and the Portuguese Agency for Investment and Foreign Trade (AICEP), with the aim of promoting Portugal's image abroad.

6. Descolonizando is a Facebook group composed of "researchers, teachers, artists, and activists from different nationalities" whose aim is "reflecting, discussing, and acting to promote the construction of a critical narrative and the elimination of racism and inequality" (https://www.facebook.com/Descolonizando-1948301182079309).

WORKS CITED

Appadurai, Arjun. 1990. "Disjuncture and Difference in the Global Cultural Economy." *Theory, Culture & Society* 7 (2–3): 295–310.

Assmann, Aleida. 2010. "From Collective Violence to a Common Future: Four Models for Dealing with a Traumatic Past." In *Conflict, Memory Transfers and the Reshaping of Europe*, edited by Helena Gonçalves da Silva, Adriana Alves de Paula Martins, Filomena Viana Guarda, and José Miguel Sardica, 8–23. Newcastle upon Tyne: Cambridge Scholars Publishing.

Barros, Filomena. 2017. "Padre António Vieira: Feita justiça a 'um símbolo' que deixou 'um legado imenso.'" Rádio Renascença, June 22, 2017. https://rr.sapo.pt/2017/06/23/religiao/padre-antonio-vieira-feita-justica-a-um-simbolo-que-deixou-um-legado-imenso/noticia/86965/.

Bell, Duncan S. A. 2003. "Mythscapes: Memory, Mythology, and National Identity." *British Journal of Sociology* 54 (1): 63–81.

Behr, Hartmut, and Yannis A. Stivachtis, eds. 2015. *Revisiting the European Union as Empire.* London: Routledge.

Bethencourt, Francisco. 1999. "A memória da expansão." In *Último império e recentramento (1930–1998)*, edited by Francisco Bethencourt and Kirti Chaudhuri, 442–80. Vol. 5 of *História da Expansão Portuguesa*. Lisboa: Círculo de Leitores.

Blaut, James M. 1993. *The Colonizer's Model of the World*. New York: The Guilford Press.

Buettner, Elizabeth. 2016. *Europe after Empire: Decolonization, Society, and Culture.* Cambridge: Cambridge University Press.

———. 2018. "European Entanglements." In *Keywords/ECHOES: European Colonial Heritage Modalities in Entangled Cities*. https://keywordsechoes.com/european-entanglements.

Cabecinhas, Rosa, and Luís Cunha. 2003. "Colonialismo, identidade nacional e representações do 'negro.'" *Estudos do Século XX*, no. 3, 157–84.

Cadete, Miguel, Alexandra Carita, and Hugo Franco. 2017. "Museu de Arte Antiga abre as portas a obras suspeitas." *Expresso*, February 21, 2017. https://expresso.pt/cultura/2017-02-21-Museu-de-Arte-Antiga-abre-as-portas-a-obras-suspeitas.

Câmara Municipal de Lisboa. 2009. "Carta estratégica 2010-2024 – Relatório da Pergunta 5." https://www.lisboa.pt/fileadmin/municipio/camara/documentos/Relatorio_5_Identidade_Cultura.pdf.

Castelo, Cláudia. 1999. *'O modo português de estar no mundo': O luso-tropicalismo e a ideologia colonial portuguesa, 1933–1961*. Porto: Afrontamento.

Clifford, James. 2007. "Quai Branly in Process." *October*, no. 120 (Spring): 3–23.

Curto, Diogo Ramada. 2017. "Lisboa era uma cidade global?" *Expresso*, February 26, 2017. https://expresso.pt/cultura/2017-02-26-Lisboa-era-uma-cidade-global--1.

De L'Estoile, Benoit. 2008. "The Past as It Lives Now: An Anthropology of Colonial Legacies." *Social Anthropology* 16 (3): 267–79.

Derrida, Jacques. 1992. *The Other Heading: Reflections on Today's Europe*. Bloomington: Indiana University Press.

Devezas, Tessaleno, and Jorge Nascimento Rodrigues. 2007. *Portugal: O pioneiro da globalização*. Lisboa: Edições Centro Atlântico.

Diário de Notícias. 2017. "Um regresso ao passado em Gorée: Não em nosso nome." April 19, 2017. https://www.dn.pt/portugal/um-regresso-ao-passado-em-goree-nao-em-nosso-nome-6228800.html.

Djass (@associacao.djass). 2017. "Queremos erigir em Lisboa um Memorial às Vítimas da Escravatura." Facebook, November 2, 2017. https://www.facebook.com/associacao.djass/posts/1759579381004239.

Exposição Mundial de Lisboa. 1998. *Relatório final da exposição*. Lisboa: Parque Expo.

Ferreira, Claudino. 2005. *A Expo'98 e os imaginários do Portugal contemporâneo: Cultura, celebração e políticas de representação*. PhD diss., Universidade de Coimbra.

Frangella, Simone. 2013. "'Fomos conhecer um tal de Arroios': Construção de um lugar na imigração brasileira em Lisboa." In *Cidade e Império: Dinâmicas coloniais e reconfigurações pós-coloniais*, edited by Nuno Domingos and Elsa Peralta, 463–502. Lisboa: Edições 70.

Gilroy, Paul. 2005. *Postcolonial Melancholia*. New York: Columbia University Press.

GoLisbon. 2021. "Europe Starts Here—Welcome to Europe's West Coast!" https://www.golisbon.com/.

Goody, Jack. 2006. *The Theft of History*. Cambridge: Cambridge University Press.

Gschwend, Annemarie Jordan, and K. J. P. Lowe. 2015. *The Global City: On the Streets of Renaissance Lisbon*. London: Paul Holberton Publishing.

Hall, Catherine, and Sonya O. Rose, eds. 2006. *At Home with the Empire: Metropolitan Culture and the Imperial World*. Cambridge: Cambridge University Press.

Hannerz, Ulf. 1990. "Cosmopolitans and Locals in World Culture." *Theory, Culture & Society* 7 (2–3): 237–51.

Harrison, David, and Michael Hitchcock, eds. 2005. *The Politics of World Heritage: Negotiating Tourism and Conservation*. Wiltshire: Cromwell Press.

Koshar, Rudy. 2000. *From Monuments to Traces: Artifacts of German Memory 1870–1990*. Berkeley: University of California Press.

Laschi, Giuliana, Valeria Deplano, and Alessandro Pes, eds. 2020. *Europe between Migrations, Decolonization and Integration (1945–1992)*. London: Routledge.

Levy, Daniel, and Natan Sznaider. 2002. *The Holocaust and Memory in the Global Age*. Philadelphia: Temple University Press.

Loftsdóttir, Kristín, and Lars Jensen, eds. 2012. *Whiteness and Postcolonialism in the Nordic Region: Exceptionalism, Migrant Others, and National Identities*. London: Routledge.

Lusa. 2017a. "Portugal reconheceu injustiça da escravatura quando a aboliu em 1761, diz Marcelo." *Público*, April 13, 2017. https://www.publico.pt/2017/04/13/politica/noticia/portugal-reconheceu-injustica-da-escravatura-quando-a-aboliu-em-1761-diz-marcelo-1768680.

———. 2017b. "Projecto *Testemunhos da Escravatura: Memória africana* apresentado em Lisboa." *Público Ípsilon*, April 22, 2017. https://www.publico.pt/2017/04/22/culturaipsilon/noticia/projeto-testemunhos-da-escravatura-memoria-africana-e-hoje-apresentado-em-lisboa-1769684.

———. 2017c. "Web Summit: Medina presenteia fundador com astrolábio, que marca uma nova aventura." *Diário de Notícias*, November 6, 2017. https://www.dn.pt/lusa/web-summit-medina-presenteia-fundador-com-astrolabio-que-marca-uma-nova-aventura-8898766.html.

MacKenzie, John, ed. 1986. *Imperialism and Popular Culture*. Manchester: Manchester University Press.

Margato, Cristina. 2018. "A controvérsia sobre um Museu que ainda não existe: Descobertas ou Expansão?" *Expresso*, April 18, 2018. https://expresso.pt/cultura/2018-04-12-A-controversia-sobre-um-Museu-que-ainda-nao-existe.-Descobertas-ou-Expansao-.

Museu Nacional da Arte Antiga. 2017. "A cidade global: Lisboa no Renascimento." http://museudearteantiga.pt/exposicoes/a-cidade-global.

———. 2009. *Encompassing the Globe: Portugal e o mundo nos séculos XVI e XVII*. Lisboa: Museu Nacional da Arte Antiga. Exhibition catalog.

Neves, José. 2019. *Portugal, uma Retrospectiva: 1998*. Lisboa: Tinta-da-China.

Oliveira, António de. 2003. "The Activities of the CNCDP: A Preliminary Assessment." *e-Journal of Portuguese History* 1 (1): 1–12.

Oliveira, Nuno. 2013. "Lisboa redescobre-se: A governança da diversidade cultural na cidade pós-colonial; A *scenescape* da Mouraria." In *Cidade e Império: Dinâmicas coloniais e reconfigurações pós-coloniais*, edited by Nuno Domingos and Elsa Peralta, 557–602. Lisboa: Edições 70.

Oliveira, Pedro Aires. 2017. "As condições políticas e sociais da descolonização." In *Retornar: Traços de memória do fim do Império*, edited by Elsa Peralta, Bruno Góis, and Joana Oliveira, 45–62. Lisboa: Edições 70.

Padrão dos Descobrimentos. 2017. "Racismo e cidadania." https://padraodosdescobrimentos.pt/publicacao/racismo-e-cidadania/.

Peralta, Elsa. 2017. *Lisboa e a memória do Império: Património, museus e espaço público*. Lisboa: Deriva/Le Monde Diplomatique.

Peralta, Elsa, and Nuno Domingos. 2019. "Lisbon: Reading the (Post-)Colonial city from the Nineteenth to the Twenty-First Century." *Urban History* 46 (2): 246–65.

Peralta, Elsa, and Lars Jensen. 2017. "From Austerity to Postcolonial Nostalgia: Crisis and National Identity in Portugal and Denmark." In *Austere Histories in European Societies: Social Exclusion and the Contest of Colonial Memories*, edited by Stefan Jonsson and Julia Willén, 74–91. Abingdon: Routledge.

Pereira, Patrícia. 2018. *Lisboa: Uma montra da Metrópole à Beira Tejo*. Lisboa: Editora Mundos Sociais.

Power, Marcus, and James D. Sidaway. 2005. "Deconstructing Twinned Towers: Lisbon's Expo'98 and the Occluded Geographies of Discovery." *Social & Cultural Geography* 6 (6): 865–83.

Silva, João Céu e. 2020. "Fernando Medina: 'Lisboa vai ter um memorial à escravatura.'" *Diário de Notícias*, June 12, 2020. https://www.dn.pt/edicao-do-dia/14-jun-2020/fernando-medina-lisboa-vai-ter-um-memorial-a-escravatura-12305662.html.

Smith, Anthony. 1999. *Myths and Memories of the Nation*. Oxford: Oxford University Press.

UNESCO. n.d. "Monastery of the Hieronymites and Tower of Belém in Lisbon." Accessed May 20, 2021. http://whc.unesco.org/en/list/263.

Wood, Allen W. 1998. "Kant's Project for Perpetual Peace." In *Cosmopolitics: Thinking and Feeling beyond the Nation*, edited by Pheng Cheah and Bruce Robbins, 59–76. Minneapolis: University of Minnesota Press.

Wolfe, Patrick. 1997. "History and Imperialism: A Century of Theory, from Marx to Postcolonialism." *American Historical Review*, no. 102, 406–9.

ELSA PERALTA holds a PhD in Anthropology from the University of Lisbon (UL) and is currently a senior research fellow at UL's Center for Comparative Studies (CEC) and an associate researcher with the Institute of Social Sciences (ICS-UL). Her interdisciplinary work focuses on the intersection between private and public modes of recall of past events, particularly the colonial past. In CEC, she coordinates the line of research on "Legacies of Empire and Colonialism in Comparative Perspective" and is the principal investigator of the project funded by the Portuguese Foundation for Science and Technology (FCT), "Constellations of Memory: A Multidirectional Study of Postcolonial Migration and Remembering" (PTDC/SOC-ANT/4292/2021). She has published several articles, chapters, and books, and was the curator of the exhibition *Return—Traces of Memory*, produced by Lisbon's City Council in 2015.

INÊS BELEZA BARREIROS

Heritage of Portuguese Influence as Erasure: Critical Perspectives on the Recreation of the Past in the Present[1]

ABSTRACT: Several attempts have been made to define and catalogue the "heritage of Portuguese influence," but none has critically addressed the politics at work in such heritage. The colonial violence that effectively scattered this heritage across the world has often been erased and replaced by the exaltation of a Portuguese imperial past expressed through aestheticization. This paper exposes the materiality of such heritage through discourse analysis, starting by unpacking one concrete example, the Sete Maravilhas de Origem Portuguesa no Mundo competition in 2009, and tracking down the conditions of possibility (when, how, and why) for this discourse practice to emerge in the Jornadas Luso-Brasileiras do Património (1984) and the Primeiro Congresso do Património Construído Luso no Mundo (1987) and to endure in such objects as *História da arte portuguesa no mundo* (1998–99) and *Património de origem portuguesa no mundo* (2010–11) as part of a visual economy that entails the spatial and temporal flow of images and discourses. This paper also examines the endurance of an imperial episteme that feeds on the idea of a supposed "Portuguese world" and gives form to its complex.

KEYWORDS: coloniality, imperial episteme, visuality, "Portuguese world" complex

RESUMO: Várias tentativas foram feitas para definir e catalogar "o património de influência portuguesa," mas nenhuma delas abordou criticamente a política que impregna esse mesmo património. Frequentemente a violência colonial que, justamente, fez com que esse património esteja hoje espalhado pelo mundo inteiro é apagada em favor da exaltação do passado imperial português expresso sobretudo através da estetização deste património. Este artigo examina, através de uma análise discursiva, esta materialidade tomando como ponto de partida o concurso das Sete Maravilhas da Origem Portuguesa no Mundo (2009) e rastreando as condições de possibilidade (quando, como e porquê) desta prática discursiva até às Jornadas Luso-Brasileiras do Património (1984) e ao Primeiro Congresso do Património Construído Luso no Mundo (1987), para igualmente analisar a sua permanência em objectos como a *História da arte portuguesa no mundo* (1999) e *Património de origem portuguesa no mundo* (2010) como parte de uma economia visual que pressupõe o fluxo espácio-temporal de imagens e discursos. Este artigo também aborda criticamente a sobrevivência de uma episteme imperial que se alimenta de um suposto "Mundo Português" e dá forma ao seu complexo.

PALAVRAS-CHAVE: colonialidade, episteme imperial, visualidade, complexo do "Mundo Português"

Introduction: The "Wonders" Effect (or Heritage as Entertainment)

Sete Maravilhas de Origem Portuguesa no Mundo (Seven Wonders of Portuguese Origin in the World) was a 2009 national popular competition whose goal was to publicize the "heritage" of Portuguese expansion. Few objects of critique have manifested quite so literally the endurance of an imperial episteme in the present. My use of imperial "episteme" follows Michel Foucault's conceptualization of an unconscious apparatus that underlies the "conditions of possibility" for (imperial) knowledge to emerge, i.e., what can and cannot be said in a given time and place, whether in theory or silently invested in a practice, and what endures (Foucault [1966] 2005, xxiii-xxiv). The competition can be understood as a symptom of this underlying episteme.

Sete Maravilhas de Origem Portuguesa no Mundo [Sete Maravilhas] followed two previous and associated competitions, one global and one local. The New Seven Wonders of the World, sponsored by UNESCO, aimed at redefining the original seven wonders established two thousand years ago by Philon of Byzantium.[2] Its goal was to stimulate "global memory."[3] Portugal's Seven Wonders was held at the same time, followed similar selection and voting processes, and had sponsors at the highest levels, including Portugal's Ministry of Culture, IPPAR (Portuguese Institute for Architectural and Archaeological Herit age), and the University of Évora.[4] Both events concluded in a ceremony held in Lisbon on July 7, 2007, and led to the establishment of the Seven Wonders Portugal Foundation. Two years later, this Foundation would organize the Sete Maravilhas analyzed here and subsequent competitions: Portugal's Seven Natural Wonders (2010), Seven Gastronomic Wonders (2011), Seven Beach Wonders (2012), Seven Village Wonders (2017),[5] Seven Gourmet Regional Wonders (2018), Seven Pastry Wonders (2019), and, most recently, Seven Pop Culture Wonders (2020). This generated a "wonders effect" as a means of branding Portugal for domestic consumption, unparalleled since António Ferro's pursuit as head of the Estado Novo's Secretariat for National Propaganda (SPN, later SNI) in the 1930s and 1940s, which molded the regime's "politics of spirit" (Ferro 1950, 29).[6] Now it had become a capitalist endeavor dressed in national attire.

The Sete Maravilhas competition nominated 27 archetypal buildings spread across three continents, 22 of which were already classified as UNESCO World Heritage sites. Crucially, the competition had the support of the CPLP (Community of Portuguese-Language Countries). It also counted on IPPAR, the Ministries of Education and Culture, the Camões Institute, the University of Coimbra, and the National Commission of UNESCO. The kickoff press conference was held, symbolically, at Torre de Belém, and its commissioner, ex-minister António Vitorino, stated on the occasion: "We are a people who are proud of our history, and we continue to be a people of Diaspora. This project is a unique opportunity to reencounter our history" ("Património da Humanidade" 2008).[7] Luís Segadães, CEO of the New Seven Wonders Foundation, on the other hand, stressed that "Portuguese monuments can be found all over the world, which clearly shows the dimension and influence of the Portuguese presence on a global scale. Globalization began with the Portuguese" ("Património da Humanidade" 2008). Both statements set the tone for Sete Maravilhas: it was to be a celebration of the imperial narrative, here reframed as "diaspora" and "globalization"—euphemisms often used to this day to refer to the colonial enterprise.

The competition was eventually postponed due to the criticism that the selection criteria lacked scientific basis. Walter Rossa, Pedro Dias, and Paulo Varela Gomes, three art historians from the University of Coimbra, argued that some examples on the list "were not of Portuguese origin" (Rossa) or not what "the Portuguese did best" (Dias); there was also an "excess" of African locations and Brazilian historical cities (Varela Gomes) and the exclusion of key places like Cidade Velha in Cabo Verde (Andrade 2008). After these criticisms were considered and Pedro Dias invited as scientific supervisor, some of the originally excluded locations were included in the competition, but the "entertaining vocation" didn't really changed (Andrade 2009). The seven winning monuments were the Diu Fortress in India; the Mazagão Fortress in Morocco; the Basilica of Bom Jesus de Goa in India; Cidade Velha/Ribeira Grande in Santiago Island, Cabo Verde; Saint Paul's Church in Macau; Church of Saint Francis of Assisi in Ouro Preto, Brazil; and the Convent of Saint Francis in São Salvador da Bahia, Brazil.[8]

Fig. 1. “7 Wonders of Portuguese Origin in the World: Promoting National Identity since 2007” (https://projetos.7maravilhas.pt/)

This list reflects the imperial (and imperialist) narrative of a country “scattered” across different continents, while also occluding the colonial violence that effectively prompted this heritage to be built all over the world. Indeed, the voting website failed to mention that some of the sites bore concrete connections to the transatlantic slave trade (some were actual slave ports or warehouses), despite the fact that UNESCO had registered them as heritage of the Atlantic slave route (UNESCO 2021). Furthermore, when visiting or studying such heritage, one is often led to forget that gilded wood carvings, luxurious marbles, exotic woods, precious metals, and gemstones, which embellish several of these monuments, are products of slave labor and extractivism forged by modernity/coloniality.[9]

Nevertheless, the competition stirred controversy among a few scholars, such as Gerhard Seibert (2009) who criticized the negation and manipulation of history operated by the competition, and Brazilian historian Ana Lucia Araujo, who, along with other colleagues, wrote an open letter stressing the violent histories connected to “these sites of death and tragedy” and calling for “respect to the history and the memory of millions of victims of the Atlantic slave trade” (“Carta aberta” 2009).[10] By the same token, Boaventura de Sousa Santos (2009) insightfully pointed out that “the gaze that is oriented to see the beauty of [these] monuments” within the competition is “also oriented not to see the unspeakable suffering of millions of Africans who . . . sacrificed their lives so that many of these monuments would come to life.”

The competition’s exaltation of a “glorious” Portuguese past expressed through the aesthetic value of this heritage ignored, by design, the sites’ contradictory and violent roles within the colonial project. It therefore expressed the coloniality at work in the present. With Sete Maravilhas, heritage thus became entertainment intended for mass consumption. This operation was performed with the complicity not only of the media, but also UNESCO, the Portuguese state and its institutions, and, most strikingly, the University of Coimbra under the sponsorship of its rector, Fernando Seabra Santos.

Such widespread consensus is hardly surprising, however. It demonstrates the extensive range of the imperial episteme at work and its manifestation in resilient and recursive forms that, as Ann Laura Stoler noted, although they "don't look or feel quite the same" as in the past, nevertheless "reenact" the imperial narrative in the present (2012, 501). This reenactment relies substantially on images and their circulation, as well as on the miniaturization and consequent portability of the empire, features that also mark other objects to be analyzed here (*História da arte portuguesa no mundo*, *Património de origem portuguesa no mundo*, and the portal *Patrimónios de influência portuguesa no mundo*). In this way, and through these means, the imperial past is not really past but a hegemonic position taken up in the present and/or reactivated and put into motion whenever necessary. But what were/are the exact conditions of possibility—when, why, and how—for this discourse to reemerge in the present?

This article performs a genealogical exploration that, unlike history, places the past in the present, questions the conceptual frame used to understand and study this heritage, and, in doing so, reproblematizes it: why and how "that-which-is" called "património de origem/influência portuguesa no mundo" may no longer be "that-which-is."[11]

The "Portuguese World" Complex

Colonial domination, as Edward Said (1994) pointed out, was not based on violence and exploitation alone but also on cultural domination. This domination was impelled by "ideological formations" expressed through discourses that generated a "consolidated vision" manifested aesthetically.[12] This vision was further intensified by the late colonial state, which, as Benedict Anderson ([1983] 2010, 185) stressed, employed a unique way of imagining: by serialization.[13] Through infinite replication, this "late colonial imagining" was what made nations, their citizens, and a "national series" possible, enduring far beyond the end of colonialism, to be embraced by the postcolonial state.

Acting as the motor that propelled a "colonial imagining" and a "national series," the 1940 Portuguese World Exposition put in place by the Estado Novo dictatorship (1933–74) would, for the first time, produce a "visuality" in the sense defined by Nicholas Mirzoeff: as "a discursive practice for rendering and regulating the real" (2011, 3). By invoking and summarizing a scattered, preexisting imperial vocabulary and archive—historical characters, national heroes, myths, places, dates, and metropolitan and overseas folklore—and by coherently "serializing" them, the Exposition posited "the Discoveries" as Portugal's golden age, telling the "exceptional" history of a small country that resisted the Moorish and the Spanish conquests, went to sea to escape its fate, "discovered" different lands, Christianized Africans and Amerindians, and finally found in Salazar a guide who would forge a new era of prosperity in a Europe divided by war. Immersed within the exposition, visitors could therefore travel from one historical moment to the next, from the colonies to the rural continental provinces and back, diving into the life of their ancestors and the glory of their past (*Comemorações centenárias* 1940; Acciaiuoli 1998; Vargaftig 2016).

Capturing the past, the present, and the future of an aspirational Portuguese world, visitors of the Exposition were led to believe that they indeed belonged to a particular world, simultaneously modern and traditional, colonial and metropolitan, urban and rural— in an "all-embracing aesthetics" (Bennett 2004).[14] This procedure is what Walter Benjamin famously labeled as the "aestheticization of politics" of fascist regimes aimed at "masking" their social tensions ([1936] 2006, 260)[15] or what Hannah Arendt has described as what distinguishes a totalitarian regime: it "thrives on this escape from reality into fiction, from coincidence into consistency" ([1951] 1962, 361).

As a deeply rooted consistency, this highly aesthetic and fictitious "Portuguese world" expressed in the Portuguese World Exposition and in a number of satellite events, such as the Portuguese World Conference,[16] established an ensemble of practices and discourses that came to define the truth claims so as to provoke a *belief*. The regime therefore created a naturalized and self-authorized worldview, the "Portuguese world," and gave shape to its complex. A complex, Mirzoeff tells us, is a "life-world" to be "visualized" and, above all, "inhabited" in order for authority to be "administered" (2011, 5). The Portuguese world complex forged within the Portuguese World Exposition was an "imperial complex" (13) that proposed an ideal world, simultaneously fascist and colonial.[17] This complex would translate into forms that have merged and accommodated palimpsestically long after the empire's decreed end.

Indeed, April 25, 1974, brought the end of Portugal as an imperial nation in praxis, but not the end of its "imagination," as Eduardo Lourenço (1983) warned us.[18] With the establishment of democracy and Portugal's integration into the European Union in 1986, this imperial complex was reconfigured, mostly through the work of the Comissão Nacional para as Comemorações dos Descobrimentos Portugueses (National Commission for the Commemoration of Portuguese Discoveries), established that same year. In a formulation reminiscent of the 1940 Portuguese World Exposition, the commission's main objective was to remember Portugal's "epic effort" and to teach the "Portuguese of today" about its "great goals."[19] Promoted by the highest ranks of the state, this heavily financed hegemonic operation enable the continuity of an imperial episteme and its complex. The objects studied here make this imperial episteme and complex tangible and show the role of economic, political, and cultural elites alike in promoting it and ensuring its survival,[20] even if unintentionally. Such is the work of coloniality.

***Património Luso no Mundo*: Heritage as Erasure**

It was against this unsettling (post)colonial backdrop that two events conveyed the foundation of Portugal's heritage policies: the Primeiras Jornadas Luso-Brasileiras do Património (First Luso-Brazilian Heritage Days), in 1984, and the Primeiro Congresso do Património Construído Luso no Mundo (First Conference of Lusitanian-Built Heritage in the World), in 1987. Heritage has always been mobilized in concrete moments in time, its very concept having grown out of nineteenth-century European fears of cultural decadence and political and social change. The Jornadas and the Congresso were not, however, the first time that efforts were made to define and preserve this heritage around the world. Indeed, the Estado Novo seemed to possess an understanding of the political value of "overseas heritage" at least since the 1930s and 1940s, as Vera Félix Maris (2016) has shown. The regime attempted to affirm its colonial policy through the conservation, restoration, and dissemination of its so-called heritage abroad, particularly after 1958, when it tried to refute worldwide condemnation and legitimize itself under the pressure of rising independence movements. A clear step to this end was creating a centralized model for safeguarding such heritage with the publication of the Decree no. 41787 of August 8, 1958.[21]

The Primeiras Jornadas Luso-Brasileiras do Património were held on March 12–16, 1984, at the Calouste Gulbenkian Foundation in Lisbon. Alfredo Viana de Lima (1913–91), a Portuguese architect with extensive experience in Brazil who was behind the classification of much of that heritage within UNESCO, set the basis of the Jornadas by referring to Portugal's "dilated dimension": "Throughout the fifteenth, sixteenth, and seventeenth centuries, there was a culture that dimensioned and . . . motivated cultures that were so different from each other.

. . . That culture was the Luso culture (we don't say Portuguese because it has a political content that the other term does not possess)" (Lima 1984, 18). He proceeded to highlight the role of both Portugal and Brazil in the making of a particular cultural and political geography:

> Brazil and Portugal should keep in mind the primordial role that other peoples . . . played in the construction of an identity full of affinities. From the far reaches of the Orient, passing through the Arab world, to the African immensity, as we know, we have received indelible marks that the genius and art of different peoples brought to the building of our heritage. There is therefore a Lusíada community, in which so many fundamental moments of an already universal culture are merged. (18)

Sponsored by the Gulbenkian Foundation (Portugal), the Roberto Marinho Foundation (Brazil), the Instituto da Cultura e Língua Portuguesa (Portugal), and the Fundação Nacional Pró-Memória (Brazil), among others, the main topics of the Jornadas were: Administrative Instruments for the Preservation of Built Heritage; Philosophy of Safeguarding Interventions; the Historical and Traditional Agglomerates and Their Surrounding Environment; and Frameworks and Public Participation in the Preservation of Common Heritage. The event, therefore, lay the foundations for a political and cultural geography that would come to be implemented in other events and objects. For example, Cidade Velha in Cabo Verde was already mentioned at the Jornadas as worthy of preservation (in the paper "Legislação existente ou a propor em Cabo Verde" by António Delgado). There was also an allusion to the Roberto Marinho Foundation's campaign to "preserve national memory," with references to Rio de Janeiro, Ouro Preto, Paraty, Curitiba, and Salvador, which came to be bastions of this heritage in Brazil ("Fundação Roberto Marinho: Campanha de Preservação da Memória Nacional" by José Carlos Barbosa de Oliveira).[22]

Architect and President of the Scientific Council of the Department of Architecture of ESBAL (Escola Superior de Belas Artes; School of Fine Arts) at the University of Lisbon, Augusto Pereira Brandão (1930–2018), who in those years was struggling to turn ESBAL's architecture department into an autonomous school (he eventually succeeded and became known as "the father" of the Faculdade de Arquitectura de Lisboa), forged a tentative concept to classify this heritage in his closing remarks at the Jornadas: "Património de Comunidade Mundial" (World Community Heritage). In hindsight, this concept seems sharper than those that followed, although Brandão's proposal ends up falling in the same "originary" traps as future conceptualizations when he states that this heritage owes its "paternity" to Brazil and Portugal. According to his definition, "Luso-Brazilian heritage" was part of a much wider whole and its study should be extended "to all nations that contain portions of that heritage" (Brandão 1984, 200).[23]

Building on the foundations laid by the Jornadas Luso-Brasileiras, the Primeiro Congresso do Património Construído Luso no Mundo was held three years later, mobilizing a large community. It was organized by the Grupo para o Estudo do Património Arquitectónico Português fora da Europa (Group for the Study of Portuguese Heritage Outside of Europe) from the Faculdade de Arquitectura, by now part of Lisbon's Technical University. The group was formed by Ana Maria Figueiredo, Isabel Galvão Lucas, Margarida Valla, Nuno Ludovice, and Paula Ramos, most of whom were architects. Similar to the Jornadas, the Congresso was an event that had substantial political, social, and financial support. Its Honorary Commission included President Mário Soares, Prime Minister Aníbal Cavaco Silva, several ministers, rectors of Portugal's public universities, the president of the Calouste Gulbenkian Foundation, and the president of the UNESCO National Commission. There was also a Portuguese Executive Commission composed of several architects, an Executive Commission for Brazil, an Advisory Commission, and a large number of sponsors (several ministries, the government of Macau, Brazil's Ministry of Culture, Lisbon City Hall, Fundação Nacional Pró-Memória, the Calouste Gulbenkian Foundation, the Roberto Marinho Foundation, public companies such as Petrogal and TAP–Air Portugal, and private enterprises, such as Central de Cervejas and Grão Pará).

The three goals of the Congresso, according to opening remarks by Brandão, who was part of the Advisory Commission and had delivered the closing remarks of the Jornadas in 1984, were, first, "to make people aware" of "the great strength" of the "Lusitanian heritage" spread all over the "tropical world"; second, "to examine and to impress on our minds that one of the characteristics of this heritage is its formal nomadism" derived from "an enormous variety of overlapping cultures" that have "different attributes, according to their location, their origin, and the region and area where they are situated"; and, third, to learn more about the heritage's "state of conservation" as it "began before the majority of existing nations" (Brandão 1987b).

The different papers drew a particular geopolitical landscape of heritage recognized in later objects: once again, the importance of Brazil stood out, and the inventory and classification of Brazilian heritage, namely in the context of the "Lusitanian colonization" of Santa Catarina. Other sites highlighted were the state of Minas Gerais; the historic cities of São Luís, Santos, Goiás, Salvador, and Diamantina; the Island of Mozambique; and Uruguay's Colonia del Sacramento. Interestingly, there were also mentions of Singapore's conservation efforts, Portuguese military architecture in Oman and Ormuz, coastal Portuguese settlements in Morocco, and even Beijing and Senegambia. Some of the participants would later publish on the topic they first presented at the Congresso, such as art historian Rafael Moreira, architect José Manuel Fernandes, architect Nuno Teotónio Pereira, and architects Fernando Távora and Alexandre Alves Costa.

In the inaugural session, Isabel Margato Valladares gave a paper entitled "Para uma definição do Património Construído Luso no Mundo" (Towards a Definition of the Lusitanian Built Heritage in the World), and later in the week there was another collective effort to define "Portuguese world heritage" in a presentation with the same exact title by the Grupo para o Estudo do Património Arquitectónico Português fora da Europa, the research group in Lisbon's School of Architecture that, since November 1983, had been engaged in an exhaustive documental and bibliographic survey of "Lusitanian heritage." Unfortunately, no conference proceedings were published after the Congresso, and therefore there is no way to access the definitions proposed in both presentations. However, the tone of the conference can be inferred from the paper titles published in the program brochure, in which, similarly to the Jornadas Luso-Brasileiras, descriptors like "Luso" and "Lusitanian" were employed at large to conceptualize this heritage.[24]

In addition, there was an entire section of the Congress devoted to the social function of heritage, conservation theories, methods, and even politics, such as "The History of the Portuguese Presence in Macau Is Told by the Portuguese and Chinese in Different Ways" (Francisco Figueira). Architect and theorist of architecture Michel Toussaint focused on the conservation of twentieth-century heritage ("Is the Twentieth-Century Architectonic Patrimony at Risk?"), a relatively undiscussed issue at the time, but which would become a central concern of his work. There were also papers on Macau, the Fortress of Diu, Ouro Preto, Pernambuco, the Cape of Good Hope, Alcácer Quibir, and an inventory of Portuguese settlements along the African coast—stressing a political and cultural geography in the making. Some proposals addressed the future of such heritage, as was the case of papers "Towards the Management of the Lusitanian Built Patrimony in the World" by the museum specialist Maria Natália Correia

Guedes—who had been head of the Direcção-Geral do Património Cultural (Directorate-General for Cultural Heritage) between 1979 and 1980 and the first President of the Instituto Português do Património Cultural (Portuguese Cultural Heritage Institute) between 1980 and 1984—and "The Role of National and International Authorities in Actions to be Developed" by architect and professor of Lisbon's School of Architecture Fernando Moreira da Silva. Furthermore, and similar to what happened in the Jornadas, the Congresso also entailed guided visits to national heritage classics, such as the Jerónimos Monastery, and cultural trips to Sintra, Mafra, Óbidos, and Évora. A reception in the São Jorge Castle and a cultural session at Padrão dos Descobrimentos completed the program.

Importantly, the Congresso was coupled with an exhibition, the result of a survey on "Lusitanian built heritage in the world" carried out by the Grupo para o Estudo do Património Arquitectónico Português fora da Europa ("Catálogo" 1987). It contemplated four main topics: (1) spatial, chronological and typological characterization, a world map with the location of the main sites where they exist or existed, and the heritage that had already been subjected to inventory; (2) presentations of a few representative documents: cities and sites, civil architecture, religious architecture, military architecture, architectural language, building techniques, decoration, and iconography; (3) samples of paradigmatic heritage in five different sites: Mazaan (Morocco), Diu (India), Malacca (Malaysia), Colonia del Sacramento (Uruguay), São Luís do Maranhão (Brazil); and (4) examples of protective actions already undertaken (Macau, Toyyan, Imperial Palace, and Rio de Janeiro) and the presentation of restoration works that are urgently needed ("Catálogo" 1987). Writing in the (not randomly) trilingual catalogue, Augusto Pereira Brandão summed up what seemed to be the overall tone of the exhibition, a "Lusitanian heritage panorama":

> The Lusitanian Culture is not one of domination and influence, it is rather a culture of symbiosis and as such a culture of exchanges. Throughout this exhibition, the Lusitanian world comes up with no compulsory expressions, creating a leitmotiv, but as agglutinant factors. From Ethiopia to China, such different moldings in form and in time! . . . From Malaca to S. Luís of Maranhão, what dispersal! . . . From Cachéu to Amboíno, what contrast! . . . From Rio de Janeiro to Mozambique island, how complementary! It is this vast and "sacred" panorama we attempt to show to whoever wants to see, feel, and love. (Brandão 1987a)[25]

The conference and the associated exhibition were thus the first survey and bibliographic, cartographic, and iconographic effort to define this heritage, "seeking to fit the different urban morphologies and architectonic types into a whole, so as to facilitate the perception of fundamental features in its chronological evolution," according to the Grupo para o Estudo do Património Arquitectónico Português fora da Europa. It aimed at educating and holding all cultural entities to account, in order "to perform, as quickly as possible, such actions as to avoid its irreparable loss" ("Catálogo" 1987).

Looking back, it seems that the Jornadas and the Congresso were a national response to the UNESCO Convention Concerning the Protection of World Cultural and National Heritage, which Portugal had signed in 1979. Both events proposed a preservation doctrine, in which such heritage is understood as unique, its study is the domain of experts (architects, museum specialists, and historians), and its significance is immutable and lies in the past. While the proposed concept—Património Construído Luso no Mundo (Lusitanian Built Heritage in the World)—did not stick, both events shaped a geopolitical framework that enabled the endurance of the imperial and fascist "Portuguese World" complex, as forged by the 1940 Exposition long before the regime's demise. This complex manifested itself in an uncritical discourse on such heritage—one of erasure and naturalization of the colonial past, which also helped appease the anxieties of a "return to Europe" for Portugal.

História da Arte Portuguesa no Mundo: Heritage as Aestheticization

If the 1980s events—the Jornadas and the Congresso—were responding to an anxiety crisis over the loss of the empire in 1974 and Portugal's entry into the European Union in 1986, then in the 1990s the field of Portuguese art history developed a new subfield with its own specialists, projects, and conceptual vocabulary that continued to make the empire's materiality an opportune (and opportunistic) topic of inquiry. These were building on previous works, such as German Bazin's *L'architecture religieuse au Brésil* and Mário Tavares Chicó's *A cidade ideal do Renascimento e as cidades portuguesas da Índia*, both published in 1956, which had enlarged the scope of Portuguese historiographical research to artistic productions resulting from colonial expansion.

In a way, it was art historians' response to the architects' protagonism in the aforementioned events and in studying the objects of imperial heritage.[26] Furthermore, as in the past, the field was also responding to a specific context,

Fig. 2. Heritage as aesthetics: Pedro Dias, *A história da arte portuguesa no mundo: O espaço do Índico, 1415–1822* (1998)

in which Portugal was trying to forge a neocolonial policy that materialized in a "humanist" rhetoric: Lusofonia, a geopolitical space "united" by the Portuguese language.[27] This new rhetoric became official through the establishment of the CPLP in 1996, in which Portugal claimed a sort of sovereignty over the language, the "proper" way of speaking and writing it, as the (empire of) language became a prosthetic entity substituting for the loss of the real empire.[28] Historical idiosyncrasies prevented the establishment of Lusofonia as a fully neocolonialist endeavor; it emerged instead as a postcolonial myth with similar ideological purposes to those of the past (see Santos 2001). One event that particularly took hold of this transmutation process was the 1998 Lisbon World Exposition, or Expo'98. Dedicated to the theme of "The Oceans, a Heritage for the Future," its official mission statement nevertheless espoused a discourse similar to that of the Portuguese World Exposition, though tempered by the quest for "knowledge about the oceans" (*Relatório* 1999, 18).[29] Expo'98 became a mirror of the Portuguese World Exposition, and its site, Parque das Nações, the mirror of Belém. By portraying Portugal both as a depoliticized empire without colonies and as a pioneer of a brotherly globalization that promoted a friendly encounter between cultures, Expo'98 expunged Portuguese colonialism of any violence, confining this aspect of its history to the realm of a well-kept family secret.

Pedro Dias's *História da arte portuguesa no mundo*, a two-volume work published in 1998 and 1999, not only reflects this sociopolitical context but is shaped by the same lingering "imperial complex" (Mirzoeff 2011) forged within the Portuguese World Exposition and reconceptualized by Expo'98, while reproducing an ambiguous discourse on colonialism. Its two volumes, respectively dedicated to the "space of the Indic" (covering East Africa, the Middle East, India, and Asia) and "the space of the Atlantic" (covering the west coast of Africa, Brazil, and the Atlantic islands of Cabo Verde, São Tomé, Madeira, and the Azores), establish a chronology between the conquest of Ceuta (1415) and the "loss" of Brazil (1822). This chronology, in turn, reflects a particular ideology, expressed on the back cover of both volumes: "After this date, neither in Portugal nor in any of its overseas territories was reality the same as before; without Brazil, *we* lost our richest land and the most dynamic part of our society, beginning an irreversible decline, which practically returned *us* to the material and immaterial limits of 1444" (Dias 1998, 1999; my emphases).

On the same back cover, the oeuvre's goals are clearly stated: to study "the artistic phenomena resulting from the maritime discoveries and *our* territorial expansion," having as object "the aesthetics that *we* took overseas, to inhabited or uninhabited lands, and that, there, we practiced for *our* use . . . on equal terms with everything that resulted from the miscegenation of European art with the art of the people with whom *we* interacted" (Dias 1998, 1999; my emphases). The recurrent use of the first-person plural by Dias exposes an overidentification between the author and his subject, a common practice in the intellectual production of experts during the Estado Novo. In addition, the use of the term "interacted" (interagimos) is a widespread euphemism to refer to the violence of colonial encounters. Reflecting the tradition of art history within which it is inscribed, this wide-ranging work sought to include all artistic disciplines: urbanism, architecture, sculpture, painting, goldsmithing, furniture, fabrics, and even everyday objects.

Perhaps the clearest symptom of the imperial episteme and complex at work in the book is the fact that each chapter starts with an introduction referring to the role of the Portuguese here and there: "Portuguese in Ceylon"; "Portuguese Presence in the Persian Gulf and Middle East"; "The Portuguese in Malacca"; "The Establishment of the Portuguese in China"; "The Portuguese Presence in Japan," etc. "Presence" or "establishment," like "interaction," are euphemisms, and at no time is the word "colonialism" mentioned. This is a striking omission,

Fig. 3. Heritage as aesthetics: Pedro Dias, *A história da arte portuguesa no mundo: O espaço do Atlântico, 1415-1822* (1999)

given that fortresses are one of the main typologies throughout the different territories in a variety of forms and scales, a typology that the Portuguese indeed mastered and is, perhaps, the most poignant manifestation of such heritage. One cannot help but wonder why the Portuguese came to excel in the construction of fortresses wherever they set foot. Or, better put: why did the Portuguese need to build fortresses in the first place?

The euphemisms continue throughout the book: the contacts (*contactos*) and the bridging (*pontes*), not the violence; the shipments (*envios*) and the exchanges (*trocas*), not the conquests; the collection (*recolhas*) and the arrival of the works (*o chegar das obras*), not the result of the lootings. When mentioning the stay of Vasco da Gama's warship in India, Dias notes it "didn't result in any construction" (1998, 10). Perhaps Gama was too busy setting vessels and buildings on fire. Dias establishes an entire narrative of "interchanging" of art works and precious objects or "diplomatic offerings" that were transported "in the chambers of the ships"—so much so that they resembled "royal chambers" (18). Besides being loaded with "gifts," those very same ships were full of other cargo never acknowledged throughout the two volumes—enslaved people. Moreover, silver and gold objects are referenced with no acknowledgement of the violence that produced them, be it slave labor or extractivism.

In the second volume, focused on the "Atlantic space," a section of more than two hundred pages dedicated to Brazil effectively confirms the terms of Brazilian independence, determined by a white oligarchy willing to preserve, at least at the beginning, as much as it could of its European legacy that could also attest to its whiteness. The words "discovery" and "first contacts" (Dias 1999, 306) are used to exhaustion, as in a prayer that must be repeated to become truth. There is even a chapter entitled: "Brancos, Pretos [*sic*] e Mulatos na Criação de uma Arte Tricontinental" (Whites, Negroes, and Mulattos in the Creation of a Tricontinental Art) (321), using the word *pretos* with no mention of its particular genealogy and racist overtones. Cidade Velha occupies six pages, but, as in the competition Sete Maravilhas, no mention whatsoever is made of its crucial role in the Atlantic slave trade (112–18).

It is a true feat to elaborate on the topic of colonial heritage so extensively, while expunging the one thing that constructed it. Perhaps this explains the lack of a conclusion and/or thesis—but the lack thereof is arguably a thesis in itself. A thesis that consists of a list of places, monuments, and objects indeed attests a Portuguese "art history in the world" to a particular aesthetics, but does not do so without violence. By not acknowledging the colonial violence, the oeuvre inevitably adds to it; its aesthetics of erasure is violent in and of itself. Ten years later, Pedro Dias (2008) repeated the feat, with the newspaper *Público* promoting an expanded, fifteen-volume version of *História da arte portuguesa no mundo*, now available to an even wider audience. There was a slight mutation in the title—*Arte de Portugal no mundo* (The Art of Portugal in the World)—but the rhetoric remained.

By producing what Michel-Rolph Trouillot (1997, 29) called a "bundle of silences" in the moments of "assembly," "retrieval," and "retrospective,"[30] Dias's oeuvre becomes part of the same hegemonic historiography, with its inability to analyze the empire in a broader context and its propensity for an overidentification with its topic.[31] Such inability derives from the weight of an ideological historiography stimulated by the Estado Novo, which dictated the prevalence of provincial and exceptionalist readings of the empire. That such an ideological approach continues to endure long after the end of the dictatorship owes a great deal to the Comissão Nacional para as Comemorações dos Descobrimentos Portugueses.[32] Its extinction in 2002 and a concomitant shift in the related scholarship from French to Anglo-American influences coincided with the emergence

Fig. 4. The Empire in a Box: *Património de origem portuguesa*, edited by José Mattoso (Calouste Gulbenkian Foundation, 2010–11)

of other readings, namely in the works of Francisco Bethencourt around the same time and under the same editorial umbrella as Dias's—the Círculo de Leitores, intended for a large audience and wide circulation.[33]

Referring to studies on twentieth-century Portuguese architectural heritage in Africa by architects and historians of architecture José Manuel Fernandes and Ana Tostões, Nuno Domingos noted how, through the "aestheticization of history," heritage "became a tale of empire" (2016, 8). Elsewhere, Domingos also stresses the role of an uncritical discourse on heritage that ends up naturalizing colonialism and reifying the grand narrative on Portuguese colonial rule (2015, 251–52). This naturalization is precisely what Dias's oeuvre accomplishes overall. Dias's *História da arte portuguesa no mundo* is a clear product of the specificities and even inabilities of art history in Portugal, demonstrating how it is shaped by the weight of architects and historians alike. As keepers of an "Authorized Heritage Discourse" (AHD), according to their own ideological agenda, they tend to focus more on chronology and on formal and aesthetic features and less on the fact that such heritage is constructed, as Laurajane Smith has pointed out, through a continuous process of (colonial) conflict, being a "struggle over power" (2006, 281; see also Smith 2012). It is as if both the object and the exercise of art history existed outside of power relations, specifically those forged by colonialism and its legacies. But heritage is never about aesthetics (even when it is), but about how power has been expressed and negotiated, then and now.

The Empire in a Box: Heritage as Miniaturization

The most recent attempt to frame and reconceptualize this heritage is a monumental three-volume work published in 2010, *Património de origem portuguesa no mundo*.[34] The work took three years to produce and was edited by historian José

Fig. 5. *Património de origem portuguesa no mundo*, vol. 1: América do Sul, edited by Renata Melchior Araújo

Mattoso and commissioned by the Calouste Gulbenkian Foundation's then-president, Rui Vilar. In its atlas-like form, it systematizes knowledge related to "Portuguese heritage around the world," focusing on architecture and urbanism and listing it by region and in alphabetical order. It includes 2,300 buildings and about 530 sites—churches, fortresses, prisons, warehouses, manors, palaces, private houses, large residential buildings, hotels, banks, high schools, cinemas, post offices, factories, gardens, streets, and squares—in Brazil, Angola, Mozambique, São Tomé, Cabo Verde, Timor, and India; in addition to Uruguay, Sri Lanka, Macau, Indonesia, Ethiopia, and Tanzania. Its publication was the corollary of previous actions promoted by the Gulbenkian Foundation, from the support it gave to the events previously discussed here—the Jornadas Luso-Brasileiras and the Congresso do Património Construído Luso no Mundo—to the restoration of buildings and monuments, beginning shortly after the foundation's inception in 1956.[35] *Património* is therefore partially a showcase of Gulbenkian's actions and its role in the "making" of such heritage.

In the general introduction to the work, Mattoso explains that the choice of the inventory model was deliberate, but that each volume is preceded by a study

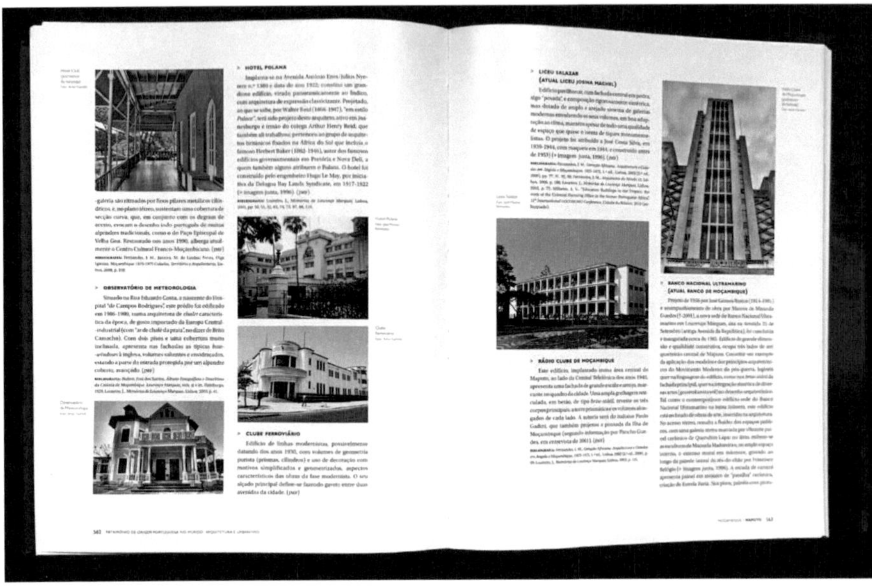

Fig. 6. *Património de origem portuguesa no mundo*, vol. 2: África, Mar Vermelho e Golfo Pérsico, edited by José Manuel Fernandes and Filipe Themudo Barata

in which the historical and cultural issues pertaining to each case are considered, framed, and given meaning, placing the objects within a geographic, diachronic, and civilizational context (Mattoso 2010, 1:15–16). Mattoso also stresses that there was no intention to produce "new research" but only to present a "state of the art" (15), systematizing information dispersed in specialized publications. The goal was to create a corpus and an object of study—that of the "heritage of Portuguese origin" as the result of an "encounter of cultures" (15). This discourse translates, even if unintentionally, the same orthodox position in regards to the history of the Portuguese empire and its heritage as described above. It is the same orthodoxy that leads Mattoso to advise against value judgments about the past, namely in historical research (12), so as not to project present contingencies onto the past (13). Mattoso seems to disregard that history is always a construction of the past in the present, and that referring to such heritage as a product of a "meeting of cultures," as he does—using a contemporary conceptual framework—is also anachronistic on its own terms. Heritage (as history), as Rodney Harrison points out, is "always chosen, recreated and renegotiated in the present" (2013, 169).

The first volume of *Património* is dedicated to South America and coordinated by architect Renata Malcher Araújo, with academic contributions from Portugal and Brazil. It is divided in four sub-areas, which correspond, roughly, to the main stages of Portuguese colonization, starting on the coast ("A costa"), advancing south ("O sul"), then entering the hinterland ("O sertão") and, finally, the Amazonian region ("A selva"). Some of the places included that preserve a more extensive and significant set of heritage are Diamantina and Ouro Preto, in the state of Minas Gerais; Salvador, in Bahia; as well as Belém, Goiás, and Natal. The chronology is focused on seventeenth- and eighteenth-century buildings based on metropolitan models, and successively linked to the sugar, gold, and diamond cycles in a historical period marked by the exploitation of slave labor.

The second volume of the set is divided in two parts: one devoted to Northern Africa, the Persian Gulf, and the Red Sea (coordinated by Filipe Themudo Barata) and the other dedicated to Sub-Saharan Africa, which includes Cabo Verde, the Gulf of Guinea, São Tomé, Angola, Mozambique, and East Africa (coordinated by José Manuel Fernandes). Predominant places include warehouses and fortresses on the coast to serve the "India Run" (Carreira das Índias) and the slave traffic. Inland presence became more common later on, starting in the nineteenth century, with the construction of military structures in river valleys and structures for the exploration of raw materials. The third volume, dedicated to Asia and under the coordination of Walter Rossa, is mostly focused on the heritage of the State of India and related to the Portuguese Patronage of the East, including Sri Lanka, Bengal, Macau, Nagasaki, and Timor.

The project reveals different sensibilities towards Portuguese imperial heritage, not only throughout the oeuvre, but also in the public presentation of the book and in a 2011 conference that followed. For the president of the Calouste Gulbenkian Foundation, this historical heritage is "one of the perennial testimonies of the passage across the globe by the Portuguese, the fingerprint of the authors of the *first globalization*" (Rolim 2010; original emphasis), echoing the discourses given just a year before by the sponsors of the Sete Maravilhas. Mattoso, on the other hand, in contrast to his introductory text to the oeuvre, emphasized in the newspaper *Público* that realism "rejects fantasies and illusions" and that remembering such heritage "in the midst of a financial and economic crisis [of 2010–15]" can "serve as a stimulus" to "overcome yet another difficult step in our history." Surprisingly, he concluded that

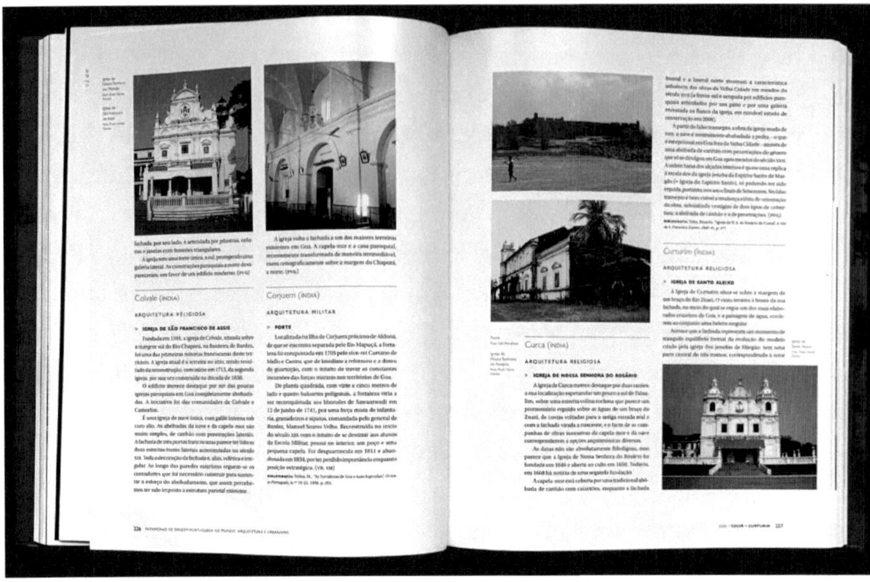

Fig. 7. *Património de origem portuguesa no mundo*, vol. 3: Ásia e Oceania, edited by Walter Rossa

> we should not, however, forget a fundamental difference: in the past, overcoming the European crisis took place, to a large extent, at the expense of the life and work of thousands and thousands of slaves: today, it can only be achieved through effort, solidarity, and the intelligence of a free citizenship, conscious of human rights. (Coelho 2011)

Mattoso's ambiguous discourse finds echo in the distinct positions of the coordinators of the three volumes, revealing a certain conceptual unease. For Filipe Themudo Barata, the heritage of Portuguese origin "is that which would serve the strategic, colonial interests of the Portuguese empire" (Coelho 2011); Fernandes, on the other hand, prefers the term "matrix" because the Portuguese presence or influence was spatially and chronologically diverse and expressed in a variety of typologies and styles (Coelho 2011). In his introduction to the second volume, Barata (2010, 23–33) does not question the term, and neither does co-editor Fernandes, who asserts the "specificity" of such heritage in terms of implantation, structural feature, urbanism, scale, and the use of accessory materials (Fernandes 2010, 185). On the other hand, Araújo (2010, 20–45), in her introduction to the first volume, stresses she uses the term "heritage of Portuguese origin" because "it is part of the Portuguese cultural heritage in the broad sense. . . . Not because the Portuguese have bequeathed it to other cultures, but because they share it and carry it as their own cultural baggage" (23). Of all four authors, Rossa is the most critical of the term, proposing "influence" instead of "origin," elaborating that "in the case of Asia, if one used the concept of origin, it would have to considerably reduce the number of items" (Coelho 2011). In his introduction to the third volume Rossa (2010, 20-61) implies that the concept of "influence" is less restrictive, which is crucial in the case of Asia due to the "polysemic" way in which this heritage manifests (21). The diversity of colonization, including through religion, the state, miscegenation, and individual adventurers, makes it difficult to speak of origin: "the border between what can be considered to be of origin is ambiguous. . . . What should count? The order? The authorship? The program? The formal expression?" (59).[36] Rossa ventures further to define heritage as "not history, but something that the present witnesses," entailing not only "contextualization," but also "questioning" (23).

The diverse sensibilities expressed in the respective introductions reflect different stances toward Portuguese colonial heritage, but throughout the oeuvre it seems consensual that heritage is less about historical ownership and more about something that can only be understood as "shared." Two years later, in 2012, the launching of an interactive public portal associated with the project, the HPIP Portal (História do Património de Influência Portuguesa; History of the Heritage of Portuguese Influence, www.hpip.org) translated what Rossa had already proposed in *Património*, consolidating yet another shift in the narrative: from *origin* to *influence*. Conceived as complementary to the volumes and as a perpetual "work in progress," this bilingual portal enables various forms of research: by authorship, by chronology, by location, or by name. The heritage inventoried in the portal, ranging from 1415 to 1999, is open to collaborations, which means that any user can add text, send photos, or make corrections (which are subsequently assessed by the portal's managers, the Universities of Coimbra, Évora, Técnica, and Nova de Lisboa) (Lopes 2012). The portal therefore democratizes the production of knowledge by enabling this repository of heritage to be accessible worldwide and open to updates.

Since the publication of the three volumes of *Património* in 2010 and of the portal, an international PhD program was launched at the University of Coimbra in collaboration with several universities from the ex-colonies, including Universidade Federal Fluminense (Brazil) and Universidade Eduardo Mondlane

(Mozambique). Like *Património*, the program is partnered with institutions such as Calouste Gulbenkian Foundation and UNESCO, and it has recently been designated as the "Cátedra UNESCO em Diálogo Intercultural em Patrimónios de Influência Portuguesa" (UNESCO Chair in Intercultural Dialogue in Heritage of Portuguese Influence). Its goal is to "contribute to the construction of alternative views to the hegemonic agendas of globalization" ("Apresentação" 2016). The PhD program seems to be the corollary of previous efforts promoted by the university, including two meetings of WHPO (World Heritage of Portuguese Origin network), the second of which culminated in the (rather slippery) *Declaration of Coimbra*.[37] Named Patrimónios de Influência Portuguesa (Heritages of Portuguese Influence), the PhD program expresses yet another change in the lexicon: besides the switch from origin to influence with the launching of the Património portal, now "heritage" becomes "heritages," in the plural. In 2015, Rossa and Margarida Calafate Ribeiro justified these shifts in a book with the same title as the PhD program:

> There is no heritage with a single origin. . . . Everything depends on the context from which the gaze falls, with Portuguese influence being the common operator that, using history, organizes and disciplines the limits, without, however, constraining them. Influence at different levels and heights of interculturality: formal and informal, administrative or spiritual, commercial or migratory, colonial and postcolonial. . . . The Portuguese influence overflows in space and time the formal limits of the empire's successive geopolitical configurations, producing intense and diffuse transculturalities, celebrated and hidden, ostensible and sensitive, that postcolonialism fragmentally absorbs. (Rossa and Ribeiro 2015, 20–21)

In the same volume, Renata Malcher Araújo (2015), the editor of the volume dedicated to South America in the three-volume *Património*, distinguishes between the concepts of influence, origin, and matrix, signaling the conceptual and political discussions that animated the years 2010 to 2015. These discussions are imprinted on *Património*, the online portal, and the PhD program and Araújo sums them up. The title of the three-volume set began as *Património português no mundo* (Portuguese Heritage in the World), which ultimately became *Património de origem portuguesa no mundo* (Heritage of Portuguese Origin in the World). The published English translation, however, carries the title *Portuguese Heritage around the World*.[38] The discussion of the database after editing the volumes resulted in the name Patrimónios de Influência Portuguesa (Heritages of Portuguese Influence), the same as the PhD program at the University of Coimbra (Araújo 2015, 58). Araújo further explains that, in the Gulbenkian project, both "matrix" and "origin" refer to the chronologies in which the heritage from different parts of the world was or is linked to Portugal, as the project relied mainly on a chronological framework. Both words imply a Portuguese "lineage." The idea of origin implies the existence of a formal lineage that seeks to internationally affirm a particular geography and its diffusion, claiming it as identity. Because matrix is related to the diffusion of forms, the formalist hierarchy does not consider the countless exchanges, negotiations, and transformations that inform heritage. Influence, in turn, is more fluid, but ambiguous enough to risk sublimating or whitewashing the violence of colonization. Still, according to Araújo, influence enables the possibility to think about the resistances and cultural hybridizations. However coercive the "methods of influence" may be, its outcomes are not entirely predictable and often result from elected or imposed reciprocal processes (2015, 57–59).

The concept of "influence" took hold, and Rossa (2015) published an article for a wider audience in the newspaper *Público* the same year, emphasizing precisely this formulation. At the same time, he suggested that, because this heritage does not belong to Portugal, its destruction must be accepted and entered into the (colonial) equation. Rossa's position seems to insinuate that the very process of "ruination" and its study as actual "ruin," as Ana Laura Stoler (2013, 1–37) noted, opens up the possibility of another history of the Portuguese empire and, concomitantly, of uncovering, understanding, and perhaps overcoming its afterlives.

Such stance entails more than changing the noun when the problem is the adjective (not insignificantly, the PhD program is now known by its nickname, Patrimónios). It also entails refusing the impulse to miniaturize the empire for consumption—be it in a luxury box as in *Património de origem portuguesa* or with a click as in the digital portal Património de Influência Portuguesa—a process that has traumatic contours, in which repetition and wide circulation are key.

Conclusion: Heritage as Colonial History of the Present

In this article, I have unfolded a genealogy intended to track down "afterlives" (Stoler 2016) of the Portuguese empire, i.e., the endurance, reproduction, and consumption of an imperial episteme and its complex at work in the present.

Departing from the analysis of the Sete Maravilhas competition (heritage as entertainment), I identify the first efforts to resuscitate this heritage through the conceptual lens of the term "Património luso no mundo" in the Jornadas Luso-Brasileiras do Património and the Primeiro Congresso de Património Construído Luso no Mundo in the 1980s (heritage as erasure of colonialism); the aestheticization performed by art history in *História da arte portuguesa no mundo* in the 1990s (heritage as aestheticization); and the forging of *Património de origem portuguesa* and its dilution into *influence* in the form of high-fashioned objects in the 2000s and 2010s (heritage as miniaturization of the empire). Furthermore, I show that this heritage, like the writing of history, has more to do with the present than with the past. Indeed, the objects I analyzed here frequently responded to the sociopolitical anxieties of their respective presents: the "loss" of the empire (1974–75) and the entrance into the European Union (1986); the incapacity of pursuing an effective neocolonial politics through CPLP (1994), or Lusofonia, and the handover of Macau (1999); and the financial crisis (2010–15).

In tracing this genealogy, I aim to shed light on the failed attempts to find a proper word with which to label Portuguese colonial heritage around the world. This unsettling process expresses what Stoler (2011) designates as "colonial aphasia," that is, "a dismembering, a difficulty speaking, a difficulty generating a vocabulary that associates appropriate words and concepts with appropriate things" (25). This "colonial aphasia" manifests in a difficulty of understanding the relevance of known and spoken truths that are systematically silenced and/or made invisible. For Stoler, this is not a problem of memory, nor a product of amnesia or ignorance, but, very often, of "active occlusion of knowledge" (2011, 25).

After all, the "heritage(s) of Portuguese influence" is not an ensemble of sites and buildings, as the objects analyzed here propose in their erasure, aestheticization, and/or miniaturization of the empire. Rather, it is what has occurred, and still occurs, at the sites themselves. Further, it is who decides which monuments are worth preserving and for whom. Indeed, to reproblematize this heritage, to make the problem problematic, academics must question as well who has been determining it to be Portuguese and, for that matter, that people need to know about it today and in what terms. Who continues producing knowledge about this heritage and who still profits from it? How is this knowledge being produced? To what end?

In this regard, I implicitly argue that a "coloniality of seeing" sustains the "coloniality of knowledge," and that the objects I analyze here materialize this colonial equation; they are situated at the very heart of the process of knowledge production and accumulation fundamental to the colonial project.[39] Indeed, colonialism inaugurated an epistemological tradition still in place today, molded by image-making and image-reading: images do not illustrate arguments; they are themselves the colonial argument. Sixteenth-century atlases and maps, with their "view from nowhere," first inaugurated a colonial imagination that established a "proto-orientalist reasoning," which obfuscated its very locus of enunciation—the West (Mignolo 1995, 327–29). This colonial imagination was then fully rationalized in the Enlightenment, namely through the *Encyclopedia* of Diderot and d'Alembert and nineteenth-century scientific atlases, as a new, vision-based scientific reasoning aimed at standardizing objects, preserving the ephemeral, and distributing the inaccessible, in order to train the "expert's eye" (Daston and Galison 1992, 85) and help built scientific "objectivity" (Daston and Galison 2010). Twentieth-century colonial photographic albums provide yet another layer to this genealogy of "technologies of colonial rule" (Stoler 2002). These technologies, which also include colonial architecture, monuments, and archives, as well as the scientific disciplines that flourished under the domain of colonial institutions, were essential to the construction and narration of empires and function as idealizations, redemptions, and purifications of the violent history of colonialism.

Therefore, colonial domination relied on a long lineage of objects, which the objects analyzed here belong to and speak to, which help convey a "consolidated vision" (Said 1994) and a particular way of "imagining"—by way of "serialization." This "imagining" endured beyond the end of colonialism and permeated not only the postcolonial state (Anderson 2006), but most importantly knowledge production to which the objects analyzed in this article attest: they compile, serialize, and visualize the Portuguese empire through "its" heritage spread across the world. As such, the objects studied here are not only key players in the narration and memorialization of the nation; most significantly, through the process of miniaturization of the empire and its portability in luxurious bindings, they are part of a whole "visual economy" (Poole 1997, 3–12). This economy entails the spatial and temporal flow of colonial discourses and images and recreates the past in the present.

Invested with a documental power and in the name of "historical truth" and "objectivity," these memorialist pieces, in their format, reproduction, and massification, paradoxically serve one purpose: to politically and ideologically eternalize a colonial epistemicide and, through this process, fabricate ways of eternalizing it in the present. In so doing, these objects manufacture a postcolonial identity dependent upon an imperial "visuality" (Mirzoeff 2011) that feeds on the idea of an alleged "Portuguese world" and its "wonders," enabling the enduring of the Portuguese-world complex, an "imperial complex" first forged within the Portuguese World Exposition (1940), in the present. Along with other books that have focused on colonial and imperial visuality, namely photography, these pieces perpetuate the spell of the empire they often seek to unpack, reframe, or resituate. In doing so, they nostalgically reverberate an imperial episteme that ends up becoming a prosthetic substitute for a politically repressed absence. As I have also tried to demonstrate, this episteme, in turn, can reconstitute its imperial subjects and their subjectivity at any point in time.

Because of this, the objects analyzed here are part of the colonial histories of the present. As academics, we need to start questioning the (colonial) ontology of our own work and forge new ways of producing knowledge on this heritage without trying to control the narrative or stop time through old conceptual frames. Heritage is more than inherence. It is the very experience of movement—i.e., time itself. Rather than preserving and studying heritage as such, academics should also study this movement, what has happened to it over time: the ruination, devastation, and even its (iconoclastic) destruction. Because the Portuguese empire lives on in complex ways, this destruction is part of history as well (though it has not yet touched historiography, which, a bit naively, still believes in the untouchability of heritage). In studying this heritage, it is not so much a history that is needed, but rather a phenomenology that can unleash the very *experience* of such heritage. Only in this way will we be able to give shape to another history, redeeming history and its images from historiography and historians.

NOTES

1. I would like to acknowledge the invaluable input of the reviewer, of editor Anna Klobucka, and of João Mário Grilo.

2. The seven wonders of the ancient world were the Pyramid of Giza, the Colossus of Rhodes, the Hanging Gardens of Babylon, the Lighthouse of Alexandria, the Mausoleum at Halicarnassus, the Statue of Zeus at Olympia, and the Temple of Artemis, all located in the Mediterranean basin.

3. People from across the world chose from 21 monuments narrowed down from an original list of 177. The new seven wonders are the Great Wall of China, the city of Petra in Jordan, the Inca city of Machu Picchu in Peru, the Mayan pyramid of Chichen Itza in Mexico, the Taj Mahal in India, the Coliseum in Rome, Italy, and the statue of Christ the Redeemer in Rio de Janeiro, Brazil. Two other international competitions followed, the New Seven Wonders of Nature and the New Seven Urban Wonders. See https://about.new7wonders.com/.

4. 793 monuments were filtered down to 77 by experts, and then further down to a final list of 21 by an advisory board from the University of Évora. Portugal's Seven Wonders are now the Tower of Belém, the Monastery of Jerónimos, the Guimarães Castle, the Monastery of Batalha, the Monastery of Alcobaça, the Pena Palace, and the Óbidos Castle. See https://projetos.7maravilhas.pt/.

5. This competition received by far the most attention from the public and was strikingly similar to the contest to elect the most Portuguese village held in 1938 by the Estado Novo, which culminated in the election of the village of Monsanto, to this day still known by that label.

6. Ferro coined this term in his celebrated 1939 speech, "Politics of the Spirit," delivered before Salazar in order to establish his own agenda. In 1943, taking stock of his ten years at the head of the SNP's cultural policies, Ferro declared that he hated "modernism," preferring the term "vanguardism" to characterize his "Politics of the Spirit." However, this vanguardism was to be divorced from internationalism through the "work of nationalization." In this way, Ferro laid the foundations for a nationalist avant-garde based on a return to tradition and a "revival of folk art" (Ferro 1943, 17–18). For Ferro's role in this process, see Acciaiuoli (2013).

7. Unless otherwise indicated, all translations from Portuguese are mine.

8. See the list of the contest's finalists and winners at https://projetos.7maravilhas.pt/portfolio-items/7-maravilhas-de-origem-portuguesa-no-mundo/#Vencedores-Mundo.

9. Decolonial authors have shown that coloniality is constitutive of modernity and described how power is structured within it. There is no modernity without the production and reproduction of coloniality, which, as Walter Mignolo pointed out, is the "dark side of modernity". See, among others, Mignolo (1995) and Quijano (1992).

10. This open letter was signed by 802 people, among them historians Arlindo Manuel Caldeira (the only Portuguese historian who signed), Mariana P. Candido, Michel Cahen, Christine Chivallon, Myriam Cottias, Hebe Mattos, Maurice Jackson, Hendrik Kraay, Jane Landers, and Jean-Marc Masseaut.

11. Drawing from Nietzsche, Foucault's genealogy is a form of "effective" history without recourse to a chronological interpretation of events. Genealogy is the history of knowledge that is to be determined. In other words, it uses the forms that have escaped the institutionalization of knowledge in various cultural and social structures without reinterpreting, discovering, or emphasizing new events in order to discover hidden meanings that have been neglected by history. Instead, genealogy is an attempt to reproblematize the event, to make the problem problematic, not to find a truer history: "the final trait of effective history is its affirmation of knowledge as perspective" (Foucault 1984, 90).

12. For Said (1994, 62–189), this manifested in nineteenth-century literature at the height of empire. I argue here that this operation is still in place today through academic works, in particular those aimed at wider audiences.

13. Anderson's main thesis is that communities are distinguished not by being false or authentic, but by the way or style in which they are imagined. Imagination implies creation rather than mere invention, which entails seeing the nation as a cultural artifact in its own right, narrated by other cultural artifacts that endow the nation with a sense of tangible reality ([1983] 2010).

14. Tony Bennett (2004) has explored the ways in which expositions from the nineteenth and twentieth centuries produced an "exhibitionary complex" aimed at a "specular dominance of totality" that "sought to make the whole world, past and present, metonymically available in the assemblages of objects and people [it] brought together . . . to lay them before a controlling vision." Furthermore, this exhibitionary complex constituted a gaze that placed the visitors "on the side of power" and by doing so visitors interiorized the idealized view of colonial-fascist power (122).

15. For a thorough analysis of Benjamin's aestheticization of politics see Jay (1992).

16. The conference, which in effect was a series of events, took place between July and November of 1940, in Lisbon, Porto, and Coimbra, with the participation of many Portuguese and foreign historians; its proceedings were published in nineteen volumes. See *Congresso do Mundo Português*, 19 vols. (Lisbon: Comissão Executiva dos Centenários, 1940).

17. Mirzoeff (2011) establishes three complexes within "visuality": the "Plantation complex" (1660–1860), the "Imperial complex" (1860–1945), and the "Military-Industrial complex" (1945–present).

18. Lourenço put it bluntly: "Salazar's mythology of ourselves, proven to be untrue in practice, has triumphed at a symbolic level. We can continue to be the *same* although we are now *different*. Once again the manipulation of discourse saves us an examination of our conscience" (1983, 20; original emphases).

19. The decree that created the Comissão states: "500 years . . . have passed since some of the most important discoveries, with special emphasis on the rounding of the Cape of Good Hope (1487), the arrival in India (1498) and the discovery of Brazil (1500). . . . The scientific character, careful preparation and firm definition of goals and their pursuit deserve to be remembered as a project of mobilization on a nation-wide scale by the Portuguese of today, who can draw valuable lessons from the values and determination that enabled reaching such vast and great goals." Decree 391/86, November 22, 1986. https://dre.tretas.org/dre/8391/decreto-lei-391-86-de-22-de-novembro.

20. I am alluding to the work of Antonio Gramsci (1971), who defined hegemony as the cultural and ideological means whereby the dominant groups in society, including, fundamentally but not exclusively, the ruling class, maintain their dominance by securing the "spontaneous consent" of subordinate groups, including the working class. This objective is achieved through the work of "organic intellectuals" and it entails a negotiated construction of a political and ideological consensus, which incorporates both dominant and dominated groups.

21. This law expanded the tasks of the Direcção-Geral de Obras Públicas e Comunicações (General Directorate of Public Works and Communications) from architecture and urbanism to covering "monuments of national interest." Thus, the Directorate would be responsible for the inventory, classification, conservation, and restoration of Portuguese monuments erected overseas (Maris 2016, 175–98). See also *Diário do Governo* no. 172/1958, Série I (August 7, 1958), https://dre.pt/web/guest/pesquisa/-/search/351913/details/normal?q=41787.

22. I thank the anonymous reviewer of this article for calling my attention to the fact that the Roberto Marinho Foundation publicized its crucial role in the preservation of heritage in Brazil, albeit mostly by using public funding.

23. Brandão expands on this: "Never again will Portugal be able to speak, in an exclusive way, of its capacity to build, to make heritage, as never again can Brazil consider the heritage built within its borders only its own. . . . The current geographical coordinates of the two countries are a hoax when we try to understand and study their cultural past. It is enough to determine that the Portuguese-Brazilian cultural framework goes with Martins Afonso de Souza to India and accompanies Tomé de Souza from Portugal and India to Brazil; it reaches Brazil and Angola with Salvador Correia de Sá. This cultural past lives in those segregated people who traveled, from Monomotapa, from Goa, from Moluccas to Brazil, or in João Ramalho siring hundreds of children in the plateaus of São Paulo. A great cultural blending overtook the world all over the place where Portuguese culture crossed. . . . The entire world community changed with this amazing cultural miscegenation of which our two countries are today a product and the outcome" (Brandão 1984, 200).

24. The titles in English here are as translated in the program: "A Question of Genetics, a Question of Soul" (Márcio Viana), "Morphology of the Lusitanian Town" (Maria João Madeira Rodrigues), "Defense and Praise of a Safeguarding Attitude about the Calouste Gulbenkian

Foundation's Basic Contribution towards the Protection of the Patrimony Built by the Portuguese in the World" (João Campos), "The ICOMOS, the Letter of Venice and the Lusitanian Built Patrimony in the World" (Sérgio Infante), "The Portuguese Route" (Rogério Lobo), "The Cultural Heritage: Portugal and the Cultural Patrimony's Protection in the New Portuguese Speaking Countries" (Francisco Keil do Amaral), "Goa, Malaca and Ormuz or 6 Reasons for Defending the Portuguese Built Patrimony in the World" (Eduardo Kol de Carvalho), "Reflections on the Defense and Conservation of the Patrimony Built by the Portuguese in the Non-European World or Variations about an Ambition" (Carlos Antero Figueiredo), "There Is Interbreeding in Every Culture [*todas as culturas se amestiçam*]" (Michel Parent), "Lusitanian Pillories in the World" (Vasco Salema). Program of the 1.º Congresso do Património Construído Luso no Mundo, Faculdade de Arquitectura de Lisboa, March 23–27, 1987.

25. Original English translation in the catalogue.

26. The two events seem to have contributed to the autonomy of architecture from Lisbon's Fine Arts School, as a more technical discipline in need of a school of its own, separated from painting and sculpture. Concomitantly, at the time, Portuguese art history was also working towards its establishment as a discipline independent from history departments.

27. The invention of Lusofonia, according to Alfredo Margarido, was enabled by collective amnesia in relation to the violence that had been exerted on the vast majority of those who speak Portuguese in the world today (2000, 6).

28. Eduardo Lourenço (1999) has noted that Lusofonia fills an imaginary space of imperial nostalgia, but it can only be lived as a "multipolar space" (164) within which each subject must open up and listen to the other, without any pretensions of "communion or universalism" (188): an "old and mythical common house of all and of no one" (192).

29. "To commemorate the historical significance of the Portuguese Discoveries in the final decades of the fifteenth century, which culminated in the first sea voyage to India made by Vasco da Gama in 1498, and the commemoration of the arrival of Pedro Álvares Cabral in Brazil in 1500. The thematic aspect of EXPO'98 was nevertheless not merely limited to the aforementioned historical commemoration . . . the aim of which was to place the oceans, their diversity and essential role in the equilibrium of the planet, at the center of the attention of the international community. . . . A strictly historical approach was therefore eschewed in favor of an orientation that approached the theme in terms of its future and related it to science, politics, technology, and art" (*Relatório* 1999, 18).

30. Trouillot explains: "Silences enter the process of historical production at four crucial moments: the moment of fact creation (the making of *sources*); the moment of fact assembly (the making of *archives*); the moment of fact retrieval (the making of *narratives*); and the moments of retrospective significance (the making of *history* in the final instance)" (1997, 29; original emphases).

31. For a recent discussion on Portuguese imperial historiography see Ferreira (2016). For a revision of the bibliography on the empire, see Curto (2015).

32. In 2003, Francisco Bethencourt opined that in the "game of compartmentalized and routine studies, reproduced in an environment of university libraries of an appalling poverty, numbed by individual and group quarrels without any intellectual interest, historiography is the poor relative of the creative movement of deconstruction of the imperial memory" (2003, 77).

33. See Bethencourt and Chaudhuri (1998). Later contributions include those of Diogo Ramada Curto (2007, with Francisco Bethencourt) and Miguel Bandeira Jerónimo (2010), not to mention Brazilian scholars such as Luiz Felipe Alencastro (2000), João José Reis (1993; 2015), Roquinaldo Ferreira (2012), and Mariana P. Cândido (2013). These new developments, however, have rarely resonated outside of academia and Brazilian historiographical contributions have had almost no echo in Portugal.

34. This work was published in English as *Portuguese Heritage around the World*.

35. These monuments include the Fort of Príncipe da Beira, in Rondônia (Brazil); the House of Nacarelo, in Colonia del Sacramento (Uruguay); the Fortress of Arzila and the Portuguese cathedral of Safim (Morocco); the Fort of São João Batista de Ajudá (Benin); the Fort of Jesus, in Mombasa (Kenya); the Fort of Quíloa (Tanzania); the Fortresses of Hormuz and Qeshm (Iran); the Church of the Rosary in Dhaka (Bangladesh); the Portuguese Feitoria de Ayutthaya (Thailand); and the Church of São Paulo in Malacca (Malaysia). There were also interventions to preserve cultural assets in museums, and dedicated to the inventory and classification of archives (Maris 2016, 167–75).

36. This leads Rossa to even question the widespread term "Indo-Portuguese," which is perceived as limited when comparing it with other taxonomies—northern, Goan, Malabar (2010, 55–56).

37. In 2006, the University of Coimbra hosted the first international meeting of WHPO, promoted by the Portuguese National Commission of UNESCO, the IGESPAR (Institute for Heritage Management), and the Portuguese Committee of ICOMOS, which established principles of conservation. In the 2010 meeting, WHPO formulated its goals in the *Declaration of Coimbra*, signed by dozens of conservation experts and representatives of twenty-five countries. The signing ceremony was presided over by the UC rector, the President of Portugal, and representatives of the Portuguese government. For more details, see Amendoeira and Aguiar (2015).

38. José Mattoso, ed., *Portuguese Heritage around the World*, 3 vols. (Lisbon: Calouste Gulbenkian Foundation, 2010–12).

39. The coloniality of seeing is an optical unconscious that consists of a series of superpositions, derivations, and hierarchical recombinations, which interconnect, in their discontinuity, the fifteenth century with the twenty-first, the sixteenth with the nineteenth, and so on (Barriendos 2011). The coloniality of knowledge is the ongoing colonial access to knowledge and its distribution, production, and reproduction; a process that excludes and occludes other epistemes and disregards other ways of knowing and producing knowledge (Mignolo 1995).

WORKS CITED

Acciaiuoli, Margarida. 2013. *António Ferro: A vertigem da palavra; Retórica, política e propaganda no Estado Novo*. Lisboa: Bizâncio.

———. 1998. *Exposições do Estado Novo, 1934–1940*. Lisboa: Livros Horizonte.

Alencastro, Luiz Felipe. 2000. *O trato dos viventes: Formação do Brasil no Atlântico Sul*. São Paulo: Companhia das Letras.

Amendoeira, Ana Paula, and José Aguiar. 2015. "O mar foi ontem o que o património pode ser hoje, basta vencer alguns Adamastores." In *Preservar o património português além-mar: Portugueses e a salvaguarda do património edificado português no mundo*, edited by Joaquim Rodrigues dos Santos, 298–302. Casal de Cambra: Caleidoscópio.

Anderson, Benedict. (1983) 2010. *Imagined Communities: Reflections on the Origin and Spread of Nationalism*. London: Verso.

Andrade, Sérgio C. 2008. "Património Maravilhas portuguesas adiadas e polémicas." *Público*, December 7, 2008. https://www.publico.pt/2008/12/07/jornal/patrimonio-maravilhas-portuguesas-adiadas-e-polemicas-287094.

———. 2009. "Sete Maravilhas criticado por escamotear esclavagismo." *Público*, June 3, 2009. https://www.publico.pt/2009/06/03/jornal/sete-maravilhas-criticado-por-escamotear-esclavagismo-308727.

"Apresentação." 2016. O Patrimónios/Curso de Doutoramento. https://doutoramento.patrimonios.pt/apresentacao/.

Araújo, Renata Malcher. 2015. "Influência, origem, matriz." In *Patrimónios de influência portuguesa: Modos de olhar*, edited by Walter Rossa and Margarida Calafate Ribeiro, 47–63. Coimbra: Imprensa da Universidade de Coimbra.

———. 2010. "Património de origem portuguesa na América do Sul: Arquitectura e urbanismo." In Mattoso, *Património*, vol. 1, 20–45.

Arendt, Hannah. (1951) 1962. *The Origins of Totalitarianism*. Cleveland, OH: Meridian Books.

Barata, Filipe Themudo. 2010. "Os portugueses no mundo islâmico." In Mattoso, *Património* vol. 2, 23–33.

Barriendos, Joaquín. 2011. "La colonialidad del ver: Hacia un nuevo diálogo interepistémico." *Nómadas*, no. 35, 13–29.

Bazin, German. 1956. *L'architecture religieuse au Brésil: Étude historique et morphologique*. Paris: Librairie Plon.

Benjamin, Walter. (1936) 2006. "The Work of Art in the Age of Its Mechanical Reproducibility." In *Selected Writings*, edited by Howard Eiland and Michael Jennings, vol. 4 (1938–40), 251–83. Cambridge, MA: Harvard University Press.

Bennett, Tony. 2004. "The Exhibitionary Complex." In *The Nineteenth Century Visual Culture Reader*, edited by Vanessa R. Schwartz and Jeannene M. Przyblyski, 117–29. New York: Routledge.

Bethencourt, Francisco. 2003. "Desconstrução da memória imperial: Literatura, arte e historiografia." In *Fantasmas e fantasias imperiais no imaginário português contemporâneo*, edited by Margarida Calafate Ribeiro and Ana Paula Ferreira, 69–81. Porto: Campo das Letras.

Bethencourt, Francisco, and Kirty Chaudhuri, eds. 1998. *História da expansão portuguesa*. 5 vols. Lisboa: Círculo de Leitores.

Brandão, Augusto Pereira. 1987a. *Catálogo do 1.º Congresso do Património Construído Luso no Mundo (23–27 de março de 1987)*. Lisboa: Faculdade de Arquitectura da Universidade Técnica de Lisboa.

———. 1984. "Discurso de encerramento." In *Primeiras Jornadas Luso-Brasileiras do Património, Departamento de Arquitectura da Escola Superior de Belas-Artes (12 a 16 de março de 1984)*, 199–200. Lisboa: Fundação Calouste Gulbenkian.

———. 1987b. *Programa do 1.º Congresso do Património Construído Luso no Mundo (23–27 de março de 1987)*. Lisboa: Faculdade de Arquitectura da Universidade Técnica de Lisboa.

Cândido, Mariana P. 2013. *An African Slaving Port and the Atlantic World: Benguela and Its Hinterland*. New York: Cambridge University Press.

"Carta aberta: O concurso 'As 7 maravilhas portuguesas no mundo' ignora a história da escravidão e do tráfico atlântico." 2009. *Lusotopie* 16 (2): xiii-xvii.

"Catálogo da exposição." 1987. *1.º Congresso do Património Construído Luso no Mundo (23 de março–5 de abril de 1987)*. Lisboa: Faculdade de Arquitectura de Lisboa and Fundação Calouste Gulbenkian.

Chicó, Mário Tavares. 1956. *A cidade ideal do Renascimento e as cidades portuguesas da Índia*. Lisboa: Junta das Missões Geográficas e de Investigações do Ultramar.

Comemorações centenárias: Programa oficial. 1940. Lisboa: Secretariado Nacional de Informação.

Coelho, Alexandra Prado. 2011. "O mapa mundo do património português." *Público*, January 18, 2011. https://www.publico.pt/2011/01/18/culturaipsilon/noticia/o-mapamundo-do-patrimonio-portugues-1475878.

Curto, Diogo Ramada. 2015. "A memória dos Descobrimentos, da Expansão e do Império Colonial." In *Este país não existe*, edited by Bruno Monteiro and Nuno Domingos, 95–107. Lisboa: Le Monde Diplomatique/Deriva.

Curto, Diogo Ramada, and Francisco Bethencourt, eds. 2007. *Portuguese Oceanic Expansion, 1400–1800*. New York: Cambridge University Press.

Daston, Lorraine and Peter Galison. 1992. "The Image of Objectivity." *Representations*, no. 40, 81–128.

———. 2010. *Objectivity*. New York: Zone Books.

Dias, Pedro. 2008. *Arte de Portugal no mundo*. 15 vols. Lisboa: Público.

———. 1998. *A história da arte portuguesa no mundo, 1415–1822: O espaço do Índico*. Lisboa: Círculo de Leitores.

———. 1999. *A história da arte portuguesa no mundo, 1415–1822: O espaço do Atlântico*. Lisboa: Círculo de Leitores.

Domingos, Nuno. 2015. "Colonial Architectures, Urban Planning and the Representation of Portugal's Imperial History." *Portuguese Journal of Social Sciences* 14 (3): 235–55.

———. 2016. "Les reconfigurations de la mémoire du colonialisme portugais: Récit et esthétisation de l'histoire." *Histoire@Politique*, no. 29, 41–59.

Fernandes, José António. 2010. "Arquitectura e urbanismo na África Subsariana: Uma leitura." In Mattoso, *Património*, vol. 2, 183–275.

Ferreira, Roquinaldo. 2012. *Cross-Cultural Exchange in the Atlantic World: Angola and Brazil during the Era of the Slave Trade*. New York: Cambridge University Press, 2012.

———. 2016. "Taking Stock: Portuguese Imperial Historiography Twelve Years after the e-JPH Debate." *e-journal of Portuguese History* 14 (1): 55–70.

Ferro, António. 1943. *10 anos de política do espírito*. Lisboa: Secretariado de Propaganda Nacional.

———. 1950. *Prémios literários*. Lisboa: Secretariado Nacional de Informação.

Foucault, Michel. 1984. "Nietzsche, Genealogy, History." *The Foucault Reader*, edited by Paul Rabinow, 76–100. New York: Pantheon.

———. (1966) 2005. *The Order of Things: An Archeology of the Human Sciences*. New York: Routledge.

Gramsci, Antonio. 1971. *Selections from the Prison Notebooks*. New York: International Publishers.

Harrison, Rodney. 2013. *Heritage: Critical Approaches*. New York: Routledge.

Jay, Martin. 1992. "'The Aesthetic Ideology' as Ideology; or, What Does It Mean to Aestheticize Politics?" *Cultural Critique*, no. 21, 41–61.

Jerónimo, Miguel Bandeira. 2015. *The "Civilizing Mission" of Portuguese Colonialism (c.1870–1930)*. London: Palgrave.

Lima, Alfredo Viana de. 1984. "Discurso de inauguração por Portugal." In *Primeiras Jornadas Luso-Brasileiras do Património, Departamento de Arquitectura da Escola Superior de Belas-Artes (12 a 16 de março de 1984)*, 17–20. Lisboa: Fundação Calouste Gulbenkian.

Lopes, Mário. 2012. "Seis séculos de património acessível a todos." *Público*, April 17, 2012. https://www.publico.pt/2012/04/17/jornal/seis-seculos-de-patrimonio-acessivel-a-todos-onlinesensibilizar-para-a-preservacao-24383612.

Lourenço, Eduardo. 1983. "Crise de identidade ou ressaca imperial." *Prelo*, no. 1, 15–22.

———. 1999. *A nau de Ícaro seguido de imagem e miragem da Lusofonia*. Lisboa: Gradiva.

Margarido, Alfredo. 2000. *A Lusofonia e os lusófonos: Novos mitos portugueses*. Lisboa: Edições Universitárias Lusófonas.

Maris, Vera Félix. 2016. *A "memória do Império" ou o "Império da memória": A salvaguarda do património arquitectónico português ultramarino (1930–1974)*. PhD diss., Faculdade de Letras, Universidade de Lisboa.

Mattoso, José, ed. 2010. *Património de origem portuguesa no mundo: Arquitectura e Urbanismo*. 3 vols. Lisboa: Fundação Calouste Gulbenkian.
Mignolo, Walter. 1995. *The Darker Side of the Renaissance: Literacy, Territoriality, and Colonization*. Ann Arbor: University of Michigan Press.
Mirzoeff, Nicholas. 2011. *The Right to Look: A Counterhistory of Visuality*. Durham, NC: Duke University Press.
"Património da Humanidade." 2008. *Maravilhas de origem portuguesa no mundo*. Comunidade dos Países de Língua Portuguesa, Notícias, November 12, 2008. https://www.cplp.org/Default.aspx?ID=4211&PID=10035&M=NewsV2&NewsId=584&currentPage=43.
Poole, Deborah. 1997. *Vision, Race and Modernity: A Visual Economy of the Andean Image World*. Princeton: Princeton University Press.
Quijano, Anibal, and Immanuel Wallerstein. 1992. "Americanity as a Concept, or the Americas in the Modern World-System." *International Social Science Journal* 134 (1):5549–57.
Reis, João José. 2015. *Divining Slavery and Freedom*. New York: Cambridge University Press.
———. 1993. *Slave Rebellion in Brazil*. Baltimore: John Hopkins University Press.
Relatório final: Exposição Mundial de Lisboa. 1999. Lisboa: Parque Expo.
Rolim, Maria Luiza. 2010. "Identificado património de origem portuguesa no mundo." *Expresso*, May 27, 2010. https://expresso.pt/actualidade/identificado-patrimonio-de-origem-portuguesa-no-mundo=f585067.
Rosaldo, Renato. 1989. "Imperialist Nostalgia." *Representations*, no. 26, 107–22.
Rossa, Walter. 2010. "Enquadramento geral: Os quês deste volume." In Mattoso, *Património*, vol. 3, 20–61.
———. 2015. "A fénix do património colonial." *Público*, January 15, 2015. https://www.publico.pt/2015/01/15/culturaipsilon/noticia/a-fenix-do-patrimonio-colonial-1682208.
Rossa, Walter, and Margarida Calafate Ribeiro, eds. 2015. *Patrimónios de influência portuguesa: Modos de olhar*. Coimbra: Imprensa da Universidade de Coimbra.
Said, Edward. 1994. *Culture and Imperialism*. London: Vintage Books.
Santos, Boaventura de Sousa. 2001. "Entre Prospero e Caliban: colonialismo, pós-colonialismo e inter-identidade." In *Entre ser e estar: Raízes, percursos e discursos da identidade*, edited by Maria Irene Ramalho and António Sousa Ribeiro, 23–85. Porto: Afrontamento.
———. 2009. "Monumentos e colonialismo." *Visão*, May 7, 2009. http://visao.sapo.pt/opiniao/opiniao_boaventurasousasantos/monumentos-e-colonialismo=f507455.
Seibert, Gerhard. 2009. "As 7 maravilhas de origem portuguesa e o tráfico de escravos." *Público*, March 18, 2009. https://www.publico.pt/2009/03/18/jornal/as-7-maravilhas-de-origem-portuguesa-e-o-trafico-de-escravos-299492.

Smith, Laurajane. 2012. "Editorial." *International Journal of Heritage Studies* 18 (6): 533–40.

———. 2006. *Uses of Heritage*. New York: Routledge.

Stoler, Ann Laura. 2012. "Ann Laura Stoler Interviewed by E. V. Daniel." *Public Culture* 24 (3): 493–514.

———. 2011. "Colonial Aphasia: Race and Disabled Histories in France." *Public Culture*, 23 (1): 121–56

———. 2002. "Colonial Archives and the Arts of Governance." *Archival Science*, no. 2, 87–109.

———. 2013. "The Rot Remains: From Ruins to Ruination." In *Imperial Debris: On Ruins and Ruination*, 1–37. Durham, NC: Duke University Press.

Trouillot, Michel-Rolph. 1997. *Silencing the Past: Power and the Production of History*. Boston: Beacon Press.

UNESCO. 2021. "The Slave Route." https://en.unesco.org/themes/fostering-rights-inclusion/slave-route#Collection.

Vargaftig, Nadia. 2016. *Des empires en carton: Les expositions coloniales au Portugal et en Italie, 1918–1940*. Madrid: Casa de Velázquez.

INÊS BELEZA BARREIROS is a cultural and art historian interested in the migration of images across time and space and the ways in which the coloniality of seeing sustains the coloniality of knowledge. She is an integrated researcher at ICNOVA, FCSH-UNL, and editor of *La Rampa—Art, Life and Beyond*, and she has been working in documentary films that explore the relationship of cinema with other arts, such as architecture, landscape, and painting. She holds a PhD in Media, Culture and Communication from New York University, an MA in Contemporary Art History from FCSH-UNL, and a BA in History and Art History from Faculdade de Letras da Universidade de Lisboa. Among several articles and book chapters, she is the author of "*Sob o olhar de deuses sem vergonha*": *Cultura visual e paisagens contemporâneas* (2009).

ANA BALONA DE OLIVEIRA

Decolonial Imagination and the Unmaking of (Post) Colonial Cities and Tongues: History, Memory, and Futurity in the Work of Angolan, Mozambican, São Tomean, Cabo Verdean, and Portuguese Contemporary Artists

ABSTRACT: This essay argues for the importance of attending to the visual production of contemporary artists concerning critical, decolonizing perspectives on notions of Portuguese heritage and influence in Portuguese-speaking African countries. Several artists have been looking critically at sculptural, architectural, and linguistic structures, to name a few, left by Portuguese colonialism in Angola, Mozambique, São Tomé and Príncipe, Cabo Verde, and Guinea-Bissau, as well as in Portugal's urban landscapes. The examined case studies are relevant works by the artists Kiluanji Kia Henda (Angola, b. 1979); Ângela Ferreira (Mozambique, b. 1958); Filipa César (Portugal, b. 1975); Olavo Amado (São Tomé and Príncipe, b. 1979); Filipe Branquinho (Mozambique, b. 1977); Mónica de Miranda (Portugal, b. 1976); René Tavares (São Tomé and Príncipe, b. 1983); Irineu Destourelles (Cabo Verde, b. 1974); and Grada Kilomba (Portugal, b. 1968). These artists bring such physical and linguistic colonial remnants to light from an ethico-political perspective with inventiveness and wit, employing artistic disruption in order to think critically about psychic and systemic coloniality in the postcolonial present and to conceive of decolonized futures.

KEYWORDS: contemporary art; decolonizing heritage and influence; cities, architectures, and languages; history, memory, and futurity

RESUMO: Este ensaio argumenta no sentido de se reconhecer a importância da produção visual dos artistas contemporâneos no que a perspectivas críticas e descolonizadoras das noções de património e influência portuguesa nos países africanos de língua oficial portuguesa diz respeito. Vários artistas têm olhado criticamente para as estruturas escultóricas, arquitectónicas e linguísticas, entre outras, que foram deixadas pelo colonialismo português em Angola, Moçambique, São Tomé e Príncipe, Cabo Verde e

Guiné-Bissau, assim como nas paisagens urbanas de Portugal. Os estudos de caso em análise são obras relevantes dos artistas Kiluanji Kia Henda (Angola, 1979), Ângela Ferreira (Moçambique, 1958), Filipa César (Portugal, 1975), Olavo Amado (São Tomé e Príncipe, 1979), Filipe Branquinho (Moçambique, 1977), Mónica de Miranda (Portugal, 1976), René Tavares (São Tomé e Príncipe, 1983), Irineu Destourelles (Cabo Verde, 1974), e Grada Kilomba (Portugal, 1968). Com inventividade e humor, estes artistas trazem à luz ético-politicamente e perturbam artisticamente tais vestígios coloniais físicos e linguísticos, com o intuito de pensar criticamente sobre a colonialidade psíquica e sistémica no presente pós-colonial, e de conceber futuros descolonizados.

PALAVRAS-CHAVE: arte contemporânea; descolonizar património e influência; cidades, arquitecturas e línguas; história, memória e futuridade

---

In this essay, I will argue for the importance of attending to the visual production of contemporary artists concerning decolonizing perspectives on notions of Portuguese heritage and influence in Portuguese-speaking African countries. Several artists have been looking critically at sculptural, architectural, and linguistic structures (among other kinds) left by Portuguese colonialism in Angola, Mozambique, São Tomé and Príncipe, Cabo Verde, and Guinea-Bissau, as well as in Portugal's urban landscapes. These artists bring such physical and linguistic colonial remnants to light from an ethico-political perspective with inventiveness and wit, employing artistic disruption in order to think critically about psychic and systemic coloniality in the postcolonial present and to conceive of decolonized futures (Quijano 2000; Mignolo 2000 and 2011; Sousa Santos 2010; Mbembe 2001).

According to Ann Stoler's elaborations on imperial debris as both ruins and ruinations, such "leftovers" are neither merely "rendered into neglect" nor simply "valorized for insistent remembrance" (2013, x). Following her suggestion, my decolonial analysis is sustained by the recognition that one must move

> away from the nostalgic European gaze upon ruins, . . . treat them as symptom and substance of history's destructive force, . . . take the measure of the "fragility" of capitalist culture from the decaying structures left scattered across our urban and rural geographies, . . . attend to the force of these fragments and the traces of violence left in its wake. (Stoler 2013, ix)

This approach implies a turn to material ruins as forms of socioeconomic, environmental, and psychic ruination, that is, as not simply "memorialized, monumental 'leftovers' or relics" but mostly "what people are *left with*": "what remains blocking livelihoods and health, . . . the aftershocks of imperial assault, . . . the social afterlife of structures, sensibilities, and things" (Stoler 2013, 9; original emphasis). These effects are to be found "in the corroded hollows of landscapes, in the gutted infrastructures of segregated cityscapes and in the microecologies of matter and mind" (9). Thus, by looking at apparently "inert remains," I examine "their vital refiguration" with Stoler's "pointed" question in mind: "How do imperial formations persist in their material debris, in ruined landscapes and through the social ruination of people's lives?" (9).

My case studies are manifold, which gives this essay a panoramic nature, although it is also structured along three main axes of analysis: colonial monuments (the longest section, which requires further segmentation for the sake of clarity); modernist architecture; and language and text. In the first section, I examine works by Kiluanji Kia Henda, Filipa César, Olavo Amado, and Ângela Ferreira around colonial statuary in Angola, Guinea-Bissau, São Tomé and Príncipe, and Portugal (which also necessitates a brief discussion on a postcolonial statue in Luanda and an anticolonial photograph, agronomy, and militant film in Guinea-Bissau). In the second section, I focus on instances of modernist architecture built by the Portuguese in Mozambique and Angola through works by Filipe Branquinho, Kiluanji Kia Henda, and Mónica de Miranda (while not forgetting Cold War-era examples of socialist modernism built by the Soviets in Luanda). In the third section, I analyze works by René Tavares, Irineu Destourelles, and Grada Kilomba, which address the coloniality imbedded in language and text, as well as historical and contemporary strategies of resistance and reinvention.

1. Decolonizing Colonial Monuments

1.1 Kiluanji Kia Henda's *Homem Novo: Balumuka* and *Redefining the Power*

In the twelve-part photographic work *Balumuka (Ambush)* (2010) (Figs. 1–2),[1] Kiluanji Kia Henda (Angola, b. 1979) has appropriated colonial ruins—and their attendant ruinations—in the urban landscape of Luanda in order to "ruin" them actively; that is, he has brought them to the visible surface of photography in order to undermine whatever symbolic power they might still embody. Such leftover structures of Portuguese colonialism have included fallen and broken colonial statues of male so-called heroes (Diogo Cão, Paulo Dias de Novais, Pedro Alexandrino, Afonso Henriques, Luís Vaz de Camões, among others),[2] "ambushed" at the São Miguel fortress by the upright solidity of the Angolan Queen Njinga Mbandi.[3] In Kia Henda's images, the queen temporarily "reenacts" her resistance against colonial occupation in the seventeenth century while the Kinaxixi square, where her pedestal used to stand, undergoes a profound and as yet unfinished urban transformation.[4] Awaiting the completion of the construction works, her bronze statue has been placed at the São Miguel fortress, where the Museum of the Armed Forces has been housed since independence, albeit neglected and closed for a long period due to the civil war (1975–2002) and the lack of appropriate conditions. Kia Henda photographed the fortress-museum before its renovation, reopening, and renaming as the National Museum of Military History were completed in 2013 (that is, before there was a definitive idea of what to do with these colonial leftovers) and when the construction works taking place both at Kinaxixi and the museum put the statues in motion, permitting their encounter. They were ultimately incorporated into the reopened museum's collection and display, with Njinga's statue prominently placed at the entrance, where it remains today.

Figs. 1-2. Kiluanji Kia Henda, part of *Balumuka (Ambush)*, 2010. Twelve digital chromogenic prints on matte paper mounted on aluminium, 166 x 110 cm each. From the series *Homem Novo*, 2009–2013. © Kiluanji Kia Henda. Courtesy of the artist.

At the time of *Balumuka* (and the earlier and related *Transit*, from 2009),[5] this colonial statuary was still "stranded," while awaiting some sort of final destination. According to Kia Henda, it was impossible to exhibit after independence; ironically replicating the migratory discourse of "Fortress Europe," he equated these monuments to citizens with expired visas, waiting for deportation (Kia Henda 2010; Kia Henda in Knoppers 2015; Kia Henda in Hossfeld 2018, 68). He added that they could be exchanged for all the Angolan objects taken by the Portuguese during colonialism, which currently belong to Portuguese museums (Kia Henda in Knoppers 2015). Because these statues were expelled to the

FAA-8060

fortress—a colonial "embassy" of sorts, erected in 1575 by Dias de Novais—where they remained exiled, unwanted, and out of sight, they have shared the space with military equipment from several historical periods: the Portuguese colonial occupation from the sixteenth century onwards; the mass settlement of the hinterland during the so-called pacification military campaigns of the late nineteenth and early twentieth centuries, which occurred in the wake of the Berlin Conference of 1884–85; the liberation war (1961–74); and the civil war (1975–2002). That is to say, the statues have mingled with colonial, anticolonial, and Cold War traces left on Angolan soil by Angolans, Portuguese, Soviets, Cubans, and South Africans, among others. In Kia Henda's work, the then-decayed colonial fortress/postcolonial museum emerges as a palimpsest of Angola's various times (and spaces) of occupation, struggle, and resistance—a material archive opening onto the transnational and transhistorical complexity of Angolan colonial and postcolonial history, with lingering effects in the present.[6]

The leftover structures examined by Kia Henda also included the colonial pedestals left vacant by the "ambushed" and "stranded" statues, as is evident in *Redefining the Power* (2011) (Fig. 3). Here, the artist collaboratively orchestrated and photographed the pedestals' temporary occupation or squatting by several young performers, who are poets, designers, and activists; friends and fellow cultural workers he admires. Both *Balumuka* and *Redefining the Power* form an integral part of the series *Homem Novo* (New Man) (2009–13), the title of which is indebted to the Marxist-Leninist conception of revolutionary subjectivity and nationhood. Similarly to many other revolutionary contexts, the expression "new man" also infused the rhetoric of revolutionary Angola, and is still inscribed in the country's national anthem.[7] As a whole, the *Homem Novo* series carries out a heterogeneous, critical, and ironic investigation not only of colonial, anticolonial, post-independence, and Cold War remnants, but also of the new post–Cold War and post–civil war symbols and heroes of the nation. As opposed to both the orthodox "new man" of the socialist revolution and the politicians, oligarchs, and media entertainers of global capitalism, to which Angola now fully belongs, Kia Henda celebrates other revolutionary subjects, artistic work and creativity, friendship and collaboration, activism and nonnormative genders and sexualities, as contributing to a more democratic society. Real and fictive; solid and transient; stone-made, metallic, and human; sculptural and performative—Kia Henda shows the nation's old and new symbols as not only enmeshed in Luanda's urban space, but also made visible so as to upset

Fig. 3. Kiluanji Kia Henda, *Redefining the Power III*, 2011. Three photographic prints on aluminium, 80 × 120 cm. From the series *Homem Novo*, 2009–13. © Kiluanji Kia Henda. Courtesy of the artist.

neoliberal views of progress and development and patriarchal conceptions of subjectivity, including the revolutionary. Njinga's imposing figure and opposing gesture, alongside those of the performers Shunnuz Fiel, Didi Fernandes, and Miguel Prince on the vacant pedestals, might be said to call for the imagination of other, decolonial futures.[8]

1.2 Filipa César's *The Embassy, Cuba*, and *Cacheu*

As far as colonial embassies, fortresses, archives, and statues are concerned, the work of Filipa César (Portugal, b. 1975) similarly demands our attention. In *The Embassy* (2011) (Fig. 4), César filmed the "gazing" hands of the Guinean archivist Armando Lona perusing a colonial photo album of the National Historical Archives in Bissau. The work's title pays homage to Chris Marker's *The Embassy* (1973), a Super 8 short feature film depicting a large crowd of asylum seekers packed into a foreign embassy. Although the country where the tense events unfold is not identified, it becomes clear that it is Chile after Pinochet's military coup on 11 September 1973. Loosely inspired by Marker's *Embassy*, while also departing from it, César's film ascribes the status of the embassy to the archive, insofar as the latter is shown to be a space similarly leading towards a foreign country of sorts—in this case, the past (Lowenthal 1985). César thus transferred Marker's spatial and geographical elaborations on border-crossing to time and

Fig. 4. Filipa César, *The Embassy*, 2011. Video still. © Filipa César. Courtesy of the artist and Cristina Guerra Contemporary Art, Lisbon.

history, while both artists can be said to have filmed these passages from an ethico-political perspective. In César's video, Lona's "viewing" hands and words point to and contextualize, respectively, the photographs in the colonial album, whereby he not only takes the spectator to the colonial past but, most importantly, deconstructs the colonial gaze that fixed and catalogued bodies and landscapes—including urban spaces with their colonial statues and monuments.[9] This decolonizing gesture culminates in the image of a loose photograph, found in between the album's last pages, of a PAIGC school in a liberated zone.[10] This is an image of struggle and revolution that highlights the fundamental role that education and culture played (Cabral 2013, 267–82, 283–98; Vaz Borges 2019). However, revolution is not devoid of contradiction in this image; in fact, Lona concludes by commenting on how the symbol of the party, inscribed on the cover of the PAIGC school book being read by the students in the photo, became the symbol of the nation in an entanglement marked by "fusion or confusion" (César 2011).

Thereafter, César made other films about another archive, the remains of which she found in peril of disappearance in 2011. *Cuba* (2012), *Conakry* (2012), and subsequent films in what she has named the *Luta ca caba inda* project, revisit the history of the National Film and Audiovisual Institute (INCA) of Guinea-Bissau, in the framework of the PAIGC liberation struggle and post-independence nation building.[11] Founded in 1977, the institute holds films made before and after independence by filmmakers such as Flora Gomes, Sana na N'Hada, and the late Josefina Lopes Crato and José Bolama Cobumba, as well as films from countries supporting the Guinean struggle, some films from Portugal, and copies of films left by Marker when he visited the country in 1979.[12] The leader of the PAIGC, Amílcar Cabral, had sent Gomes, N'Hada, Crato, and Cobumba to Cuba to train with Santiago Álvarez at the Institute of Cinematographic Art and Industry (ICAIC) in 1967.

In *Cuba*, images of Álvarez's *Año 7* (Year 7) (1966) and of Cobumba, Crato, Gomes, and N'Hada's unfinished *Guiné-Bissau: 6 anos depois* (Guinea-Bissau: 6 Years Later) (1980) unfold on a screen and on the bodies of three performers: the Guinean filmmaker Suleimane Biai; INCA's former director, the Guinean Carlos Vaz; and the Portuguese actress Joana Barrios. They read aloud excerpts from Cabral's *Estudos agrários* (Agrarian Studies) (1988), which gathers his agronomic texts from 1949 to 1960, and from his "A arma da teoria" (The Weapon of Theory), the lecture he gave at the Tricontinental Conference in Cuba in 1966 (Cabral 2013, 239–56). *Cuba* initiated César's ongoing examination of the role played by Guinean militant cinema and its internationalist networks of solidarity in both recording and strengthening the liberation struggle and the decolonizing nation building. These processes were, in turn, deeply nourished by Cabral's agronomic knowledge and experience of land and soil (acquired in Cuba, in the Alentejo region of Portugal, in the final course of study for his agronomy degree, and later in Guinea-Bissau and Angola), and by the emancipatory relevance he ascribed to theory and culture.[13]

César filmed *Cacheu* (2012) in between the more literally archival *The Embassy* and *Cuba*, while anticipating the latter's cinematic focus (and marking the actual inception of *Luta ca caba inda*) (Fig. 5). Somewhat similarly to Kia Henda's *Balumuka* at the São Miguel fortress in Luanda, *Cacheu* harnesses the haunted atmosphere of the Cacheu fortress (built in 1588), in northwestern Guinea-Bissau, for an active work of remembrance. Both Kia Henda and César choreograph a dance of ghosts performed by the stone specters of colonial statues: dead and yet hauntingly present (Derrida 1994; Gordon 2008), fallen from their pedestals, lying broken in graveyards of imperial debris (Stoler 2013), and yet demanding the living to recognize the enduring violence of their fallen gestures. Even more demanding, however, of both the living and these colonial dead, are the

Fig. 5. Filipa César, *Cacheu*, 2012. Video still. © Filipa César. Courtesy of the artist and Cristina Guerra Contemporary Art, Lisbon.

statue-less ghosts of the millions of enslaved Africans who were taken through Cacheu, São Miguel, and all the other fortresses on African shores toward the Americas (Sharpe 2002).

Beginning a strategy that César would use in subsequent films of the *Luta ca caba inda* project, *Cacheu* comprises a 16 mm single shot of a performative lecture on, and in front of, a screening. The performer, Joana Barrios, analyzes various screened images of the Cacheu fortress and of the Portuguese statues that, depicting figures from different colonial periods (Teixeira Pinto, Honório Barreto, Nuno Tristão, and Diogo Cão), were relocated to the fort in postcolonial times.[14] The visual analysis allows Barrios to delve into the centuries-old history of occupation and enslavement led by the Portuguese in the region, and of the Guinean resistance and struggle. The images include photos of Cacheu's statues from 2010 and 2012, and fragments from several films: César's *The Embassy* (the moment when Lona signals the photo where the statue of Teixeira Pinto is still standing on its pedestal); Marker's *Sans soleil* (Sunless) (1983), which shows Pinto's and Barreto's fallen, broken statues;[15] and Gomes's *Mortu nega* (*Death Denied* or *Those Whom Death Refused*) (1988), with Tristão's and Cão's statues standing on the floor before relocation.[16] In her lecture, Barrios comments on Cacheu's photos with slightly adapted script excerpts from Marker, Alain

Resnais, Ghislain Cloquet's *Les statues meurent aussi* (*Statues Also Die*) (1953), and Alexander Kluge and Peter Schamoni's *Brutalität in Stein* (*Brutality in Stone*) (1961), as well as the linguist Daniel Duku's reflections on decolonizing the language of the so-called discoveries.[17] In an important moment, Barrios is interrupted by a recorded Guinean voice of a man recounting his memories of these statues in his own Creole words. Just before the end, *Cacheu* lingers briefly on the moving image of a cauldron where food for enslaved people was once cooked, which, placed at the center of the fortress, memorializes the violence of enslavement and its legacies, and pays homage to those who died, survived, and resisted.

Although these dead colonial statues have been "buried" in Cacheu, the undying haunting of their violent histories and legacies, made visible on the screen, lives on beneath the veil of denial and amnesia. Although monuments celebrating colonial figures have fallen in the past and continue to fall, and while important counter-monuments have often been erected in their place through activism and art (even if only temporarily, at times), such a fall must be made truly deadly as an actual epistemic and structural decolonization and reparation.[18] Otherwise, no matter how fallen, broken, and out of sight, such statues will keep haunting lives undyingly. In Stoler's (2013, 9) terms, these ruins' violent histories and legacies must be remembered and examined so that their attendant social and psychic ruinations are, themselves, ruined. According to Derrida's hauntological spectropoetics—which is "not only but also, a *politics* of memory, of inheritance, and of generations"—in order to live "more justly" one must "learn to live *with* ghosts, in the upkeep, the conversation, the company, or the companionship, in the commerce without commerce of ghosts" (1994, exordium; original emphases). This "being-with specters" (Derrida 1994, exordium) should aim at the decolonial healing afforded by the possibility to "properly bury" the traumatic past (Sharpe 2002; Kilomba 2008, 146), which requires remembrance first and foremost, and the desire for a future otherwise. Significantly, for Derrida, spectral justice concerns responsibility for those who are "not yet" as much as "those who are no longer" (1994, exordium).

1.3 Olavo Amado's *(Re)Descobertos*

As opposed to the colonial statues' ruined condition in Kia Henda's photographs and César's video, in Olavo Amado's (São Tomé and Príncipe, b. 1979) sartorial intervention for the camera in the photographic series *(Re)Descobertos* ([Re] Discovered) (2013) (Fig. 6), they seem to have risen again, but only ostensibly.[19]

Fig. 6. Olavo Amado, *(Re)Descobertos*, 2013. Inkjet print on matte paper, 70 x 100 cm. From the series *(Re)Descobertos*, 2013. © Olavo Amado. Courtesy of the artist.

In fact, despite the statues' fairly well-preserved condition, the artist's gesture of dressing them up in colorful African-cloth garments necessarily and humorously disturbs any heroic grandeur they could evoke, especially considering their eminent placement at the entrance of São Tomé's National Museum, at the São Sebastião fortress. Amado critically acknowledges the prominent visibility ascribed to the statues by their location as he mocks it. His intervention makes them even more conspicuous, but in a noncelebratory and humorous fashion: it reverses the colonial relationship of "discoverer versus discovered" by turning the Portuguese into the (re)discovered, as the title suggests. They also emerge as reappropriated and Africanized by São Tomeans, and therefore much more in line with the histories of struggle and resistance told by the National Museum's display. Finally, the work's title warns against not only the untruth of the so-called discoveries, but also the dangers of ongoing patterns of coloniality and the neocolonialism at work in capitalist forms of European "rediscovery."

1.4 Kiluanji Kia Henda's *A descoberta* and Ângela Ferreira's *Messy Colonialism, Wild Decolonization*

In Lisbon, Kia Henda, Ângela Ferreira (Mozambique, b. 1958) and others have also looked at the ways in which the grand narrative of the so-called discoveries continues to deny the violent histories and memories of slavery and colonialism. This denialist narrative, in addition to thriving at all levels of public education (including many sectors of Portuguese academia), remains deeply embedded in celebratory monuments, many of which were built under the aegis of the Estado Novo dictatorial regime (1926–74), while others have been erected much more recently.[20] This denial contributes to perpetuating the present-day legacies of such violent pasts in the form of an enduring structural racism in contemporary Portuguese society, conveniently swept under the carpet of an anxiously maintained lusotropicalism, now repackaged as *lusofonia* and the idea of a benign Portuguese influence around the world.[21] Due to intersections of race, class, and gender, those who continue to carry the heavy burden of such a collective denial are, today as much as yesterday, nonwhite bodies (Black, Romany, and other racialized communities) and, in particular, cis- and transgender racialized women (hooks 2015; Davis 1983; Collins 2009; Crenshaw 1989; Vergès 2019). After many decades of resistance and struggle, antiracist and intersectional feminist grassroots organizations are bringing structural racism and the processes of memorialization of slavery and colonialism into the public sphere with increasing visibility.[22]

Ferreira's video and sculptural installation *Messy Colonialism, Wild Decolonization* (2015) (Fig. 8), like much of her other work, involved exploring several archives. In the Portuguese Film Archive and in open-access online archives, she found filmic and photographic material relating to the Padrão dos Descobrimentos (Monument to the Discoveries) in the Praça do Império (Empire Square) in Belém, Lisbon. The monument had previously been the setting of Kia Henda's

Fig. 7. Kiluanji Kia Henda, *A descoberta*, 2007. Inkjet print on cotton paper, 188 x 120 cm. © Kiluanji Kia Henda. Courtesy of the artist.

A descoberta (The Discovery) (2007) (Fig. 7), which depicts black youth squatting the structure, as choreographed by the artist, and mockingly "discovering" it.[23] The image brings to the fore the black subjectivity that remains structurally marginalized in Portuguese society through urban segregation—a powerful legacy of the colonial and enslaving violence that is silenced by the monument's celebratory narrative.

Almost a decade later, Ferreira used her archival material to make a video to be screened on a wooden sculpture that recreates the crates and boxes of the Portuguese settlers who left the former colonies in 1975.[24] The video and the sculpture intend to reflect on how the site of the Padrão dos Descobrimentos symbolically marked both the beginning of the Portuguese colonial enterprise as envisioned by the Estado Novo regime from the late 1930s and its collapse in the mid-1970s, after thirteen years of war waged against the Angolan, Mozambican, and Guinean liberation movements (1961–74). The first, temporary version of the Padrão was inaugurated at the Exhibition of the Portuguese World, organized by the regime in 1940 to celebrate the anniversary of Portugal's founding in 1140 and Portuguese independence from Spain in 1640. A permanent version of the monument was inaugurated in 1960, in commemoration of the anniversary of the death of Henry the Navigator—the inaugural figure, both historical and mythical, of the so-called age of the discoveries—in 1460.[25] Ferreira's video begins with images of the Padrão's construction, pertaining to the newsreels *Imagens de Portugal* (Images of Portugal) nr. 186 (1959) and nr. 193 (1960), the latter of which depicts the building of the sculptures that became the Padrão's main decorative elements at the atelier of Leopoldo de Almeida.

The sides of the monument, in the shape of a caravel facing the Tagus estuary, are occupied by an ascending parade of kings, conquerors, explorers, scholars, and poets, led by Henry the Navigator, and sculpted in the large-scale, epic style typical of Estado Novo statuary—stone heroes demonumentalized by Kia Henda's black subjects. The façade takes the form of a cross, within which appears the image of a sword—a powerful metaphor for the entanglements between the discoveries, evangelizing/civilizing mission, and conquest.[26] The films that Ferreira uses to recall these histories were also made in the context of the Estado Novo's propaganda initiatives.[27] Her short-length silent video piece is a potent reminder of the regime's ideological investment in grand cultural events, monumental public sculpture, architecture, and cinema in order to promote and celebrate itself; and of the fact that the histories of some of these

Fig. 8. Ângela Ferreira, *Messy Colonialism, Wild Decolonization*, 2015. Installation view, GIBCA—Gothenburg International Biennial of Contemporary Art, Roda Sten Konsthall, Gothenburg, 2015. © Hendrik Zeitler. Courtesy of the artist.

cultural productions have still not been critically reexamined outside of some academic circles.[28]

The fact that such newsreels were sponsored and controlled by the Estado Novo underscores the importance of what comes next in Ferreira's video piece. About forty years later, the wooden crates of returning settlers piled up at this very same site—the Padrão monument—some of them remaining there for years awaiting clearance, caught up amid the revolutionary period. The video ends with two images taken by the photojournalist Alfredo Cunha in 1975, depicting what Ferreira terms the "spoils of the end of colonialism . . . standing up against the Monument to the Discoveries" (Ferreira 2015): the crates and boxes that the installation renders sculpturally.[29] Cunha's images poignantly testify to the ironies of history in showing what remained of the so-called discoveries next to their very monument: a hurriedly "crated empire" in pieces.[30] Shipped to Portugal and stacked next to the Padrão, the crates ultimately demonumentalized it.

In this investigation and many others, Ferreira looks at historical events in a way that does justice to their complexities and contradictions, inviting us to do the same. She confronts us with the absence of a rigorous public debate on the violence of the colonial enterprise—a colonial violence that goes back to the beginning of the Portuguese empire and far predates the Estado Novo (as was made evident by its own cultural manifestations celebrating historical moments of colonial discovery and conquest, which the regime powerfully reconfigured within its own dictatorial framework). Ferreira also considers, however, the difficulties and consequences of a decolonization process that involved the sudden mass arrival of many Portuguese from the former colonies who were practically strangers in the former metropole. Many of them resented the loss of the empire and were undesirous of and unwanted by the revolution. Far from victimizing former settlers, Ferreira is interested in examining how decolonization remained psychically unfinished.[31] The violence of colonial exploitation and the loss of the empire in a bloody war were silenced to the extent that Portuguese society has become amnesiac and nostalgic, repressing and whitewashing the colonial past and, as elaborated by Paul Gilroy (2004) with regards to the British context, ultimately disallowing a thorough consideration of its enduring legacies.

2. Decolonizing Modernist Architecture

Some artists have also examined the ways in which the remnants of the modernist architecture left by the Portuguese in the former African colonies have been reappropriated in postcolonial times. Mostly through photography and video, Kia Henda and Mónica de Miranda (Portugal, b. 1976) in Angola, and Filipe Branquinho (Mozambique, b. 1977) in Mozambique, among others, reflect on the many pasts—colonial, post-independence, post–Cold War, post–civil war—told by the often decaying, and yet reinhabited, modernist buildings of 1950s and 1960s Luanda, Maputo, and elsewhere. These artists, gazing without nostalgia at these pasts through architecture, critically engage with a present marked by oligarchic capitalism and its neoliberal conceptions of progress and development, which prompts them to imagine other futurities. Particularly in Luanda, such conceptions have been materialized in, and through, the neglect and demolition of downtown architectural heritage and the forced eviction of inner-city slum dwellers to make way for the glossy skyscrapers and waterfronts of a deeply segregated and gentrified urban space.[32]

Branquinho, who has a background in architecture, photographed contemporary Maputo in the *Interior Landscapes* series (2011–15) (Fig. 9) by examining the exterior views (building façades and a coastline panorama) and, especially, the

Fig. 9. Filipe Branquinho, *Cine Theater Africa, Audience*, 2011. Inkjet print, variable dimensions. From the series *Interior Landscapes*, 2011–15. © Filipe Branquinho. Courtesy of the artist and Galerie Magnin-A, Paris.

indoors of several iconic buildings of the city's colonial and postcolonial history and cultural life: the Scala, Africa, and Gil Vicente movie theaters, the Iron House, the Natural History Museum, the Historical Archive, the Mozambican Radio, the Center for Photographic Education, among several others (Pinho 2015). Unlike in previous series, which relied more heavily on portrait,[33] the artist depicts a profound sense of inhabitation of many of these interiors through close attention to architectural structures such as corridors, doors, walls, and windows, as well as furniture and other objects evincing human presence in seemingly vacant spaces, with few photographic subjects posing for the camera. The series shows most of these buildings as not only fairly preserved (with some exceptions), but also, importantly, in active use as spaces for labor, study, leisure, commerce, and religion, despite the apparent human absence.

As a whole, the series becomes a visual archive and cartography of sorts, mapping a possible journey across the city's past and present through an architecture that is notably (though not exclusively) modernist. Particularly in Mozambique and Angola, modernist architecture became an integral part of the so-called

Figs. 10-11. Kiluanji Kia Henda, *The Spaceship Icarus 13, Luanda*, 2008, and *The Astronomy Observatory, Namib Desert*, 2008. Photographs mounted on acrylic frame, 120 x 80 cm each. From *Icarus 13*, 2008. © Kiluanji Kia Henda. Courtesy of the artist.

modernizing plans of the last decades of Portuguese colonialism. Maputo, Luanda, and other cities were sites of architectural, urban, and social experimentation by more progressive architects, where racial segregation nonetheless persisted, and finally became spaces for a reappropriated, recreated modernity to be inhabited by Mozambicans and Angolans after independence. Thus, despite the buildings' colonial origin, Branquinho's photographs avoid the dangers of nostalgia by highlighting their contemporary life and their status as Mozambican historical and architectural heritage.

However, the modernist architecture examined by contemporary artists also includes post-independence constructions from the Cold War period, especially in Angola. The mausoleum where Agostinho Neto is supposedly buried was built in Luanda by the Soviet Union in 1982, three years after his death in Moscow.[34] Kia Henda's *Icarus 13* (2008), inspired by Cold War histories and fictions of space conquest as well as Western antiquity myths, humorously reconfigures the mausoleum into the Icarus 13 spaceship (Fig. 10), which, thanks to the creative efforts of a team of Angolan scientists, successfully completed humankind's first journey to the sun in 2006.[35] Other shots in Kia Henda's script include those of the Astronomy Observatory in the Namib desert (Fig. 11)—in fact, the Cine-Estúdio, an abandoned modernist movie theater left unfinished by the Portuguese in the city of Namibe in 1975.[36] Kia Henda's subsequent film, *Concrete Affection—Zopo Lady* (2014–15), draws on the Polish journalist Richard Kapuścinski's 1976 book *Another Day of Life* and uses the quasi-sculptural vestiges of architectural modernism in contemporary Luanda to narrate a fictionalized story of sudden departure in the chaotic summer of 1975, when the Portuguese desperately packed their belongings in crates and massively abandoned the city on the verge of civil war.[37]

Miranda's *Panorama* series (2017–18) also draws on modernist architecture in Angola. Her previous work, *Hotel Globo* (2014–15), had already critically examined the changing urban surface of Luanda through video, photographic, and performative incursions into the interior landscapes of the 1950s Hotel Globo. Until recently, the modernist hotel had still functioned in downtown Luanda, where, as stated earlier, the architectural heritage has been increasingly replaced with luxurious high-rise buildings.[38] In Miranda's work, modernist buildings, including the Hotel Globo and, subsequently, the Hotel Panorama and the Karl Marx Cinema (called Avis before independence; see Fig. 12), become spatio-temporal and affective "lenses" through which her own and her collaborators' bodies gaze at, inhabit, and reappropriate the multiple geographies and histories of the

Fig. 12. Mónica de Miranda, *Cinema Karl Marx*, 2017. Inkjet print on fine art paper, 103 x 249 cm. From the series *Panorama*, 2017–18. © Mónica de Miranda. Courtesy of the artist.

city.[39] As a diasporic subject between Portugal and Angola, Europe and Africa, Miranda negotiates double and doubling experiences of belonging, including those inherited from her Angolan family, from which an unbelonged sense of shared, communal dwelling might be said to emerge.[40]

3. Decolonizing Language and Text

As the post-independence renaming of the Avis Cinema in Luanda as Karl Marx Cinema makes evident, language is inextricable from power.[41] In fact, the Portuguese language as heritage and influence in African countries that were formerly Portuguese colonies has played a major problematic role not only in the postcolonial project of lusofonia, but especially as a so-called civilizing tool during colonialism: its top-down spread, more institutional than real, involved many forms of symbolic and epistemic violence. The mastery of the Portuguese language was imposed as evidence of civilization, and as one of the many conditions for African subjects to gain access to a never-fully-equal citizenship.[42] Thus, the creoles of Cabo Verde, Guinea-Bissau, and São Tomé and Príncipe, alongside the many national languages that have survived in Angola, Mozambique, and Guinea-Bissau, are living proof of resistance. Although the post-independence governments opted for Portuguese as the official language in their unifying nation-building efforts and in order to avoid ethnic divisions, the Portuguese language in Africa has often become more institutional than quotidian. Moreover, Portuguese spoken around the world is recognized as plural and increasingly hybridized, while Portugal's version of the language has become provincialized

(Chakrabarty 2008). However, two decolonial tasks remain unfinished: countering the notion that Portugal's version of the language is the original and correct one (as opposed to all the allegedly subsidiary and distorted variants), and revaluing African languages and creoles. Significantly, several governments in Cabo Verde have had it on their agendas to make Creole the country's official language, followed by Portuguese as the second.[43]

In line with the resistance historically inscribed in the creole languages and other forms of cultural creolization (Glissant 1997) and hybridity (Bhabha 1994), René Tavares (São Tomé and Príncipe, b. 1983) has reflected through painting, drawing, and photography on the African reinventions of European traditions at work in the Tchiloli theater, dance, and music performances of São Tomé and Príncipe, notably in his series *Tchiloli Family* (2011) and *Tchiloli Unlimited* (2019) (Tavares 2020) (Fig. 13), among others.[44] The Tchiloli (meaning "theater" or "tragedy" in São Tomean Creole) retrieves medieval stories around Charlemagne, following a 1540 text by the blind Madeiran playwright Baltazar Dias, *A tragédia do Marquês de Mântua e do Imperador Carlos Magno* (The tragedy of the Marquis of Mantua and the Emperor Charlemagne) (Valverde 2000; Seibert 2009; Barros 2010).[45] It tells the story of the murder of Valdevinos (the nephew of the Marquis of Mantua) by Dom Carloto (the son of and heir to the Emperor Charlemagne), who, despite being Valdevinos's best friend, was in love with his wife Sibila. The story ends with the emperor ordering the execution of his own son, as a justice-restoring punishment for his crime.

The circumstances of the introduction of Dias's play in São Tomé are contentious, with some scholars proposing that it was taken to the archipelago, in the form of its nineteenth-century adaptation as found in Almeida Garrett's *Romanceiro* and other sources, by São Tomeans travelling from Lisbon (Seibert 2009; Valverde 2000). However, despite the lack of archival evidence, other scholars seem to accept that Dias's play might have been introduced around the time of its writing by sugar-plantation owners and other travelers from Madeira—an account initially propagated in the 1960s by Portuguese intellectuals indebted to lusotropicalism (Seibert 2009). Whichever the case, it seems that an appealing factor for the strong penetration and local reinvention of this text by São Tomeans might have been its thematic focus on issues of legal justice and equality and its evidence of retribution for the transgressions committed by those in power, at a time (depending on which version one follows) either of slavery in the sugar plantations (sixteenth century) or of forced labor in the cocoa- and coffee-producing *roças* (from the late nineteenth century).[46] Despite lusotropicalist

Fig. 13. René Tavares, *Tchiloli Unlimited,* 2019. China ink and pigment on rice paper, 46 x 77 cm. From the series *Tchiloli Unlimited*, 2019. © René Tavares. Courtesy of the artist.

interpretations of the Tchiloli as an instance of so-called harmonious cultural encounter between the Portuguese and the São Tomeans, this practice seems to have emerged as a cultural expression of resistance against colonialism.

Having worked previously around the plastic qualities of theater through painting and drawing, Tavares's interest in the Tchiloli grew over the years out of a concern with São Tomé's cultural identity, history, and heritage—a creole African identity arising from a long and complex history of resistance to Portuguese colonialism, slavery, and forced labor, embedded in richly inventive forms of material and immaterial cultural heritage, including the Tchiloli.[47] Despite the form's European source, Tchiloli performances are deeply informed by various story-telling, acting, dancing, musical, and spiritual African traditions. The cultural creolization and hybridity at work in the Tchiloli should not be mistaken, therefore, for fraternal acculturation.[48]

For his part, Irineu Destourelles (Cabo Verde, b. 1974) has critically examined the coloniality that continues to pervade psychic and social lives in Cabo

Verde by devising a hybrid language that is a sort of anti-creole for video. In *New Words for Mindelo's Urban Creole* (2014) (Fig. 14), besides resisting the potentially fetishistic traps of representing bodies and landscapes by replacing them with text, Destourelles ironically presents a new glossary made from a mix of references from Greek mythology and names from Portuguese colonial history, which seems to have been emptied of African influences. These neologisms (made up of old words) appear consecutively as dictionary entries in white font on a single black screen, the rhythm of their sequential emergence signaled by a repetitive sound. Their definitions describe contemporary phenomena, which, although apparently recent, testify to enduring class-, race-, and gender-based legacies (under new guises) of slavery and colonialism in the postsocialist, neoliberal, globalized, and touristic present. The entries refer to situations of colonial amnesia and Eurocentric alienation (some of which resonate with the works examined earlier, such as "dysnomia, *v.* to let a colonial building become derelict; to avoid analyzing and understanding colonial events"; "amechanon, *n.* a fanatic supporter of a European football team"); racism and colorism ("arminisme, *v.* to want to have a child with a person with lighter skin, preferably a Caucasoid"); kleptocracy and corruption ("adefage, *v.* to appropriate governmental funds to set up a private construction company"; "apatesme, *v.* to receive money from a drug baron to finance political or economic projects"); the oversexualization and sexual exploitation of black bodies by white tourists and "expats" ("agriuse, *n.* a child sex tourist"); among other aspects (Destourelles 2014).

Destourelles's ironic and critical invention of these new words arose from his awareness that the coloniality they describe often remains silenced and unaddressed in the Creole-speaking Cabo Verdean daily life, particularly in Mindelo (where he has lived, having been born on the island of Santo Antão), the capital of the island of São Vicente and commonly referred to as the country's so-called cultural city. Compared to other islands in the archipelago, São Vicente's permanent colonial settlement took place much later (only in the nineteenth century); and, with more of a commercial (ship supply) than agricultural nature, it is generally thought to be less marked by the centuries-old importation of enslaved labor from West Africa (which occurred in islands such as Santiago, the first to be colonized in the fifteenth century) than by a purportedly cosmopolitan mix of traders and seafarers, particularly British. Of course, the complex migratory history within the archipelago complicates this narrative. In any case, distinct colonization patterns seem to have resulted in a contemporary condition in

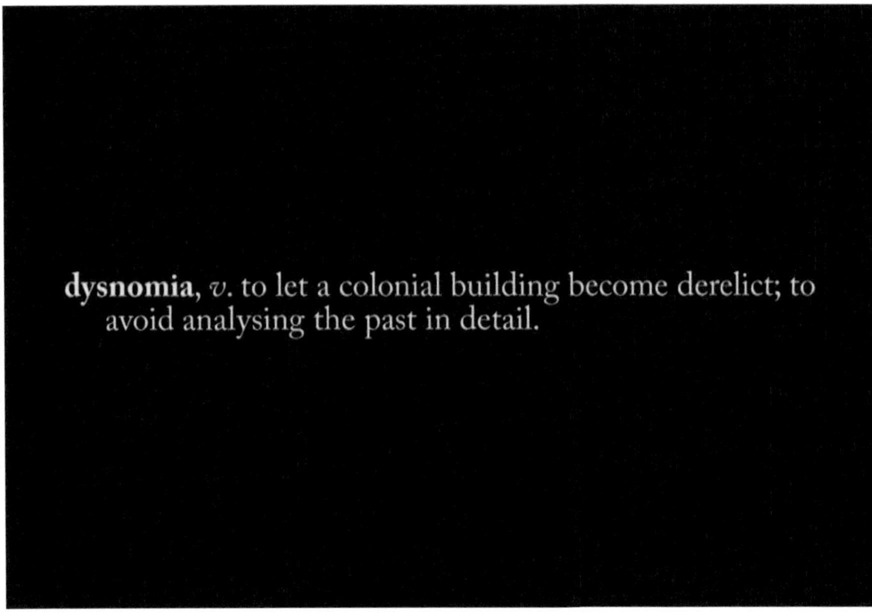

Fig. 14. Irineu Destourelles, *New Words for Mindelo's Urban Creole*, 2014. Video still. © Irineu Destourelles. Courtesy of the artist.

which relationships to the colonial past and African heritage differ across Cabo Verde's islands, with Mindelo's inhabitants often perceived as, and critiqued for, being more Eurocentric. Although the title of Destourelles's work underscores Mindelo's social and psychic realities through language, the work as a whole speaks critically of the country's postcolonial and postsocialist condition of enduring coloniality.[49]

Inasmuch as language has played a key role both in colonialism's strategies of domination and in postcolonial regimes of coloniality, it remains a site of resistance and a fundamental part of any real project of epistemic decolonization. *The Most Beautiful Language*, to quote the title of one of Grada Kilomba's (Portugal, b. 1968) two solo exhibitions in Lisbon in 2017, should be the one whose dictionary includes the living words, meanings, and practices of consecutive negation, frustration, ambivalence, identification, and decolonization as the necessary decolonial steps for black subjects. As far as white subjectivity is concerned, such a process should be one of successive denial, guilt, shame, recognition, and reparation (Kilomba 2008).[50] Although Kilomba elaborates on both psychic trajectories in her book *Plantation Memories* (2008), it is in the silent

Fig. 15. Grada Kilomba, *The Dictionary*, 2017. Installation View, *Grada Kilomba, The Most Beautiful Language*, Galeria Av. da Índia, Lisbon, 2017–18. © Bruno Lopes. Courtesy of the artist and EGEAC/ Galerias Municipais, Lisbon.

video piece *The Dictionary* (2017) (Fig. 15), which was on view in *The Most Beautiful Language*, that she invites not only her readers but also her viewers, particularly white ones, in gallery and museum settings, to read her dictionary entries for denial, guilt, shame, recognition, and reparation.[51] These appear sequentially in small white font on five black screens, demanding the viewer's proximity and dislocation. The screens' slightly mirroring surfaces, in turn, return the viewer's own image, inviting self-reflection (at once visual and epistemic, physical and psychic) and self-implication (Kilomba and Escórcio 2017). In fact, although reparation is the ultimate goal, Kilomba's inclusion of the preceding words/stages in *Dictionary* highlights the protracted temporality of what should be envisaged positively as an ethico-political, rather than moral, continual process of reckoning and accountability, awareness and responsibility, the discomfort of which is to be welcomed and embraced.

In conclusion, these reflections on the decolonial images and imaginations, by means of which contemporary artists from Angola, Mozambique, São Tomé and Príncipe, Cabo Verde, and Portugal have examined critically notions of heritage and influence in Portuguese-speaking African countries (and in Lisbon's cityscapes), offer a panoramic and inescapably partial view of diverse artistic practices, trajectories, and contexts. Each of these artists has unearthed histories and memories and envisioned futurities from the standpoint of hyper-specific social contexts and personal experiences, and through fairly distinctive and deeply collaborative practices. Despite the limitations inherent to any selection—which I have nonetheless tried to sustain by highlighting aesthetic and ethico-political connections among the works—I hope to have made my own decolonial contribution by historicizing these artists' significant gestures. They can be said to ultimately assemble in their shared urging for critical remembrance and imagination, and for decolonizing strategies of systemic reparation.

NOTES

1. *Balumuka* means "to stand up" or "to rise," as well as "to ambush" (in military jargon) in Kimbundo (Kia Henda in Hossfeld 2018, 68).

2. Diogo Cão was the first known European to arrive at the mouth of the Congo River in 1482; Paulo Dias de Novais was the first Portuguese governor of Angola and the so-called founder of Luanda in 1576; Pedro Alexandrino was a nineteenth-century explorer and governor of Angola; Afonso Henriques was the first king of Portugal in the twelfth century; Luís Vaz de Camões was the sixteenth-century poet who wrote *Os Lusíadas* (*The Lusiads*) (1572), an epic poem about the so-called discoveries, and is a major figure of Portuguese literary history.

3. Daughter of Ngola Kiluanji (the ruler of the Ndongo kingdom in the sixteenth century), Njinga Mbandi (1582–1663) was the queen of the Ndongo and Matamba kingdoms in the seventeenth century and a skilled military strategist and diplomat, who is still seen in present-day Angola as a symbol of resistance against Portuguese occupation (Heywood 2017).

4. Njinga's pedestal goes back to the colonial period: from 1937, it held a World War I memorial depicting an allegory of Victory (by the Portuguese sculptor Henrique Moreira); however, the statue was commonly referred to as Maria da Fonte (the nineteenth-century leader of a popular revolt in northern Portugal). Although formally named Largo dos Lusíadas, the square was commonly referred to as Largo Maria da Fonte or Largo do Kinaxixi (due to the neighbouring Kinaxixi market, built in 1950–52, in turn named after the Kinaxixi lagoon). The Victory statue was dynamited in 1974 and replaced with a Soviet tank (supposedly the one in which Agostinho Neto, the anticolonial leader and first president of independent Angola, entered Luanda to proclaim independence). Njinga's statue was commissioned by the state, produced by the North Korean Mansudae art studio, and placed on an altered version of the pedestal in 2002, where it remained until

the beginning of the construction works in the Kinaxixi square in 2008. The modernist Kinaxixi market (by the Portuguese architect Vasco Vieira da Costa), the Cuca building, and other structures were demolished to make space for a shopping mall and luxury high-rise buildings. An empty remnant of the pedestal remains amid the construction works, halted since the 2014 oil crisis. Kia Henda is currently working on a project about this site's history: *Red Light Square—History is a Bitch: Kinaxixi.*

5. *Transit* is a photographic work depicting the disassembled statue of Paulo Dias de Novais, with its four pieces lying on the ground.

6. See also Alfredo Jaar's video *Muxima* (2005) and Jo Ractliffe's photographic series *Details of Tiled Murals at the Fortaleza de São Miguel, Depicting Portuguese Explorations in Africa* (2007) (Ractliffe 2008). These tiled murals were made for the Museum of Angola, installed in the fortress in 1939. With the beginning of the liberation war in 1961, the fortress became the headquarters of the Portuguese armed forces.

7. The lyrics of Angola's national anthem, "Angola Avante" (Forward Angola) (1975), were written by the writer Manuel Rui and the music composed by Rui Mingas.

8. On Kia Henda's *Homem Novo*, see also Siegert (2017).

9. Hands have also played an important part in Chris Marker's *Le fond de l'air est rouge* (A Grin without a Cat) (1977).

10. The PAIGC (Partido Africano para a Independência da Guiné e Cabo Verde) was the Marxist-Leninist liberation movement led by Amílcar Cabral until his assassination on 20 January 1973. The liberated zones were the areas, in southern Guinea-Bissau, from which the PAIGC armed struggle (begun in 1963) had managed to expel the Portuguese armed forces, and where the independent nation-state was rehearsed before the unilateral proclamation of independence in September 1973. Portugal recognized the independence of Guinea-Bissau after the Carnation Revolution (which overthrew the Estado Novo on 25 April 1974) in September 1974.

11. Since then, César has made *Mined Soil* (2014), *Transmission from the Liberated Zones* (2016), *Spell Reel* (2017), and *Quantum Creole* (2019), among other films. *Luta ca caba inda* is the Guinean Creole for "a luta continua" (the struggle goes on). On this project, see, among others, César and Smith (2011); Moukouri (2012); César (2016; 2018a; 2018b); and César et al. (2017).

12. The Guinean films were digitized at the Arsenal—Institute for Film and Video Art in Berlin in 2012 (César 2016). Marker was invited to Bissau by Mário Pinto de Andrade, the Angolan poet who was a founding figure of the MPLA (Movimento Popular para a Libertação de Angola) and its first president between 1960 and 1962. Clashing with the party's more totalitarian wing, he and his brother Joaquim Pinto de Andrade led the Revolta Activa group in 1974. Forced into exile, he left for Guinea-Bissau, where he became minister of information and culture in 1978–80. He was the partner of the French-Guadeloupian filmmaker Sarah Maldoror.

13. Ângela Ferreira has also examined important connections between militant film, farming, and other collective activities in the context of FRELIMO's liberation struggle and decolonization in Mozambique, most notably in *Political Cameras* (2011) (Balona de Oliveira 2016c).

14. Teixeira Pinto was the army officer leading the so-called pacification campaign in Guinea-Bissau in 1913–15. Honório Barreto was a nineteenth-century governor and slave trader. Nuno Tristão was the first known European to reach Guinea's coast in 1445. Diogo Cão was the first known European to arrive at the mouth of the Congo River in 1482.

15. Marker's *Sans soleil* includes footage of the Bissau carnival that was likely filmed by N'Hada and Gomes, as they were both (with Jean-Michel Humeau) camera operators in Sarah Maldoror's *À Bissau, le carnaval (Carnival in Bissau)* (1980), the film for which, according to Maldoror, such footage was originally shot. Together with Thierry Sabatier, Josefina Lopes Crato worked on the sound. In his film, Marker thanked N'Hada—who, at the time, was INCA's president—for the carnival images (Piçarra 2020).

16. Importantly, those whom death refused in Gomes's film are the Guineans who, having fought against Portuguese colonialism and survived the war of liberation, had to continue the struggle of post-independence nation building.

17. Marker's script ("the society of statues is mortal. One day, their faces of stone crumble and fall to earth. . . . An object dies when the living glance trained upon it disappears" [1953]) is quoted out of sequence in different moments. Barrios's final statements on these statues ("The living intentions behind their original production seem to keep them undead. . . . Although they seem haunted, death refuses to take them" [César 2012]) echo, in addition to Gomes's film, Kluge and Schamoni's critical reflection on Nazi built heritage: "Every structure left to us by history expresses the spirit of its builder, even if later used for other purposes. The abandoned buildings of the Nazi party serve as witnesses in stone to a time that played host to the most terrible events in German history (1961)."

18. Recent falls occurred with the Rhodes Must Fall (RMF) movement in South Africa in 2015, to confederate monuments with the Black Lives Matter (BLM) movement in the US, and, after George Floyd's murder by the police in Minneapolis on 25 May 2020, to colonial and white-supremacist statues in the US, the UK, Belgium, etc. As to counter-monuments, see, for instance, the unveiling of Kehinde Wiley's *Rumors of War* (2019) in Times Square, New York, in September 2019, and its permanent placement in Richmond, Virginia, in December 2019, countering the history told by the city's many confederate monuments (Ugwu 2019; Stamberg 2020). See also Marc Quinn's controversial *A Surge of Power (Jen Reid)*, a sculpture installed overnight on the empty pedestal of slaver Edward Colston's fallen statue in Bristol on 15 June 2020. Because there was no public debate on its placement, it sparked intense criticism from many black British artists, who rightly saw it as an instance of white appropriation (Price 2020). Quinn's work was taken down the following day by local authorities, who intend to initiate a public discussion involving the black community on what to do with the vacant pedestal.

19. The three statues represent the Portuguese Pêro Escobar, João de Santarém, and João de Paiva. Escobar and Santarém are known as the first Portuguese to arrive in the archipelago—its so-called discoverers—and Paiva was one of its first colonizers.

20. In 2017, a statue of the seventeenth-century Portuguese Jesuit priest and writer Padre António Vieira was erected in Lisbon, raising criticism from antiracist activists and scholars due to its representation of Vieira converting three childlike indigenous people from Brazil, where he lived, and the fact that it was built with public funds and without public debate. Although Vieira considered that indigenous peoples should not be enslaved, he nonetheless defended their conversion, as well as the enslaving of Africans, facts which are usually silenced in Portugal, where Vieira is celebrated as a so-called precursor of human rights.

21. After the Second World War, The Estado Novo appropriated lusotropicalism, a concept originally theorized by the Brazilian sociologist Gilberto Freyre in the 1930s, to justify Portugal's maintenance of its African colonies when other European countries started to decolonize. It propagated the idea that the Portuguese mixed more with the African populations they colonized and were more benevolent toward them than the other European colonizers, ideas that still pervade in Portuguese society (Castelo 1998; Anderson et al. 2019). "Lusofonia" generally refers to the group of Portuguese-speaking countries—Portugal and its former colonies—and operates institutionally through the Community of Portuguese Language Countries (CPLP), an international organization founded in 1996 that works along the lines of the British Commonwealth and the Francophonie. On critical perspectives around lusofonia, see Cahen (1997); Margarido (2000); Barros (2009); Barros Varela and Costa (2009); and Barros Varela (2014).

22. An important memorialization initiative countering the celebratory narrative was the proposal by Djass—Association of Afro-descendants for a Memorial to Enslaved People in Lisbon, which was chosen by the people of Lisbon through the municipal participatory budget voting process in 2017. Subsequently, Djass invited the artists Grada Kilomba (Portugal), Kiluanji Kia Henda (Angola), and Jaime Lauriano (Brazil) to present their proposals for the memorial, which were voted on in six public gatherings across the city, notably in the Lisbon suburbs where many African and Afro-descendant communities live; these communities were especially invited to participate. The winning proposal was Kia Henda's. Djass's modus operandi contrasted enormously with Lisbon mayor's tourism-driven, top-down plan for a Discoveries Museum, which received fierce opposition from activists, artists, and academics.

23. Kia Henda carried out this work in collaboration with the TDK Association from Bairro da Quinta Grande, in Lisbon's northern periphery. Other artists, such as Jota Mombaça and the authors and actors from the play *Aurora negra* (Black Dawn) (2000), Cleo Diára, Isabél Zuaa, and Nádia Yracema, have also performed at the Padrão. On the ways in which the memory of the empire is celebrated in Lisbon's urban space, particularly in the Belém area, see Peralta (2013; 2017) and Peralta and Domingos (2019).

24. More than half a million Portuguese departed from the former colonies, some of them second- and third-generation settlers who had never been to Portugal. Arriving in the former metropole, these immigrants were commonly referred to as *retornados* or returnees, a name that persists today, but with which these former settlers never identified since they felt they were arriving in a foreign place rather than returning home. The Institute for the Support of the Return of National Citizens (IARN—Instituto de Apoio ao Retorno de Nacionais) was created by the revolutionary government in 1975 in order to support the relocation of these former settlers; it was closed in 1981. On the retornados, see Peralta and Oliveira (2016); Peralta et al. (2017); and Peralta (2019a; 2019b).

25. The temporary version of the Padrão was designed by the architect Cottinelli Telmo in collaboration with the sculptor Leopoldo de Almeida. Telmo's design was kept for the permanent construction, led by António Pardal Monteiro (Telmo had died in 1948), while Almeida himself recovered his original sculptural design. On the colonial section of the 1940 Exhibition of the Portuguese World and other colonial exhibitions in Portugal and abroad, see Ferraz de Matos (2006).

26. The sword, in turn, is decorated with the cross of the Ordem de Avis, a military and religious order devoted to the conquest of land from the Moors and the expansion of Christianity in Portugal in the twelfth century; the Avis dynasty—which initiated the so-called discoveries in the fifteenth century—was connected to this order. Below, Avis will reappear as the colonial name of a modernist cinema in Luanda.

27. The newsreels *Imagens de Portugal* were made in three series between 1953 and 1970 (Piçarra 2015, 144–223). The images used by Ferreira belong to the second series (1958–61), produced by Doperfilme under the direction of Perdigão Queiroga (Piçarra 2015, 152–68).

28. The square in front of the Padrão is decorated with a large-scale floor piece in limestone designed by Luís Cristino da Silva, depicting a compass rose and a world map of the routes taken by the Portuguese during the so-called age of the discoveries. This square was offered to Portugal by apartheid South Africa in 1960 (at the time of the Padrão's permanent construction), a fact that is seldom referenced.

29. The video's script unfolds on Cunha's images. For a history and visual analysis of the Padrão, in the context of the Exhibition of the Portuguese World in 1940, its permanent construction in 1960, and Cunha's photographs in 1975, see Sapega (2002; 2008).

30. Ferreira used the phrase *império encaixotado* (boxed or crated empire) as the subtitle of her work on at least two occasions: in her contract with the Portuguese Film Archive for access to the newsreels and in the solo exhibition *Ressignificação* (Resignification) at the Colégio das Artes in Coimbra in 2016 (Olaio and Carvalho 2017). For now, this remains the only time when the work (which has traveled extensively) was exhibited in Portugal, in a version made in collaboration with students from the University of Coimbra.

31. On the nonvictimization of former settlers, as well as the limits of the Padrão not only as a monument but also as a container and archive of objects and events, see

Ferreira (2017). On this and other works on mass settler return from the former colonies, see Balona de Oliveira (2016a; 2017a).

32. Regarding post–civil war Angola, see Soares de Oliveira (2015) and Schubert (2015). After a post-war period of accelerated growth in Angola, the decrease in oil prices from 2014 onwards caused a severe economic and financial crisis, which halted the construction of many of these skyscrapers. Both this interruption and the exorbitant prices of finished buildings have produced an urban landscape of new empty ruins alongside the old.

33. Some of Branquinho's portrait series include *Ocupações* (Occupations) (2011) and *Showtime* (2012–13).

34. Agostinho Neto was the leader of the MPLA between 1962 and 1979 and independent Angola's first president. The mausoleum was completed and repaired by the North Korean Mansudae art studio only after the end of the civil war, and it was officially inaugurated on 17 September 2012 in commemoration of the ninetieth anniversary of Neto's birth. Neto's sarcophagus is secured in a central and closed area of the mausoleum, out of visitors' sight (Siegert and Vanin 2019; Martins and Cardina 2019). See also Jo Ractliffe's photographic work *Mausoléu de Agostinho Neto* (Agostinho Neto's Mausoleum) (2007) (Ractliffe 2008) and Ondjaki (2008), which features the mausoleum and its surroundings prominently.

35. Although turning the mausoleum into a spaceship obviously involves fiction, the project was faithful to what Luandans commonly call the mausoleum: *foguetão* (spaceship). Further, the spaceship aesthetics was intentional on the part of the Soviets, inspired by Neto's renowned poem, "O caminho das estrelas" ("The Path of the Stars") (1953) (Neto 1977), which can be read on its interior walls, among other poems, speech fragments, and a eulogy. For an in-depth analysis of Kia Henda's *Icarus 13*, see Balona de Oliveira (2019b).

36. The Cine-Estúdio was designed by Botelho Vasconcelos of the Atelier Boper (Hurst and Fernandes 2015, 166–77).

37. For an in-depth analysis of this work, see Balona de Oliveira (2016a; 2017a).

38. The Hotel Globo has also been an important artistic hub: it harbored artists' studios and the nearby SOSO gallery (an exhibiting space for the Luanda Triennial), and has hosted the Fuckin' Globo exhibitions since 2015 and the Ateliê Mutamba and the Jahmek gallery since 2022. For an in-depth analysis of Miranda's *Hotel Globo*, see Balona de Oliveira (2016b; 2017b; 2019a).

39. Designed by the Portuguese architect Carlos Moutinho very likely between the 1950s and 1960s, the iconic Hotel Panorama decayed progressively during the civil war and was eventually abandoned. A renovation and expansion plan was designed in 2007 but never carried out (Magalhães and Gonçalves 2009, 61, 211). The Cinema Karl Marx was designed in the early 1960s by João Garcia de Castilho, the Portuguese architect of many other modernist buildings in the city (such as the open-air Cine-Miramar, designed with his brother Luís Garcia de Castilho in 1964) (Hurst and Fernandes 2015, 221).

40. For an in-depth analysis of Miranda's *Panorama*, see Balona de Oliveira (2017c; 2018; 2019c).

41. The colonial nomenclature for some African countries, cities, and streets was widely changed upon independence. In Luanda and Maputo, for example, many streets and squares were named in homage to heroes of the liberation struggle as well as socialist and pan-Africanist figures.

42. The mastery of Portuguese, among other requirements, was formalized through successive legislation comprising the *Estatuto do Indígenato*, which, until 1961, distinguished between *indígenas* (indigenous), *assimilados* (assimilated), and whites. The assimilados were considered civilized and therefore "almost" Portuguese, while the indígenas were seen as uncivilized and occupied the bottom of the colonial social hierarchy. On the Portuguese so-called civilizing mission between the late nineteenth and the early twentieth century, see Bandeira Jerónimo (2009). On the Portuguese classification of Africans throughout several colonial periods, see Castro Henriques (2019).

43. Creole is the maternal language of Cabo Verdeans, while Portuguese is the country's official language, although Article 9 of Cabo Verde's constitution declares that the state should promote the conditions for the former to become official on an equal footing with Portuguese (Direção de Serviços Parlamentares 2010, 28). See, for example, Céu e Silva (2017). For a more in-depth analysis, see Veiga (2009).

44. According to some, Tchiloli derives etymologically from the Portuguese *tiroliro* (fife), the transverse flute used in the play (Seibert 2009). While the Tchiloli is most common in São Tomé, in Príncipe its equivalent is the *Auto de Floripes*. On the latter, see Lemos Martins and Palinhos (2013).

45. Dias's text was presumably written in 1540 but published only in 1665 in Lisbon (Valverde 2000).

46. The formal abolition of slavery in São Tomé and Príncipe took place in 1875 but it continued in practice as forced labor. Enslaved people were replaced by *serviçais*, subsequently called *contratados*. It should be added that São Tomeans' historical resistance (escapes, hinterland *quilombos* or *mocambos*, revolts, etc.) to both slavery and the subsequent forced labor culminated, firstly, in the destruction of many sugar plantations in the sixteenth century and the concomitant decline of sugar production, which was transferred to Brazil and later replaced by cocoa and coffee, and, secondly, in the importation of forced labor (serviçais and contratados) from Cabo Verde, Angola, and Mozambique after abolition. The surviving former forced laborers, who stayed in the archipelago after independence in 1975, and their descendants comprise contemporary São Tomean society, with the inherited colonial hierarchy that kept them at the bottom having far from disappeared in the postcolonial period. On this colonial hierarchy and its legacies, see Seibert (2015). On São Tomean *quilombolas* and their descendants, the *Angolares*, the 1595 slave revolt led by Amador, and the lusotropicalist denial of São Tomean resistance by the geographer

Francisco Tenreiro, see Seibert (2004; 2012). On the continuities between slavery and forced labor, see Bandeira Jerónimo and Monteiro (2019) and Castro Henriques (2019). On forced labor until 1962, see Monteiro (2018).

47. The application of the Tchiloli for inclusion in UNESCO's immaterial world heritage list was first announced in 2009 and reiterated, most recently, in 2018 (Lopes 2018).

48. On Tavares's Tchiloli-related work, see also Nolasco (2020).

49. On Cabo Verde's colonial history and its contemporary legacies, see Barros Varela (2014); Cabral (2015); and Lima and Robalo (2018). On Cabo Verde's discomfort with its anti-colonial history from the 1990s onwards, see Cardina and Nascimento Rodrigues (2020). On Destourelles's work, see also Nolasco and Destourelles (2016).

50. *The Most Beautiful Language* took place at Galeria Av. da Índia in Lisbon between October 2017 and March 2018 (Rapazote 2018). Kilomba's other 2017 exhibition in Lisbon, *Secrets to Tell*, was on view at MAAT from October 2017 to February 2018 (Ferreira de Carvalho 2017).

51. Besides the 2008 book format, *Plantation Memories* also took the shape of a performative video in 2015. For an in-depth analysis of this and other works by Kilomba, see Balona de Oliveira (2020a; 2020b).

WORKS CITED

Anderson, Warwick, Ricardo Roque, and Ricardo Ventura Santos, eds. 2019. *Luso-Tropicalism and its Discontents: The Making and Unmaking of Racial Exceptionalism*. New York: Berghahn Books.

Balona de Oliveira, Ana. 2020a. "Breaking Canons: Intersectional Feminism and Anti-Racism in the Work of Black Women Artists." *Vista: Revista de cultura visual*, no. 6, 79–100.

———. 2016a. "Decolonization in, of and through the Archival 'Moving Images' of Artistic Practice." *Comunicação e sociedade*, no. 29, 131–52.

———. 2017a. "A Decolonizing Impulse: Artists in the Colonial and Post-Colonial Archive, Or the Boxes of Departing Settlers between Maputo, Luanda and Lisbon." In *(Re)Imagining African Independence: Film, Visual Arts and the Fall of the Portuguese Empire*, edited by Maria do Carmo Piçarra and Teresa Castro, 185–204. Oxford: Peter Lang.

———. 2019a. "Diálogos artísticos, transdisciplinares e intergeracionais: Práticas artísticas contemporâneas e o imaginário de Ruy Duarte de Carvalho." In *Diálogos com Ruy Duarte de Carvalho*, edited by Ana Balona de Oliveira, Manuela Ribeiro Sanches, Marta Lança and Rita Chaves, 165–84. Lisboa: Buala/CEC-FLUL.

———. 2019b. "Falling Radio Towers and Flying Mausoleums: Iconographies of Revolution and Utopia in the Work of Ângela Ferreira and Kiluanji Kia Henda." In *Revolution 3.0: Iconographies of Radical Change*, edited by Katharina Fink, Nadine Siegert, Ulf Vierke and Ute Fendler, 284–328. Münster: AVM.edition.

———. 2017b. "Globo Lodgers: (Un-)Mapping the Memory of the Vertical City with the Horizontality of the Body." In *Mónica de Miranda: Geography of Affections 2012–2016*, edited by Mónica de Miranda, 111–23. Lisbon: Self-published.

———. 2016b. "Os hóspedes do globo: (Des-)mapeando a memória da cidade vertical com a horizontalidade do corpo." *Buala*, November 8, 2016. http://www.buala.org/pt/vou-la-visitar/os-hospedes-do-globo-des-mapeando-a-memoria-da-cidade-vertical-com-a-horizontalidad-o.

———. 2016c. "Images and Sounds of Revolution between the Towering and the Underground." In *Ângela Ferreira: Underground Cinemas and Towering Radios*, edited by Manuela Costa, 65–88. Lisbon: EGEAC/Galerias Municipais.

———. 2019c. "Panoramas de fragmentos móveis, ou visões gémeas de (des)pertença na obra de Mónica de Miranda." *Vazantes* 3 (1): 5–16.

———. 2017c. "Panoramic in Moving Fragments, or Mónica de Miranda's Twin Visions of (Un-)Belonging." *Buala*, July 5, 2017. http://www.buala.org/en/ill-visit/panoramic-in-moving-fragments-or-monica-de-miranda-s-twin-visions-of-unbelonging.

———. 2018. "Panoramic in Moving Fragments, or Mónica de Miranda's Twin Visions of (Un)Belonging." In *Atlantica: Contemporary Art from Angola and Its Diaspora*, edited by Afonso Dias Ramos, Ana Balona de Oliveira, Marissa Moorman, and Mónica de Miranda, 177–86. Lisbon: Hangar Books.

———. 2020b. "*Plantation Memories*, Anastácia, Dandara, and Zumbi, the Slave Ship São José, and the Farms of São Tomé, or Slavery, Colonialism, and Racism in the Work of Women Artists." Special issue of *Observatorio (OBS*)*, 88–107.

Bandeira Jerónimo, Miguel. 2009. *Livros brancos, almas negras: A missão "civilizadora" do colonialismo português, 1870–1930*. Lisboa: Imprensa de Ciências Sociais.

Bandeira Jerónimo, Miguel, and José Pedro Monteiro, eds. 2019. *O direito sobre si mesmo: 150 anos da abolição da escravatura no Império Português*. Lisboa: Assembleia da República, Direção de Informação e Cultura.

Barros, Agnela. 2010. "Tchiloli de S. Tomé ou Carlos Magno em África." *Buala*, August 11, 2010. https://www.buala.org/pt/palcos/tchiloli-de-stome-ou-carlos-magno-em-africa.

Barros, Víctor. 2009. "A lusofonía como espellismo dunha casa miticamente común." *Tempo exterior: Revista de análise e estudos internacionais*, no. 19, 7–21.

Barros Varela, Odair. 2014. "Manifesto 'lusofóbico': Crítica da identidade cultural 'lusófona' em Cabo Verde." *Desafios – Revista da Cátedra Amílcar Cabral*, no. 2, 1–24.

Barros Varela, Odair, and Suzano Costa. 2009. "Comunidade dos Países de Língua Portuguesa (CPLP): Comunidade 'lusófona' ou fictícia?" *Tempo Exterior – Revista de Análise e Estudos Internacionais*, no. 19, 23–46.

Bhabha, Homi K. 1994. *The Location of Culture*. London: Routledge.

Cabral, Amílcar. 2013. *A arma da teoria: Unidade e luta I*. Praia: Fundação Amílcar Cabral.

———. 1988. *Estudos agrários de Amílcar Cabral*. Lisboa and Bissau: Instituto de Investigação Científica Tropical/Instituto Nacional de Estudos e Pesquisa.

Cabral, Iva. 2015. *A primeira elite colonial atlântica: Dos "homens honrados brancos" de Santiago à "nobreza da terra."* Praia: Pedro Cardoso.

Cahen, Michel. 1997. "Des caravelles pour le futur? Discours politique et idéologie dans l'institutionnalisation de la communauté des pays de langue portugaise." *Lusotopie*, no. 4, 391–433.

Cardina, Miguel, and Inês Nascimento Rodrigues. 2020. "The Mnemonic Transition: The Rise of an Anti-Anticolonial Memoryscape in Cape Verde." *Memory Studies* 14 (2): 380–94.

Castelo, Cláudia. 1998. *O modo português de estar no mundo: O lusotropicalismo e a ideologia colonial portuguesa, 1933–1961*. Porto: Afrontamento.

Castro Henriques, Isabel. 2019. *De escravos a indígenas: O longo processo de instrumentalização dos africanos (séculos XV–XX)*. Lisboa: Caleidoscópio.

César, Filipa. 2012. *Cacheu*. 16 mm film transferred to HD video, color, sound, 10:20.

———. 2011. *The Embassy*. HD video, color, sound, 37:06.

———. 2016. "A Grin without Marker." *Decolonizing Archives – Internationale Online*. https://www.internationaleonline.org/research/decolonising_practices/59_a_grin_without_marker.

———. 2018a. "Meteorisations: Reading Amílcar Cabral's Agronomy of Liberation." *Third Text* 32 (2–3): 254–72.

———, ed. 2018b. *The Struggle Is Not Over Yet: An Archive in Relation*. Berlin: Archive Books.

César, Filipa, Tobias Hering, and Carolina Rito, eds. 2017. *Luta ca caba inda: Time Place Matter Voice 1967–2017*. Berlin: Archive Books.

César, Filipa, and Valerie Smith, eds. 2011. *Labor Berlin 5: Filipa César*. Berlin: Haus der Kulturen der Welt.

Céu e Silva, João. 2017. "Abraão Vicente: 'O crioulo deve ter a dignidade de ser a língua oficial de Cabo Verde.'" *Diário de Notícias*, October 30, 2017. https://www.dn.pt/artes/abraao-vicente-o-crioulo-deve-ter-a-dignidade-de-ser-a-lingua-oficial-de-cabo-verde-8881572.html.

Chakrabarty, Dipesh. 2008. *Provincializing Europe: Postcolonial Thought and Historical Difference*. Princeton, NJ: Princeton University Press.

Collins, Patricia Hill. 2009. *Black Feminist Thought: Knowledge, Consciousness, and the Politics of Empowerment*. New York: Routledge.

Crenshaw, Kimberlé. 1989. "Demarginalizing the Intersection of Race and Sex: A Black Feminist Critique of Antidiscrimination Doctrine, Feminist Theory and Antiracist Politics." *University of Chicago Legal Forum* 1989 (1): 139–67.

Davis, Angela. 1983. *Women, Race and Class*. New York: Vintage Books.

Derrida, Jacques. 1994. *The Specters of Marx: The State of the Debt, The Work of Mourning, and the New International*. London: Routledge. Kindle.

Destourelles, Irineu. 2014. *New Words for Mindelo's Urban Creole*. HD video, black and white, sound, 10:26.

Direcção de Serviços Parlamentares. 2010. *Constituição da República de Cabo Verde*. Praia: Assembleia Nacional, Divisão de Documentação e Informação Parlamentar. http://www.parlamento.cv/Downloads/Constitui%C3%A7%C3%A30%20da%20Rep%C3%BAblica%20de%20Cabo%20verde,%202010.pdf.

Ferraz de Matos, Patrícia. 2006. *As côres do Império: Representações raciais no Império Colonial Português*. Lisboa: Imprensa de Ciências Sociais.

Ferreira, Ângela. 2017. "Os limites do poder do Padrão dos Descobrimentos e o retorno ao arquivo." In *Retornar: Traços de memória do fim do Império*, edited by Elsa Peralta, Joana Oliveira, and Bruno Góis, 353–62. Lisboa: Edições 70.

———. 2015. *Messy Colonialism, Wild Decolonization*. Single channel video projection, black and white, silent, 5:56.

Ferreira de Carvalho, Nuno, ed. 2017. *Grada Kilomba: Secrets to Tell*. Lisbon: Fundação EDP/MAAT.

Gilroy, Paul. 2004. *Postcolonial Melancholia*. New York: Columbia University Press.

Glissant, Édouard. 1997. *The Poetics of Relation*. Ann Arbor: University of Michigan Press.

Gordon, Avery. 2008. *Ghostly Matters: Haunting and the Sociological Imagination*, Minneapolis: University of Minnesota Press.

Heywood, Linda. 2017. *Njinga of Angola: Africa's Warrior Queen*. Cambridge, MA: Harvard University Press.

Hooks, bell. 2015. *Ain't I a Woman: Black Women and Feminism*. New York: Routledge.

Hossfeld, Johannes, ed. 2018. *Kiluanji Kia Henda: Travelling to the Sun through the Night/ Viajando ao Sol durante a noite*. Göttingen and Munich: Steidl/Goethe Institut.

Hurst, Miguel, and Walter Fernandes. 2015. *Angola Cinemas: A Fiction of Freedom*. Berlin and Luanda: Steidl Verlag/Goethe-Institut Angola.

Kia Henda, Kiluanji. 2010. "Part 4: Kiluanji Kia Henda." In *After Post-Colonialism: Transnationalism or Essentialism?* London: Tate Modern. https://www.tate.org.uk/context-comment/audio/after-post-colonialism-transnationalism-or-essentialism-audio-recordings.

Kilomba, Grada. 2008. *Plantation Memories: Episodes of Everyday Racism*. Münster: Unrast Verlag.

Kilomba, Grada, and Sílvia Escórcio. 2017. "Grada Kilomba." *Contemporânea* 12. https://contemporanea.pt/edicoes/12-2017/grada-kilomba.

Kluge, Alexander; Schamoni, Peter (dir.), 1961, *Brutalität in Stein*, Germany, 12:00.

Knoppers, Kim. 2015. "Interview with Kiluanji Kia Henda." *Foam Magazine*, May 20, 2015. https://www.foam.org/talent/spotlight/interview-with-kiluanji-kia-henda.

Lemos Martins, Moisés de, and Jorge Palinhos. 2013. "Teatro popular português: *Auto de Floripes* e as origens e significado do teatro do espaço lusófono." *Ensaio geral* 5 (10): 114–31.

Lima, Redy Wilson, and Alexssandro Robalo. 2019. "Entre o mito da *morabeza* e a (negada) questão racial em Cabo Verde: Um olhar contracolonial." In *Tecendo redes antirracistas: Áfricas, Brasis, Portugal*, edited by Anderson Ribeiro Oliva, Marjorie Nogueira Chaves, Renísia Garcia Filipe, and Wanderson Flor do Nascimento, 77–97. Belo Horizonte: Autêntica Editora.

Lopes, Mário. 2018. "São Tomé e Príncipe: Tchiloli poderá ser candidata a património mundial." *São Tomé Digital*. https://stpdigital.net/2018/07/08/tchiloli-podera-ser-candidata-a-patrimonio-mundial/. Accessed November 20, 2019.

Lowenthal, David. 1985. *The Past is a Foreign Country*. Cambridge: Cambridge University Press.

Magalhães, Ana, and Inês Gonçalves. 2009. *Moderno tropical: Arquitectura em Angola e Moçambique, 1948–1975*. Lisboa: Tinta da China.

Margarido, Alfredo. 2000. *A Lusofonia e os lusófonos: Novos mitos portugueses*. Lisboa: Edições Universitárias Lusófonas.

Marker, Chris, Resnais, Alain, Cloquet, Ghislain (dir.), 1953, *Les statues meurent aussi*, France, 30:00.

Martins, Vasco, and Miguel Cardina. 2019. "A Memory of Concrete: Politics of Representation and Silence in the Agostinho Neto Memorial." *Kronos* 45 (1): 46–64.

Mbembe, Achille. 2001. *On the Postcolony*. Berkeley: University of California Press.

Mignolo, Walter D. 2011. *The Darker Side of Western Modernity: Global Futures, Decolonial Options*. Durham, NC: Duke University Press.

———. 2000. *Local Histories/Global Designs: Coloniality, Subaltern Knowledges, and Border Thinking*. Princeton, NJ: Princeton University Press.

Monteiro, José Pedro. 2018. *Portugal e a questão do trabalho forçado: Um império sob escrutínio (1944–1962)*. Lisboa: Edições 70.

Mourouki, Laetitia, ed. 2012. *Filipa César: Luta ca caba inda (La lutte n'est pas finie)*. Paris: Jeu de Paume.

Neto, Agostinho. 1977. *Sagrada esperança*. Luanda: União dos Escritores Angolanos.

Nolasco, Ana. 2020. "Gazes from the South: The Tchiloli and the Work of René Tavares." *African Arts* 53 (3): 44–57.

Nolasco, Ana, and Irineu Destourelles. 2016. "Entrevista com Irineu Destourelles—Verifebura: Prática colonial e consciência pós-colonial." *Buala*, March 28, 2016. https://www.buala.org/pt/cara-a-cara/entrevista-com-irineu-destourelles-0.

Olaio, António, and José Maças de Carvalho. 2017. *Ângela Ferreira: Ressignificação*. Coimbra: Colégio das Artes da Universidade de Coimbra.

Ondjaki, 2008. *Avó Dezanove e o segredo do soviético*. Lisboa: Caminho.

Peralta, Elsa. 2013. "A composição de um complexo de memória: O caso de Belém, Lisboa." In *Cidade e império: Dinâmicas coloniais e reconfigurações pós-coloniais*, edited by Elsa Peralta and Nuno Domingos, 361–407. Lisboa: Edições 70.

———. 2019a."A integração dos 'retornados' na sociedade portuguesa: Identidade, desidentificação e ocultação." *Análise Social* 231 (2): 310–37.

———. 2017. *Lisboa e a memória do império: Património, museus e espaço público*. Lisboa: Le Monde diplomatique/Outro Modo.

———. 2019b. "The Return from Africa: Illegitimacy, Concealment, and the Non-Memory of Portugal's Imperial Collapse." *Memory Studies* (May 2019): 1–18. https://doi.org/10.1177/1750698019849704.

Peralta, Elsa, and Joana Oliveira. 2016. *Retornar: Traços de memória/Traces of Memory*. Lisboa: EGEAC/Galerias Municipais.

Peralta, Elsa, Joana Oliveira, and Bruno Góis, eds. 2017. *Retornar: Traços de memória do fim do império*. Lisboa: Edições 70.

Peralta, Elsa, and Nuno Domingos. 2019. "Lisbon: Reading the (Post-)Colonial City from the Nineteenth to the Twenty-First Century." *Urban History* 46 (2): 246–65.

Piçarra, Maria do Carmo. 2015. *Azuis ultramarinos: Propaganda colonial e censura no cinema do Estado Novo*. Lisboa: Edições 70.

———. 2020. "Resistance and Political Awareness through the Eye-Camera of Sarah Maldoror." In *Contemporary Lusophone African Film: Transnational Communities and Alternative Modernities*, edited by Paulo de Medeiros and Livia Apa, 63–79. London: Routledge.

Pinho, Alexandra, ed. 2015. *Filipe Branquinho: Paisagens interiores*. Lisboa: EGEAC/Galerias Municipais.

Price, Thomas J. 2020. "The Problem with Marc Quinn's Black Lives Matter Sculpture." *The Art Newspaper*, July 16, 2020. https://www.theartnewspaper.com/comment/a-votive-statue-to-appropriation-the-problem-with-marc-quinn-s-black-lives-matter-sculpture.

Quijano, Aníbal. 2000. "Coloniality of Power, Eurocentrism and Latin America." *Nepantla: Views from South* 1 (3): 533–80.

Ractliffe, Jo. 2008. *Terreno ocupado*. Johannesburg: Warren Siebrits.

Rapazote, João, ed. 2018. *Grada Kilomba: The Most Beautiful Language*. Lisboa: EGEAC/Galerias Municipais.

Sapega, Ellen W. 2008. *Consensus and Debate in Salazar's Portugal: Visual and Literary Negotiations of the National Text, 1933–1948*. University Park: Pennsylvania State University Press.

———. 2002. "Image and Counter-Image: The Place of Salazarist Images of National Identity in Contemporary Portuguese Visual Culture." *Luso-Brazilian Review* 39 (2): 45–64.

Sharpe, Jenny. 2002. *Ghosts of Slavery: A Literary Archaeology of Black Women's Lives.* Minneapolis: University of Minnesota Press.

Schubert, Jon. 2015. "2002, Year Zero: History as Anti-Politics in the 'New Angola.'" *Journal of Southern African Studies* 41 (4): 835–53.

Seibert, Gerhard. 2004. "Os Angolares da Ilha de São Tomé: Náufragos, autóctones ou quilombolas?" *Textos de história: Revista da pós-graduação em história da Universidade de Brasília* 12 (1–2): 43–64.

———. 2009. "Carlos Magno no Equador: A Introdução do 'Tchiloli' em São Tomé." *Latitudes: Cahiers lusophones*, no. 36, 16–20.

———. 2015. "Colonialismo em São Tomé e Príncipe: Hierarquização, classificação e segregação da vida social." *Anuário antropológico*, no. 2, 99–120.

———. 2012. "Tenreiro, Amador e os Angolares ou a reinvenção da história da Ilha de São Tomé." *Realis: Revista de estudos anti-utilitaristas e pós-coloniais* 2 (2): 21–40.

Siegert, Nadine. 2017. "Art Topples Monuments: Artistic Practice and Colonial/Postcolonial Relations in the Public Space of Luanda." *Portuguese Literary and Cultural Studies* no. 30/31, 150–73.

Siegert, Nadine, and Fabio Vanin. 2019. "The António Agostinho Neto Memorial." In *Revolution 3.0: Iconographies of Radical Change*, edited by Katharina Fink, Nadine Siegert, Ulf Vierke, and Ute Fendler, 200–204. Munich: AVM.edition.

Soares de Oliveira, Ricardo. 2015. *Magnificent and Beggar Land: Angola since the Civil War.* London: C. Hurst & Co.

Sousa Santos, Boaventura, and Maria Paula Meneses, eds. 2010. *Epistemologias do Sul.* Coimbra: Almedina.

Stamberg, Susan. 2020. "'Rumors of War' in Richmond Marks a Monumentally Unequal America." NPR, June 25, 2020. https://www.npr.org/2020/06/25/878822835/rumors-of-war-in-richmond-marks-a-monumentally-unequal-america?t=1596547470674.

Stoler, Ann L., ed. 2013. *Imperial Debris: On Ruins and Ruination.* Durham, NC: Duke University Press.

Tavares, René, ed. 2020. *Tchiloli Unlimited.* Lisboa: Self-published.

Ugwu, Reggie. 2019. "Kehinde Wiley's Times Square Monument: That's No Robert E. Lee." *New York Times*, September 27, 2019. https://www.nytimes.com/2019/09/27/arts/design/kehinde-wiley-times-square-statue.html.

Valverde, Paulo. 2000. *Máscara, mato e morte em São Tomé.* Oeiras: Celta.

Vaz Borges, Sónia. 2019. *Militant Education, Liberation Struggle, Consciousness: The PAIGC Education in Guinea Bissau 1963–1978.* Oxford: Peter Lang.

Veiga, Manuel. 2009. "O crioulo e o português em Cabo Verde." *Sibila: Revista de poesia e crítica literária*, April 1, 2009. https://sibila.com.br/mapa-da-lingua/o-crioulo-e-o-portugues-em-cabo-verde/2753.

Vergès, Françoise. 2019. *Un féminisme décolonial.* Paris: La Fabrique.

ANA BALONA DE OLIVEIRA is FCT Researcher (CEEC 2017) at the Institute for Art History, Nova University of Lisbon, where she co-coordinates the cluster "Transnational Perspectives on Contemporary Art." She holds a PhD in History of Art (Modern and Contemporary) from the Courtauld Institute of Art, University of London (2012) and received doctoral (2008) and postdoctoral (2012) grants from FCT, Portugal. She has lectured and published extensively in Portugal and abroad (*Nka*, *Third Text*, *African Arts*, etc.) and has curated several solo and group exhibitions, notably by António Ole, Edson Chagas, and Ângela Ferreira, among others.

MIRIAN TAVARES

Da ruína como discurso: Apontamentos sobre cinematografias pós-coloniais

RESUMO: O cinema foi inventado na tarda-modernidade, engendrando um discurso, um aparelho, uma arquitetura e uma proposição. Para perceber o seu alcance, não pode ser retirado do contexto em que nasceu e nem se podem ignorar as implicações espácio-temporais que o visionamento dos filmes provocou nos seus contemporâneos. De que maneira, então, os realizadores dos países africanos de língua portuguesa constroem um discurso próprio, dentro de um dispositivo herdado do período colonial? Como colabora o cinema no processo de construção identitária? De que maneira alguns cineastas habitam as ruínas do colonialismo? E como eles subvertem o conceito tradicional de ruínas, que se transforma num modelo de resistência ao novo, ao estrangeiro? Através da análise de alguns filmes de realizadores de Moçambique, Cabo Verde e Guiné-Bissau, procuro perceber as semelhanças e dissemelhanças do uso do dispositivo cinematográfico na construção de discursos audiovisuais no período pós-colonial.

PALAVRAS-CHAVE: cinema africano, ruínas, identidade, representação

ABSTRACT: Having been invented in the late modernity, cinema has engendered its own discourse, apparatus, architecture, and propositions. To acknowledge a film's full scope, one must not neglect the context in which it was created; nor can one ignore the space-time implications it has had for its contemporary spectators. In what manner have directors from African Portuguese-speaking countries constructed their own discourse within a device inherited from the colonial period? And how have they subverted the traditional concept of ruin, which has become a model of resistance to what is new, to what is foreign? How do some directors inhabit the ruins of colonialism? Through the analysis of some films from countries such as Mozambique, Cape Verde, and Guinea Bissau, I attempt to understand the similarities and dissimilarities in the use of cinematographic devices in the construction of audiovisual discourses in the postcolonial period.

KEYWORDS: African cinema, ruins, identity, representation

1. Das ruínas como reinvenção

A ideia de ruína remete, de um modo geral, para uma edificação que sobreviveu, desfigurada, e que conta uma história ou faz parte da história de uma nação. Quando se fala do passado, mesmo que recente, como o período da descolonização dos países africanos de língua oficial portuguesa, assomam imagens ruinosas que contemplam edificações destruídas ou abandonadas, afetadas pelas guerras que assolaram alguns desses países. Guerras que afetaram o território, alteraram cartografias e deixaram marcas que persistem. Neste texto, procuro refletir sobre a maneira como alguns cineastas desses países erigiram, sobre as ruínas do colonialismo conceptual e concreto, as suas cinematografias.

As ruínas arquitetónicas costumam ser associadas ao conceito de restos, sobras, ou mesmo de fracasso. A partir do Romantismo, a ideia de ruína adquire novos sentidos na cultura ocidental, devido ao reaproveitamento de ruínas, reais ou imaginárias. Com elas, os românticos construíram um presente com História, ou uma nova História do presente. Ao falar sobre arquitetura, Schopenhauer (2012) ressalta o seu caráter concreto e, paradoxalmente, diáfano: "Architecture has this distinction from plastic art and poetry: it does not give us a copy but the thing itself" (1803). Para o filósofo, a arquitetura era "a coisa mesma" (*the thing itself*) e a sua razão de ser a constante tensão entre a gravidade e a pedra, entre o espaço ocupado e a luz.

Como a arquitetura, o cinema é uma arte do espaço e do tempo, que reproduz, ou reinventa o fora de si, convertendo tudo em imagem, através do uso controlado da luz. As imagens cinematográficas, assim como as arquitetónicas, exigem e existem num contexto, e são influenciadas pelas suas circunstâncias. Nesse sentido, recupero a ideia de ruína do Romantismo para fazer apontamentos sobre a obra de quatro cineastas de países africanos de língua oficial portuguesa, na tentativa de revelar modos de produção-criação que emergem sobre as ruínas do colonialismo. Entendo que a maneira de reabitar espaços ruinosos é, também, uma maneira de criar uma cinematografia própria, que reflete a sua circunstância. Numa atitude de resistência, mas nunca de negação do passado, cineastas como José Cardoso, Licínio de Azevedo, Flora Gomes e Leão Lopes atuaram sobre o território, usando os seus filmes como ferramenta na tentativa de contar as histórias que não haviam sido contadas, ou que, de alguma maneira, foram ocultadas.

Laure Brayer (2016, 184–89) refere que as imagens são dispositivos úteis para se compreender as cidades contemporâneas, e afirma que o cinema é a imagem que reflete, de forma mais abarcável e quotidiana, a cidade. As imagens do cinema aproximam de nós o espaço urbano ao banalizar a complexidade do espaço, tornando-o compreensível e apreensível. O espaço torna-se o lugar do sensível e dos sentidos. Ao mesmo tempo, revela ritmos e nuances invisíveis ao olho nu.

Da mesma forma que o cinema torna mais abarcável a cidade contemporânea, ao tornar o espaço o lugar do sensível, como disse Brayer, considero que torna também mais abarcável a História, ou as histórias, que os lugares contêm. Talvez por isso, desde o primeiro instante, os movimentos de libertação de Moçambique e da Guiné-Bissau tenham apostado no cinema como um dispositivo capaz de os ajudar a reconstruir a identidade perdida, ou fragmentada, pelas guerras de independência. Recorro aqui ao sentido foucaultiano de dispositivo, de acordo com a leitura de Giorgio Agamben (2014, 8): não um aparelho ou um evento discursivo; não um edifício nem uma proposição filosófica; o dispositivo é, em suma, a rede que estabelece um diálogo entre todos estes sistemas, reais e virtuais, e tem um papel estratégico relacionado sempre a uma vontade de poder.

O cinema foi levado aos países africanos pelos europeus, como um poderoso instrumento de conversão, não de almas, mas de sentidos. Fruto da tarda-modernidade, o dispositivo cinematográfico reflete e reproduz um modelo civilizacional, uma mundivisão. Assim, questiono-me como o cinema deixou de ser uma arma de dominação para se tornar um mecanismo de denúncia e de resistência. Num universo bastante vasto de realizadores e de cinematografias, escolhi um *corpus* que inclui os realizadores Flora Gomes (Guiné-Bissau), José Cardoso, Licínio de Azevedo (Moçambique) e Leão Lopes (Cabo Verde). Esta escolha deve-se ao facto de ter conhecido mais de perto as obras de cada um desses realizadores, em conjunto, ou de forma particular, ao longo de trabalhos de pesquisa académica que supervisionei. Além disso, dentro do contexto da cinematografia da Guiné-Bissau, Flora Gomes é um pioneiro e, como os realizadores da primeira vaga do cinema pós-colonial em Moçambique (José Cardoso e Licínio de Azevedo), frequentou a escola de cinema cubana, influenciada pelo modelo soviético, que privilegiava o cinema de carácter coletivo e politizado. Apesar de pertencer à mesma geração, Leão Lopes tem uma formação diversa, até porque a própria história do cinema pós-colonial em Cabo Verde não é semelhante à de Angola, Moçambique ou Guiné-Bissau. Mas é, também ele, um pioneiro e um artista que cumpre a múltipla função de professor, cineasta, produtor e agitador cultural.

Nos filmes de cada um desses cineastas, somos confrontados com as ruínas, reais e metafóricas, que persistem (ou que resistem) no período pós-colonial. A ruína, de acordo com Walter Benjamin (1994), é portadora de "aura": "Em suma, o que é aura? É uma figura singular, composta de elementos espaciais e temporais: a aparição única de uma coisa distante, por mais perto que ela esteja" (170). A ruína aproxima de nós o passado sem, no entanto, o presentificar na sua plenitude. Ela é um fragmento da História, ou de uma história, e suscita a lembrança, e a vivência, de algo que, estando presente, já não está diante de nós. Mas uma ruína funciona como um palimpsesto composto de camadas de tempo, nenhuma delas reprodutível, mas todas, ao mesmo tempo, memoráveis. Como disse Benjamin ao refletir sobre o conceito de História, "O passado traz consigo um índice misterioso, que o impele à redenção. Pois não somos tocados por um sopro de ar que foi respirado antes?" (1994, 223).

A redenção do objeto passado no presente pode se dar através da sua ruína, das sobras ou fragmentos daquilo que ele representou e, sobretudo, através da sua ressignificação. Pensar os cinemas pós-coloniais é também pensar de que maneira cada uma dessas cinematografias reflete e refletiu sobre a História que é composta, como tal, de restos, de ruínas, de sobras.

2. As ruínas da/na colónia

Ao contrário da literatura, o cinema português levou algum tempo até transformar em imagens o trauma da colonização do ponto de vista do colonizador. Portugal deixou de ser o país transcontinental da narrativa do Estado Novo, para voltar a ser um pequeno país obrigado a reerguer-se através de uma afirmação europeia após o período colonial. Entre outros, realizadores como Manoel de Oliveira, Pedro Costa e Margarida Cardoso converteram em filmes a passagem de Portugal por África, e os resultados desse processo no país. Dessa cinematografia de reflexão sobre a História, interessa-me particularmente o filme *Ruínas* (2009), realizado por Manuel Mozos, que mostra o passado recente de Portugal através de uma geografia banal, composta de pequenos gestos quotidianos, distanciada dos grandes gestos do passado de glórias lusitanas.

Ao falar sobre o *Ruínas*—filme composto por imagens de prédios, ou de espaços, em estado ruinoso, transformados numa visão poética—Susana Viegas ressalta que esta seleção de imagens não tem um caráter melancólico nem enuncia a nostalgia (lusitana) de um passado grandioso. Segundo ela, Mozos quer mostrar apenas "a simples passagem do tempo e a mudança de hábitos de vida, de tudo que não parece ter relevância histórica: a passagem inexorável do quotidiano, os pequenos despojos dos dias, como uma ementa gastronómica ou os banais pedidos feitos a um hotel" (Viegas 2011, 48–49). As ruínas são reabitadas, ou ressignificadas, e funcionam como um comentário, não uma lamentação. De alguma forma, o realizador usa a seu favor a grande magia do cinema: "dar vida ao que já morreu" (19).

Se, no conceito benjaminiano de aura, Georges Didi-Huberman (2015) encontra uma visão do passado reconstruído, uma retrama dos acontecimentos, podemos pensar o cinema como o lugar onde são tecidas as novas narrativas sobre uma velha história—a do colonialismo europeu, ou ocidental, revisitado pelo olhar daqueles que sobreviveram e que retomaram para si o país, e o direito de contar, à sua maneira, o passado—e de construir uma nova narrativa no presente. Estas cinematografias, como o cinema feito em Portugal desde o 25 de Abril de 1974, como que retramam o passado, usando o dispositivo cinematográfico como lugar do híbrido, das mestiçagens, da reutilização ruinosa de espaços coloniais ou do aproveitamento destes mesmos espaços numa lógica outra, assegurando, no entanto, a ideia de pertencimento e de apropriação.

A relação entre o cinema e a História não é nova. Diversos teóricos fizeram leituras que aproximam a fábula cinematográfica da História dos historiadores. Marc Ferro (1992) escreveu a obra seminal sobre as relações, ou sobre as não relações, entre o cinema e a História, ou pelo menos sobre o papel que o cinema ocupa, e o que deveria ocupar, como ferramenta para os historiadores. De facto, durante muitos anos o cinema foi visto como uma diversão que contribuía, a maior parte das vezes, para deturpar a História. O que se ignorava era o panorama mais vasto em que a própria História se desenrola, pois, mesmo que os filmes não se constituam como documentos-fontes fiáveis, constituem-se como uma poderosa ferramenta para se analisar o período histórico que deu origem a determinada cinematografia. Cada época viu e retratou a História de acordo com o pensamento dominante. É interessante perceber quais foram os elementos, os momentos e os heróis que o cinema decidiu, em dada altura, consagrar ou ignorar. Do cinema pós-colonial dos países de língua portuguesa, ou mesmo dos processos de descolonização, começam a aparecer registos que dão conta, de forma aturada, do que efetivamente se passou e do que está, alguns anos depois, a decorrer nestes territórios.

O cinema é sempre um documento, ou um registo, do visível, ou do que se viu. E quem está por trás da câmara tem o poder de mostrar(-se) e de presentificar, diante de todos, ausências e lacunas. O filme de Mozos, *Ruínas*, é composto a partir dessa particularidade da imagem cinematográfica, a de tornar visível o invisível, de transformar sombras em edifícios, de converter ruínas em metáforas. Nesse sentido, consigo relacionar o seu filme, e a sua cinematografia, àquela realizada nos países africanos outrora colonizados por Portugal: com as devidas diferenças, a função primordial dos filmes destes países é iluminar as sombras do passado e, sobretudo, refletir sobre o presente possível.

3. Os cinemas africanos—O lugar do passado no presente

Para Achille Mbembe (2018), "écrire le monde depuis l'Afrique, inscrire l'Afrique dans le monde ou comme un fragment du monde, voilà bien une tâche grisante et, la plupart du temps, propre à la perplexité" (escrever o mundo a partir da África, inscrever a África no mundo ou como um fragmento do mundo, essa é de facto uma tarefa estimulante e, na maioria das vezes, causadora de perplexidade) (143).[1] Há, desde algum tempo, uma reivindicação, sobretudo dos filósofos do continente africano, por um lugar no campo da teoria e da filosofia, não apenas um lugar na etnografia (como se este fosse o desígnio único do ser africano, um campo de experimentações teóricas, políticas ou sociais). Ryan M. Nefdt (2017), num ensaio a que chamou "Decolonizing Philosophy," reflete sobre o papel dos filósofos negros sul-africanos e sobre a ausência dos mesmos dos *curricula* universitários, ou dos debates, afirmando que aparecem apenas como "a curiosity or an exotic side thought." Cita Edourd Glissant, que afirma "the West is not the West: it is a project, not a place" (Nefdt 2017, 145). No mesmo sentido, Mbembe sugere que a teoria não é somente o nome da tentativa ocidental de domesticar a contingência, mas sim a maneira ocidental de se distinguir do resto. E o resto é relegado ao lugar da etnografia.

A obrigação de o ser "africano" cumprir um desígnio deixa parte da população, sobretudo os jovens, entre duas atitudes: a aceitação ou a revolta. E há nuances que este maniqueísmo não contempla, ou que um certo pensamento paternalista não enxerga. Após a colonização propriamente dita, resta uma colonização do desígnio. John Peffer (2013) fala sobre a juventude malinesa, que decidiu explorar a sua emancipação de maneira paradoxal: "Elle souhaitait se détacher par elle-même de ce qu'elle analysait comme mentalité colonisée et vielles costumes de la génération de ses aînés" (Ela [a juventude] quer desligar-se do que via como mentalidade colonizada e também dos velhos costumes das gerações anteriores) (54). Sem, no entanto, corresponder ao ideário marxista do período revolucionário, nem recorrer ao revisionismo dos teóricos da independência, a sua revolução foi feita através da internacionalização dos costumes, ou, como afirma Diawara (citado por Peffer), a juventude manifesta a sua rebelião contra seus pais, juntando-se à "diáspora estética" (54) do pan-africanismo. Aos ídolos locais acrescentam igualmente Jimi Hendrix ou Françoise Hardy. Reclamam, enfim, o direito ao cosmopolitismo, não numa atitude subserviente ou colonizada, mas numa atitude rebelde e antropofágica.

Neste contexto, a arte, e sobretudo a fotografia e o cinema, nos países africanos pós-coloniais, busca refletir não a África etnográfica, mas a do quotidiano de cada um, tradicional e moderna, nova e velha, fruto dos fluxos diversos de pessoas através do continente e para fora dele. Assim sendo, o cinema feito em Moçambique, Cabo Verde e Guiné-Bissau assume esta atitude rebelde e que não obedece ao modelo apriorístico de um cinema internacional, mas permite-se o exercício da liberdade, e neste exercício aparece, claramente, o seu caráter internacional e cosmopolita.

No texto de abertura do número da revista *Politique africaine* dedicado a analisar o audiovisual africano na lógica do capitalismo global, Alessandro Jedlowski (2019) traça uma breve história do audiovisual nos países africanos subsaarianos e reflete sobre o impacto das novas tecnologias em contextos de profundas revoluções político-económicas decorridas nos últimos quarenta anos. Uma das questões que levanta é exatamente a inadequabilidade das teorias "clássicas," que, debruçando-se sobre as culturas africanas pós-coloniais, promoviam uma visão imobilista, ou imobilizadora, destas culturas e das suas manifestações: "La production audiovisuelle africaine des premières décennies a été principalement analysée à travers le paradigme théorique, d'inspiration militante, du '*Third Cinema*'" (A produção audiovisual africana das primeiras décadas tem sido analisada principalmente através do paradigma teórico, de inspiração ativista, do "*Third Cinema*") (Jedlowski 2019, 9). Este autor refere ainda que outra das grandes correntes de estudos do audiovisual africano provém da antropologia e aponta os textos de Karin Barber e Johannes Fabian, que se debruçaram sobre as culturas populares urbanas na África pós-colonial, agregando o conceito de "Indústria Cultural Artesanal," que se estabelece de forma mais ou menos organizada e compete com os monopólios globais que dominam aquilo a que Barber e Fabian chamam "indústrias culturais monopolíticas." O objeto preferencial destes estudos é o cinema nigeriano, ou "Nollywood," fenómeno único no continente africano de produção massiva e de filme de género, que se desenvolveu ainda mais com a difusão das novas tecnologias no continente, entre a década de 1990 e o início do século XXI. Apesar de haver um grupo já significativo de estudos sobre os países africanos de língua oficial portuguesa, grande parte da bibliografia internacional sobre o cinema subsaariano dedica-se ao estudo do caso Nollywood.

De acordo com Jedlowski, "Au cours des années 90 et au début des années 2000, ces acteurs traditionnels ont été progressivement marginalisés par l'émergence d'une économie de petits entrepreneurs qui produisaient des contenus médiatiques avec des budgets limités et des technologies bas de gamme, destinés à une distribution locale via des réseaux principalement informels" (Durante a década de 90 e início dos anos 2000, os produtores tradicionais foram gradualmente marginalizados devido ao surgimento duma economia de pequenos empresários que produziam conteúdos com orçamentos limitados e tecnologias de baixo custo, destinadas à distribuição local feita, principalmente, através de redes informais) (2019, 8). As novas tecnologias incrementaram, quer a produção quer a distribuição dos filmes em países como a Nigéria, o Gana, a Uganda e outros da África subsaariana, cujo mercado alternativo, com tecnologias de baixo custo (VHS e DVD), é rapidamente substituído pela tecnologia digital, que reforça a rede de projeção das produções locais, sem, no entanto, resolver completamente o problema da distribuição. O canal mais óbvio de escoamento destas produções, as salas de cinema, está destinado aos sucessos internacionais e poucos são os países (p.ex., Costa do Marfim e a República Democrática do Congo) que possuem canais de televisão com espaço dedicado ao audiovisual nacional. No caso dos países que constituem o *corpus* aqui analisado, os canais de televisão nacionais não se dedicam à distribuição dos filmes produzidos nos próprios países, e as salas de cinema, quando as há, não exibem a cinematografia nacional.

Assim, entre uma visão que demanda um tipo de produção politizada, ou autoral, e outra que contempla o contexto tecnológico e político mais contemporâneo, a produção audiovisual dos países africanos subsaarianos continua a enfrentar uma série de questões que, de alguma maneira, tendem a engessar, senão a produção em si, pelo menos a maneira como esta produção é estudada e difundida.

Se tomarmos o exemplo da Nigéria, para criar um paralelo em relação à situação de países como Moçambique, Cabo Verde ou Guiné-Bissau, cujos filmes começam a circular no mercado mundial através de plataformas como a Netflix, deparamo-nos com uma produção diversificada que ora responde aos ensejos da corrente do *Third Cinema* (filmes que recuperam as tradições locais),[2] ora reflete os efeitos do panafricanismo ou da chamada afromodernidade, e que narra histórias do quotidiano, de uma minoria da população, completamente integrada ao sistema neoliberal e consumista das políticas mundiais. Não sendo o meu objetivo estudar o cinema produzido na Nigéria, ou em países africanos francófonos ou anglófonos, mas sim nos países de expressão portuguesa, recorro ao exemplo de Nollywood como contraponto, por ser o mais próximo que o continente possui de uma indústria cultural no campo da produção audiovisual. No caso dos cinemas de países de expressão portuguesa não há indícios de industrialização dos processos, nem de produção, nem de distribuição. No entanto, em termos de linguagem fílmica, há uma aproximação estética que revela o sincretismo, ou a antropofagia, das obras realizadas no período pós-colonial, financiadas ou não pelos estados nacionais.[3] Moçambique oferece, quiçá, o caso mais emblemático de uma cinematografia pós-colonial que surge como uma demanda do próprio Estado após as lutas de libertação.

4. O cinema através dos cineastas

4.1. José Cardoso: Da cinefilia à realização

Após a independência, o cinema moçambicano ganha um fôlego extra graças à criação do Instituto Nacional de Cinema (INC) e ao investimento feito pelo governo de Samora Machel na formação de técnicos e realizadores. Tudo começara ainda na década de 1950, como um projeto de amadores e cinéfilos como José Cardoso, considerado o pai do cinema de Moçambique. Através da análise do seu filme de estreia, percebemos que, sem fugir dos impositivos que o dispositivo cinematográfico e a sua linguagem impõem, o realizador se apropria das imagens que viu e cria uma cinematografia própria, que já anuncia a crise do sistema colonial, usando, no entanto, a poética do cinema europeu da altura.

Segundo o testemunho do próprio Cardoso, "Era menino ainda quando aprendi a sonhar. E foi na adolescência da vida que me ofuscou a aurora do deslumbramento. Então criei. Dei voz e palavra à imagem, à luz e ao movimento e então aconteceram estas histórias verdadeiras de desamor e revolta, no limitado e humilde espaço de uma película de oito milímetros."[4] Antes de ser realizador, em 1958 Cardoso fundara com outros amantes do cinema o Cineclube da Beira, que rapidamente se tornou o segundo maior cineclube de todo o império português, ficando apenas atrás do Cineclube do Porto. É importante referir que a ditadura exercia um controlo da distribuição dos filmes mais apertado em Portugal do que nas colónias, o que permitia ao cineclube moçambicano exibir obras que só muito mais tarde tiveram permissão para exibição na metrópole.

Através da atividade cineclubista, Cardoso e outros companheiros enveredaram pela produção e realização de filmes, a princípio em Super 8, que era o meio mais acessível, permitindo a realização de cinema a baixo custo, longe dos grandes centros de produção cinematográfica. Por outro lado, esse formato permitia maior liberdade de ação e de escolha do tema, ao mesmo tempo que dava resposta a um modelo seguido por aqueles que, como Cardoso, começaram a fazer cinema em Moçambique na década de 1960, o do neorrealismo italiano e do cinema produzido nos países que então viviam sob regimes comunistas, como a Polónia, a Checoslováquia e, posteriormente, Cuba.

O cinema moçambicano tem um cariz documental bastante marcado, devido às suas raízes e, mais tarde, devido à criação, pelo INC, dos jornais cinematográficos *Kuxa kanema*. Se, por um lado, as questões de produção se constituem como uma razão concreta para a escolha do modo documental, por outro, os temas e os meios de produção exigem um tratamento mais realista, fazendo com que cineastas como Licínio de Azevedo optem por um formato misto, que avança no tempo com uma proposta de transversalidade entre o documentário e a ficção, criando ficções documentais e vice-versa, hoje muito praticada em diversas cinematografias.

José Cardoso, mais conhecido pelo seu filme emblemático *O vento sopra do Norte* (1987), que inaugura a ficção na cinematografia moçambicana, declarou numa entrevista ao jornal *@Verdade* que a sua carreira como profissional começou em 1976, embora desde a fundação do Cineclube da Beira tenha realizado vários filmes de "cinema não profissional," expressão que prefere ao de "cinema amador," pois esta categoria albergava uma diversidade de praticantes com os quais ele nem sempre se identificava (Cardoso 2013).[5] É sobre a sua primeira experiência como cineasta que agora me vou debruçar. *Anúncio*, curta-metragem em oito milímetros realizada em 1966, é um filme estético e tematicamente próximo ao cinema neorrealista italiano. Cardoso conta-nos o drama de um desempregado à procura de trabalho. Se, por um lado, o tema reforça o caráter documental do filme, por outro nega a documentabilidade através da escolha meticulosa dos planos, da montagem rigorosa e das referências cinematográficas que possui e que se revelam em diversos momentos.

A personagem principal de *Anúncio*, um homem à procura de emprego, é representada pelo próprio realizador. Durante a produção recebe a visita do amigo Zeca Afonso (cantautor da resistência ao regime de Salazar), que se entusiasma com o filme e escreve para sua banda sonora a balada "Vejam bem." Há ainda outra referência musical fundamental para a história, uma citação do filme

Orfeu negro, realizado em 1959 por Marcel Camus e baseado na obra de Vinícius de Morais. A escolha das músicas não é apenas casual, mas demonstra uma opção consciente do caminho que o filme, e parte significativa da produção posterior de Cardoso, trilham: o papel das artes na política e a filiação cinéfila do realizador. Entre a citação e o documento, *Anúncio* é um filme que, sem ser panfletário, reclama para si um papel ativo na política do país, então ainda uma colónia portuguesa, sem descurar, no entanto, a criação das imagens que refletem a sofisticação do realizador no seu tratamento, e revelam um conhecimento profundo do cinema que era feito então.

Anúncio foi apresentado no Primeiro Festival de Cinema de Amadores de Aveiro, em 1967, e recebeu uma crítica muito elogiosa de Fernando Gonçalves Lavador, no número 291 da revista *Vértice*: "Do ponto de vista formal, apresenta qualidades que vão desde uma utilização inteligente e adequada da banda sonora e de oportunas elipses integradas . . . até uma interpretação simples e sóbria" (cit. em Cardoso 2014). O filme não possui diálogos e é através da música, e da imagem, que é apresentada a história de um homem desesperado, famélico, à procura de trabalho em pleno período de Carnaval, e que acaba por se envolver com um grupo de foliões mascarados que celebram o entrudo.

O filme, que segue as diretivas do Cinema Novo brasileiro tal como foram proferidas por Glauber Rocha—uma ideia na cabeça e uma câmara na mão—, não se parece nada com o produto típico do cinema amador. Os planos, cuidadosamente pensados e executados, os *raccords* de continuidade sem falhas e as imagens, cujo valor simbólico é evidente, ultrapassam a sua condição de filme de estreia e revelam o cineasta que desponta a partir daí. Numa das cenas, a personagem principal está sentada à beira do passeio, a tentar consertar os sapatos e, através dos seus olhos (numa utilização narrativa e sensível da câmara subjetiva), vemos aparecer um polícia que não precisa dizer nada: a sua presença imponente, vislumbrada num contra-*plongée* bem executado, revela-se apenas, de forma metonímica, através da visão das pernas, qual colunas fixadas diante dos olhos do homem sentado. Sem um movimento, a Lei impõe a ordem através da imagem.

É pela imagem que o filme nos fala. Uma imagem, em movimento constante, através das ruas da cidade segue o homem que vagueia à procura de trabalho e de comida, o que o leva, e que nos leva junto com ele, a um baile de mascarados. A cidade não aparece na sua plenitude; temos acesso apenas a fragmentos, recortes, pontos de vista. A sua geografia é a do cinema, não respeita o traçado urbanístico que se inscreve no real. A cidade levada pelos colonizadores é desmontada pelo realizador através dos planos cinematográficos. Se a parte inicial do filme é calcada em imagens documentais, quase etnográficas, a segunda parte, cuja música de fundo é a do referido filme de Marcel Camus, remete-nos, em simultâneo, ao neorrealismo e ao surrealismo de Jean Cocteau. Enquanto a música cita Camus, as imagens referem-se ao *Orfeu* de Cocteau, através das máscaras e do clima feérico que se instaura na narrativa a partir desse inusitado encontro entre a fome e a festa.

Anúncio é um filme experimental em muitas dimensões, mas é, sobretudo, um filme iniciático que traça o percurso do seu realizador, cuja escola de cinema é composta dos filmes que viu e cujos princípios políticos, que nunca ocultou, transparecem nas imagens de um cinema meticuloso que trata com mestria dos temas locais. Cardoso é um cineasta nascido em Moçambique, mas o seu cinema pertence ao grupo mais vasto dos autores que contribuíram para a construção de um imaginário, e de uma gramática, do audiovisual no mundo. Este filme, como os muitos que vai realizar ao longo da sua carreira, é antes de tudo, um exercício de subversão de um dispositivo que engendra modos de ver e de mostrar. O espaço urbano é, aqui, pano de fundo. E serve apenas como cenário de um drama que se desenrola diante de nós e que possui um caráter universal.

4.2. Licínio de Azevedo—Reabitando velhos espaços

Há, no cinema de ficção moçambicano, em geral, uma opção pelos planos fechados, nos quais a personagem se destaca da paisagem circundante, e se torna o centro do interesse da trama. A descrição, se e quando há, está contida no arrastar das imagens que, de fragmento em fragmento, remontam um espaço. E o espaço, muitas vezes, é uma ruína, ou um resto, de edifícios erigidos no período colonial, reaproveitados, ou ressignificados por novos usos que a população local lhes dá. É possível vislumbrar esta ideia de ocupação das ruínas, ou de estetização das mesmas, em filmes como *O Grande Bazar* (2006), de Licínio de Azevedo, em particular nas cenas em que a cidade nos é apresentada pela janela do comboio, ou quando vemos o Grande Bazar, um mercado informal, com uma arquitetura própria, labiríntica e efémera, como tantos mercados africanos. Em Maputo, como noutras cidades do país, há mercados construídos seguindo o modelo português. No entanto, os mercados verdadeiramente "habitados" são semelhantes ao que aparece no filme de Azevedo.

Um exemplo genial desta apropriação criativa do dispositivo pode ser visto no curta-metragem de 2001, assinado por Orlando Mesquita, A *bola*. O filme foi realizado por Azevedo que, como já não podia concorrer naquele ano aos fundos de apoio ao cinema, pediu a Mesquita que o fizesse em seu nome, num mecanismo que revela adaptação a um sistema de produção viciado, dependente de uma demanda externa de fundos estrangeiros que determinam os temas a serem tratados nas produções audiovisuais. *A bola* faz parte de um conjunto de produções que visam sensibilizar a população do país para o uso do preservativo, como forma de evitar a propagação da SIDA. No entanto, a parte mais pedagógica é deixada para o final, e o curta-metragem narra, através de imagens, uma partida de futebol entre meninos da periferia de uma cidade não especificada.

Quando se fala do cinema como dispositivo, há que levar em conta as condições de produção. Neste filme em particular, feito por um cineasta que nasceu no Brasil, mas se considera um realizador moçambicano, o sistema é usado a seu favor. Licínio de Azevedo faz o filme que quer, mesmo que não o assine, demonstrando o seu domínio da narrativa audiovisual através dos planos e cortes, do uso do *raccord* de continuidade e do enquadramento do espaço. Repete, de forma consciente, o *modus operandi* imposto pelo modelo do cinema *mainstream*, para contar uma outra história de um espaço outro: periférico e não-metropolitano. Apropria-se de um modelo que, na cinematografia ocidental, passou a ser considerado desfasado e ruinoso, reinventando, como os meninos, um jogo que se joga aqui conforme novas regras. Reinventa, ou reabita assim, um dispositivo outrora de dominação, para se dar a ver, ou exibir-se.

4.3. Flora Gomes—As ruínas dos espaços coloniais

Não são apenas os cineastas moçambicanos a recorrer a este procedimento—o de aproveitar edifícios, ou espaços urbanos, que foram construídos pelos colonizadores como palco para encenar novas vivências. O que outrora eram ruínas, edificações desgastadas que simbolizavam o próprio desgaste dos sistemas de poder, é revisitado, por várias cinematografias, como espaços alternativos, ou de uma habitabilidade outra. Recuperam, de alguma maneira, a beleza das ruínas, que se convertem em discurso do novo que irrompe e que altera o espaço à sua volta. Não negam o passado, mas, como parte desta contemporaneidade diaspórica, reapropriam-se dos lugares e criam neles novos sentidos, revolucionários, sincréticos—resultado de uma nova forma de (vi)ver.

No seu longa-metragem de estreia, *Mortu nega* (1988), Flora Gomes faz um exercício de rememoração, e de escritura, da história do seu país, Guiné-Bissau, através do cinema. O filme narra os acontecimentos que precederam o fim do colonialismo e o começo de uma nova ordem, ainda maculada por velhos vícios, mas buscando aprender com o passado para a construção de um presente diverso. Numa das cenas do filme, assistimos a uma aula de cidadania nas ruínas de um edifício, transformado em escola. Crianças e adultos estão a aprender a escrever, a ler, não apenas a decorar palavras. O professor insiste no significado profundo dos termos, simbólico e material. Só se aprende a ler, verdadeiramente, quando as palavras se tornam vivas e prenhes de sentido. A beleza da cena, filmada de modo clássico, ou convencional, é acentuada pelo paradoxo do lugar: nas ruínas do velho mundo, constrói-se uma nova geração. Para Jusciele Oliveira (2019), o título do filme, *Mortu nega*, que significa em crioulo da Guiné-Bissau "aqueles que a morte rejeitou," conecta o filme à cultura oral daquele país, bem como constrói uma ponte entre a História e o presente.

Na sua tese de doutoramento, que orientei, Oliveira (2018) defende que o cinema de Flora Gomes é, sobretudo, um cinema de autor. Ao contrário do que ocorre no cinema da Nigéria, que copia um modelo hollywoodiano de uma cinematografia de géneros, os cinemas dos países de língua portuguesa optaram pelo modelo europeu ou latino-americano, de cunho mais autoral. No caso do cinema moçambicano, que começa por ser financiado pelo Estado, mas que perde rapidamente esse apoio, há uma tendência de se fazer um cinema comandado pelas demandas das organizações não governamentais que financiam muitos dos filmes e que exigem que os mesmos tratem de assuntos específicos, como a prevenção da SIDA, a violência contra a mulher ou a necessidade da educação. Há realizadores que encontram forma de escapar a tais exigências sem, no entanto, abrir mão do financiamento, fazendo o filme que querem, mesmo que tenham de trabalhar a partir de argumentos encomendados, como já tinha sido referido a propósito do filme *A bola* de Orlando Mesquita e Licínio de Azevedo.

Em 2010, Sílvia Vieira e Bruno Silva realizaram o documentário *Assim estamos livres: Cinema moçambicano 1975–2010*. Através de um conjunto de entrevistas aos principais realizadores, produtores e técnicos do cinema moçambicano, conseguimos perceber o percurso traçado pelo cinema naquele país após o período colonial. São os próprios realizadores que falam do apoio inicial dado pelo Estado, que concebeu o Instituto Nacional de Cinema e que, aos poucos, por razões diversas, foi retirando verbas destinadas ao cinema, o que obrigou os profissionais do setor a procurar financiamentos alternativos. Neste sentido, é possível afirmar que a temática do cinema moçambicano, pelo menos entre as décadas de 1980 e 2010, estava muito restringida às causas das entidades financiadoras, o que, de alguma forma, põe em causa o conceito de um cinema autoral nesse país. O caso de Angola é semelhante, mas o mesmo não ocorreu na Guiné-Bissau ou em Cabo Verde.

A Guiné-Bissau investiu na produção cinematográfica, em especial em dois realizadores que foram enviados para estudar cinema em Cuba e que voltaram para contar, cada um a sua maneira, a história do país: Flora Gomes e Sana Na N'Hada. O primeiro longa-metragem de ficção de Gomes, *Mortu nega*, é lançado em 1987 e obtém sucesso no circuito internacional dos festivais. O reconhecimento internacional e o apoio do Estado permitem-lhe criar uma cinematografia peculiar, na qual o passado, o presente e até o futuro, são convocados para falar do país, das vicissitudes pelas quais seus habitantes passaram e o que é que os identifica com a Guiné-Bissau. De alguma forma o cinema funcionou nessas nações pós-coloniais como a literatura e as artes plásticas funcionaram no Romantismo, reforçando a ideia de identidade local e de pertença.

Flora Gomes nega a categorização de cinema etnográfico que, de um modo geral, é atribuído à cinematografia africana subsaariana. Seus filmes retratam o seu país, e as ruínas do seu país, de maneira a criar um retrato vivo e atual da realidade que a Guiné-Bissau atravessa, e que atravessou, no período pós-colonial. O conceito de pan-africanismo pode ser aqui reencontrado, mesmo que não possamos comparar a sua produção àquela feita em Nollywood. "Gomes's work diverts from the ethnographic cinema that tries to reproduce or document African reality as fixed, immutable, and primitive, leaving aside also the modernity of the continent, urban spaces, cities and city landscapes" (Oliveira 2019, 6).

4.4. Leão Lopes—O impossível retorno

Do mesmo modo que vários realizadores moçambicanos se viram na obrigaçao de trabalhar como produtores dos seus próprios filmes, para que os mesmos fossem distribuídos e vistos para além do sistema dos festivais, Leão Lopes assumiu múltiplas funções em Cabo Verde. Professor, jornalista, agitador cultural, artista plástico, escritor e realizador, a obra de Lopes não pode ser resumida à sua carreira no cinema. Porém, aquilo que ele faz nos e com os seus filmes é um reflexo desta multiplicidade de funções que tomou para si, e que se traduzem no seu esforço de promover a formação e a capacitação local. A sua cinematografia é também uma escola para técnicos, atores, produtores e cenógrafos, que convivem lado a lado com profissionais consagrados e com eles aprendem. Flora

Gomes criou igualmente a sua escola porque, como Lopes, acredita que o cinema é uma forma de resgatar a autoestima da população que se vê envolvida e representada nos grandes ecrãs, não como personagens de uma etnografia a ser estudada, mas como pessoas reais que vivem histórias que precisam ser contadas.

Em 2009 o realizador cabo-verdiano lançou o documentário *Os últimos contratados*. O filme relata a história dos homens e mulheres cabo-verdianos que foram levados para trabalhar nas roças de São Tomé e Príncipe. Passado o período áureo da produção agrícola local, muitos regressaram e outros tantos ficaram pelo caminho. É uma daquelas histórias nunca contadas, de pessoas comuns, obrigadas a realizar um movimento diaspórico e depois a ficarem retidos num espaço "entre," pois perderam as suas raízes e não se conseguiram fixar no novo país. Em S. Tomé são tratados como pessoas de segunda ou de terceira categoria, sendo quase invisíveis para o grande espectro da população. O filme começa com a imagem de um cais que se prolonga até ao fim do horizonte contemplado pelo ecrã. Um homem caminha e a câmara capta o movimento, mudando a angulação, o que deixa o espetador, num primeiro momento, sem saber se o homem vai ou vem, como se este executasse um movimento pendular, indo em direção ao mar e regressando, sem, no entanto, deixar o cais. De seguida o ecrã escurece e vemos escrita a história que se vai relatar. Numa síntese que pretende iluminadora, Lopes dá conta de quem são os últimos contratados.

Algumas das casas senhoriais, das antigas plantações de cacau, agora em plena decadência, aparecem reabitadas no filme, transformadas em prédios de habitação, ou melhor, lugar de abrigo daqueles que não têm para onde ir. A estrutura da casa mantém-se, mesmo que esventrada, e os salões, quartos e cozinhas são convertidos em espaços de ocupação comum. Sobre as ruínas edifica-se um novo espaço, também ele ruinoso, composto de seres periféricos e desterrados, assim simbolizando uma vitória incompleta, ou ainda em curso, do processo revolucionário.

5. Conclusão

Como disse Edourd Glissant, o Ocidente não é um lugar, é um projeto. E o cinema foi utilizado para garantir que esse projeto se espraiasse pelo resto do mundo. O poder de sedução das imagens em movimento, sobretudo quando controladas, enquadradas e dispostas numa ordem narrativa que prevê um fim, continua bastante significativo. Tomando a formulação tarkovskiana, o cinema é *a arte de esculpir o tempo*, de reescrever a memória, ou de dar sentido aos restos que a História não contempla, pois a História, já se sabe, ocupa-se em consagrar os vencedores. A capacidade do cinema, enquanto dispositivo, de converter espaço em tempo e vice-versa, recupera o caráter aurático dos lugares que são revelados a cada *frame*, ou imagem, porque estamos diante de uma ruína, ou de uma imagem ruinosa, sombras de algo que esteve em presença da câmara, mas que não está, efetivamente, diante de nós.

A imagem previsível do filme, fruto de uma sequência lógica de *raccords*, é uma linguagem que se estabeleceu ao longo do século XX e que contaminou outras linguagens audiovisuais. É também uma linguagem impura, maculada, reescrita a cada novo filme ou cinematografia que diverge, que propõe disrupção, que contraria o *raccord* de continuidade, que (re)instaura novas, ou velhas, temporalidades. O cinema foi uma das arenas de eleição em que se encenou, e se encena, os dramas pós-coloniais.

Os realizadores destes países, como os de muitos outros que não possuem uma máquina de apoio do Estado a todas as produções, nem um conjunto robusto de indústrias culturais, usam o dispositivo para promover um diálogo entre o passado e o presente, o velho e o novo, o ancestral e o contemporâneo, numa atitude disruptiva e diaspórica, negando-se a cumprir um desígnio puramente etnográfico. Numa época de globalismo, a linguagem do audiovisual se tornou monolítica e a forma de resistir ao mesmo é criar o outro, com a consciência de que não se consegue superar, ou destruir, um modelo tão bem estabelecido.

Como no filme de Manuel Mozos, *Ruínas*, as cinematografias de países como Moçambique, Cabo-Verde ou Guiné-Bissau mostram-nos o passado, e os restos, fragmentos ou sobras, não numa atitude de lamentação, mas sim numa postura de reconstrução, ou melhor, de adaptação e mudança, de transformação. O romântico sentimento de melancolia, que contemplava e reproduzia ruínas, é substituído pelo pragmatismo da ação sobre as edificações, simbólicas e reais. Reabitar o espaço é criar novas memórias sem, no entanto, apagar o passado. É evitar que ele volte ao presente, como farsa, ou como novas formas de colonização.

NOTAS

1. Todas as traduções são de minha autoria.

2. Num texto sobre o audiovisual nigeriano, Françoise Ugochukwu (2013) fala sobre a produção mais recente do cinema de Nollywood que tem a História do país como pano de fundo, ou como foco central das narrativas, e que utiliza, de forma muito particular, a tradição oral que continua vigente: "Ce canal de transmission endosse en outre le rôle didactique des contes, assurant non seulement la transmission des cultures et de l'histoire du pays mais également celle des leçons qu'en ont tiré les milieux populaires. Cet héritage oral des vidéo films nigérians n'a pas encore été vraiment étudié" (Esse canal de transmissão também assume o papel didático de contar histórias, garantindo não só a transmissão das culturas e da História do país, mas também das lições que delas tiraram os meios populares. Esta herança oral dos vídeo-filmes nigerianos ainda não foi totalmente estudada) (330).

3. "Flora Gomes, cineasta da Guiné-Bissau, repete muitas vezes que fazer cinema é bastante difícil e fazer cinema em África é uma insanidade total. Após a independência, Moçambique investiu na produção cinematográfica como forma de propaganda do novo regime, na tentativa de criar uma imagem do país para ser consumida por uma nação fragmentada" (Tavares 2015, 373). Os governos pós-coloniais de Moçambique, Guiné-Bissau e Angola investiram, em maior ou menor grau, na produção de uma cinematografia própria como mais uma arma de propagação das ideias revolucionárias.

4. Depoimento enviado pelo realizador à equipa do KUGOMA—Festival de Curtas-metragens de Moçambique, coordenado e produzido por Diana Manhiça, responsável pela reedição dos três primeiros filmes de José Cardoso em DVD (Cardoso 2014).

5. A entrevista, conduzida pouco antes do falecimento do realizador, foi publicada postumamente.

OBRAS CITADAS

Agamben, Giorgio. 2014. *Qu'est-ce qu'un dispositive?* Paris: Éditions Payot et Rivages.

Benjamin, Walter. 1994. *Obras escolhidas: Magia e técnica, arte e política*. São Paulo: Brasiliense.

Brayer, Laure. 2016. "Les images filmiques et la part insignifiante de l'expérience urbaine." *Multitudes* 65 (4): 184–89.

Cardoso, José. 2014. *8mm: Os 3 primeiros filmes de José Cardoso*. DVD. Prod. Diana Manhiça KUGOMA.

———. 2013. "'Eu fui, sou e serei sempre comunista': José Cardoso (1930–2013)." Entrevista. *@Verdade*, 30 de outubro de 2013. https://verdade.co.mz/eu-fui-sou-e-serei-sempre-comunista/.

Didi-Huberman, Georges. 2015. *Diante do tempo: História da arte e anacronismo das imagens.* Belo Horizonte: Editora UFMG.

Ferro, Marc. 1992. *Cinema e História.* São Paulo: Paz e Terra.

Jedlowski, Alessandro. 2019. "L'audiovisuel africain et le capitalisme global." *Politique africaine*, no. 153, 7–27.

Mbembe, Achille. 2018. "L'Afrique en théorie." *Multitudes* 73 (4): 143–52.

Nefdt, Ryan M. 2017. "Decolonizing Philosophy." *Africa Is a Country*, 30 de junho de 2017. https://africasacountry.com/2017/06/decolonizing-philosophy/.

Oliveira, Jusciele. 2019. "'I Make Films to Be Seen': The Narrative Issue of Flora Gomes." *Journal of Science and Technology of the Arts* 11 (1): 1–9.

———. 2018. *Precisamos vestirmo-nos com a luz negra: uma análise autoral nos cinemas africanos—o caso Flora Gomes.* Tese de doutoramento, Universidade do Algarve.

Peffer, John. 2013. "La diaspora des images de l'Afrique." *Multitude* 53 (2): 47–58.

Schopenhauer, Arthur. 2012. *The Selected Works of Arthur Schopenhauer.* New York: Library of Alexandria. Kindle.

Tavares, Mirian. 2015. "Cinema: Tempos e movimentos." *Patrimónios de influência portuguesa: Modos de olhar*, coord. Walter Rossa and Margarida Calafate Ribeiro, 351–75. Coimbra: Imprensa da Universidade de Coimbra.

Ugochukwu, Françoise I. 2013. "Le vidéo-film nigérian dans le prolongement de l'histoire orale." *Littérature orale africaine: Décryptage, reconstruction et canonisation*, ed. Alain Cyr Pangop Kameni and Clément Dili Palaï, 329–44. Paris: Harmattan.

Viegas, Susana. 2011. "Efabulações de um país sem imagem: De *Ruínas* a *Fantasia Lusitana*." *Drama: Revista de cinema e teatro*, no. 3, 48–49.

Filmografia

Azevedo, Licínio, realizador. *O Grande Bazar.* 2006.

Cardoso, José, realizador. *O anúncio.* 1966.

Gomes, Flora, realizador. *Mortu nega.* 1988.

Lopes, Leão, realizador. *Os últimos contratados.* 2009.

Mesquita, Orlando (Licínio de Azevedo), realizador. *A bola.* 2001.

Mozos, Manuel, realizador. *Ruínas.* 2009.

Vieira, Sílvia, e Bruno Silva, realizadores. *Assim estamos livres!* 2010.

MIRIAN NOGUEIRA TAVARES é professora associada da Universidade do Algarve. Com formação académica nas Ciências da Comunicação, na Semiótica e nos Estudos Culturais (doutorou-se em Comunicação e Culturas Contemporâneas pela Universidade Federal da Bahia), tem desenvolvido o seu trabalho de investigação e de produção teórica nas áreas das estéticas fílmica e artística. Como professora da Universidade do Algarve, participou na elaboração do projeto de licenciatura em Artes Visuais, do mestrado e doutoramento em Comunicação, Cultura e Artes e do doutoramento em Média-Arte Digital. Atualmente é Coordenadora do CIAC (Centro de Investigação em Artes e Comunicação) e Diretora do doutoramento em Média-Arte Digital.

KIMBERLY DACOSTA HOLTON

Troubling the Good Time Blues: Fado Performance, Placemaking, and Border Crossing in the United States[1]

ABSTRACT: This paper examines fado's powerful relationship to deterritorialization and the complex spatial poetics that condition fado in diaspora. Immigrant enclaves, often defined by frames of spatial multiplicity, where lives are contextualized according to places left and places arrived at, are fertile ground for the study of a musical genre like fado, known both for its topophilia, or love of place, and for its intense focus on making absent places present. This paper explores the ways in which multiple spatial frames inform and influence fado performance in New Jersey. The closing of Newark's last casa de fado has forced the genre into "tight spaces" where fado performers and aficionados share evenings of entertainment with other musical genres and audiences. Some view this hybrid format as a positive development, others as a negative one. Those who see fado's unmooring from traditional performance spaces as the cause of repertoire diminishment and audience misbehavior have pushed fado into spaces associated with education as well as into small, private, home-like settings. Lastly, fado's increasing vulnerability within the space of the enclave has resulted in charged border crossings and the emergence of a more heterogenous group of fado performers and enthusiasts. These border crossings are contextualized against the backdrop of a history of ethnic tensions in Newark's Ironbound neighborhood, and a move among some artists and community leaders to embrace a paradigm of mixture and exchange, with fado as a key expressive laboratory for such a shift.

KEYWORDS: fado, diaspora, Portuguese Americans, Newark, Ironbound, migration, performance, music

RESUMO: Este ensaio examina a relação poderosa entre o fado e a desterritorialização, além da poética complexa que condiciona a performance do fado em diáspora. Enclaves de imigrantes, muitas vezes definidos por quadros de multiplicidade espacial, onde as vidas individuais são contextualizadas de acordo com os espaços que ficaram atrás e os espaços de chegada, constituem-se em território fértil para o estudo de um género musical como o fado, reconhecido pela sua topofilia, ou amor ao espaço, e pelo seu enfoque intenso de tornar presentes os espaços ausentes. Este artigo explora as maneiras como múltiplas espacialidades informam e influenciam a performance do fado no estado de Nova Jersey. O encerramento de última casa de fado em Newark forçou o género a estabelecer-se nos "espaços apertados" onde os fadistas e os seus aficionados partilham noites de entretenimento com outros géneros musicais e outros públicos. Alguns vêm neste formato híbrido um desenvolvimento positivo, outros negativo. Os que vêm o desancorar do fado dos seus locais tradicionais como a causa do empobrecimento de repertório e do mau comportamento do público têm levado o fado para os espaços associados com a educação e para espaços íntimos, que se assemelham a lares particulares. Por último, a vulnerabilidade crescente do fado no espaço do enclave imigrante resultou em travessias de fronteira intensas e no surgimento de um grupo mais heterogéneo de fadistas e entusiastas. Estas travessias de fronteira, que serão contextualizadas na história das tensões étnicas dentro do bairro de Ironbound, em Newark, motivaram a aceitação por parte de alguns artistas e líderes da comunidade, de um novo paradigma de mistura e intercâmbio, utilizando o fado como um importante laboratório expressivo para tal mudança.

PALAVRAS-CHAVE: fado, diáspora, luso-americanos, Newark, New Jersey, Ironbound, migração, emigrantes, performance, música

---

It is a hot, humid day and the festivities have already begun. Sounds of accordions echo onto the steamy pavement as swirls of colored lights, strung across the main artery of Ferry Street, direct the eye toward the traditional parade route. It is as though you are in a Portuguese village for a summertime festival. The location, however, is thousands of miles away, in a neighborhood called the Ironbound in the east ward of Newark, New Jersey—a gritty US port city associated for much of the post–World War II period with crime and poverty, but more recently termed a "renaissance city" for its tech- and arts-driven growth, a branding shift mired in controversy.[2] Today Newark's Ironbound neighborhood prepares for the Portugal Day parade, an outdoor display of many floats, marked by the cacophonous inclusion of disparate urban institutions and ethnic denizens of all stripes and persuasions. By day's end, half a million revelers will fill the streets of the neighborhood some people call "Little Portugal."[3]

The parade won't begin for another two hours, however, and groups of friends and families gather indoors at the Sport Club Português for a pre-parade performance of a play written by East Ward Councilman Augusto Amador, entitled *Foi pelo sonho que fomos*. The play is staged high under a proscenium arch at the back of a large banquet hall. The audience pipes down as costumed actors enter the stage and sit at tavern tables under an enormous reproduction of José Malhoa's *Os bêbados* painted by a local Luso-American artist. The play, rife with poetic verses about longing for Portugal and adapting to the US, is billed as "uma viagem cultural ao fundo do tempo." The curtain opens to reveal a dizzying barrage of Portuguese props and emblems, an identificatory shorthand so well-known in this neighborhood—the flag, the rooster, the filigree jewelry, the guitarra portuguesa, the checkered tablecloth—symbols that, borrowing Cristiana Bastos's (2020, 37) terminology, reflect the Portuguese American expression of "hyperbolic" nationalism.

As the audience grapples with how to take in this colorful hodgepodge, a huge projection screen swells with black and white photos. At first there is no sound—just languorous image after image of Portuguese emigrants boarding boats in mid-century Lisbon, carrying guitars, sitting on crates, crying into kerchiefs, setting off for shores unknown. These historical images, some of them now famous—reproduced in many a book, documentary and website dedicated to the topic of Portuguese migration—seem to have a powerful effect on the audience. Then a slow, sad fado sung by legendary fadista Amália Rodrigues fills the capacious hall as the black and white photos continue, this time portraying the passage itself. Images of waves and ships, small against the vast ocean, are set to Amália's throaty dips and melismas. The terrifying uncertainty of this liminal, open-ocean phase, neither here nor there, the transition from one world to another, seems somehow perfectly expressed in Amália's vocal delivery and lyrical content. As the dramatized slideshow builds, audience members begin to weep softly, and the symbiosis between fado and immigrant passage looms large, a perfect combination, a poetics of song and experience dependent on one another and intensely felt by those in the audience who "left for the dream," embodying the title of Amador's play.

As I sat in this makeshift theater on June 11, 2011, during Portugal Day in Newark, listening to Amália sing and watching those around me weep on a day meant for revelry, I realized that fado's powerful relationship to deterritorialization and the complex spatial poetics of its performance in a US ethnic enclave would be a crucial angle to examine. Immigrant enclaves, defined always by frames of spatial multiplicity where lives are contextualized according to places left and places arrived at, not to mention the powerful in-between spaces of passage, are fertile ground for the study of a musical genre like fado, known both for its topophilia, or love of place, and for its intense focus on making absent places present.

This paper explores the ways in which multiple spatial frames inform and influence fado performance in New Jersey. The space of the ethnic enclave, a vulnerable sphere of ethnic succession and demographic turnover, has been the staging ground for the closing of the last casa de fado in Newark—potentially a signal of fado's diminishing relevance to the Portuguese American community of Northern New Jersey. However, the closing of this last traditional venue has accompanied the genre's move into "tight spaces" (Baker 2001) where fado performers and audiences share evenings of entertainment with other musical genres and companion audiences. Some view this hybrid format as a positive development, others as a negative one. Those who see fado's unmooring from traditional performance spaces as the cause of repertoire diminishment and audience misbehavior have pushed fado into spaces associated with education as well as into small, private, home-like settings. Lastly, fado's increasing vulnerability within the space of the enclave has resulted in charged border crossings and the emergence of a more heterogenous group of fado performers and aficionados. These border crossings are contextualized here against the backdrop of a history of ethnic tensions in the Ironbound neighborhood, and a move among some artists and community leaders to embrace a paradigm of mixture and exchange, with fado as a key expressive laboratory for such a shift.

This paper is based on more than ten years of ethnographic fieldwork, from 2008 to the present, and on regular attendance of fado concerts, rehearsals, and other social gatherings in the Ironbound, in New York City, and in other regional hubs of Portuguese immigration. It is also based on semi-structured, long-format ethnographic interviews with fado performers, lyricists, producers, and aficionados, primarily in Northern New Jersey, as well as the consultation of the Ironbound Oral History Project archive of interviews.[4]

Spaces Undone: Changes within Newark's Fado Cathedral

Newark's Little Portugal neighborhood, also called the Ironbound, has long been hailed as the "Catedral do Fado." This immigrant neighborhood has the most newly arrived population of Portuguese, the highest degree of Portuguese language use in the home, and the largest proportion of continentals (as opposed to Azoreans) of all of the major US hubs of Portuguese emigration (Vicente

1999). Northern New Jersey is also home to hundreds of Portuguese cultural associations, schools, clubs, and churches—most of them involved in maintaining Portuguese traditions, particularly those of an expressive nature. Perhaps the general characteristics of this ethnic enclave and the widely avowed desire on the part of the community to keep Portuguese language and culture alive into the second and third generations explain the Ironbound's label as a "Fado Cathedral." It has, in fact, spawned and supported a fado performance scene which has remained active, with seasonal ups and downs, for over five decades.

The Ironbound boasts fifteen to twenty amateur fadistas and instrumentalists who either live or regularly perform there. This group is varied. Two-thirds form what is known as the "old guard": fadistas in their fifties, sixties, and seventies, all of whom were born in Portugal and many of whom are Portuguese-language dominant. Another six to ten singers form what is increasingly called a wave of second-generation "fado jovem" (Durães 2012). All but one of this group of "young fado" singers was born in New Jersey, all are in their teens and twenties, and all are bilingual.[5] These two generations often perform together and conceive of themselves, to some degree, as part of a unified group of local fadistas, although their spatial and social practices sometimes diverge.

In the mid to late 2010s, following fado's UNESCO designation as Intangible Cultural Heritage of Humanity, fado in New Jersey seemed to hit a high-water mark; a seemingly endless array of celebratory events at clubs, ribbon cuttings, restaurant openings, and wine tastings featured fado as part of a diverse program of entertainment, with "Fado Friday" sessions sprouting up at several area restaurants, and a growing wave of young fadistas reviving the scene and capturing the public's attention anew. However, there have also been signs of change that some performers and aficionados interpret as fado's diminishment within the ethnic enclave.[6] These signs of change hinge on issues of space. One measure of the health of the fado scene in diaspora is the presence (or lack thereof) of adequate and appropriate space for performance. Fado's adaptation to increasingly awkward spaces, which are deemed at best atypical or nontraditional and at worst inappropriate or "undignified," calls into question the importance of fado to the immigrant community and sets off the perennial debate as to whether or not fado will survive into the next generation.

In order to chart the changing nature of performance venues, it is important to note that the Ironbound currently has no dedicated casa de fado. Casas de fado, intimate spaces where food and alcohol are often served and patrons listen to fado late into the night, first appeared in Lisbon, Portugal, in the early twentieth century, as part of a larger movement toward the commercialization and professionalization of fado.[7] For long stretches throughout the 1980s, 1990s, and early 2000s, the Ironbound supported at least one casa de fado. These establishments, as noted by many fado scholars, have served a variety of important social and musical functions (Nery 2004; Cordeiro 1994; Klein and Alves 1994). One central function of the casa de fado in the Portuguese context has been teaching and initiating new generations of fado singers.[8] The history of instability regarding the Ironbound's casas de fado exposes the sometimes-fragile link between fado in Portugal and fado in the Portuguese diaspora in the US.

The last Ironbound casa de fado, Quebra Bilhas, closed in the late 2000s.[9] The closing, which was in part prompted by a murder outside the front doors of the establishment, and an occasional crop of rough-and-tumble patrons, recalls fado's nineteenth-century association with Lisbon crime, prisons, and prostitution. This incident draws attention to the uncannily similar backdrop that Newark and Lisbon provide to fado lore and history. They are both port cities built around the commercial activities enabled by river transport systems. Both cities are dominated by "landscapes of voyage" (Stewart 1993). Both feature riverside neighborhoods that have been associated with vice, crime, and populational transience. Each is perched on opposing sides of the Atlantic and both have nurtured fado, known for its lyrical lamentation of difficult circumstances and its expressive portrayal of the urban spaces which provide the mise-en-scène for pleasure and hardship alike.[10]

Even though the riverside neighborhoods of Newark and Lisbon provide similarly fertile socio-spatial ground for fado performance, Newark's current lack of a casa de fado forces the genre into "tight spaces." Borrowing the term from Houston Baker (2001), dance scholar Danielle Goldman (2010, 146) analyzes the way dance improvisation necessitates "an ongoing interaction with shifting tight places." These tight spaces, "whether created by power relations, social norms, aesthetic traditions or physical technique" (146), can be viewed as constraining, liberating, or both.[11] Ironbound fado has made a forced exodus from the traditional space of the casa de fado—where mementos and memorabilia line the walls, providing visual evidence of fado's dogged persistence, and where audiences know how to behave—into "tight spaces" such as family restaurants, basements of cultural centers, and other makeshift venues originally designed for other purposes. This shift is a cause for consternation among some fadistas and puts venue owners of "tight spaces" in a difficult position as they struggle to balance competing agendas and expectations. Even though fado in Portugal has a long history of change and a wide array of changing performance contexts—from the gritty streets of portside Lisbon in the 1820s, to the bourgeois salons of the turn of the century, to the casas de fado and theater stages of the twentieth and twenty-first centuries—changing spaces play a different role in diaspora. The ethnic neighborhood is always under threat of dissolution. And this socio-spatial fragility ties into issues of belonging, visibility, and identity; the disappearance of dedicated fado venues becomes a manifestation, perhaps proof, of the ethnic succession underway.

Since the closure of Quebra Bilhas, reliable weekly opportunities to hear fado in the Ironbound have diminished. For many years, however, a restaurant called El Pastor served as a parallel space for the regular weekend performance of fado. El Pastor, originally a Spanish restaurant, entered new management in the mid-1980s under Portuguese businessman and fado enthusiast, José Marques. Marques never changed the name of his new restaurant, but he revamped the menu of weekend entertainment. "He loved fado and had a lot of faith in fado bringing in people to the restaurant" (Cirne 2020).[12] Under Marques's ownership, therefore, fado consistently anchored the weekend programming. In the early years, fado was the unequivocal musical draw—El Pastor's weekend entertainment featured three long fado sets, interspersed with shorter sets of Portuguese popular music (Cirne 2020). During many of these nights, Marques also paid extra for fado's traditional instrumentation—a solo vocalist accompanied by a Spanish guitar (or viola) and a guitarra portuguesa (a twelve-string lute-like instrument that in Lisbon fado shares the melody with the voice)—in order to guarantee an "authentic" traditional experience of fado. Because guitarra portuguesa players were in short supply in New Jersey and New York, they commanded higher fees than the "house band" comprising keyboards and percussion. But the extra outlay was worth it, particularly in the early years, as El Pastor's devotion to fado succeeded in attracting robust crowds of weekend patrons, mostly first-generation Portuguese immigrants and their families and friends, for long sessions of listening, eating, and drinking, which often lasted well past midnight (Cirne 2020).

Over time, however, as Portuguese emigration to the US slowed and Portuguese American families who had first settled in the Ironbound began moving out to neighboring towns for more green space and better school systems, El Pastor's typical weekend crowd began to change. Because it retained its Spanish-language name, the restaurant began to appeal to an increasingly broad range of Newark denizens. The changing demographics of the weekend crowd at El Pastor reflected the changing ethnic composition of the Ironbound, where the Portuguese were joined, and in part replaced, by increasing numbers of Brazilians, Ecuadorians, and other Central and South American immigrants. The owners of El Pastor modified weekend programming in response to this shift, which took place from the 1990s through the mid-2010s. Instead of interspersing fado sets with Portuguese popular music, El Pastor increasingly offered upbeat Latin dance music from South America and the Spanish-speaking Caribbean, such as salsa, cumbia, and merengue, in order to offset the melancholy of fado—which an increasing number of weekend patrons didn't know (Cirne 2020).[13]

In addition to sharing the stage with other types of music during these years, fado's instrumentation also changed over time. The death of several local guitarra portuguesa players made securing traditional accompaniment challenging. Fado vocalists, therefore, ended up being routinely accompanied at El Pastor by the long-standing Duo Suave, comprising musical director/keyboardist Tony Cirne and percussionist Victor Fonseca.[14] The disappearance of traditional fado accompaniment displeased some fado performers, as well as some die-hard fado aficionados who regularly patronized El Pastor. As ethnomusicologist Salwa El-Shawan Castelo-Branco (1994, 127) states, "Tanto o público como os intérpretes do fado consideram o acompanhamento instrumental, sobretudo o da guitarra, como o elemento indispensável para a interpretação do fado, e um dos seus mais poderosos símbolos." The traditional pairing of two string instruments and a vocalist is essential to the musical dialogue created by fado performers where the guitarra acts as second soloist (Castelo-Branco 1994, 135, 131). Consequently, the loss of two local guitarra players and a viola player left weekend fado programming in a bind. As the culminating event in this narrative of change and accommodation, fado's multi-decade relationship with the venue of El Pastor ended completely in the mid-2010s, when the establishment closed its doors for good.

Even though El Pastor has closed, ending a long-lived commitment to fado programming, this collaboration represents an important phase in Newark's fado history that warrants examination and analysis. By examining fado's tenure at El Pastor, we can better understand how New Jersey's community of fado performers, aficionados, and venue owners responded to change over time. We can explore the limits of which aesthetic accommodations were seen as permissible in the context of diaspora, and which "crossed the line," threatening the definitional frameworks for what constitutes fado. We can understand what kind of "tight space" El Pastor constituted and whether accompanying changes in performance format, instrumentation, repertoire, and taste publics signaled constraint or liberation or a combination of both.

Fadistas are often divided in their reflections on the role of El Pastor in the fado community. On the one hand, many of the old guard were regular weekend patrons there. Male fado performers would sit around the big wooden bar after work and watch soccer matches on TV, while female singers shared meals with friends and family in the dining room, listened to other fadistas, danced, or occasionally sat in on someone else's set. Certain fado regulars—either performers or aficionados—even had their own special tables reserved for them week after week. El Pastor was an important social hub for this generation. The younger singers also have an attachment to El Pastor, even though their peers typically didn't socialize there. Many young fadistas associate El Pastor with early performance opportunities and their first interactions with the old-guard fadistas. The restaurant owners and Tony Cirne typically welcomed new talent and provided important exposure for those new to the scene. A 2012 feature in the local Portuguese paper confirmed, for example, that "segundo Tony Cirne, o director musical do El Pastor, 'a aposta na juventude será, sem dúvida, uma das características desta nova época'" (Durães 2012, 14). El Pastor, therefore, played a crucial role as the brick-and-mortar anchor for fado performing, listening, and networking, greasing the wheels of exchange and interplay by "putting experience into circulation," to borrow Victor Turner's (1991) phrase. In this sense, inasmuch as El Pastor's "tight space" provided an essential outlet for the sociability of fado performers while enabling the music's continuation and growth through regular performance opportunities, it can be thought of as generative, but perhaps not exactly liberating.

On the other hand, some performers and fado enthusiasts complained about the restaurant's environment, suggesting that the formatting and instrumentation constraints compromised core ingredients of fado's defining framework. High on the list of complaints was the dancing component of the weekend programming, which patrons saw as derailing the proper emotional environment for fado listening and, therefore, for fado performance.

On a chilly Saturday night in September of 2012, El Pastor's dining room/performance space was filled to capacity. Several long tables accommodated parties of twenty or more, as well as many of the usual four-tops. Cirne, the keyboardist and master of ceremonies, joked with the audience all night in three languages—Italian, Spanish, and Portuguese. Indeed, there was a big extended family of Italians celebrating a birthday, several tables of Portuguese and Brazilian families, and a smattering of Galicians and Central Americans—ethnic groups that reflect the demographics of Newark's East and North Wards. Before playing a merengue, Cirne, a native Portuguese speaker, encouraged the audience to get up and dance in Spanish. "Arriba! Arriba!!" he shouted playfully. Not needing much cajoling in any language, seven or eight pairs of middle-aged and even elderly patrons crowded onto the small dance floor, laughing and moving adroitly to the fast-paced Dominican rhythms. Clearly this part of the evening—during which Cirne, an instrumentalist, producer, and composer, bantered with the audience, DJ-ed requested tunes, and sang over recorded dance tracks—had gained an enthusiastic following over the years. Many people there had come to dance. And with the rotating disco ball poised over the dance floor and the DJ's masterful polyglot jocularity and spinning of upbeat Latin rhythms, this segment of the audience clearly got what they came for.

And then the fado portion began. As Cirne descended from the small stage he had been perched on all night and began to walk through the crowded dining room, I wondered how he would get the boisterous crowd to quiet down enough for young fadista Pedro Botas to begin his set. As fado aficionados know, audience behavior is a crucial element in successful fado performance. Some fado scholars describe the intense interchange between vocalist and audience members during peak performative moments as quasi-religious. Graça Índia Cordeiro states, for example:

> A emoção que atravessa a voz e a postura do cantador transmite-se, por contágio, aos ouvintes que o acompanham em todos os pormenores, e é neste momento, quase religioso, de comunicação, criada uma ligação sensitiva entre todos os participantes—*é tão fadista quem canta como quem ouve*—que se vive a partilha de uma narrativa, de um sentimento, numa espécie de comunhão entre todos. (1994, 68; italics in the original)

A key ingredient that enables this intense relationship between fado performer and audience is silence. Based on her research of amateur fado in Lisbon, Lila Ellen Gray observes:

> Silence can be qualitative; singers and fans might speak of a venue in terms of the quality of its silence, where an audience who knows how to be silent is one that knows how to listen with the same intensity with which the fadista is singing, thus entering into the fado and thus into the feeling. (2013, 38)

Given that "high quality" silence paves the way for an audience/singer exchange essential to "entering into the fado," Cirne had his work cut out for him as he threaded his way through tables without his microphone, presenting information in an unamplified voice that no one could hear. It was the first time all night that he spoke without a microphone; clearly, this was his strategy for transitioning into an acoustic-type environment, where patrons had to be especially quiet to hear voices whose only projection came from the diaphragm. As he continued to speak, looking almost as if he were in a silent film, a few patrons noticed him, halted their conversations, and elbowed and shushed their dining companions. It took five or six minutes, but the silent-film trick seemed to work. As the audience finally came to full attention, Tony introduced Pedro. Pedro took a deep breath, looked to the heavens, and began to sing the mournful melodies and lyrics of the Sérgio Nunes fado "Lenda da fonte." He has a deep resonant voice and an earnest delivery, and he sang beautifully despite the nerve-racking battle for silence that preceded his set and the absence of string accompaniment.

Four or five tables of people—perhaps a third of the audience—seemed to have come for fado, and the rest for the dancing and conviviality. Botas concentrated on those particularly fado-friendly tables and finished a set of three passionately delivered fados. Some of the other tables of non-Portuguese seemed to be listening out of respect; others responded more viscerally to the songs and joined the fado-friendly tables in applauding during the singer's last crescendo—a gesture of appreciation and shared emotion. Still others seemed not to know the fado audience protocol and were not particularly interested in this segment of the evening's programming. In short, it was not an unfriendly crowd, but an audience of extremely diverse taste publics that displayed a range of interest in and appreciation for the fado component of the evening. El Pastor's musical programming would continue in this vein until well after midnight, alternating between DJ-ed Latin dance tunes and short sets of fado.

So what can we make of the disparate musics and leisure time pursuits that share a "tight space"—some nights amicably, other nights awkwardly? Maria de São José Corte-Real (2010; 1991), who spent a year doing fieldwork in the

Ironbound in the early nineties, documented a similar space-sharing arrangement between what she described as "lambada" dance sets and fado sets. Her latest analytical take on these strange bedfellows is that the fado audiences she observed begrudgingly obeyed a Salazar-era pressure to reminisce through expressive modalities, which they found unsatisfying. She creates an analytical dichotomy where fado consumption is obligatory and Latin dancing is liberating: "The intensity of the participation left . . . the impression that the audience was more identified with the lambada dance than with the fados offered up" (2010, 88). She furthers her analysis by arguing that the tension between these two different strategies of identification and belonging resulted in frustration for the audience (87–88).

I agree that the alternating sets produced tension and perhaps at times frustration for some audience members, at least among those I met at El Pastor. However, a couple of factors may muddy the waters here, potentially disrupting a dichotomous reading, at least by the 2010s. One is the diversity of the audience in many venues across the Ironbound—increasing throughout the 1990s, 2000s, and 2010s—and a concomitant range of familiarity with fado. My reading of audience frustration is that in a room full of urban denizens, immigrants from different countries with different musical tastes, habits, languages, and leisure-time agendas, who share a dance floor and who share the consumption of what is essentially a variety show, there will always be certain music and dance sets that appeal to some audience members more than others. In an urban environment like Newark's Ironbound, the heterogeneity of the audience is an essential factor that disrupts a reading of a generalized Portuguese emigrant preference for Latin dance music over fado. The audience at El Pastor from the nineties until its closing was rarely one hundred percent Portuguese.

The second factor that complicates a dichotomous reading of the musical variety at El Pastor is the possibility that the same Portuguese audience members could simultaneously enjoy both expressive modalities without conflict and frustration. Fado vocalist and guitarist Francisco Chuva (2008) suggests, in fact, that the mix of fado and Latin dance music is what most middle-aged Portuguese Americans want on the weekends. As he states,

> há muita gente que vem aqui [El Pastor] porque gostam do fado, jantam a ver fado, têm que ter música para dançar um pouquinho também. . . . As casas do fado só dão fado, não dão mais nada. Aquilo não pode ser, a pessoa tem

uma semana de trabalho bastante grande, às vezes com bastantes horas. Eu ao sábado quero desistir um pouco, quero uma musiquinha para dançar, para afastar o stress.

In other parts of the interview, Chuva elaborates on this point, positing the need for stress release through a mixture of upbeat dancing and fado-inspired reminiscing as unique to the immigrant experience in the US. He explains that many of his coethnics have an intense attitude toward work, given that there is only one generation to make an economic impact, to make the migratory rupture worthwhile. He describes his own work week at a metal plant that begins at five a.m. and ends at eight p.m., "with just enough time in between to get the courage up to start all over again the next day" (Chuva 2008). Intense work experiences are related to the types of blue-collar jobs available to many foreign-born Portuguese who arrived between 1960 and 1980, often with little formal education and limited English. These experiences are compounded by US habits of working overtime, often through lunch and on weekends, with little to no vacation time—markedly different, according to Chuva, from what is permissible and habitual in Portugal. According to Chuva's testimony, then, the leisure-time desires of the Portuguese in the US may be different from those in Portugal. He is not, however, implying that there is no place for fado in the US diaspora. In fact, for Chuva and others in his generation, performing and listening to fado, especially in the context of diaspora, is often linked to important memory work and the cathartic experience of reminiscing about the past. Attending fado performances that actively conjure absent places, people, and eras—memory work wrapped up in the feeling of saudade—has been termed by one scholar of Portuguese emigration a "palliative tool" for dealing with the challenges of deterritorialization (Wieczorek, forthcoming). So, according to Chuva, the setup at El Pastor functioned well for many: Portuguese emigrants had access to live performances of fado as well as other livelier music and dance forms, all in one tight place, for ease of access and variety, designed for those working toward the American Dream, with limited free time, intense work weeks, and a desire to "afastar o stress" and "matar saudades" in a one-stop-shop experience on a Saturday night.

Spaces Remade: A Circus of Audience Cultivation

While Chuva casts fado's Ironbound adaptation in a largely positive light, there are others who are not as sanguine about changes in performance contexts that lead to uncontrollable audiences and, as a result, to repertoire diminishment.

As we transition from the discussion of El Pastor to an analysis of "special event" fado performance, it becomes evident that venues can influence audience composition and expectation, which can, in turn, lead to changes in fado repertoire. José Luís Iglesias, a longtime resident of Northern New Jersey, has waged a lengthy battle to create a stimulating performance scene for Portuguese American artists, musicians, and lyricists. Iglesias taught himself to play guitarra portuguesa in response to the shortage of local string players and has become an important force in the New Jersey/New York fado scene. He describes performing fado for an audience of five hundred Portuguese Americans during a gala dinner to inaugurate the Portugal Day weekend:

> Sendo fado e não havendo mais nenhuma atração numa festa destas, nós quando começamos, as pessoas não interromperam nada a conversa que estavam a ter, nada. Tocamos um fado. O segundo era "O abandono" do David Mourão-Ferreira. Eu tive que me levantar do meu lugar e fui ao microfone, e fui dizer às pessoas que a gente estaria à espera até estarem todos calados. Porque eu expliquei, aqui há quem goste de fado, eventualmente há quem não goste, mas quem não goste devia arriscar e até ir a ver, tentar ver o que há no fado que pode ser atraente, ou pelo menos respeitar o gosto dos outros. (Iglesias 2009)

Iglesias attributes part of the problem in audience comportment to the diverse venues and events that fado musicians are thrown into—contexts where Portuguese American audiences, only some of whom appreciate fado, have lost the "humility and respect" that they would have possessed in Portugal, taking on foreign attitudes of disrespect and rowdiness. He goes on to say that some local fadistas, who are invited to perform for club anniversaries, Portugal Day celebrations, wine tastings, and other one-time events where audience interest in fado cannot be predicted, have tailored their repertoire to the lowest common denominator.

The fados that are sure crowd-pleasers, that are upbeat and possess a sing-along aspect, become de rigueur for many special-event contexts where fadistas must reign in boisterous crowds. Iglesias contends that this type of repertoire diminishment, choosing "fados que não exigem," creates a circus-like environment:

> Cantam imediatamente determinados fados que pessoas já conhecem, são fados fáceis de ouvir, mas as letras não têm realmente, não têm significado às tantas, aquilo não atrasa nem adianta. Mas as pessoas reconhecem-se, porque

> é como ver um jogo de futebol, é de adesão imediata, é uma coisa, é energia, é intuitivo, não tem nada a ver com o aspecto musical. (Iglesias 2009)[15]

Iglesias's testimony here and above points to a complex of frustrations, which deal with issues of assimilation into a new cultural environment and the potential incompatibility of fado with swathes of the Portuguese American community who have acquired new goals, desires, and habits. The "unchallenging" fados give immediate satisfaction; they possess an "intuitive" energy and spark in-the-moment engagement with sound that is tailor-made to match the US environment of fast food, pop-up shops, and throw-away merchandise. It is not just the fast-paced rhythms and penchant for immediate gratification of US life that undergird Iglesias's description, but also the mainstream US value system, which he posits as less conducive to soulful, in-depth, quiet reflection. According to Iglesias's testimony, this value system seems to have rubbed off on segments of the special-event fado crowds he plays for: "Aqui há um novo-riquismo, as pessoas gostam de ir a uma festa mostrar-se, mas lá dentro não tem nada" (Iglesias 2009).

The concern about newly acquired materialism that may condition indifference toward the immaterial riches of music among those whose expressive habits are oriented toward festive ostentation finds its way into the lyrics of a fado written by local New Jersey poet João S. Martins. In his "Fado da noite do fado," the Ironbound's main artery, Ferry Street, is central to a discussion of immigrant dreams and realities. In his middle three stanzas, Martins (2015, 36) writes:

> nas vozes que a noite esconde
> por muito escuro que faça
> uma luzinha presença
> brilha por trás da vidraça
>
> vendem-se imagens e luzes
> nas janelas da ilusão
> capa que encobre a tristeza
> das noites de solidão
>
> nas estrelas que viajam
> há uma esperança e uma prece
> sonhos das horas que passam
> enquanto a noite adormece

The play between night and day is a backdrop for the glittering shop windows full of promise and illusion, beckoning immigrant pedestrians who traffic along Ferry Street on their way to work and back home again. "Images are sold" on Ferry Street, but we get the sense in this fado that those who buy into the dream do not get what they've paid for, calling into question the migratory project, bolstered as it is by the promise of economic betterment within the capitalist framework of capital accumulation and consumerism.

A growing group of fado performers has addressed the indifference sometimes exhibited by special-event audiences with a fresh approach that focuses on audience cultivation. In a way, teaching audiences to appreciate fado could be viewed as a type of a remediation for those who were seduced by the glittering windows and bought into a potentially bankrupt American dream. By instructing Portuguese American audiences how to listen to fado, these musicians orchestrate a relearning of expressive modalities from worlds left behind, a remembering of the culturally coded sounds of lament, and a guided reconnection to modes of comportment, ways of thinking, and neglected cultural roots. To this end, Iglesias and other like-minded artists have begun performing fado with a distinctively didactic bent in secondary schools, universities, and libraries. Teaching the listening public about Portuguese music accompanies the search for new venues, both within and outside the Ironbound enclave, and a drive to expand fado's horizons and secure its positive reception.

One 2008 performance at Newark's Sport Clube Português, for example, carried the title *All That Fado!*—a spinoff on the 1930s American musical *All That Jazz!*, which had been revived in part through the Broadway hit *Chicago*. Iglesias and Santos included several pages of background on the history of fado in the photocopied program handed out to each audience member. The program was printed completely in English. Santos and Iglesias introduced songs throughout the evening with bilingual explanations of lyrics. The audience of about fifty to sixty people, including Ironbound regulars, extended families of Portuguese Americans, and a large group of Seton Hall University students, filled the intimate space and remained attentive and engaged throughout the evening. Santos and Iglesias's repertoire was more ample than in the typical special-event performances and included fados de Coimbra, politically charged fados like "Abandono," and newer fados based on the verses of canonical Portuguese poets. At this event, which was part musical demonstration, part history lesson, and part performance, the ambiance was formal and respectful. Following the concert, audience members approached the performers as they packed up their sound equipment to ask questions about the lyrics. Two students asked Iglesias if they could hold the guitarra portuguesa, plucking at the strings reverently as they asked questions about the instrument.

In the many fado performances I've seen over the years in New Jersey and New York, I rarely saw audience members, complete strangers, approach fadistas with questions following the performance. The structure created by the bilingual playbill, featuring components like a precise listing and order of fados to be played—an unorthodox element even in high-profile venues like Mariza's Carnegie Hall concerts—communicates a desire to inform and instruct. And this, in turn, creates an opening for questions and inquiries, precisely the type of engaged dialogue Iglesias and Santos want to nurture. This approach might mute the potential emotional "communion" between audience and performer; such heightened feeling seems to feed on the improvised quality of a musical climax that takes one by surprise, a dynamic perhaps impeded by the cerebral contemplation of lyrics, history, and instrumentation. But what this didactic fado approach may sacrifice in shared emotion, it gains in audience cultivation and enrichment. This heuristic orientation not only structures a specific type of fado performance, it also informs a willing, respectful public and expands the horizons of Portuguese music using immigrant musicians as intermediaries for larger pedagogical purposes.

> The true fadista wants to be heard in restricted spaces, where intimacy can and should exist. The true fadista wants to talk, sing with the people right in front of him. The true fadista doesn't want to sing what he sang and how he sang yesterday. . . . The true fadista refuses the "more-than-tested and predictably successful" recipe. The true fadista is an inveterate gambler: he wants to risk, risk, and risk. (Iglesias 2019)

Parting the Codfish Curtain: Fado's Charged Border Crossing

The production company "Fátima Santos Presents" is another platform designed to further cultivate audiences through the didactic presentation of fado in new places and through collaboration with other musicians. Local fadista Fátima Santos has experimented with different programming efforts in many spaces throughout the Ironbound and surrounding areas. For various periods in the mid-2010s, Fátima Santos Presents organized regular concerts at the Café Concerto, a corner space in the basement of the Ironbound's Sport Clube Português, adjacent to a bar frequented mostly by older Portuguese men involved in sueca games and long evenings of drinking and banter. An unlikely spot for musical experimentation, the Café Concerto became the venue for jazz concerts featuring New York musicians and bossa nova evenings with Brazilian musicians, as well as other players and genres from outside the Ironbound enclave. Met with varying degrees of success and interest, these Fatima Santos Presents concerts marked a broadening of the fado scene—a dynamic that continues today within other local venues, involving wider circles of fadistas and the integration of outsider musicians.

The musical programming of several gala events in the last ten years reflects a desire to expose the Ironbound's Portuguese emigrant public to different musical traditions and to place fado within a multicontinental orbit of Lusophone cultural exchange. For example, the literary group ProVerbo, which operates out of the Sport Clube Português and comprises twenty to thirty regular members, organizes a gala dinner every year where typically one high-profile musician or writer is invited from Portugal to perform alongside local Portuguese immigrant musicians. For some galas, however, program organizers include other musics from around the Lusophone world. In 2009, for example, the ProVerbo gala featured a broad program of live music including morna and batuque from Cabo Verde, performed by local Cabo Verdean emigrants, Brazilian gaúcho performance featuring Brazilian American second-generation youth, and local Portuguese fado and rancho performances. Glória de Melo and João Martins, founders of ProVerbo, constituted the force behind this programming expansion. They aimed to emphasize "cooperation" across the Portuguese-speaking world by focusing on the musical history of broad Lusophone interchange, as opposed to a bounded presentation of exclusively Portuguese genres.[16] The fact that some of the audience accepted this paradigm of Lusophone exchange while others left early, grumbling about the absence of the usual nationalistic model of programming, underscores the tension within the enclave over issues of ethnic isolation versus assimilation. It also points to a taste for expressions of "hyperbolic" nationalism among some Luso-Americans, as Cristiana Bastos (2020) argues.

The wave of musicians, writers, and community leaders who are pushing to expand fado's presentation and arguing for models of exchange, integration, and innovation run up against a more conservative streak within the community that reflects the desire to cordon off and preserve Portuguese culture. This attitude toward expressive culture is paralleled by the geography of Ironbound, an area of Newark that is literally "bound" and kept separate by elevated train tracks to the west and enormous interstate highways around much of the rest of the neighborhood. For this reason, and because the Ironbound's Portuguese community has been known for its insularity, the boundaries separating the ethnic enclave from the rest of the city and beyond have been dubbed "The Codfish Curtain" by local Luso-American resident and scholar Linda Rodrigues (Smothers 1997).

The tensions over "bounded" isolation versus unbound mixing, which sometimes play out among the audiences of Ironbound banquet halls, reflect more everyday tensions within an ethnic enclave in the midst of a demographic shift. As ethnographers have documented in Ironbound high schools (Ramos-Zayas 2009) and in neighborhood festivals and outdoor celebrations (Holton 2006b), some segments of the Ironbound population clash over simmering postcolonial prejudices and preconceptions. Viewed from one angle, the tension involves one group's demographic diminishment and another group's rise. The Portuguese, who arrived en masse in Newark between 1960 and 1980, have been joined and are perhaps slowly being replaced in the East Ward by Brazilians and Central Americans, most of whom began arriving in the 1990s.[17] It is a classic story of ethnic succession, where an urban community of immigrants, now in the second and third generations, begins to assimilate into the mainstream and move out toward the suburbs or neighboring cities in search of better school systems and more green space. There are still many Portuguese families living in the Ironbound, but they are aging. Most of those who have moved out to nearby towns still come back regularly to the Ironbound for grocery shopping, to attend mass, to see friends, and to spend time at clubs and cultural centers. But the Portuguese component to the neighborhood is not what it used to be, and people sense that the Ironbound's "Little Portugal" era may be in decline.

In its more complex form, the Ironbound conflict extends beyond the fragility of one group's attachment to place during a moment of demographic transition. The situation in the Ironbound is more complicated because, in large part, the group being replaced and the group doing the replacing share a colonial history and a language. According to the testimonies of several hundred Portuguese and Brazilian immigrants interviewed for the Ironbound Oral History Project (IOHP), what divides and unites these two ethnic groups, resettled side by side in the US in an era of postcolonialism, is very much in contention.[18] Both groups come to the fresh start provided by migration with colonial baggage and the vestiges of old wounds and prejudices that inflect present day interaction and sometimes thwart a peaceable coexistence in diaspora.

Although a discourse analysis of the IOHP interviews shows a narrative strain emphasizing Portuguese-Brazilian cooperation, the more dominant narrative is one of cultural misunderstanding, strife, and a markedly dissociative way of defining Portuguese and Brazilian identity in diaspora. There are incendiary charges in both directions: IOHP testimonies by Brazilians link charges of racial prejudice, closed-mindedness, and conservatism to Portugal's history as a colonial power and to its leadership role in the slave trade.[19] Charges in the other direction emphasize Brazil's "tropical" orientation and what is characterized as a companion attitude of liberalism and moral permissiveness.[20] Persuasive evidence of these oppositional attitudes, according to the testimonies, is found in the expressive forms that have come to symbolize cultural difference in this Newark neighborhood (Holton 2006b). Although there are performance forms popular in the Ironbound, such as Portuguese rancho groups and Brazilian gaúcho groups, that are quite similar in their presentational styles, performance circuits, and social purpose as positive leisure-time activities for second-generation urban youth, not one person interviewed mentioned them as proof of the ways in which Portuguese and Brazilians are similar. Instead, many testimonies focused on the ways in which the two "national song forms"—fado and samba—perfectly expressed the North-South divide and the reasons that cultural habits developed in Brazil and Portugal, respectively, are inherently and forever opposed. In short, fado and samba both bolster and justify Luso-Brazilian conflict in the Ironbound.

As John M. O'Connell (2010, vii) states, "music can be used to identify conflict by examining the manifestations of discord in musical discourse and in musical practice." Discourse about the way in which musical forms represent cultural difference and justify quotidian antagonisms elucidate conservative attitudes concerning the preservation and protection of Portugal's "national song." Against this backdrop, one can begin to understand why there is resistance to fado's border crossing, both in its mixing with other Lusophone music genres and in its role as a platform for the expressive talents of immigrant musicians and lyricists. If fado is an essential (and essentialized) symbol of Portuguese identity in diaspora in the context of Luso-Brazilian tension, then it is not difficult to see why multiethnic teams of fado musicians and vocalists would draw complaint from the more conservative sector of the population. To stir the pot even further, scholars are increasingly in agreement that Portugal's "national song" has Afro-Brazilian roots (among other early influences), and that the first documented mention of the cultural form "fado"—then more of a danced than sung form—actually appeared in Brazil in the 1700s.[21] It is easy to understand, then, why singing "Estranha forma da vida," an Amália Rodrigues classic, in a Brazilian accent, or adding a bossa nova syncopation to fado guitar arrangements, or splicing together fado and samba verses and performing them in drag—all formal experimentations that have occurred in this region over the past decade—would offend a conservative standpoint. It follows that special-event programming like ProVerbo's gala, curated to demonstrate the easy cohabitation and expressive kinship between Lusophone musical genres such as fado, morna, bossa nova, and samba, would provoke the early departure of those audience members wishing the codfish curtain had never been lifted.

Despite the insular reputation of this ethnic enclave, a gingerly established paradigm of mixture seems to be gaining support, as more and more fado enthusiasts and musicians from the community and beyond push the boundaries of instrumentation, arrangement, and venue. This sometimes involves expanding the cast of fado performers into multiethnic, plurilingual teams rallied around the beauty of a musical form—making a de facto argument for pan-Lusophone exchange and collaboration. As Dan Lundburg (2010) notes in his study of Middle Eastern musicians in Germany, the diasporic context can encourage interethnic cooperation among musicians—partnerships that might not be possible in other sociogeographic spaces. Scholars like Barbara Kirshenblatt-Gimblett (1988) have also argued that the diasporic context can be a liberating space of formal musical innovation—as was the case with her study of US klezmer musicians. Until relatively recently, however, this has not been true for fado in Northern New Jersey. Unlike the easy integration of non-Portuguese and Portuguese instrumentalists in Rhode Island bandas that Katherine Brucher (2009) documents, this relatively recent inclusion of foreign singers and instrumentalists in the fado scene of New Jersey and New York City has taken a while to become accepted wholesale by the Ironbound fado community.

A constellation of factors has facilitated fado's particularly intense border crossing in the New Jersey/New York region. First, the shortage of instrumentalists and the closing of the last casa de fado, ostensibly constraining factors, paradoxically forced fado performance to extend into new venues, open up to new audiences, and expand its usual cast of performers to include musicians and vocalists from other ethnic groups. Second, while the Ironbound's demographic shift and the Portuguese community's slowly diminishing residential presence have indeed produced tension and anxiety, they have also spawned a paradigm of mixture—if not always out of desire, then out of necessity—and certain Portuguese American community and cultural leaders have been vocal advocates of this turn.[22]

In addition, a shift in fado historiography and representation has spread across the Atlantic. More definitive arguments by scholars such as Rui Vieira Nery (2004) and José Tinhorão (1994) have found their way into New Jersey's Portuguese community, expanding residents' understanding of fado's early history and the triangulation of cultural influences that circulated among port cities in Brazil, Africa, and Portugal and gave rise to the song/dance form in its earliest incantation. Aside from reading newspaper articles and reviews about fado in the local paper *LusoAmericano* and online, attending guest lectures at area universities by visiting musicologists such as Salwa Castelo-Branco, and participating in classes (such as the recent Citylore workshops) dedicated to dispelling myths about fado's early history, many local fado enthusiasts and performers have seen Carlos Saura's film *Fados* (2007).[23] Saura's cinematic portrayal of fado in all its diversity, with attendant pluricontinental influences and proliferation, has impacted New Jersey's local fado community by exposing narrative inroads for viewing fado more broadly, as "world heritage" along the lines of its UNESCO designation in 2011, instead of a narrowly defined national form to be protected from outside participation and alteration.

Lastly, the codfish curtain has been opened, allowing for broader trafficking of new multiethnic casts of fado performers, due in part to the emergence of a young crop of second-generation fadistas. Although it is beyond the purview of this paper (and has been treated at some length elsewhere), it is worth noting that these younger Northern New Jersey fadistas are using online technology, bilingualism, and more expansive spatial practices to connect Newark to New York City, thus opening up the fado performance scene even further.[24] The scene's expansion beyond the local enclave can also be linked to the rise of several Portuguese restaurants in New York City that have offered weekly fado sessions on and off over the past several decades. Because of this partnership, homegrown US fado has garnered a broader, more diverse audience, and New Jersey fadistas increasingly engage other genres and ways of thinking about music and spectacle.

Conclusion

This paper has explored fado's placemaking and border crossing against the backdrop of the changing space of the immigrant enclave. As Michael Colvin (2008; 2016) underscores, fado has a long history of association with vulnerable urban spaces and transient populations. In the case of the Ironbound, socio-spatial vulnerability is tied to processes of ethnic succession, the slow dissolution of Newark's "Little Portugal" and concomitant concerns surrounding belonging and identity in diaspora. Tracking down and securing the "tight spaces" where fado can thrive in diaspora is a bulwark against the threat of disappearance and the "perilous territory of not-belonging" (Said 2010, 359). In the process of accommodating challenges to venue, instrumentation, and changing public tastes, Ironbound fado became increasingly accustomed to sharing the stage with more up-tempo Latin American and Caribbean musics. The one-stop Saturday night experience, where a diverse, polyglot public can reminisce about the past while dancing away the stresses of the present, seemed to work for a contingent of first-generation fado enthusiasts.

For some, these accommodations signal an erosion of social meaning and threaten the cultural integrity of fado as a genre. Some worry that the kind of "high-quality silence" needed from fado audiences is at odds with US ideologies and habits and the dizzying rhythms of urban life. To ward against the erasure or diminishment of fado's more "difficult" repertoire, some New Jersey fadistas have borrowed the tools and structures of education to create an environment for preserving and understanding fado in all of its lyrical and philosophical depth. Similarly, new social pathways facilitate border crossing, and paradigms of mixture and exchange have broadened the range of fado's publics and performers, creating a more dynamic and multidirectional circuitry between the Ironbound and New York City and between Portugal and Newark.

Ultimately, the perennial anxiety over fado's survival in the US can be quieted by an understanding of the genre's special link to the experience of deterritorialization, and to those who have experienced loss by way of migration. In the words of New Jersey fado guitarist Francisco Chuva (2008),

> o fado [conta] histórias do português que foi para o estrangeiro, do pescador que saiu pelo mar, disilusões da vida. Tem a ver com a saudade. Eu acho [que] a gente aqui, os portugueses aqui sentem mais o fado do que os portugueses lá. Não quero dizer que os portugueses lá não gostam do fado . . . mas acho

que o afastamento do nosso país e a saudade leva-nos a gostar mais do fado. . . . E eu penso que no geral toda a gente pensa na mesma maneira.

NOTES

1. I would like to thank the many fado performers and aficionados who shared their thoughts and insights with me over the years, sometimes sitting for multiple interviews and fielding questions of all sorts. Without their time and generosity, this research would not have been possible. Any errors or shortcomings are my own.

2. Newark's late twentieth- and early twenty-first-century history has been greatly impacted by the 1967 uprisings and subsequent legislative and grassroots attempts to ameliorate the unjust structures and practices that provoked them. In July 1967, Newark's disenfranchised, largely African American residents responded to institutionalized racism, lack of political representation, a white vice grip on local political and commercial power, police brutality, segregation, and "legal" displacement through use of eminent domain laws by rising up against systemic injustice. The violence and unrest that ensued ended up in the destruction of property and businesses. The events also set off an exodus of "white flight" to the suburbs and years of more general population loss for Newark. Racist redlining practices made it difficult for working-class people of color to rebuild. In the last fifteen years, there has been some progress in addressing the practices, laws, and attitudes that set off the 1967 uprisings, but a 2019 report entitled "Recent Wealth Divide in Newark" shows that "despite Newark's ongoing renaissance as a corporate and cultural hub, the new wealth is not, for the most part, flowing to much of its population—the communities of color that make up the majority of city residents" (Flanagan 2019). It is for these reasons and others that the "renaissance city" designation for Newark inspires controversy.

3. The Bernardino Coutinho family started the Portugal Day parade in the early 1980s. It began as a small, intimate urban parade celebrating Portugal's different regions, but has grown in recent years into an enormous two-week series of concerts, exhibits, dinners, and lectures culminating in the Portugal Day parade. The parade itself and some of the corollary events have taken on a broader, more inclusive orientation, involving various associations and populations from Newark's different neighborhoods and throughout Northern New Jersey. At one point, a committee of organizers considered calling it the "Immigrant Parade" and disassociating it from the Portuguese altogether. Ultimately this was voted down, but the parade itself remains a wide-ranging hodgepodge of municipal, county, and even suburban groups and organizations, ranging from Scottish bagpipe players, African American step groups, and Brazilian samba performers to Portuguese folkloric troupes and beyond.

4. The Ironbound Oral History Project was started in 2000 by the author. It is a repository of more than 250 oral history interviews with Portuguese-speaking migrants and

their descendants residing in Northern New Jersey. The collection of interviews has been conducted and transcribed by undergraduate students at Rutgers University in Newark, and is growing every year.

5. For more on second-generation fado performers in New Jersey and in California, see Holton (2016; 2020).

6. For as long as I have been doing fieldwork within the fado scene of New Jersey, there have been discussions of fado's impending disappearance. The anxiety over whether or not fado will "survive" in this Portuguese American immigrant hub has recently been revealed, for example, through the dynamic online discussion following guitarist José Luis Iglesias's Facebook post entitled "Is There Still Fado in New Jersey?" An essay form of this post was subsequently published in *eMagazine* (Iglesias 2019).

7. According to Alexandra Klein and Vera Alves (1994, 37), during the period before dedicated casas de fado emerged, fado was performed throughout Lisbon in an "unprogrammed way" as the "fado vadio," literally "vagabond fado," performed "na rua, na taberna, no bordel, e depois, a par destes, no salão aristicrático e nas esperas de toiros."

8. According to Leonor Losa's (2019, 133) recent dissertation on fado performance in Lisbon, the importance of the casa de fado to the nurturing of young talent has ebbed and flowed over the years. Analyzing the practices of lauded younger generation fadista Ricardo Ribeiro, Losa states that "a centralidade que a presença na casa de fados ocupa na vida de Ricardo não é típica da nova geração de fadistas cujas carreiras, como a de Ricardo, se desenvolvem centralmente em trabalhos gravados e espectáculos, sendo que o eixo da apresentação nestes espaços é cada vez menos relevante." So while the lack of a casa de fado in the Ironbound is sometimes used as a negative indicator of the health of the fado scene in diaspora, its importance in securing a new generation of fado singers in Lisbon seems to vary and shift. The same can be said for the younger generation of fadistas in Northern New Jersey, many of whom rely on audio recordings and online performance videos for practice and learning (Holton 2016).

9. The link between Lisbon and Newark can be seen in the name of this Ironbound casa de fado, established by fadista-proprietor Rosalina Silva and her husband. Quebra Bilhas was the name of a well-known casa de fado on the outskirts of Lisbon. Rosalina Silva became enchanted with the name of the establishment in her home country and decided to duplicate it when she opened her own fado house in Newark.

10. Several Newark-based Portuguese American writers have penned literary works centering on Newark's Ironbound neighborhood, where the Ironbound is even featured as a protagonist—personified as a lover, a mother, or a friend. Hugo dos Santos (2012), for example, wrote an extended literary piece along these lines, entitled "Ironbound, A Blog," which he describes as a "love letter to the place where I grew up." Writers João S. Martins (2015), Marina Carreira (2017; 2018), paulA neves and Nick Kline (2017), Gloria de Melo (1998), and others have also written fado poems focused on Newark or the relationship

between Newark and Lisbon. This intense literary focus on the space of the neighborhood, applying affective frameworks of topophilia to the hyperlocal, thus characterizes fado lyrics in both riverside locations, further unifying Newark and Lisbon as urban environments that inspire the creation and performance of fado.

11. It is interesting to note the genealogy of this term and its increasing relevance to studies of improvisation. Houston Baker first used "tight spaces" in his book *Turning South Again: Re-Thinking Modernism/Re-Reading Booker T* (2001), followed by an expanding cadre of dance scholars who use it to analyze the dynamic between spatial or social constraint and aesthetic improvisation and emancipation (see Midgelow 2019; Browning 2011).

12. Throughout this essay I use real names of cited performers with permission.

13. Klein and Alves (1994, 39) trace a similar dynamic beginning in late-1920s Lisbon, where the increasingly commercial strategy that linked profit with greater diversity of musical programming produced dedicated fado houses and fado salons, "procurando atingir um público vasto de modo a rentabilizarem-se. . . . Deste modo, não é por acaso que muitas vezes o fado era apresentado em conjunto com outros géneros musicais, também em voga: o foxtrot, o tango, a valsa, e o jazz."

14. The New Jersey/New York fado scene is still in the midst of what many deem an "instrument crisis," due to the lack of dedicated fado string players. Fifteen years ago, there were three area "parelhas" or pairs of viola/guitarra players who regularly accompanied local fado singers. At one point there were also several young Luso-American instrumentalists who seemed promising replacements for the aging first-generation players. However, due to illness, aging, and emigration, suddenly the local scene found itself in the mid-2010s with no solid guitarra player and only one seasoned viola player. Interestingly, the fado scene responded using several different strategies. For higher profile events with ample programming budgets, José Silva and Viriato Ferreira, the well-known parelha from Southern New England, travel five hours south to perform. For more routine performances in venues like El Pastor, nontraditional instrumentation such as electric keyboard and percussion is used as a stand-in. And in some venues, special occasions that feature guitarra accompaniment are advertised in local papers as a special draw (Durães 2012). For performances outside the enclave with fewer Portuguese immigrants in the audience, a handful of non-Portuguese instrumentalists sometimes accompany fadistas. This last strategy, which marks an opening up of the guitar-playing circuit, has been largely spearheaded by José Luís Iglesias, an accomplished Portuguese-born guitarist who played with Zeca Afonso in his younger years, holds a master's degree in jazz studies, and has put an enduring interest in the confluence of Portuguese traditional musics with other expressive forms into practice through local performance, teaching, and recording. Iglesias began teaching himself to play the guitarra portuguesa around 2012 and is now the most reliable player in the area. Loic da Silva, a Luso-French accordion player who moved to New Jersey/New York in 2017, has also entered the scene as a guitarra player to positive local reviews.

15. Tony Cirne (2020) stated that on nights at El Pastor when there seemed to be fewer fado enthusiasts in the audience, and the majority of the room wanted to dance, he would encourage the fadistas to sing more upbeat fados—at least for the first set, until the unaccustomed could get used to the silence required from the audience. According to Cirne, the fadistas did not always take his advice. Some of them, despite the challenging conditions, would continue with plans to sing the "heavier" fados and let the chips fall where there may. Pedro Botas (2012) affirms that the choice and sequencing of fados is sometimes tailored to the room at the last minute.

16. Melo and Martins first introduced these ideas in an interview with Delisa Snowden (2007) for the Portuguese cable TV program *EUA Contacto*—the desire to use the annual ProVerbo gala not only to bring important Portuguese musicians to perform in Newark but also to showcase musicians from other Lusophone countries in order to highlight "cooperation" and commonality across the Portuguese-speaking world. These objectives continue into the present. The organizing committee for the ProVerbo gala in 2019, for example, put out a social-media call for volunteers to compose music to a poem by local Brazilian American journalist Vera Reis entitled "Fado and Samba." The idea was to present the same poem in two different versions at the 2019 gala—one set to music in the style of a fado and the other in the style of a samba. As stated elsewhere in this paper, the two "national" musical forms, samba and fado, are often invoked as cultural evidence of the differences and tensions between local Portuguese and Brazilian emigrant communities. But in this example the musics are used for different discursive and social purposes: fado and samba are joined together, sharing the same poem, in an orchestration of proximity and sociomusical dialogue.

17. Records show that the Portuguese found their way to New Jersey as early as 1725. But more consistent arrivals did not begin until the 1850s. Promise of factory work became a draw in the early twentieth century, and by the 1920s and 1930s there were six Portuguese-language newspapers published in Newark ("Roots of the Portuguese" 1997). However, the wave of Portuguese emigration from 1960 to 1980, spurred by changes in US immigration laws as well as by political repression and mandatory military service to fight in Portugal's unpopular colonial wars, produced the greatest numbers of Portuguese settlement in New Jersey to date.

18. Sociologist Glória de Sá (n.d.) has also researched the comingling of Portuguese and Brazilians immigrants in the US, but within a different regional context, that of Southeastern New England.

19. These ideas became the core of a local conflict regarding a statue of Queen Catherine. The New York City borough of Queens is thought to be named after Portuguese Queen Catherine of Bragança, and artist Audrey Flack spent a decade during the 1990s creating models for a statue to honor her. But controversy arose among the city's residents when Queen Catherine's slaveholding history was brought to the public's attention. A group

called "Friends of Queen Catherine," involving some wealthy Portuguese Americans, tried to fight for the statue's placement, but in the end it was not given a home in Queens due to the link between Portugal and the slave trade. The twists and turns of this controversy received ample coverage in Newark's local Portuguese-language paper, *LusoAmericano*, as well as in larger papers such as *The New York Times*. For more on this incident, see Bastos (2020) and Kilgannon (2017).

20. This perception of moral permissiveness conflicts with the reality of Brazilian American religious practices as demonstrated by the influx of Brazilians into Newark's conservative Evangelical churches---seen as more conservative than the Old-World Catholicism of the Portuguese.

21. For more on this history, see Nery (2004) and Tinhorão (1994); for a discussion of fado historiography and origins debate, see Holton (2006a).

22. In addition to the ProVerbo gala discussed in this paper, there is "Ferry Street," a literary/musical/graphic design project celebrating the multiethnic space of the Ironbound's main artery that culminated in a book of original poems and paintings, live concerts, and local gallery exhibitions (Silva, Martins, and Iglesias 2015). One could also read the expansion of the Portugal Day parade in similar terms, and the orientation of the Coutinho family who founded the parade as supporting the mixture/exchange paradigm. Lastly, a series of weekly workshops organized by visiting Portuguese actress Ana Sofia Paiva and funded by the New York City nonprofit Citylore also furthered the fado mixture/exchange orientation. The workshops took place in the Ironbound in spring 2012, comprising several months of weekly two- to three-hour sessions focused on fado history, song taxonomy, and lyric writing, and involving a core group of twenty first- and second-generation poets and musicians. These workshops culminated in a large outdoor concert, which featured original fado lyrics, compositions, and performances by a multiethnic cast of performers.

23. *Fados*, screened locally in New York City starting in March 2009, was promoted with a splashy review in *The New York Times* (see Dargis 2009). Since then, excerpts have been widely viewed on YouTube and spoken and blogged about on local fadistas' personal websites and Facebook pages.

24. It is also important to note that the most sought-after first- and second-generation fadistas are often asked to perform for special-event occasions beyond the borders of New York and New Jersey, in other hubs of Portuguese emigration in the US, such as Providence, RI; Fall River, MA; Palm Coast, FL; and California's Central Valley. This diasporic performance circuit has been in place for many decades.

WORKS CITED

Baker Jr., Houston A. 2001. *Turning South Again: Re-Thinking Modernism/Re-Reading Booker T.* Durham, NC: Duke University Press.

Bastos, Cristiana. 2020. "Intersections of Empire, Post-Empire and Diaspora: De-Imperializing Lusophone Studies." *Journal of Lusophone Studies* 5 (2): 27–54.

Botas, Pedro. 2012. Interview with author, audio recording. Newark, NJ, September 17, 2012.

Brito, Joaquim Pais de, ed. 1994. *Fado: Vozes e sombras*. Lisboa: Lisboa 94.

Browning, Barbara. 2011. "Dancing Samba in Tight Spaces." *Critical Studies in Improvisation* 7 (1): 1–3.

Brucher, Katherine. 2009. "Viva Rhode Island, Viva Portugal! Performance and Tourism in Portuguese-American Bands." In *Community, Culture and the Makings of Identity: Portuguese-Americans along the Eastern Seaboard*, edited by Kimberly DaCosta Holton and Andrea Klimt, 203–26. Dartmouth, MA: Tagus Press.

Carreira, Marina. 2017. *I Sing to That Bird Knowing He Won't Sing Back*. Georgetown, KY: Finishing Line Press.

———. 2018. *Save the Bathwater*. Union, NJ: Get Fresh Books.

Castelo-Branco, Salwa El-Shawan. 1994. "Vozes e guitarras na prática interpretativa do fado." In Brito, *Fado*, 125–40.

Chuva, Francisco. 2008. Interview with author, audio recording. Newark, NJ, June 7, 2008.

Cirne, Tony. 2020. Interview with author, Zoom audio recording. November 5, 2020.

Colvin, Michael. 2016. *Fado and the Urban Poor in Portuguese Cinema in the 1930s and 1940s*. Suffolk, UK: Boydell & Brewer.

———. 2008. *The Reconstruction of Lisbon: Severa's Legacy and the Fado's Rewriting of Urban History*. Lewisburg, PA: Bucknell University Press.

Cordeiro, Graca Índia. 1994. "O Fado no Bairro da Bica: a Casa da Milú." In Brito, *Fado*, 57–72.

Corte-Real, Maria de São José. 1991. "Retention of Musical Models: Fado Performance among Portuguese Migrants in New York." Unpublished master's thesis, Columbia University.

———. 2010. "Revising Citizenship: Migration and Fado in the Play of Identities in the United States." *Migrações*: Music and Migration, no. 7 (October): 73–96.

Dargis, Manohla. 2009. "Guitars, Whores and Sin: The World of the Fadista." *The New York Times*, March 5, 2009.

Durães, Ricky. 2012. "Fado regressa ao El Pastor no próximo fim-de-semana: fado jovem abre temporada e David Couto e Pedro Botas são cabeça de cartaz." *LusoAmericano*, September 7, 2012.

Flanagan, Brenda. 2019. "Report: Newark's Renaissance Presents a Tale of Two Cities." *NJ Spotlight News*, October 31, 2019. https://njspotlight.com/news/video/report-newarks-renaissance-presents-a-tale-of-two-cities/.

Goldman, Danielle. 2010. *I Want to Be Ready: Improvised Dance as a Practice of Freedom*. Ann Arbor: University of Michigan Press.

Gray, Lila Ellen. 2013. *Fado Resounding: Affective Politics and Urban Life*. Durham, NC: Duke University Press.

Holton, Kimberly DaCosta. 2016. "Fado in Diaspora: Online Internships and Self-Display among YouTube Generation's Performers in the US." *Luso-Brazilian Review* 53 (1): 210–32.

———. 2006a. "Old Myths and New Frontiers: Fado Historiography." *P: Portuguese Cultural Studies* 0 (Winter): 1–17.

———. 2020. "Sound Travel: Fadocore in California." In *Transnational Portuguese Studies*, edited by Hilary Owen and Claire Williams, 317–35. Liverpool: Liverpool University Press.

———. 2006b. "Thugs and Prostitutes, Nuns and Rustics: The Politics and Poetics of Portuguese-Brazilian Conflict in Newark, NJ." Paper presented at the Northeast Modern Language Association, Philadelphia, March 2006.

Iglesias, José Luís. 2009. Interview with author, audio recording. Newark, NJ, June 2009.

———. 2019. "Is There Still Fado In New Jersey?" *Feel Portugal in the USA E-Magazine*, August 27, 2019. https://feelportugal.com/2019/08/27/is-there-still-fado-in-new-jersey/.

Kilgannon, Corey. 2017. "The Statue that Never Was." *The New York Times*, November 9, 2017.

Kirshenblatt-Gimblett, Barbara. 1998. "Sounds of Sensibility." In "Klezmer: History & Culture," special issue, *Judaism: A Quarterly Journal of Jewish Life and Thought* 47 (1): 49–78.

Klein, Alexandra Naia, and Vera Marques Alves. 1994. "Casas do fado." In Brito, *Fado*, 37–56.

Losa, Leonor. 2019. "Ser fadista é maior que ser cantor: Intersubjectividade, voz e ethos da memória." PhD diss., FSCH, Universidade Nova de Lisboa.

Lundberg, Dan. 2010. "Music as Identity Marker: Individual vs. Collective." *Migracões: Music and Migration* 7 (October): 30–43.

Martins, João S. 2015. "Fado da noite do fado." In *Ferry Street: Rua da palavra*, edited by Fernando Silva, João S. Martins, and José Luís Iglesias, 36–37. Newark, NJ: Marques & Pereira.

Melo, Glória de. 1998. *A minha mão esquerda*. East Providence, RI: Peregrinação Publications.

Midgelow, Vida L. 2019. "Introduction: Improvising Dance: A Way of Going About Things." In *The Oxford Handbook of Improvisation in Dance*, edited by Vida L. Midgelow, 1–25. Oxford: Oxford University Press.

Nery, Rui Vieira. 2004. *Para uma história do fado*. Lisbon: Público.

Neves, paulA, and Nick Kline. 2017. *Shirts and Skins*. Newark, NJ: Shine Portrait Studio Press.

O'Connell, John Morgan. 2010. "Preface." In *Music and Conflict*, edited by John Morgan O'Connell and Salwa El-Shawan Castelo-Branco, vii–viii. Urbana: University of Illinois Press.

Ramos-Zayas, Ana Yolanda. 2009. "Stereotypes of the Tropics in 'Portuguese Newark': Brazilian Women, Urban Erotics and the Phantom of Blackness." In *Community, Culture and the Makings of Identity: Portuguese-Americans along the Eastern Seaboard*, edited by Kimberly DaCosta Holton and Andrea Klimt, 431–60. Dartmouth, MA: Tagus Press.

"Roots of the Portuguese in Newark Can Be Found in Three from Old Guard." 1997. *Knowing Newark*, Newark Public Library, June 5, 1997. https://knowingnewark.npl.org/roots-of-the-portuguese-in-newark-can-be-found-in-three-from-old-guard/.

Sá, Maria da Glória de. n.d. "Old-Timers and Newcomers: Portuguese and Brazilians in New Bedford and Fall River, Massachusetts." Unpublished manuscript.

Said, Edward. 2010. "Reflections on Exile." In *Out There: Marginalization and Contemporary Cultures*, edited by Russell Ferguson, Martha Gerver, Trinh T. Minh-ha, and Cornel West, 357–66. Cambridge, MA: MIT Press.

Santos, Hugo dos. 2012. *Ironbound: A Blog*. Self-published. Kindle.

Saura, Carlos, dir. 2007. *Fados*. New York: Zeitgeist Films.

Silva, Fernando, João S. Martins, and José Luís Iglesias. 2015. *Ferry Street: Rua da palavra*. Newark: Marques & Pereira.

Smothers, Ronald. 1997. "In Newark's Museum, an Exhibit Honors the City's Portuguese." *The New York Times*, December 4, 1997. https://www.nytimes.com/1997/12/04/nyregion/in-newark-s-museum-an-exhibit-honors-the-city-s-portuguese.html.

Snowden, Delisa. 2007. "Gala Proverbo 2007." *EUA Contacto*. Video, 7:59. Accessed November 11, 2020. https://www.dailymotion.com/video/x2shwww.

Stewart, Susan. 1993. *On Longing: Narratives of the Miniature, the Gigantic, the Souvenir, the Collection*. Durham, NC: Duke University Press.

Tinhorão, José. 1994. *Fado: Dança do Brasil, cantar de Lisboa. O fim do mito*. Lisboa: Caminho.

Turner, Victor. 1986. "Dewey, Dilthey and Drama: An Essay in the Anthropology of Experience." In *The Anthropology of Experience*, edited by Victor Turner and Edward Bruner, 33–44. Urbana: University of Illinois Press.

Vicente, António Luís. 1999. *Os portugueses nos Estados Unidos: Política de comunidades e comunidade política*. Lisboa: Fundação Luso-Americana para o Desenvolvimento.

Wieczorek, Marta. Forthcoming. "Portuguese Saudade, the Trajectories of Longing and Desire: Phenomenological Interpretations from Macau." *Current Anthropology*.

KIMBERLY DACOSTA HOLTON is Professor in the Department of Spanish and Portuguese Studies at Rutgers University, Newark. The recipient of fellowships from the Ford Foundation and the Social Science Research Council, Holton has published widely on expressive culture, literature, and migration in the Lusophone world. She is the author of *Performing Folklore: Ranchos Folclóricos from Lisbon to Newark* (Indiana UP, 2005) and co-editor with Andrea Klimt of *Community, Culture and the Makings of Identity: Portuguese-Americans along the Eastern Seaboard* (Tagus Press, 2009). Holton is currently working on a book about Portuguese fado performance in the US diaspora.

KRISTA BRUNE

The Temporalities of Diasporic Heritage in New York

ABSTRACT: Critical approaches to heritage invite reflections on how Portuguese-speaking diasporic communities in the New York metropolitan area articulate forms of community, collective memory, and embodied culture. While the region's Portuguese and Brazilian immigrants and their descendants recognize their shared language through educational and linguistic initiatives, they celebrate their national differences during annual festivals of Portugal Day in Newark in June and Brazilian Day in New York in September. These festivities exemplify the function of heritage as a comment on the past constructed in the present through displays of cultural practices and traditions. To examine the manifestations and repercussions of heritage work among diasporic communities, this article analyzes how Portugal Day and Brazilian Day serve to foster collectivity among immigrant groups on the basis of national affiliations and also commodify their cultures as temporally and/or spatially "other" and, thus, exotic for contemporary residents of the New York area. The performances at Portugal Day and Brazilian Day as "authentic" expressions of national cultures differ, however, especially with respect to temporalities. An interest in preserving cultural traditions from previous centuries permeates Portugal Day, which contrasts with the greater emphasis on contemporary musicians and artists at Brazilian Day. I suggest that these temporal orientations point to different strains of national identity and culture as encapsulated by the concept of saudade in Portugal and the idea of Brazil as "the country of the future" and, moreover, the distinct histories of Portuguese and Brazilian migration to the United States.

KEYWORDS: Portuguese and Brazilian immigrants, ethnic celebrations, New York, national identity, cultural heritage

RESUMO: As aproximações críticas ao patrimônio convidam reflexões sobre como as comunidades da diáspora lusófona na área metropolitana de Nova Iorque articulam formas de comunidade, memória coletiva e cultura encarnada. Enquanto os imigrantes portugueses e brasileiros e seus descendentes reconhecem sua língua compartilhada em iniciativas educacionais e linguísticas, ao mesmo tempo as duas comunidades celebram suas diferenças nacionais durante os festivais anuais do Dia Portugal em Newark em junho e o Dia Brasileiro em Nova Iorque em setembro. Essas festas exemplificam a função de patrimônio como um comentário sobre o passado construído no presente via as exibições das práticas e tradições culturais. Para examinar as manifestações e repercussões do patrimônio entre comunidades diaspóricas, este artigo analisa como o Dia Portugal e o Dia Brasileiro fomentam o sentido de coletividade entre grupos de imigrantes com base nas afiliações nacionais e, ao mesmo tempo, mercantilizam suas culturas como "outras" em termos temporais e/ou espaciais e, por isso, exóticas para os residentes contemporâneos de Nova Iorque. As representações durante o Dia Portugal e o Dia Brasileiro como expressões "autênticas" das culturas nacionais diferem, especialmente com respeito às temporalidades. Um interesse em preservar as tradições culturais de séculos anteriores permeia o Dia Portugal, o que contrasta com a ênfase maior nos músicos e artistas contemporâneos no Dia Brasileiro. Sugiro que essas orientações temporais indicam diferentes variedades de identidade e cultura nacionais como encapsuladas pelo conceito de saudade em Portugal e a ideia do Brasil como "o país do futuro" e, além disso, as histórias distintas da migração portuguesa e brasileira para os Estados Unidos.

PALAVRAS-CHAVE: imigrantes portugueses e brasileiros, celebrações étnicas, Nova Iorque, identidade nacional, patrimônio cultural

---

On a sunny June afternoon, sounds of European and Brazilian Portuguese, Spanish, and English intermingle on the streets of Newark's Ironbound neighborhood as bass drums from a performance of Sport Club Português's Os Tugas boom in the distance. Grills with sardines, cheese, and meats emit smoke and smells that waft through the air, mixing with the distinctive scents of fried Brazilian pastéis and grilled corn. Sipping cold beer, wine, sugar-cane juice, or other drinks, extended families of immigrants who now call the Ironbound home, visitors to Newark, and other residents celebrate Portuguese heritage at the annual Portugal Day. The event occurs on the weekend closest to June 10, the official Day of Portugal, Camões, and the Portuguese Communities. Newark's Portugal Day, which celebrated its fortieth year in 2019, consists of a multiday festival, with performances and booths selling food, drinks, clothes, and trinkets, or distributing information about local organizations or politicians, and the Sunday parade, according to the event's official website. The schedule features musicians, dance troupes, and other performers that recall folkloric cultural traditions of Portugal's rural north, the ancestral home of the majority of Portuguese who settled in northern New Jersey.

A few miles away, across the Hudson River in midtown Manhattan, on the Sunday of Labor Day weekend, streets are again overwhelmed with conversations and music in Portuguese. Now the distinctive rhythms and sounds of various forms of Brazilian Portuguese dominate as Brazil's yellow-and-green jerseys and flags substitute the red-and-green Portuguese ones that crowded the streets of Newark months earlier. Similar smells of fried pastéis and grilled meats and cheeses drift through the crowds, joined by the palm oil used to prepare acarajé and the aromas of other Brazilian treats like coxinha, pão de queijo, and feijoada. Spreading over twenty-five blocks around 46th Street's Little Brazil, Brazilian Day is promoted as the largest Brazilian celebration outside of Brazil. With performances by well-known musicians and a festive atmosphere recalling Carnival, the event attracts crowds of Brazilians who live in New York and neighboring states, busloads from immigrant communities in Massachusetts, Florida, and Texas, and other tourists and community members. The event, which celebrated its thirty-fifth year in 2019, marks both the unofficial end to summer in the United States and the commemoration of Brazil's Independence Day on September 7. The music blasting from the main stage favors currently popular styles of sertanejo, forró, funk, and samba-reggae, as well as celebrated samba performers, rock groups, and singer-songwriters.

These festivals represent articulations of cultural heritage by the two national groups, Portuguese and Brazilian, that mainly constitute the Portuguese-speaking diasporic communities in the New York metropolitan region. Both events construct a vision of national identity and culture through food, music, dance, and goods. Dislocated from places historically associated with Portuguese and Brazilian heritage, these immigrant groups and their descendants emphasize select objects and practices as essential to the expression and preservation of their culture via Portugal Day and Brazilian Day. The celebrations help to build community among immigrants through language and culture as they promote a particular vision of Portugal and Brazil in greater New York as commodities in the circuit of international and ethnic festivals. In these street-festival constructs of national culture, Portugal emerges primarily as a rural country of folkloric traditions guided by a deep sense of saudade, whereas Brazil exudes a festive energy that coincides with its label as the country of the future.[1] While the differences in the festivals reflect distinct constructions of national identity, they also point to the disparate experiences of Newark and New York as part of a shared metropolitan area. As a city still marked by the extensive repercussions of the 1967 race riots, Newark remains in the shadow of neighboring New York, a larger and more prosperous global city. Disparities in scale and visibility between Newark's Portugal Day and New York's Brazilian Day correspond, in part, to the specific profile of each city within local and global spheres.[2]

In spite of these differences in scope, both events contribute to the celebration and reification of the communities' intangible cultural heritage, which UNESCO defines as "the practices, representations, expressions, knowledge, skills—as well as the instruments, objects, artefacts and cultural spaces associated therewith—that communities, groups and, in some cases, individuals recognize as part of their cultural heritage" (UNESCO 2003). Forms of intangible cultural heritage include performing arts, oral traditions, rituals, and festive events, which manifest in Portugal Day and Brazilian Day as food, ranchos folclóricos, samba, and other rhythms and dances. Rather than remain frozen in time and space, these practices adapt to new surroundings yet maintain a discursive claim to cultural "authenticity." Rodney Harrison highlights the complex temporality of heritage, which "is formed *in the present* and reflects inherited and current concerns about the past" (2013, 14; original emphasis). In other words, heritage develops as the present creation of an imagined past. For Portuguese and Brazilian communities in Newark and New York, constructing a collective past via music, dance, and food at their annual festivals involves returning to distinct moments in national and diasporic histories and reflecting on the current realities of each nation and their immigrant communities. As celebrations that have responded to shifting tastes and demographics over the past four decades, Newark's Portugal Day and New York's Brazilian Day exemplify the living nature of intangible cultural heritage as learned from previous generations and, in the words of UNESCO, "constantly recreated by communities and groups in response to their environment, their interaction with nature and their history" (UNESCO 2003). While performers and vendors likely learn their rhythms, movements, and recipes from previous generations and will pass this knowledge on to the next, they also transform inherited forms of music, dance, and food to reflect the evolving preferences and needs of Portuguese and Brazilian communities in greater New York.

Critical heritage studies, as I propose in this article, serve as a generative lens to examine the confluence of national and diasporic identities, linguistic expressions, immigrant traditions, and cultural commodities at play in Portugal Day and Brazilian Day. In moving the discussion beyond a focus on material objects and buildings, recent approaches to heritage consider the role of intangible culture, public spaces, and nature both within and beyond the confines of nation-states or international bodies like UNESCO. This outlook invites a deeper analysis of how Portuguese-speaking communities in New York and its environs engage with visions of the past in the present to articulate distinct forms of community, collective memory, and embodied culture. Before delving into a more detailed study of Portugal Day and Brazilian Day, I provide a brief overview of Portuguese and Brazilian immigration to the region. With this background in mind, I turn my attention to the festivals and examine them as articulations of imagined pasts in the present. I conclude by considering how expressions of Portuguese and Brazilian diasporic heritage intersect with commercial interests in the production and circulation of ethnic others for residents of the New York metropolitan region.

Portuguese and Brazilian Communities in Greater New York

Though the arrival of Portuguese immigrants in Massachusetts dates to as early as the seventeenth century, this group does not become a notable presence in New York until the early twentieth century, during what Leo Pap (1981, 35) describes as the first wave of Portuguese mass immigration, peaking between 1911 and 1920. Following this swell in migration, the Ironbound neighborhood in Newark emerged in the 1920s and 1930s as a Portuguese community with a commercial district along Ferry Street and a population of about six thousand Portuguese, including American-born children, by 1940 (Pap 1981, 88). After this initial period of growth, the number of Portuguese immigrants to New Jersey surged in the 1960s and 1970s due to political and economic changes on both sides of the Atlantic. The 1965 Immigration and Nationality Act in the United States repealed the 1924 Immigration Act's quota system based on national origin and instead gave priority to skilled professionals and relatives of US citizens and permanent residents. This shift in US immigration policy coincided with a period of political instability in Portugal due to the colonial wars from 1961 to 1974 and the end of the Estado Novo's forty-eight-year dictatorship in 1974 (Holton 2009, 156). The vast majority, eighty-three percent, of New Jersey's foreign-born Portuguese population arrived between 1965 and 1980, which made it the state with the fourth largest Portuguese population, behind historic destinations of California, Massachusetts, and Rhode Island, according to the 1990 census (Holton 2009, 154–55).

Most of the Portuguese settlers in Newark have come from the rural northern states of Minho, Trás-os-Montes, and Alto Douro, the coastal region of Aveiro, or the central area of Viseu, where they worked in agriculture or fishing and had little formal education (Baptista 2009, 177). This profile of Newark's Portuguese community as predominantly continental differs from the prevalence of Azoreans who immigrated to other parts of the United States (Holton 2009, 154–55). The professed values, traditions, and cultures of Newark's Portuguese residents correspond to those associated with Portugal's more conservative and rural north. Kimberly DaCosta Holton (2009, 158–63) identifies family, respect for authority, and celebrating agrarian life as important to the Portuguese in northern New Jersey. Based on oral histories and ethnographic work, Holton suggests that ranchos folclóricos play a central role in attempting to maintain traditional values and pass them on to younger generations. Portugal Day, as I discuss further in the next section, emerges as a public stage for the expression of this imagined ideal of a folkloric Portuguese past. This vision contrasts with the current demographic composition of the Ironbound, which includes Brazilian and other Latin American immigrants alongside the Portuguese community. Lori Barcliff Baptista (2009, 197) astutely synthesizes this disconnection: "While the Ironbound is presently experiencing an influx of immigrants from Brazil, Ecuador, and Mexico, it nostalgically resonates in what performance scholar, Joseph Roach, theorizes as 'collective social memory' as a Portuguese ethnic enclave."

Baptista's observation has become even more palpable on the streets of the Ironbound since her study's publication in 2009. According to estimates from the American Community Survey (US Census Bureau 2010; 2019), 14,161 people in Newark, or 5.2 percent of the population, identified as Portuguese in 2010, while 9,272 people, or 3.3 percent of the population, did so in 2019. Similarly, in 2010, 11,332 people, or 15.9 percent of the foreign-born population, were from Europe and 49,477 (69.2 percent) were from Latin America. By 2019, 9,411 people (10.5 percent) were from Europe and 61,936 (69.2 percent) were from Latin America. Though not broken down by neighborhood to isolate the Ironbound, these statistics record the city's declining Portuguese population and corroborate Baptista's description of new immigrants arriving from Latin America. This demographic change dates to the late 1980s and early 1990s, as reported in a 1995

New York Times article on undocumented immigrants from Portugal and Brazil in the Ironbound (Dunn 1995).[3] Whereas Portuguese immigration began to slow with the improvement of Portugal's economy in the late 1980s, Brazil became a country of emigrants, rather than immigrants, for the first time that decade (Castro e Lima and Castro 2017, 13–14). Maxine Margolis locates Newark, with its itinerant Brazilian consulate and its Portuguese-speaking businesses, as a key destination for these émigrés. Brazilians now outnumber Portuguese in Newark, and Brazil ranks third among source countries of the city's foreign-born population (Margolis 2013, 80–81). While Ferry Street's restaurants and cafés suggest a coexistence of Portuguese and Brazilian in the Ironbound, the racialization and the exoticization of Brazilian women reveal a darker underside to this multiethnic milieu (Ramos-Zayas 2009).[4]

Though Brazilians, including Sousândrade, Monteiro Lobato, and Hélio Oiticica, have lived in New York in small numbers since the late nineteenth century, a more significant community did not emerge until the 1980s (Moser and Tosta 2011, xv-xxiv, 167–72).[5] Various factors motivated this increase in Brazilian immigration, most notably high rates of inflation, unemployment, and economic instability in Brazil in the late 1980s and early 1990s. According to Margolis, Brazilian immigrants in New York tend to be middle or lower middle class, fairly well educated, and from urban areas in Brazil, who arrive in the United States as "economic refugees escaping their nation's chaotic economy," rather than as political exiles (2009, x). Despite their affluence relative to other immigrants, the vast majority of Brazilians in greater New York lack the proper papers to live and work in the United States (ix).[6] In the New York/New Jersey region, where 16 percent of the estimated 1.3 million Brazilians in the United States currently reside, almost half (47 percent) have arrived since 2000 (Castro e Lima and Castro 53–54, 62, 130, 135).[7] Brazilian immigrants in this area have settled primarily in New York City, with the largest community in Astoria, Queens, and in cities in New Jersey, including Newark and Elizabeth. New York's Brazilian community is one of the largest in the United States, but, according to the 2000 US census, Brazil did not rank among the top thirty source countries for the city's foreign-born population. In Astoria, while Brazilians accounted for less than four percent of its foreign-born population per the 2000 census data, the Brazilian community has a strong commercial presence with restaurants, bakeries, specialized markets, travel agencies, salons, and boutiques (Margolis 2013, 78–84).[8] Even though few Brazilians live in Manhattan, Little Brazil continues to host the most prominent Brazilian Day festival every September. Smaller celebrations unfold on the streets of Astoria and among other pockets of the Brazilian community in the region.

Portuguese and Brazilian communities in the United States share the Portuguese language and also their perceived status as relatively invisible migrants. According to M. Estellie Smith's (1973) assessment, Portuguese Americans were an "invisible minority" due to their lack of civic and political engagement, especially in comparison to the groups of Irish or Italians. As Smith claims, a willingness to work in poor conditions without fighting to participate in decision-making and leadership roles contributed to the invisibility of the Portuguese, which, in turn, protected them from discrimination in employment that other immigrants faced. Holton (2009, 172) posits that Portuguese Americans remain invisible as a result of "scholarly inattention to these communities," an oversight her work begins to correct. Likewise, Margolis (2009, 92–93) draws scholarly attention to the comparative invisibility of Brazilian immigrants, which she attributes to North American ignorance about Brazil's languages and peoples, the lack of a cohesive Brazilian neighborhood, and minimal news coverage of Brazilians. Difficulties in classifying Brazilians within racial and ethnic categories of the US census further hinder their recognition, and official documentation, as a distinct immigrant group (Margolis 2009, 95–100).[9] The Portuguese language separates Brazilians and Portuguese from their Spanish-speaking neighbors in Latin America and Iberia, and from the US government's category for people of Hispanic origin. Linguistic and other commonalities between Portuguese and Brazilians do not result, however, in a unified vision of Luso-Brazilian identity when these groups reside in the same region or neighborhood. While official channels of the Portuguese and Brazilian consulates and the Instituto Camões work toward a common goal of promoting the Portuguese language and Lusophone cultures, Portuguese and Brazilians living in Newark differentiate themselves via idiomatic expressions, accents, and vocabulary (Ramos-Zayas 2009, 437, 454).[10] Moreover, as I discuss in the next sections, Portuguese and Brazilian communities in greater New York utilize Portugal Day and Brazilian Day to articulate and promote distinct visions of cultural heritage.

Saudade for a Rural Past at Newark's Portugal Day

Portugal Day telegraphs an idea of the Portuguese diasporic community rooted in saudade, which Bela Feldman-Bianco (2009, 51) characterizes as "a cultural construct that defines Portuguese identity in the context of multiple layers of space and (past) time." This concept relates to individual experiences of emigration and collective forms of memory that coalesce in Newark's annual Portugal Day. The event commemorates the anniversary of the death of Portugal's national poet Luís de Camões on June 10, which has been recognized since 1977 as the Day of Portugal, Camões, and the Portuguese Communities, replacing the Estado Novo-era Day of the Portuguese Race. According to Feldman-Bianco, this change in nomenclature indicated a shift in Portuguese identity whereby "the emigrant communities spread around the world replaced the former colonial dominions in the new and expanded construction of a 'global' Portuguese nation" (2009, 55). By inaugurating their celebration of Portugal Day in 1979, members of Newark's Portuguese community participated in this construction of a diasporic identity that, indirectly, lauded Camões and the imperial outlook of his 1572 epic *Os Lusíadas*. Darlene J. Sadlier (2016, 15) situates the legacy of this poem as grounded in "the image of a people on the move, undeterred by seemingly insurmountable forces. This portrait is celebrated to this day and is an indelible part of the national imaginary."

The spirit that Camões's poem embodies is central to the ethos of Newark's Portugal Day, which celebrates Portuguese Americans as a group that moved away from its rural past and overcame obstacles to live in the United States. Bernardino Coutinho, who founded the festival and directed it for more than thirty years, exemplified this ideal trajectory of a Portuguese migrant. After arriving in Newark in 1967 with scant resources, he worked at an East Orange bakery for five years while he saved enough money to open his Coutinho's Bakery in the Ironbound in 1973 (*Newark Star-Ledger* 2016). In establishing Portugal Day in the Ironbound, Coutinho and his fellow business leaders honored the role of the Portuguese community in the region as they also aimed to attract people from beyond the neighborhood to their stores and restaurants. From its origins, Newark's Portugal Day has combined a desire to promote and preserve Portuguese heritage with commercial interests. Portugal Day, which has unfolded on the streets of the Ironbound every June for the past forty years, contributes to the continued perception of the neighborhood as a Portuguese enclave, despite the arrival of Brazilian, Ecuadorian, and Mexican immigrants in recent decades. Baptista attributes this disconnect between the neighborhood's image and its reality to "how local publics have experienced the Ironbound over the course of the last twenty years through its restaurants and the Portugal Day Festival" (2009, 197).

During the festival weekend, the Ironbound presents images of a rural Portuguese past by means of music, dance, and food. Constructing the past in the present is the task of heritage, but it also suggests the temporal and spatial role of saudade in manifestations of Portuguese cultural identity. Given that Portuguese immigrants to Newark often discarded rural, preindustrial trades of farming or fishing for modes of industrial labor in factories or railyards, expressions of cultural heritage at Portugal Day tend to craft an idealized view of the rural past through folkloric music, dance, and dress. The percussion group Os Tugas of the Sport Club Português, for example, illustrate this desire to recreate cultural forms from an imagined rural past in a contemporary urban realm. Founded in 1921 as a social club for Portuguese men in Newark, Sport Club Português now functions as a community organization for all ages and genders that supports the study of Portuguese language, history, and culture. A recent addition to the club's cultural offerings, Os Tugas have performed at Portugal Day and other venues since 2015. Consisting of fifteen to twenty musicians dressed in straw hats and red or green shirts who play drums of differing sizes as they march, Os Tugas bring the percussive traditions of "Zés-Pereiras" from pilgrimages and festivals in the northern regions of Entre Douro and Minho to Newark's streets and stages. The drumbeats reverberate through the crowds gathered near the Portugal Day main stage or along the parade route, but they lack the religious resonances that they have held in northern Portuguese towns for centuries.

A similar spatial and temporal decontextualization unfolds with ranchos folclóricos, which figure prominently at Portugal Day. This revivalist folklore draws on traditions from rural Portugal to put late nineteenth-century dances, songs, and costumes into circulation in twenty-first-century Newark. According to Holton (2009, 158), there were sixteen groups active in northern New Jersey in the early 2000s, each with thirty to thirty-five musicians and dancers. Rather than embark on ethnographic research to inspire their performances, these troupes stage recreations of dances documented in books and other archival materials and performed by groups in Portugal. Holton astutely claims that dancing ranchos "promotes an embodied albeit 'invented' celebration of this rural past" (2009, 163). Inventing tradition, which involves creating the past in the present, is central to the task of heritage in the Portuguese community of greater New York (Hobsbawm [1983] 2006, 1–14).[11] Ranchos serve a dual function: on the one hand, they help Portuguese immigrants to "forget their current geographic circumstance" by transporting them spatially and temporally via memories of summer festas in Portugal's north and, on the other, perform a version of Portuguese American heritage for a diverse public in metropolitan New York (Holton 2009, 167).

With this emphasis on traditional music and folkloric dance, Portugal Day constructs an image of Portuguese identity and culture as entrenched in nostalgia. On the festival main stage in 2019, for instance, seven different groups of ranchos folclóricos performed. According to the event's official website, the schedule also featured Marante, a romantic crooner from Portugal performing with Diapasão; Tiago Marato, a young accordionist from Minho who blends traditional rhythms with more contemporary lyrics; and Luis Neves, whose repertoire includes Portuguese covers of 1970s and 1980s rock ballads. The styles and instrumentation of these musicians evoke a musical past of Portugal and its diasporic community. Alongside folkloric musicians and dancers, these performers contribute to the creation of a collective cultural past in the present. This invention of tradition addresses two distinct publics in greater New York: Portuguese immigrants and their descendants, who long to hear rhythms, genres, and lyrics sung in Portuguese that remind them of their ancestral home, and other community members or visitors who wish to hear and see an "authentic" Portugal in the simulacra of an ethnic festival. Both of these facets envision saudade as essential to Portuguese heritage and, by extension, the cultural identity of Portuguese living in New Jersey.

New York's Brazilian Day as Festive Projection of the Future

While Newark's Portugal Day, with its support from local businesses and its appeal to residents of neighboring communities, attracts hundreds of thousands of visitors, the festival lacks the prominence and global scale of New York's Brazilian Day. An estimated one million people crowd the streets of midtown Manhattan to attend the annual cultural and commercial event, which receives corporate sponsorships from airline companies Delta and Brazil-based GOL, the Brazilian media conglomerate Globo, and *The Brasilians*, an English-Portuguese newspaper published in New York since 1972, according to the event's website. Given that João de Matos, the editor of *The Brasilians*, produces Brazilian Day, the bilingual periodical advertises and reports on the celebration for months before and after the early September event. The festival commemorates Brazilian independence, primarily for Brazilians in the United States, but it also appeals to other residents of greater New York interested in Brazilian culture. The fascination of this second group suggests an impulse to consume what Graham Huggan (2001) terms the "postcolonial exotic."[12] Promotional materials address the festival's varied publics with the abbreviated moniker BR Day New York and, more importantly, slogans in English ("the green and yellow mood") and Portuguese ("ser brasileiro é simplesmente ser" [being Brazilian is simply being]). In its reference to the colors of the Brazilian flag, the English-language motto emphasizes symbolic expressions of national identity. Wearing green and yellow or, more likely, being surrounded by these colors allows non-Brazilians to be swept up in the feeling of being Brazilian. For Brazilians, the catchphrase in Portuguese suggests that their Brazilian identity does not render them as exceptional others; it is simply one way of being in the world.

These Portuguese and English expressions indicate how Brazilian Day speaks to the needs and interests of Brazilians living in the United States as well as those of non-Brazilians. Similar to Portugal Day, Brazilian Day exists as a fixture in the calendar of ethnic events held annually in the New York area. Its origins in the mid-1980s coincide with the arrival of significant numbers of Brazilian immigrants to the region and to the United States in general. Recognizing connections between histories of Brazil and Brazilian immigration and the development of New York's Brazilian Day proves critical to understanding how the festival's vision of Brazil proposes heritage work that is future oriented. Unlike Portugal Day, which conceives of Portuguese identity as a comparatively static articulation of the past, Brazilian Day crafts an understanding of the past in the present that looks toward the future. In other words, the festival constructs an image of the forward-looking Brazil of the 1980s in the contemporary moment. Even though economic instability and extreme inflation resulted in emigrants from Brazil to outnumber immigrants entering the country in the late 1980s and early 1990s, the decade represented a moment of optimism as Brazil transitioned from dictatorship to democracy (McCann 2008).[13] In subsequent decades, it seemed like Brazil, long considered the country of the future, might finally be on the cusp of achieving its perceived potential (Zweig 1941).[14] Brazilian Day's expressions of heritage reflect this fascination with Brazil's future possibilities.

Musicians and artists who perform at Brazilian Day contribute to this image of diasporic cultural heritage as expressing the potential of being Brazilian. Their relative fame also speaks to the heightened commercial interests at stake in Brazilian Day as a street festival and a televised broadcast for Globo subscribers in the United States and Brazil. In recent years, Globo television personalities

Serginho Groisman, Otaviano Costa, Ana Furtado, and Glenda Kozlowski have hosted the New York event, drawing on their experiences as hosts and actors to introduce performers and energize the crowd. By integrating known entities from Globo's programming into the festivities, Brazilian Day addresses the needs of a live audience, who seek entertainment and visceral connections, and a distant public of television viewers, for whom the host generates a sense of familiarity. These masters of ceremonies elevate Brazilian Day's performances from a series of musical acts into a televisual spectacle that celebrates Brazil's intangible cultural heritage for Brazilians and non-Brazilians, whether they are physically present at the event or accessing it through a mediated broadcast from afar.

The performers represent the variety of musical preferences, from sertanejo and pagode to samba-reggae and funk, that Brazilians in both countries hold and that non-Brazilians expect when they think of Brazilian music. In 2018, Brazilian Day featured sertanejo duo Matheus & Kauan, teenage forró singer Eduarda Brasil from Globo's talent show *The Voice Kids*, the 1980s rock band Os Paralamas do Sucesso, funk singer MC Koringa, and reggae singer Toni Garrido from the band Cidade Negra (Widyloar 2018). The lineups from the previous five years have included a similar mixture of musical styles, periods, and commercial successes to craft a soundtrack of Brazil's recent past that reverberates with live audiences and television viewers. This performance of Brazil on a midtown stage finds inspiration in the popular rhythms and beats that have resonated in Brazil and beyond since Brazilian immigrants began arriving in New York in greater numbers in the 1980s. By inventing a shared musical past, Brazilian Day helps immigrants maintain links to their nation and its culture, language, and people. At the same time, the event projects an enticing and diverse soundscape of Brazil for a foreign audience.

Commodifying Cultural Heritage

Portugal Day and Brazilian Day bookend summer festival season in greater New York as distinct ways of celebrating and commodifying the cultural heritage of diasporic Portuguese-speaking communities. As a festival featuring performances in New York of primarily Brazil-based musicians, Brazilian Day is best understood as a transnational collaboration between New York-based producer João de Matos and Brazil's Globo network with its prominent profile in the global mediascape (Appadurai 1996, 35–37). In contrast, Newark's Portugal Day parade, festival, and road races feature local sponsors, including Lusitania Savings Bank; restaurants and cafés such as Iberia, Seabra Foods, and Teixeira Bakery; media outlets like the *Luso-Americano* website and Radio Luso-American; and the Lar de Leões soccer club. While SIC Internacional, a transnational television and media corporation based in Portugal, also sponsors the event, it lacks the extensive global reach of Brazilian Day sponsor Globo. Portugal Day displays a relatively local approach to event planning that prioritizes the needs of the Ironbound and its residents as part of the broader Newark community. The commercial interests of the festival's founder Bernardino Coutinho and other local businesses have remained comparatively humble, especially when contrasted with the enterprising producer who built Brazilian Day into a behemoth of corporate sponsorships. As a result, Portugal Day has faced financial difficulties, which led to its cancelation in 2010 and revival the following year under the planning of the União de Clubes Luso-Americanos de New Jersey. In 2015, the non-profit organization Portugal Day Newark took the reins. This organizational history differs from the commercially viable path of Brazilian Day.

Both festivals construct an invented version of Portuguese and Brazilian heritage as part of the Portuguese-speaking diaspora of the New York metropolitan region, but they differ in their mode of commodifying cultural expressions and traditions for these communities and the broader public. Newark's Portugal Day displays a nostalgic version of Portuguese culture for first and second-generation Luso-Americans and other visitors who continue to frame the Ironbound as the locus of the region's Portuguese community, even as the neighborhood transforms.[15] The festival has begun to reflect the changing Ironbound by including Ecuadorian and Colombian food vendors next to booths selling Portuguese staples of sardines and wine. Brazilian Day places a less central focus on the needs of the immigrant communities in greater New York as it offers a celebration of Brazilian music, culture, and food for varied publics of Brazilians at home and abroad, tourists, and other residents of the metropolitan area. In spite of their distinct profiles, Portugal Day and Brazilian Day each aim to address the interests of their specific audiences by displaying diasporic cultural heritage.

These festivals reveal how creating the past in the present can manifest as temporalities that correlate with broader views of national identity and culture. Newark's Portuguese community looks back, both temporally and spatially, with saudade for a rural, pre-industrial Portugal, whereas New York's Brazilian residents envision a past when their nation was about to realize its potential as the perpetual country of the future. These outlooks produce expressions of cultural heritage, namely the supposedly homogenous Portuguese folkloric traditions and the diverse Brazilian musical expressions, linked to their respective pasts as nations of emigrants and immigrants. The Portuguese impulse to travel and, at times, settle abroad has often generated a more static vision of national identity and culture rooted in an idealization of the past. In contrast, Brazil's history of colonization, slavery, and immigration has resulted in ongoing intersections of people, languages, and cultures. By reenacting these established dynamics annually, Portugal Day and Brazilian Day help to preserve idealized images of national identity and culture closely associated with how these diasporic communities envision their intangible cultural heritage. Although the events have changed over the years to account for shifting demographics and musical preferences, they continue to serve as present constructs of a past era, specifically the nostalgia of Portuguese immigrants in the 1970s and the optimism of Brazilians in the 1980s. In doing so, Newark's Portugal Day and New York's Brazilian Day address the needs of immigrants to concretize collective memories and the desires of people outside the diasporic communities to consume commodified versions of Portuguese and Brazilian cultures.

NOTES

1. Saudade, roughly translated as nostalgia or melancholy, is an "untranslatable" given its philosophical, historical, and literary meanings as "the key feeling of the Portuguese soul" that "proceeds from a memory that wants to renew the present by means of the past" (Santoro 2013, 929). The idea of saudade continues to shape discussions of Portuguese identity at home and abroad.

2. It is worth noting that Newark also hosts a Brazilian Day on the first weekend of September, but it pales in comparison to the size, commercial success, and longevity of the New York festival. From 1992 to 2012, the Brazilian American United Association, a Newark-based nonprofit, sponsored the Brazilian Day celebration in the Ironbound district. The festival has continued every year, except 2014, under the organization of José Moreira and Silvana Magda and with support from a range of local businesses (A. Santos 2017).

3. According to an undocumented Portuguese resident quoted in the article, "You see a lot of Brazilians now. They are going through the same phase of the Portuguese thirty years ago" (Dunn 1995).

4. In her study, Ana Ramos-Zayas (2009) contrasts perceptions of Portuguese women as respectable and traditional with views of Brazilian women grounded in "stereotypes of the tropics" as racialized and hypersexualized.

5. Robert Moser and Antonio Luciano de Tosta (2011) outline the history and literature of Luso-Americans in the United States and Canada, with emphasis on Portuguese,

Brazilian, and Cabo Verdean communities. The introductions to the anthology and to the Brazilian section provide a useful overview and chronology of the cultural contributions of these groups.

6. When Margolis completed her ethnography in the early 1990s, 50 percent of Brazilians in New York were undocumented; by 2000, the percentage without papers had risen to 70 percent.

7. Estimates of the Brazilian population in the United States range from 335,608, based on the American Community Survey (ACS) in 2014, to between 800,000 and 1.3 million, according to Brazil's Ministério das Relações Exteriores. The US government tends to undercount Brazilians since they do not easily fit into census categories for race and ethnicity. Moreover, these immigrants often fear or are not interested in filling out census forms. The Brazilian ministry uses remittances and data from consulates and the embassy to calculate its estimate. See Margolis (2009, 6–8) for data from the US and Brazilian governments and a discussion of why Brazilians are comparatively invisible migrants.

8. Margolis (2013) notes that, in recent decades, the Brazilian community has dispersed to other areas in the greater New York region, including Mineola, Mount Vernon, Port Chester and the Catskills in New York State, Long Branch and Riverside in New Jersey, and Danbury in Connecticut.

9. The category of "Hispanic origin" used in the 2000 and 2010 census excludes Brazilians by defining "Hispanic or Latino" as "a person of Cuban, Mexican, Puerto Rican, South or Central American, or other Spanish culture or origin regardless of race." The 2020 census continued to delimit Hispanic or Latino in this manner but allowed for more flexible means of racial and ethnic self-identification in other questions.

10. Ramos-Zayas (2009) draws a parallel between how Portuguese and Brazilians in the Ironbound employ the Portuguese language and how Mexicans and Puerto Ricans in Chicago mark their differences through their distinct uses of Spanish.

11. Holton (2009) refers to Eric Hobsbawm's concept of the "invention of tradition" as she depicts the key cultural role of ranchos folclóricos among the Portuguese community of northern New Jersey.

12. Huggan (2001) frames the "exotic" as a construct that grants cultural capital to postcolonial writing. He underscores the role of the exotic in helping to legitimize marginal works and to allocate more cultural capital to writers. Though his study focuses on late-twentieth-century global Anglophone literature, the concept of the exotic plays a similar role in the accumulation of cultural capital in forms of embodied performance and intangible cultural heritage. See George Yúdice's *The Expediency of Culture* (2004) for more on the various roles of culture in the current age of globalization.

13. In *The Throes of Democracy*, Bryan McCann (2008) sketches a history of Brazil's present with a focus on possibilities and challenges of transitioning from dictatorship to democracy.

14. Stefan Zweig (1941), the Austrian Jewish writer who lived in exile in Brazil from 1940 until his death in 1942, considered Brazil "the future of our world" and a country worth emulating. Reflecting in on the rise of Brazil during the previous decade, historian Marshall Eakin (2013, 230) claimed that "the time has come to recognize that the country of the future has become the country of the present."

15. Newark native and Luso-American writer Hugo dos Santos (2017) comments on the shifting meaning of Portugal Day for Portuguese immigrants, their descendants, and the broader Newark community in a post on the Newest Americans website accompanied by colorful photographs. It remains to be seen whether the accessibility of Portugal as a popular tourist destination reconfigures Newark's Portugal Day and affects how Luso-Americans and other community members experience the celebration.

WORKS CITED

Appadurai, Arjun. 1996. *Modernity at Large: Cultural Dimensions of Globalization*. Minneapolis: University of Minnesota Press.

Baptista, Lori Barcliff. 2009. "Images of the Virgin in Portuguese Art at the Newark Museum." In Holton and Klimt, *Community, Culture and the Makings of Identity*, 175–201. Dartmouth, MA: Tagus Press.

Castro e Lima, Álvaro Eduardo de, and Alanni de Lacerda Barbosa de Castro. 2017. *Brasileiros nos Estados Unidos: Meio século (re)fazendo a América (1960-2010)*. Brasília: Fundação Alexandre de Gusmão.

Dunn, Ashley. 1995. "In Newark, Immigration Without Fear: A Neighborhood Remade by Unexpected Hands." *New York Times*, January 16, 1995.

Eakin, Marshall. 2013. "The Emergence of Brazil on the World Stage." *Latin American Research Review* 48 (3): 221–30. https://doi.org/10.1353/lar.2013.0044.

Feldman-Bianco, Bela. 2009. "Multiple Layers of Time and Space: The Construction of Class, Ethnicity, and Nationalism among Portuguese Immigrants." In Holton and Klimt, *Community, Culture and the Makings of Identity*, 51–94. Dartmouth, MA: Tagus Press.

Harrison, Rodney. 2013. *Heritage: Critical Approaches*. London: Routledge.

Hobsbawm, Eric. (1983) 2006. "Introduction: Inventing Traditions." In *The Invention of Tradition*, edited by Eric Hobsbawm and Terence Ranger, 1–14. Cambridge: Cambridge University Press.

Holton, Kimberly DaCosta. 2009. "Dancing Along the In-Between: Folklore Performance and Transmigration in Portuguese Newark." In Holton and Klimt, *Community, Culture and the Makings of Identity*, 145–74. Dartmouth, MA: Tagus Press.

Holton, Kimberly DaCosta, and Andrea Klimt, eds. 2009. *Community, Culture and the Makings of Identity: Portuguese-Americans Along the Eastern Seaboard*. Dartmouth, MA: Tagus Press.

Huggan, Graham. 2001. *Postcolonial Exotic: Marketing the Margins*. London: Routledge.

Margolis, Maxine L. 2009. *An Invisible Minority: Brazilians in New York City*. Gainesville: University Press of Florida.

———. 2013. *Goodbye Brazil: Émigrés from the Land of Soccer and Samba*. Madison: University of Wisconsin Press.

McCann, Bryan. 2008. *The Throes of Democracy: Brazil Since 1989*. New York: Zed Books.

Moser, Robert Henry, and Antonio Luciano de Andrade Tosta, eds. 2011. *Luso-American Literature: Writings by Portuguese-Speaking Authors in North America*. New Brunswick, NJ: Rutgers University Press.

Newark Star-Ledger. 2016. "Bernardino Coutinho, 1937–2016." Last modified June 7, 2016. https://obits.nj.com/obituaries/starledger/obituary.aspx?n=bernardino-coutinho&pid=180242403&fhid=26990.

Pap, Leo. 1981. *The Portuguese-Americans*. Boston: Twayne Publishers.

Ramos-Zayas, Ana Y. 2009. "Stereotypes of the Tropics in 'Portuguese Newark': Brazilian Women, Urban Erotics, and the Phantom of Blackness." In Holton and Klimt, *Community, Culture and the Makings of Identity*, 431–59. Dartmouth, MA: Tagus Press.

Sadlier, Darlene J. 2016. *The Portuguese-Speaking Diaspora: Seven Centuries of Literature and the Arts*. Austin: University of Texas Press.

Santoro, Fernando. 2013. "SAUDADE (Portuguese)." In *Dictionary of Untranslatables*, edited by Barbara Cassin, Emily Apter and Jacques Lezra, 929–31. Princeton, NJ: Princeton University Press.

Santos, Ang. 2017. "Get Ready for Brazil Week 2017 in Newark." Last modified August 30, 2017. https://www.wbgo.org/post/get-ready-brazil-week-2017-newark.

Santos, Hugo dos. 2017. "Portugal Day." *Newest Americans*. Last modified March 8, 2017. http://newestamericans.com/portugal-day/.

Smith, M. Estellie. 1973. "Portuguese Enclaves: The Invisible Minority." Paper presented at the Southern Anthropological Society meeting, Wrightsville Beach, NC, March 1973. https://eric.ed.gov/?id=ED076720.

UNESCO. 2003. "Text of the Convention for the Safeguarding of the Intangible Cultural Heritage." Last modified October 17, 2003. https://ich.unesco.org/en/convention#art2.

US Census Bureau. 2010. "Selected Social Characteristics in the United States." American Community Survey Five-Year Estimates, Newark. Last modified February 2, 2021. https://data.census.gov/cedsci/table?q=ACSDP5Y2010.DP02&g=1600000US3451000&tid=ACSDP5Y2010.DP02.

——. 2019. "Selected Social Characteristics in the United States." American Community Survey Five-Year Estimates, Newark. Last modified February 2, 2021. https://data.census.gov/cedsci/table?q=ACSDP5Y2017.DP02&g=1600000US3451000&tid=ACSDP5Y2019.DP02.

Widyloar, Keith. 2018. "Brazilian Day New York 2018 Is the Biggest Brazilian Festival outside Brazil." *New York Latin Culture Magazine*. Last modified July 31, 2018. https://www.newyorklatinculture.com/brazilian-day/.

Yúdice, George. 2004. *The Expediency of Culture: Uses of Culture in the Global Era*. Durham, NC: Duke University Press.

Zweig, Stefan. 1941. *Brazil: Land of the Future*. Translated by Andrew St. James. New York: The Viking Press.

KRISTA BRUNE is an assistant professor of Portuguese and Spanish at the Pennsylvania State University. She is the author of *Creative Transformations: Travels and Translations of Brazil in the Americas* (SUNY Press, 2020). Her articles have appeared in, among others, *Luso-Brazilian Review*, *Hispanic Review*, *Translation Review*, *Journal of Lusophone Studies*, and *Studies in Latin American Popular Culture*. Her research has received funding from Fulbright, the Tinker Foundation, FLAD, and the National Endowment for the Humanities.

Reviews

Nery, Rui Vieira.
A History of Portuguese Fado.
Translated by David Cranmer.
Lisboa: Imprensa Nacional-Casa da Moeda, 2012.

"Everything ends up coming round full circle" (52), writes Rui Vieira Nery in *A History of Portuguese Fado* (2012), translated by David Cranmer for the English edition, in which he gives a history of the genre from its itinerant beginnings as part of Afro-Brazilian, Black Atlantic repertoire to its instantiation in the mid-eighteenth century as Lisbon's urban song and then, throughout the twentieth century, as a globally-recognized and particularly Portuguese cultural expression. Nery describes his work as "a broad historical panorama of the genre's development during a period of almost two hundred years" (22). Laid out over 400 glossy pages of large text with many full color images and reproductions of illustrations, photos, booklets, posters, and other works of art, he pieces together a historical narrative through an archive of varied material taken from travelogues, fado histories, representations of fado in literature and art, promotional artwork, printed musical notation, critical reception, and fado recordings and compositions. Notably, this English version of Nery's monograph comes with a new introductory essay by the author, covering developments in fado practice and distribution that had occurred during the eight years since the original Portuguese-language publication in 2004: the increased proliferation of fado performers through recorded and mass-distributed media (CDs and DVDs), and the changing contexts of fado performances unmoored from traditional fado houses and turning up ever more frequently in concert halls and global theatres. Writing the previous sentence today in 2021 feels quaint if not completely outdated. Streaming and social media sites and applications, such as YouTube and Spotify, have transformed the consumption of popular music, consequently making CDs and DVDs seemingly relics of a long-gone past, while during the decade since publication of this English edition, Lisbon has experienced a boom of international tourism that have made amateur fado performers and fado houses permanent fixtures on tourist itineraries, as essential as a daytrip to Sintra and a mouthful of *pasteis de Belém*.

Yet, against the rapidly changing contexts of fado performance and reception, Nery's history remains a rich and necessary resource for scholars of fado and Portuguese culture, with its mission to rescue the genre from nationalist mythology and sedimented perceptions as the ever-eternal expression of Portuguese *saudade*, now made more urgent in light of Lisbon's contemporary Instagram-able iteration. Nery tells us early on of his concern to avoid the pitfalls of fado histories and misconceptions of fado origins:

> I have tried throughout to give substance to [fado's] historical manifestations and to run, like the devil from the cross, from the airy-fairy vocabulary that separates abstract concepts from the practices and real objects which embody them, and which give them their only tangible existence (in words like *saudade*, melancholy and fatalism), because I know all too well that the latter is the most direct route to the Pandora's box of pseudo-Celtic, pseudo-Arab, pseudo-troubadour myths and such like which for more than a century have overshadowed a genuinely rigorous study of Fado. (22)

Most compelling and perhaps surprising, even if not altogether new information, is the beginning chapter, innocuously entitled "From its origins to 1840: establishing the genre," that firmly places fado's beginnings in Brazil as Afro-Brazilian dance, locating the first mentions of the word *fado* (fate) linked to music as designating cultural practices witnessed in colonial Brazil as particular Afro-Brazilian dances and musical expression (33-38). The circle that Nery refers to, in which all things fado end up coming round, is what Paul Gilroy has demarcated as the Black Atlantic, what Joseph Roach calls the circum-Atlantic, and Portuguese anthropologist Miguel Vale de Almeida has dubbed the Brown Atlantic to more directly address the histories of Portuguese-speaking cultures of the Atlantic rim and beyond that were affected by Portuguese settler-colonialism, trans-Atlantic slave-trading, and Luso-Brazilian discourse on race. In this churning of power and time, Portuguese fado emerges as a repertoire of the Black Atlantic, a product of the forced displacement and transformation of African people and their cultures in the Americas. A decade before Nery's original Portuguese edition, however, Brazilian scholar and music critic José Ramos Tinhorão stated this fact outright in his book *Fado: dança do Brasil, cantar de Lisboa, o fim de um mito* (1994). Tinhorão states definitively his desire to put an end to the same fado mythology that Nery's is still contending with in his work, one which locates fado only ever in tones of Portuguese nationalist ethos and pseudo-historical claims, rather than in the encounter of Afro-Brazilian dances that included *fados* and *lumduns* with more Luso-Brazilian song forms such as *modinhas*.

The power of the myth seems to have endured, however, at least from the 1990s to 2004 and again to this English edition of 2012, as evidenced by Nery's new preface essay on changing fado contexts that do not include, despite the available historiography, a widespread acceptance of fado's Black Brazilian roots. Indeed, even Nery's title suggests his is but one history of Portuguese fado, seemingly among several potential others, belying his extensive research, and sounding more like a trepidatious claim rather than historical fact. As to fado's Afro-Brazilian origins, he further provides the disclaimer that "this Fado danced in colonial Brazil... is still distant from being the Portuguese Fado," even as he adds that it is "without a shadow of a doubt... a central starting point, from which emerge innumerable aspects that persist uninterruptedly amid Portuguese Fado practice" (38). Despite his reassurances, readers can take his research at face value and need not see these two as separate expressive forms, but rather as two points of a genre whose history is tied up in a past yet to be fully reckoned with in Portugal: the centrality of racism and violence to the machinations of Portuguese empire and contemporary society; and the permeance of this history in cultural practices and heritage subsumed as uniquely Portuguese.

Though he is cautious of his claims, Nery gives us a clear and detailed narrative of fado's development from the colonial period to present day. He traces how danced Afro-Brazilian fados turn up in Lisbon through the transit of the circum-Atlantic, and how this expressive song and dance moors itself in Lisbon's periphery and underbelly in taverns and whorehouses. Beyond musical analysis and close readings of literary references, Nery also provides historical context for fado's many transformations, showing how political upheavals and cultural changes rippled down to popular practices, and how fado's affective repertoire was attuned to the expression of quotidian experience. Through historical and visual references, Nery's outlines how, from the mid-eighteenth century on, fado's popular domain affects its practice in Lisbon and how the danced aspect of its repertoire changes as fado becomes more staged, its music annotated, its poems transcribed, and its audience more mixed, meshing Lisbon's working class with petite bourgeoise and aristocrats. Nery also shows fado's expansion through male university students to Coimbra; its transformation through musical theatre and public shows; the effect of Portuguese political change at the turn of the twentieth century on fado practice; its popularity in Brazil as part of revues; and its codification under the Estado Novo regime's fascistic scrutiny. While fado is imprinted with the voice and life of Amália Rodrigues from the mid-twentieth century onward, and Nery gives Amália and other fado stars their due credit, the reader will be well into three hundred pages of large text and captivating images before we reach the year of 1945 in this history.

Other published works may delve more deeply into fado's divas and its iterations as fascist appropriation and political resistance. Yet, the strength of Nery's book is in the early history it establishes against what Nery describes as "the silence of the historical sources" (31). More fado silences have been contested recently, with artists Fado Bicha reviving fado's queer history and refiguring its canon into bawdy expressions of queer and trans desire in tunes that are boldly antiracist and anti-homo- and transphobic. Importantly, and resonating with the global Black Lives Matter movements, activists in Lisbon have pushed back against long-enduring systemic racism, racist violence, and revisionist Portuguese history, and there is renewed interest in fado's origins as Afro-Brazilian dance. The Batoto Yetu Portugal Association, a non-profit that targets youth and underserved communities with programs on African culture, launched the Fado Dançado initiative in 2014, with recitals, lessons, and various video projects that resurface fado's early beginnings. In this way, Nery's history of Portuguese fado does begin to come full circle, and though he claims that such a definitive history is impossible, he proves otherwise in this work, unsettling a profound investment by many of fado's gatekeepers in its claim as national heritage. His work provides the ground for welcomed research that would consider what remains in today's fado of its Black Atlantic beginnings. Though the dance may have receded, the genre's expressive repertoire—one of desire and distress—stirs up a history that continues, determinedly, to resonate through Portuguese society and culture as a fado yet to be sung.

DANIEL DA SILVA is an assistant professor in the Department of Spanish and Portuguese at Rutgers University.

Alberto Pena Rodríguez.
News on the American Dream.
Translated by Serena J. Rivera with Glória de Sá.
Dartmouth, MA: Tagus Press, 2020.

Alberto Peña Rodríguez's study on the Portuguese American press is an important contribution to the growing field of Portuguese American studies, particularly for those who pursue a nuanced historical understanding of the Portuguese American community.

The detail given on the Portuguese American press by Peña Rodríguez sometimes comes with surprising findings, such as the first Portuguese American newspaper appearing in Erie, Pennsylvania. The Portuguese American press studied is that produced by immigrants originating mainly from the Azores and mainland Portugal, although there is both a brief look at the *Jornal Português* in California, whose longest editor was of Brazilian origins, and comments on how certain Portuguese American newspapers in New England have begun to include other Portuguese language communities. There is also a brief look, in Chapter 3, at the Portuguese American newspapers published in Hawaii.

Previous studies on the Portuguese American press examined specific areas. Peña Rodríguez's study provides a breadth of scope that is at once a detailed survey of the Portuguese American press landscape since 1877, and a longitudinal study of important Portuguese American newspapers, and the important figures involved, in the East and West Coasts of the United States. The painstaking archival research that the author performed to produce this study comes through in every chapter. There is also an evident amount of detective work involved in this study, as can be seen in the appendices and the bibliography, the latter organized by topic, which Peña Rodríguez generously shares so as to facilitate the access to information for anyone who wants to follow up or build upon the findings of his study. The most valuable information contained in these appendices is where to access the newspaper sources Peña Rodríguez consulted. The information contained in the endnotes and the beautiful illustrations that accompany the text in the chapters are also worthy of praise. In the endnotes, we can also see the careful work that has gone into translating this study, and the care that Tagus Press has placed in the publication.

Although there is a degree of repetition of certain ideas and conclusions from the introduction on, the intention is perhaps to facilitate the reader's dipping into individual chapters rather than the whole book. The central arguments of the study center around the idea of how the Portuguese American press was an outlet that allowed individuals to pursue their American Dream, showing the philanthropical aspect behind the publication of newspapers and the people who brought them about. Peña Rodríguez shows how the press promoted the development of a Portuguese American community through, to take an example among the many given, asking readers to support Portuguese American businesses. The study also shows how Portuguese American newspapers provided training grounds for future generations of journalists and of Portuguese American newspapers. The detailed examples provided demonstrate how Portuguese American newspapers acted as support networks that navigated the different needs of the newly-arrived immigrants as well as the long-time settled immigrants and their descendants. For example, the importance of education imparted by the Portuguese American press is shown not just in how they taught the readers about the American experience, but also about pride of origins. The study does not cover, however, some of the reactions of the Portuguese American community to how they were viewed, such as the reaction to the publication of Taft's study on child mortality in the New England mills in the late 1920s, or the Big Dan case in the 1980s.

To briefly summarise Peña Rodríguez's study, it is composed of five chapters, an introduction, a conclusion, three appendices and a bibliography organised into six areas or topics. The first chapter sets the scene for understanding how the ethnic press operates in the United States before specifically examining the Portuguese American press. Care is taken to give details of the Portuguese American communities, noting the historical factors that affected these newspaper publications. Details are also given on how rivalries between notable members of the community, some of which politically motivated, were aired in the newspapers. The second chapter looks in more detail at the content within the Portuguese American newspapers published, noting instances where newspapers reported, and formed opinions for the readership, on local and international current affairs that affected the Portuguese American community. By focusing on case studies of Portuguese American editors, this chapter examines the struggles faced by the editors and publishers in reaching readers and being economically viable; in their pursuit of a public form of expression for the Portuguese American community; in the editors' individual pursuit of community leadership; and, finally, in reporting the truth even in the face of pressure and censorship from the Estado Novo. Chapter three provides a historical study of the first years of the Portuguese American press, until 1929, examining not only the different newspapers that emerged, but also sketching an idea of the contents covered, and how the political landscape at home and in Portugal was reflected in this content, even in the public debate that was reflected in their pages. Chapter four carries on the themes in the previous chapter, this time examining the period from 1930 to 2015 at the same time as it examines how the Portuguese American press expands to different states, following the migration patterns of the community. Chapter five is a case study chapter which examines the history and importance of four Portuguese American newspapers: the *Diário de Notícias* in New Bedford, Massachusetts, which was the basis of Rui Antunes Correia's MA thesis; the *Jornal Português* in Oakland and then San Pablo, California; the *Luso Americano* in New Jersey; and, finally, *The Portuguese Times* in New Bedford and its television channel. The conclusion of this study returns to the idea of how the Portuguese American press acted as a conduit for information about Portugal and the US as well as created a space for the community to be, to feel itself as a Portuguese American community, even as this community has integrated within the wider ethnic mosaic in the US.

The final section in Chapter 5 is worth noting. This section examines how the Carnation Revolution was reported on by *The Portuguese Times*, and includes how the readers used *The Portuguese Times* to air their views and reactions to events in Portugal, and how, later, the newspaper and the community then mobilized US political figures in support of the newly-formed Portuguese democratic government. In so doing, this section provides a different image of the Portuguese American community from its portrayal as conservative and pro-fascist in the Lisbon press.

The study is a very good resource for scholars interested in the ethnic press, for those interested in seeing what the historical debates and preoccupations of the Portuguese American community were, and even for those of us who want a fuller picture of the Portuguese American community from its origins to the present day. Peña Rodríguez's study shows that the Portuguese American community was actively participating in public debates, commenting on current affairs, and visible and vocal from the outset. The study also shows that the Portuguese American press, like the community, has adjusted and adapted to internal and external factors to provide a service, and be of service, to the community it writes for, and about.

CARMEN RAMOS VILLAR is Senior Lecturer in Hispanic Studies at the University of Sheffield (UK).